Lecture Notes in Computer Science   16497

Founding Editors

Gerhard Goos
Juris Hartmanis

The series Lecture Notes in Computer Science (LNCS), including its subseries Lecture Notes in Artificial Intelligence (LNAI) and Lecture Notes in Bioinformatics (LNBI), has established itself as a medium for the publication of new developments in computer science and information technology research, teaching, and education.

LNCS enjoys close cooperation with the computer science R & D community, the series counts many renowned academics among its volume editors and paper authors, and collaborates with prestigious societies. Its mission is to serve this international community by providing an invaluable service, mainly focused on the publication of conference and workshop proceedings and postproceedings. LNCS commenced publication in 1973.

Renata Guizzardi · João Araújo

Editors

Requirements Engineering: Foundation for Software Quality

32nd International Working Conference, REFSQ 2026
Poznań, Poland, March 23–26, 2026
Proceedings

 Springer

Editors
Renata Guizzardi (iD)
University of Twente
Enschede, The Netherlands

João Araújo (iD)
NOVA LINCS, Universidade NOVA de Lisboa
Lisbon, Portugal

ISSN 0302-9743 ISSN 1611-3349 (electronic)
Lecture Notes in Computer Science
ISBN 978-3-032-21422-5 ISBN 978-3-032-21423-2 (eBook)
https://doi.org/10.1007/978-3-032-21423-2

This Springer imprint is published by the registered company Springer Nature Switzerland AG
The registered company address is: Gewerbestrasse 11, 6330 Cham, Switzerland

If disposing of this product, please recycle the paper.

Preface

This volume contains the papers presented at REFSQ 2026, the 32nd *International Working Conference on Requirements Engineering: Foundation for Software Quality*, held on March 23–26, 2026, in Poznań, Poland.

The REFSQ series was established in 1994, initially as a workshop series, and has evolved into a working conference since 2010, where significant time is dedicated to presentations, thorough discussions, and community building, and has established itself as one of the most important international scientific events in the field of Requirements Engineering, and the only one that takes place permanently in Europe, which promotes a special connection to European industry.

This year's special conference theme was "Trustworthy and Ethical Systems via Requirements Engineering". These days, we face many challenges in information systems and software engineering, motivated by continuous and rapid developments in AI. In our view, this evolution is unstoppable, and we must make the world ready for it. However, as usual, technology evolves before the methods are crafted to develop it. The Requirements Engineering community is, however, very attentive and keeps up with the trends and needs of this society. REFSQ is one of the conferences responsible for that, and this year, we continued this tradition by proposing the Trustworthy and Ethical Systems via Requirements Engineering special theme. We cannot expect novel systems to lead to trustworthy and ethical results if we do not endow requirements engineers, system designers, and developers with proper approaches focusing on trust and ethics from the early stages of the development cycle. With this special theme, we want to foment fruitful discussions emphasizing the following aspects:

- Correctness and ethics should go hand in hand with requirements elicitation, analysis, negotiation, monitoring, and assessment.
- Trust is paramount to creating a society that relies on machines for crucial processes and aspects of people's lives.
- Providing people with trustworthy, ethical, and ready information about novel technology is essential to let them choose whether and how to use it and is essential for a safe and happy world.

We were glad that the community reacted promptly to this special theme. We received several submissions on trustworthiness and ethics in the context of this conference and some of them are part of this volume.

In total, we received 67 submissions in different paper categories. In the reviewing process, each submission was reviewed by three members of the program committee, following a single-blind process, and discussed by the three reviewers aiming to reach a consensus for the final decision. Nevertheless, thirteen papers for which no consensus had been reached were discussed at an online plenary Program Committee meeting held on December 11th, 2025.

After the review and discussion process, 23 papers were accepted, where five of them were conditionally accepted to include a list of improvements to be considered in the final version of the paper, and 6 were accepted as research preview papers. The revised versions underwent a final review by program committee members who had been appointed as "gatekeepers" for the revisions. All the conditionally accepted papers and research preview papers met the conditions and were finally accepted.

Thus, of the 69 papers submitted, a total of 23 were finally accepted for presentation at REFSQ 2025 and for publication in this volume.

The acceptance rate for each paper category has been calculated as follows:

- Technical Design: 31 submissions, 7 accepted (23%)
- Scientific Evaluation: 20 submissions, 9 accepted (45%)
- Experience Report: 4 submissions, 0 accepted (0%)
- Vision Paper: 5 submissions, 0 accepted (0%)
- Research Preview: 15 submissions, 7 accepted (47%)

The acceptance rate of full contributions related to the categories Technical Design, Scientific Evaluation, and Experience Report was approximately 31.3% (16/51).

As in previous years, the main conference was organized as a three-day symposium (Tuesday to Thursday), with two days of academic presentations and one day devoted to industrial presentations.

We would like to thank all members of our community. Their commitment and the diversity of ideas in Requirements Engineering enable the continuous progress of our discipline. We express our heartfelt gratitude to the Steering Committee Chairs, the Background Chair, and all members of the Organizing Committee for their dedicated work and constant support. We also extend our sincere thanks to the Program Committee for their valuable reviews and active participation in the discussions and decision-making process concerning the papers accepted for REFSQ'26.

We are especially grateful to the Proceedings Chairs, Oliver Karras and Greta Adamo, without whom the delivery of these proceedings would not have been possible. Finally, our deepest gratitude goes to all authors who submitted their work to REFSQ'26. You are truly the essence of this conference, and we sincerely appreciate your contributions and trust.

January 2026

Renata Guizzardi
João Araújo

Organization

Program Committee

Sallam Abualhaija   University of Luxembourg, Luxembourg
Greta Adamo   Free University of Bozen-Bolzano, Italy
Carina Alves   Universidade Federal de Pernambuco, Brazil
Daniel Amyot   University of Ottawa, Canada
João Araújo   Universidade NOVA de Lisboa, Portugal
Fatma Başak Aydemir   Utrecht University, The Netherlands
Clara Ayora   Universidad de Castilla la Mancha, Spain
Nelly Bencomo   Durham University, UK
Daniel Berry   University of Waterloo, Canada
Stefanie Betz   Furtwangen University, Germany
Markus Borg   CodeScene, Sweden
Isabel Sofia Brito   Instituto Politécnico de Beja, Portugal
Jean-Michel Bruel   IRIT, France
Stan Bühne   IREB GmbH, Germany
Jaelson Castro   Universidade Federal de Pernambuco, Brazil
Ruzanna Chitchyan   University of Bristol, UK
Eduardo Cibrián   Carlos III University of Madrid, Spain
Nelly Condori Fernández   Universidad Santiago de Compostela, Spain
Fabiano Dalpiaz   Utrecht University, The Netherlands
Maya Daneva   University of Twente, The Netherlands
Marian Daun   Technical University of Applied Sciences Würzburg- Schweinfurt, Germany
Jose Luis de la Vara   University of Castilla-La Mancha, Spain
Oscar Dieste   Universidad Politécnica de Madrid, Spain
Jörg Dörr   Fraunhofer IESE, Germany
Marie Farrell   University of Manchester, UK
Henning Femmer   Fachhochschule Südwestfalen, Germany
Alessio Ferrari   ISTI-CNR, Italy
Farnaz Fotrousi   Chalmers and Gothenburg University, Sweden
Julian Frattini   Chalmers University of Technology — University of Gothenburg, Sweden
Samuel A. Fricker   University of Applied Sciences and Arts Northwestern Switzerland, Switzerland
Sepideh Ghanavati   University of Maine, USA
Martin Glinz   University of Zurich Switzerland

Enyo Gonçalves	Universidade Federal do Ceará, Brazil
Miguel Goulão	Universidade Nova de Lisboa, Portugal
Sarah Gregory	1968
Eduard C. Groen	Fraunhofer IESE, Germany
Iris Groher	Johannes Kepler University Linz, Austria
Katharina Großer	Universität Koblenz, Germany
Alicia Grubb	Smith College, USA
Paul Grünbacher	Johannes Kepler University Linz, Austria
Renata Guizzardi	University of Twente, The Netherlands
Irit Hadar	University of Haifa, Israel
Anne Hess	Technical University of Applied Sciences Würzburg- Schweinfurt, Germany
Tobias Hey	Karlsruhe Institute of Technology, Germany
Jennifer Horkoff	University of Gothenburg and Chalmers University of Technology, Sweden
Emilio Insfran	Universitat Politècnica de València, Spain
Isabel John	TH Würzburg Schweinfurt, Germany
Erik Kamsties	University of Applied Sciences and Arts Dortmund, Germany
Oliver Karras	TIB - Leibniz Information Centre for Science and Technology, Germany
Eric Knauss	Chalmers — University of Gothenburg, Sweden
Sylwia Kopczynska	Poznań University of Technology, Poland
Kim Lauenroth	University of Applied Science and Arts Dortmund, Germany
Maria Lencastre	Universidade de Pernambuco, Brazil
Emmanuel Letier	University College London, UK
Tong Li	Beijing University of Technology, China
Grischa Liebel	Reykjavik University, Iceland
Nazim Madhavji	University of Western Ontario, Canada
Anastasia Mavridou	KBR/NASA Ames Research Center, USA
Daniel Mendez	Blekinge Institute of Technology, Sweden, and fortiss, Germany
Luisa Mich	University of Trento, Italy
Quim Motger	Universitat Politècnica de Catalunya, Spain
Gunter Mussbacher	McGill University, Canada
Denisse Muñante	ENSIIE & SAMOVAR, France
Nan Niu	University of Cincinnati, USA
Rene Noel	Universidad de Valparaiso, Chile
Marc Oriol	Universitat Politècnica de Catalunya, Spain
Zachary J. Oster	University of Wisconsin-Whitewater, USA
Shola Oyedeji	LUT University, Finland

Elda Paja	IT University of Copenhagen, Denmark
Oscar Pastor	Universidad Politécnica de Valencia, Spain
Nitish Patkar	University of Applied Sciences and Arts Northwestern Switzerland Switzerland
Sven Peldszus	IT University of Copenhagen, Denmark
Anna Perini	Fondazione Bruno Kessler Trento, Italy
Tiago Prince Sales	University of Twente, The Netherlands
Adam Przybylek	University of Galway, Ireland
Jolita Ralyté	University of Geneva Switzerland
Bjorn Regnell	Lund University, Sweden
Marcela Ruiz	Zurich University of Applied Sciences Switzerland
Mehrdad Sabetzadeh	University of Ottawa, Canada
Mattia Salnitri	University of Bergamo, Italy
Simon Andre Scherr	Fraunhofer IESE, Germany
Kurt Schneider	Leibniz Universität Hannover, Germany
Laura Semini	University of Pisa, Italy
Carla Silva	Universidade Federal de Pernambuco, Brazil
Maria Spichkova	RMIT University, Australia
Paola Spoletini	Kennesaw State University, USA
Angelo Susi	Fondazione Bruno Kessler, Italy
Pablo Sánchez	University of Cantabria, Spain
Michael Vierhauser	University of Innsbruck, Austria
Andreas Vogelsang	University of Duisburg-Essen, Germany
Thorsten Weyer	Technische Hochschule Mittelhessen, Germany
Krzysztof Wnuk	Blekinge Institute of Technology, Sweden
Andrea Wohlgemuth	Utrecht University/Fachhochschule Dortmund, Germany

Additional Reviewers

Aadinehzadeh, Faranak	Saleh, Sabbir
Fotouhi, Sara	Sorokos, Ioannis
Haghighi, Sara	Vigh, Eszter
LaChance, Clark	Villela, Karina
Maksimov, Yuliyan	

Contents

User Feedback

Requirements Specification and Privacy by Design

Trustworthiness in AI and Information Systems

Formal Methods

LLMs use in RE

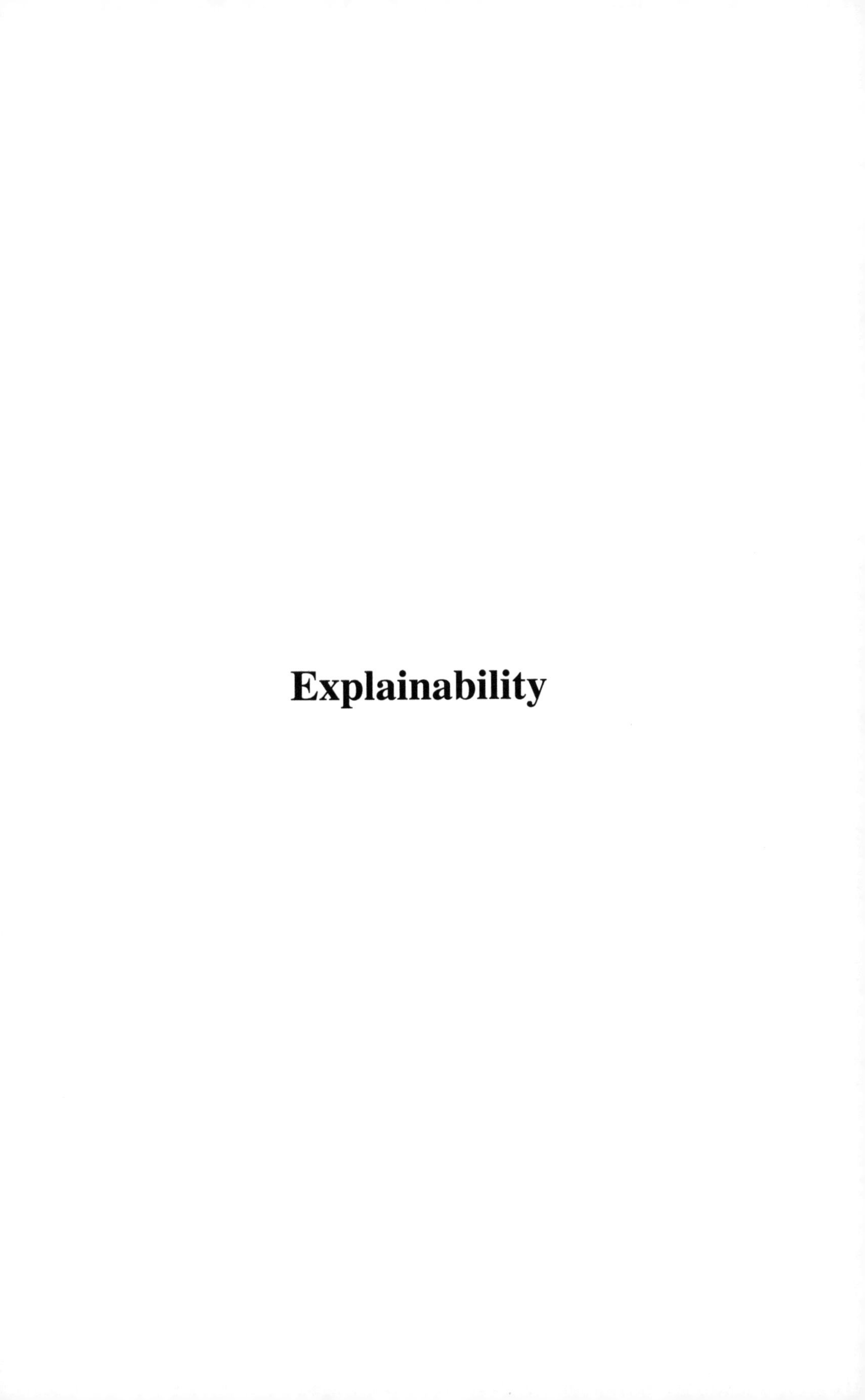# Explainability

Immersive and Enjoyable Explanations On Distinct Explainability Requirements in Games

Jakob Droste[1]([✉])(iD), Ronja Fuchs[2](iD), Hannah Deters[1](iD), Martin Obaidi[1](iD), Alexander Dockhorn[3](iD), and Kurt Schneider[1](iD)

[1] Software Engineering Group, Leibniz University Hannover, Hannover, Germany
`jakob.droste@inf.uni-hannover.de`
[2] Institute of Information Processing, Leibniz University Hannover, Hannover, Germany
[3] SDU Metaverse Lab, University of Southern Denmark, Odense, Denmark

Abstract. **[Context and motivation]** When complex systems are difficult to understand and interact with, explanations have proven effective in supporting users and enhancing user experience (UX). Explainability research has extensively examined UX factors critical to productivity software, such as trust and learnability. **[Question/problem]** However, it has largely overlooked key UX factors of entertainment software, including immersion, enjoyment, and emotional engagement. Video games provide a compelling context for investigating this research gap, as they combine complex interactive systems with rich emotional and immersive experiences. Since there is no general understanding of players as the stakeholders of software explanations, two central questions remain: (1) what types of explanations do players need, and (2) how do explanations influence players' user experience? **[Principal ideas/results]** In this work, we report on two complementary studies: a survey and a controlled experiment. The survey assessed participants' general need for explanations in digital games. The experiment involved participants playing a video game, *Ori and the Blind Forest*, either with or without explanations, and evaluating their user experience. **[Contribution]** Our findings provide two key contributions: (1) we identify explanation needs that are unique to video games and distinct from other software domains, and (2) we offer empirical evidence that explanations may enhance players' user experience, improving immersion and enjoyment.

Keywords: Explainability · Requirements Engineering · User Experience · Entertainment Software · Digital Games

1 Introduction

Explanations are an essential part of many complex software systems [21,22]. The respective non-functional requirement explainability describes the ability of a software to explain itself, its behavior, and its interactions [12,22,39]. In

R. Guizzardi and J. Araújo (Eds.): REFSQ 2026, LNCS 16497, pp. 3–19, 2026.
https://doi.org/10.1007/978-3-032-21423-2_1

recent years, explainability has gained major attention in the field of artificial intelligence (AI) [1, 39]. In particular, explanations have been used to make AI behavior and decisions more transparent and understandable to human users [12, 13, 39]. Outside of AI, software engineering research has applied explainability concepts to make system aspects such as security [4, 61] and privacy [8, 9] more understandable. Meanwhile, user experience research has identified explanations as a suitable means to guide user interactions, improving the learnability and usability of the software [3, 20, 21].

Video games and their diverse technology and gameplay features may impose various challenges on their players. Game designers walk a fine line between making their games accessible, but also challenging and engaging [41, 52]. As such, explanations have long been an essential part of many video games. One example of this are tutorials for gameplay elements that are not immediately intuitive [3, 5]. Another example are explanations within the narrative of story-driven games, which aim to construct a coherent in-game logic within the player's mind [35, 42].

Requirements engineering research has concluded that different stakeholders of a software need different explanations [13, 22, 39]. This is also true for video game research, where different works have already addressed many different explanation types [3, 35, 38]. However, these works often address explanation needs in games on a case-by-case basis, rather than approaching them under the broader term of explanation requirements. As such, there is no general understanding of players as the stakeholders of software explanations.

In this paper, we examine video games as explainable software, through the lens of requirements engineering. We discuss relevant related work from the fields of requirements engineering and human-computer interaction, and report on two complementary studies: a survey and an experiment. In the survey study, 50 participants gauged their general need for explanations in video games. In the experiment, 20 participants played Moon Studios' *Ori and the Blind Forest* – either with or without explanations. Using a post-experiment questionnaire, we analyzed their user experience and elicited explanation needs for the game. Our work contributes two major findings: 1) video games invoke a unique prioritization and categorization of explanation needs, which is distinct from other everyday software, and 2) explanations enhance players' user experience, improving their fun and immersion. These findings underline the importance of integrating explanation design into game development as a formal requirement.

The rest of this paper is structured as follows: Sect. 2 covers related work. Section 3 details the methodology of our initial research, while Sect. 4 covers the initial findings. We discuss the implications of our work as well as future research directions in Sect. 5 and conclude this paper in Sect. 6.

2   Related Work

2.1   Requirements Engineering for Explainable Systems

Explainability is an emerging non-functional requirement in complex software systems. It describes the ability of a system to provide explanations for any system aspect, making itself more understandable to its stakeholders [12,22]. With the emergence of AI, research into explainability has boomed since 2018 [26]. Most research in the field of explainable AI focuses on explaining the inner workings of the system [17,58]. However, requirements engineering for explainable systems has also been conducted in the context of non-AI software, revealing that end-users require a diverse range of software explanations. These include system aspects such as user interactions [19,22], privacy information [8,9], or domain knowledge [21,48].

Recent works in the field of requirements engineering for explainable software have focused on everyday software systems [22,59], which video games are considered to be a part of [28]. Crawling user feedback, such as app reviews, has proven particularly useful for automated need assessment [46,59]. The use of taxonomies that categorize types of explanation needs has proven to be effective in supporting discussions about these needs [21,22,59]. When combined with workshops, such taxonomies have proven to help participants to establish user-specific requirements [21,47]. However, so-called hypothetical bias [30] impedes the elicitation of explanation needs, as users find it difficult to envision what questions they might have without having used the system themselves. Considering this, prototyping [57] or elicitation during system runtime [19] are effective methods for identifying actual explanation needs.

2.2   Explanations and User Experience

User experience includes all interactions of the user with the product, the service, and the responsible company [45]. In particular, the perception and feelings of users toward the system are highlighted [2,31,32]. Orzikulova et al. [49] demonstrated that explanations can improve the user experience, especially in terms of effectiveness. This is in line with frequently stated goals of explanations, including trust, user satisfaction, and symbiosis [26]. The human-computer interaction (HCI) community even explicitly lists user experience as a goal of explainability [26]. According to El Ali et al. [25], providing good explanations includes avoiding information overload, enabling personalization, and improving the design of the explanation, i.e., its presentation and placement. Bertrand et al. [7] suggest providing selective, mutable, and dialogic explanations, emphasizing that interactive explanations increase perceived usefulness and performance.

Deters et al. [20] analyzed the influence of explainability on user experience as a whole by examining the influence on each UX factor individually. Their findings show that the influence of explanations on UX factors such as fun, immersion, and emotional engagement has not yet been reviewed by scientific literature. UX experts suspect both positive and negative influences on these factors, revealing an interesting research gap [20]. Entertainment software, including video games, offers a compelling research context to address this gap, as its design focus lies on hedonistic UX factors rather than transparency and productivity [44]. Given that game development heavily relies on non-functional dimensions (e.g., enjoyment and immersion), established requirements engineering practices and frameworks may help to assess the players' perspective [37].

2.3   Requirements Engineering for Digital Games

Kasurinen et al. [37] and Callele et al. [10] highlight the importance of requirements engineering techniques in game development processes, although they are not yet systematically applied. Given that game development tends to focus on non-functional requirements (e.g., fun and immersion), established requirements engineering practices may help to assess the players' perspective [37].

Daneva [16] analyzed gameplay requirements for massively multiplayer online role-playing games (MMORPGs). They identified *playability* as a key non-functional requirement of digital games, which, similar to usability, is closely related to explainability. Whereas a player's explanation needs specifically refer to a deficit of information during gameplay, playability needs refer to their overall capability to engage with the game. This includes explanations, but also other features such as accessibility and usability elements. Therefore, when addressing playability needs, requirements engineers can leverage explanations as a means to improve playability and, by extension, player experience.

2.4   User Experience in Digital Games

Player Experience (PX) refers to user experience in the specific context of digital games [44]. While PX shares its foundational elements with UX, it diverges in critical ways. Traditional UX often prioritizes task efficiency and functional usability, whereas PX centers on hedonic dimensions such as fun, immersion, and emotional engagement [44]. In digital games, the experience itself is the goal, making PX a more affective, enjoyment-centered construct. Game usability plays a central role in shaping PX. As Rajanen and Tapani [54] note, games – like any interactive software – require strong usability to ensure a positive experience. However, usability in games extends beyond traditional productivity software metrics. Depending on the genre, games provide challenge, support learning, and sustain player motivation through dynamic psychological components such as flow, immersion, and emotions [15,18,54]. Pedersen et al. [51] highlight challenge and learnability as key to enjoyment, especially in games with procedurally generated content. Their findings indicate that players prefer smooth progression, but also require challenge to achieve flow, underscoring the need to balance difficulty and accessibility in game design [15].

As digital games are marketed directly to individual consumers rather than organizations, a compelling and enjoyable PX directly affects product success and player retention [50]. From a software development perspective, Pagulayan et al. [50] offer a user-centered design framework for games that addresses both evaluation and optimization strategies. They emphasize that games differ from productivity applications in that their primary focus is on the process of interaction rather than outcome achievement. Games construct their own internal goals, and as such, must cater to diverse user expectations, backgrounds, and skill levels. The authors highlight the importance of accessibility, explainability, and short-term engagement, especially during early playing phases. In contrast, inadequate onboarding may disrupt the learning curve and lead to user frustration and premature disengagement [51].

2.5   Explanations in Digital Games

Explanations play an essential role in video game design, shaping how players understand gameplay mechanics, interpret feedback, and engage with both artificial and human opponents. Tutorials are a key method to explain user interactions in games, especially during onboarding [5]. Pagulayan et al. [50] stress that effective tutorials should adapt to players' skill levels and encourage hands-on learning rather than relying solely on text. Poorly written explanations can frustrate players, whereas well-written explanations do more than just provide instructions; they also direct players toward their objectives. Cao and Liu [11] argue that tutorials must deliver personalized, timely feedback, especially in the context of complex gameplay. Their findings align with broader research emphasizing the variability of optimal tutorial design across genres and demographics [29,33]. Green et al. [29] advance this by proposing AI-driven tutorials that adapt dynamically to player behavior.

Beyond onboarding, players require clear performance feedback to understand their role in competitive settings. Pfau [53] argues that vague performance feedback fosters overconfidence and toxicity, highlighting the need for explanations that reflect individual contributions in multiplayer environments. In the context of AI in games, explanations help players better understand system behavior. Molineaux et al. [43] present an NPC agent capable of explaining its behavior to players in real time, helping users interpret the rationale behind opaque decision-making. These explanations aim to reduce frustration and foster trust in AI-driven interactions. Similarly, Berger and Müller [6] examine the role of explainable AI in educational games, where transparency is essential for learning or training purposes.

Explanations are not universally beneficial in the same way for all genres and user groups. Rienzo and Cubillos [55] studied games designed for elderly players, emphasizing the need for cognitively accessible instructions. Clear rules and transparent design reduce cognitive load, which can otherwise become a significant barrier to engagement for older adults. On the opposite end of the spectrum, Väkevä et al. [60] examined FromSoftware's *Dark Souls*, a video game famous for its scarcity of explanations and high difficulty. They argue that the game's opacity positively contributes to mental resilience by encouraging players to persevere, reflect, and seek support in online communities. Here, the lack of explicit explanations becomes a feature rather than a flaw, providing a high level of difficulty that enables a positive player experience. Denisova et al. [18] argue that repeated failure in games may lead to frustration, but conversely can be considered an essential part of learning if the game provides sufficient explanations.

3   Methodology

3.1   Research Goal and Research Questions

The primary goals of this work are (1) to examine the need for explanations in video games, and (2) to evaluate the effects of explanations on underexplored

Fig. 1. Overview of the Research Procedure.

UX factors, in the context of a video game. To this end, we conducted a survey and a controlled experiment, addressing the following research questions:

RQ1 How do players prioritize explanation needs typically found in digital games?

RQ2 What new types of explanation needs can be identified from users playing the game *Ori and the Blind Forest*?

RQ3 How do explanations in the game *Ori and the Blind Forest* influence the UX factors fun, immersion, and emotion?

RQ1 explores players' general perceptions of explanations in video games, namely which types of explanations they consider more important than others. We leverage an existing taxonomy for explainability needs in everyday software [21], which digital games are considered to be a part of [28]. Based on this taxonomy, we surveyed video game players to evaluate their perceived need for different types of explanations. RQ2 examines explanation needs that fall outside Droste et al. [21]'s taxonomy. During the experiment, we elicited participants' explanation needs, clustered those that did not align with the taxonomy, and compared them against existing literature. RQ3 addresses a research gap identified by Deters et al. [20], who found that several UX factors are underrepresented in explainability research. Our experiment contributes to this discussion by providing a case example of how explanations in entertainment software can influence fun, immersion, and emotional engagement. Our research procedure is summarized in Fig. 1.

3.2 Data Collection

We collected data by conducting two empirical studies:

Survey: The first part of the survey questionnaire consisted of demographic questions, including participants' age, occupation and gaming experience (what and how often they play). The second part of the survey addressed explanation needs in games and built upon the explanation need taxonomy by Droste et al. [21]. In particular, participants used 7-point ordinal scales to gauge the importance of explanations concerning *interactions, system behavior, domain knowledge, privacy & security* and *user interface (UI)*, subdivided into their respective subcategories. The full questionnaire is available in our supplementary material [23].

The survey was published on the online message board of *Leibniz University Hannover* (Germany) in November 2024. From a total of 56 initial survey participants, 50 completed the entire survey. 37 of the participants were students,

16 were employed, and three were occupied otherwise (voluntary service). The average age was 25.3. The majority of participants (33) stated that they rarely play new games and most (32) stick to one or two genres. Most participants (31) indicated an average play time of less than ten hours per week, with only a few participants (5) stating they play more than 30 h per week.

Experiment: For the experiment, participants were invited to play the introductory sequence of the video game *Ori and the Blind Forest*. They used either an on-site computer system or *Steam Remote Play* and *Discord*. In both cases, we captured the screen recording and noted participants' behavior and verbal remarks on an observation sheet. *Ori and the Blind Forest* has an optional setting to deactivate certain interface elements, which includes tutorials and explanations for interface and gameplay elements. We divided the participants of the experiment into two groups: one group playing the game with explanations, and another group playing the game without explanations.

Before and after playing the game, participants answered questionnaires addressing their user experience. The pre-play questionnaire contained the same demographic questions as the initial survey. The post-play questionnaire contained questions to measure three user experience factors relevant to explainable systems and games: fun, immersion, and emotion [20]. In particular, we used questions from the *Game Experience Questionnaire* (GEQ) [34] to measure fun, the *Immersive Experience Questionnaire* (IEQ) [36] to measure immersion, and the *Positive and Negative Affect Schedule* (PANAS) [62] to measure emotion. To ensure that the results of the PANAS questions were not biased by participants' emotional state before the experiment, we also included PANAS questions in the pre-play questionnaire. These questions were answered on 10-point ordinal scales. Lastly, we included open questions for the elicitation of explanation needs. The full experiment questionnaires are available in our supplementary material [23].

The call for participants was posted on the same message board as the survey, in January 2025. The experiment was conducted with 20 participants, ten of whom were employed, nine of whom were students, and the remaining one was occupied otherwise. Since participation in the preceding survey was anonymous, we do not know if experiment participants had also taken part in the survey. The average age was 25.7. All participants had no prior experience with *Ori and the Blind Forest*, which was a prerequisite for participation. Again, the majority of participants (16) stated that they rarely play new games, and most played games from either one or two genres (8) or three to five genres (9). Reported weekly play time was higher than in the preceding survey, with the majority (11) playing less than ten hours, but four playing more than 30 h.

3.3   Data Analysis

Survey: The quantitative data from the online survey was analyzed using descriptive statistics. We report participants' aggregated relevance ratings for Droste et al. [21]'s explanation types, using mean ($\bar{x}$) and standard deviation (σ).

Table 1. Relevance ratings from the initial online survey. (1 – not at all important, 7 – extremely important)

Type of Need	$\bar{x}$	σ	Type of Need	$\bar{x}$	σ
User Interface	**5.04**	**1.47**	**System Behavior**	**4.42**	**1.87**
Domain Knowledge	**5.03**	**1.46**	Consequences	4.68	1.68
System-specific Elements	5.60	1.25	Bugs & Crashes	4.60	1.94
Terminology	4.46	1.66	Unexpected System Behavior	4.38	1.99
Interaction	**4.97**	**1.50**	Algorithm	4.02	1.86
Navigation	5.22	1.34	**Privacy & Security**	**3.93**	**1.92**
Operation	5.12	1.41	Privacy	3.94	1.97
Tutorials	4.56	1.76	Security	3.92	1.87

Experiment: The quantitative data from the experiment questionnaires was analyzed using two-tailed hypothesis testing. For all statistical analysis tests presented in this paper, we performed the Mann–Whitney U (MWU) test at the 5% significance level. We evaluated the effect sizes according to Cohen's guidelines [14]. Participants' qualitative feedback was categorized using two-cycle coding. To analyze their explanation needs, we performed *in vivo* coding for the first cycle and pattern coding for the second cycle, following the guidelines of Saldaña [56]. During the second coding cycle, we used the coding scheme for explanation needs provided by Droste et al. [21]. The entire coding procedure was conducted by two researchers independently. All conflicts between the two raters were discussed and resolved with the help of a third researcher. All three raters had a background in explainability research. We report the inter-rater agreement using Fleiss' κ [27]. Codes for newly identified explanation types were declared and assigned by only one researcher, but discussed and reviewed with another.

4   Findings

4.1   Explanation Type Relevance (Survey)

Table 1 shows the survey participants' aggregated ratings for different explanation types identified by Droste et al. [21]. Explanations concerning the user interface (5.04) or domain knowledge (5.03) received the highest relevance ratings from our participants. In the context of video games, domain knowledge explanations may address elements specific to a given game, such as certain items or characters, or game-specific terminology. User interface explanations concern the heads-up display (HUD) of a game and may address questions about ambiguous design elements or unexpected layout changes. Explanations concerning interactions between the user and the system (4.97) were the next most highly rated explanation types. These explanations may address the operations and navigation that players perform when interacting with a game, but also include tutorials for various gameplay features. The other explanation types, namely those that concerned system behavior (4.42) or privacy and security (3.93), received lower relevance ratings from our participants.

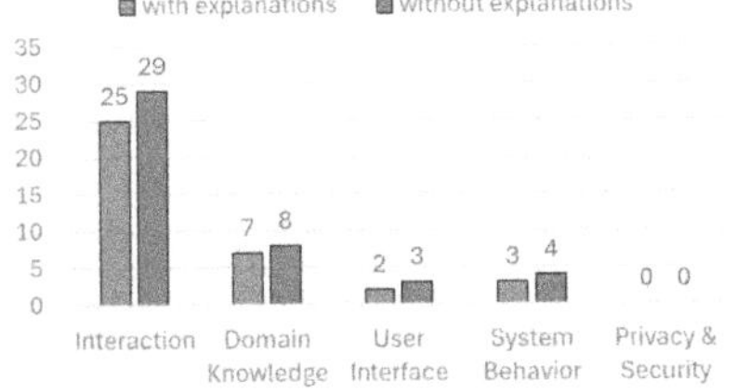
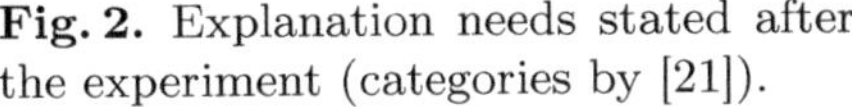

Fig. 2. Explanation needs stated after the experiment (categories by [21]).

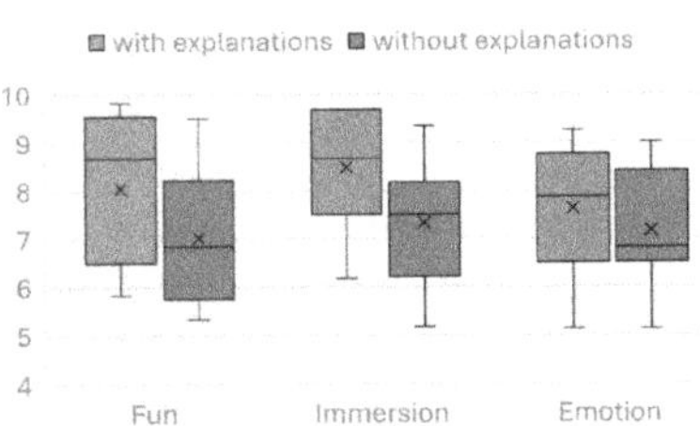

Fig. 3. Players' user experience scores reported after the experiment.

4.2 Identified Explanation Needs (Experiment)

After the experiment, participants stated explanation needs across multiple categories in their answers to the open questions. When coding these needs, we achieved an inter-rater agreement of $\kappa = 0.717$ [27]. According to Landis and Koch [40], this indicates a substantial agreement. Figure 2 shows the number of explanation needs identified in our participants' feedback. The detailed results of our coding procedure are provided in our supplementary material [23].

Known Types of Needs: In contrast to the survey's relevance ratings, needs for interaction explanations were by far the most prevalent during the experiment, followed by explanations for domain knowledge. Only few needs concerned the user interface or system behavior. Notably, participants in the group without explanations stated slightly more needs across almost all categories. The only exception were *Privacy & Security* explanations, for which no need was stated.

New Types of Needs: We observed two major discrepancies between the needs stated by our participants and the need definitions by Droste et al. [21]: (1) Ten explanation needs in the interaction category addressed the navigation of the player character within the game world, rather than the navigation of menus and complex UI elements. These worlds are a key component in many digital games, and are usually not present in other everyday software. (2) Seven explanation needs in the interaction and domain knowledge categories concerned progression within the game in a narrative sense. Specifically, participants stated that they did not understand how to progress the story of the game or what their overall goal in the in-game world was. Outside these categories, two participants explicitly stated that they did not want additional explanations and would rather explore the game themselves. As indicated by our research data [23], their demographic profile cannot be conclusively linked to their preference for no explanations.

4.3   User Experience (Experiment)

Figure 3 summarizes the three user experience factors as reported by our participants after the experiment. In particular, we evaluated whether perceived fun, immersion, and emotion differed between players who received explanations while playing and those who did not. Players with explanations reported an improved user experience across all three examined factors. The most notable difference was found for immersion, where an MWU test was just short of revealing a statistically significant difference ($p = 0.054, z = 1.928$) at the 5% level. The respective effect size ($r = 0.431$) showed that explanations had a medium effect on immersion [14]. Our evaluation of the next most notable factor, players' perceived fun, revealed no statistically significant difference ($p = 0.097, z = 1.663$) at the 5% level. Similar to our results for immersion, the effect size ($r = 0.372$) showed that explanations had a medium effect on fun [14]. Lastly, we found no statistically significant difference for emotion ($p = 0.308, z = 1.021$) at the 5% level. Furthermore, the respective effect size ($r = 0.228$) showed that explanations only had a small effect on emotion [14].

5   Discussion

5.1   Answering the Research Questions

RQ1) Priority of Known Explanation Types: The findings from our survey suggest that players have diverse explanation needs when engaging with the games they play (cf. Table 1). The aggregated scores for most categories were close to the neutral score. This indicates that while some players want explanations, they are not unanimously perceived as a critical component of games. The relative priorities of the explanation types stand in contrast to Droste et al. [21]'s findings for everyday software as a whole. This implies that explainability requirements in games might not be directly transferable from other everyday software domains.

RQ2) Distinct Explanation Needs in Games: Our findings show that players display a distinct need for explanations in games, especially concerning user-system interactions and domain-specific knowledge. The newly identified explanation types concerning software-internal worlds or narrative progression are not a part of Droste et al. [21]'s taxonomy for everyday software, which we attribute to an under-representation of digital games in their dataset.

RQ3) User Experience With(out) Explanations: Within the context of playing the introductory sequence of *Ori and the Blind Forest*, we observed an overall positive effect of explanations on players' user experience. In particular, our findings show notable improvements in player immersion and enjoyment, and a weak improvement in emotional engagement. This highlights the need to explicitly treat explainability as a non-functional requirement in game development, as well-implemented explanations directly influence key user experience factors.

5.2   Reflection on the Results

Distinct Explanation Needs in Games: Throughout our experiment, players who received in-game explanations reported improvements in their user experience. This highlights a clear demand for explanations that actively contribute to an improved player engagement. Furthermore, the distinct needs and priorities of our participants underline the importance of understanding players as the stakeholders of software explanations.

To assist game developers in creating more effective explanations, future research should explore how different types of explanations specifically influence user experience and overall player engagement. In particular, we suggest the development of a taxonomy for explanation needs in games. The taxonomy used in this paper was designed to work for everyday software systems and has been successfully used for requirements elicitation and management before [21,46, 47]. However, in the context of games as explainable software, it appears to be limited in its usefulness, as our findings were heavily skewed towards interaction explanations. In contrast to most everyday software, the focus of games lies in the enjoyment of interactions, rather than strictly increasing productivity. This also introduces distinct explanation types, such as narrative explanations, that have not been considered in requirements engineering so far. As such, video games constitute a special case of explainable software, which warrants further examination.

Balancing Challenge and Frustration: Throughout the experiment, two participants stated that they would rather not receive more explanations, even if they were helpful on paper. An essential component of player engagement and flow is the appropriate level of challenge. Determining what constitutes the right set of explanations to challenge players while not frustrating them requires nuanced consideration. This is further complicated by the differences between diverse game genres and player populations. Educational games should prioritize clear, focused explanations and avoid unnecessary challenge, as the goal is to teach or simplify interactions. Conversely, certain genres, such as the FromSoftware's *Soulslike* games, are renowned for their high difficulty and deliberate withholding of explanations, to cultivate a demanding environment, and foster resilience and perseverance among players.

Future research should investigate the complex interplay between explanations and challenge. Specifically, it should identify when explanations mitigate excessive difficulty and when they diminish intended gameplay tension. Appropriate RE methods can determine the optimal balance of providing explanations that reduce frustration and prevent disengagement, while preserving the level of challenge necessary to sustain flow.

5.3   Threats to Validity

We discuss the limitations of the validity of our research in accordance with Wohlin et al. [63]:

Construct Validity: We constructed our own PX questionnaire, building upon three established sources [34, 36, 62], instead of using the original questionnaires themselves or alternative questionnaires, which might have led to different results. Considering this limitation, the research reported in this paper should not be considered holistic. Future research should examine the validity of different measures for PX and their usefulness in the context of requirements engineering for explainable systems.

Internal Validity: Our experiment was conducted between-subjects, with a control group. Despite that, all participants played only the introductory sequence of *Ori and the Blind Forest*, instead of more challenging parts that might have led to more or different explanation needs. As such, our findings might not accurately represent how players interact with the game as a whole. Furthermore, our evaluation of PX might not be consistent with the more challenging parts of the game. A within-subjects design, in which the same participant plays different sections of the game with and without explanations, would address these concerns, trading off with the robustness offered by a between-subjects design.

Conclusion Validity: The results from our PX evaluation were not statistically significant and revealed effect sizes from medium to weak. Consequently, they might not be generalizable to a larger population and should be interpreted with caution. In contrast, our coding procedure led to substantial agreement between the raters. Considering the multi-label nature of the procedure, we are confident that our codes are representative of our participants' actual explanation needs.

External Validity: The participants were recruited from within the network of a German university. As such, our findings might not be generalizable to the international gaming community at large. Furthermore, we only experimented with one game, and other games might have led to a different distribution among the identified types of needs. Depending on the specific title and genre, other games might share some of *Ori and the Blind Forest*'s explanation requirements, but might also introduce new ones. The observation that privacy and security explanations received the lowest rating in the survey, and were not at all elicited during the experiment, could be biased by multiple factors. For one, *Ori and the Blind Forest* is a single-player game that requires no personal data from its players. Multiplayer games, where players engage with each other online, might lead to a higher need for privacy explanations. Furthermore, the need for privacy information depends on the specific participant profile, as outlined by Dupree et al. [24]. As the average age of our participants was rather young and recruitment was done in a university context, the low need for privacy explanations could also be influenced by their privacy profile.

6   Conclusion

Video games are complex software and require various explanation types to be accessible to players. Examples of this include in-game tutorials, explanations for operation and navigation, and narrative explanations that build a coherent in-game logic. This research paper addressed games as explainable software, from the perspective of requirements engineering. In particular, we report on a survey and an experiment that examine players' general explanation needs in games and the impact of explanations on players' user experience.

Our findings are twofold: 1) video games invoke distinct explanation needs and priorities, that are not yet considered in requirements engineering for explainable systems, and 2) well-integrated explanations have a positive impact on the UX factors fun and immersion. Consequently, we find that video games constitute a distinct and interesting case of explainable software that should receive special consideration in requirements engineering research.

Acknowledgments. This work was funded by the Deutsche Forschungsgemeinschaft (DFG, German Research Foundation) under Grant No.: 470146331, project softXplain (2022–2026).

Data Availability Statement. The responsible university ethics review board approves human-subjects research and they approved this project. All participants have given their informed consent to participate in the studies. To enable the verifiability of our research, we provide our questionnaires (translated to English) and all collected research data (raw) as supplementary material [23]. Qualitative feedback from our participants was anonymized as necessary.

References

1. Adadi, A., Berrada, M.: Peeking inside the black-box: a survey on explainable artificial intelligence (xai). IEEE Access **6** (2018)
2. Allam, A.H., Hussin, A.R.C., Dahlan, H.M.: User experience: challenges and opportunities. J. Inf. Syst. Res. Innov. **3**(1) (2013)
3. Andersen, E., et al.: The impact of tutorials on games of varying complexity. In: Proceedings of the SIGCHI Conference on Human Factors in Computing Systems, pp. 59–68 (2012)
4. Bender, G., Kot, L., Gehrke, J.: Explainable security for relational databases. In: Proceedings of the 2014 ACM SIGMOD International Conference on Management of Data, pp. 1411–1422 (2014)
5. Benvenuti, D., Ferro, L.S., Marrella, A., Catarci, T.: An approach to assess the impact of tutorials in video games. In: Informatics, vol. 10, p. 6. MDPI (2023)
6. Berger, F., Müller, W.: Back to basics: explainable AI for adaptive serious games. In: Fletcher, B., Ma, M., Göbel, S., Baalsrud Hauge, J., Marsh, T. (eds.) JCSG 2021. LNCS, vol. 12945, pp. 67–81. Springer, Cham (2021). https://doi.org/10.1007/978-3-030-88272-3_6

7. Bertrand, A., Viard, T., Belloum, R., Eagan, J.R., Maxwell, W.: On selective, mutable and dialogic XAI: a review of what users say about different types of interactive explanations. In: Proceedings of the 41st Conference on Human Factors in Computing Systems (CHI 2023). ACM (2023)

8. Brunotte, W., Droste, J., Schneider, K.: Context, content, consent-how to design user-centered privacy explanations (s). In: International Conference on Software Engineering and Knowledge Engineering (SEKE), pp. 86–89 (2023)

9. Brunotte, W., Specht, A., Chazette, L., Schneider, K.: Privacy explanations-a means to end-user trust. J. Syst. Softw. **195**, 111545 (2023)

10. Callele, D., Neufeld, E., Schneider, K.: Requirements engineering and the creative process in the video game industry. In: 13th IEEE International Conference on Requirements Engineering (RE'05) (2005)

11. Cao, S., Liu, F.: Learning to play: understanding in-game tutorials with a pilot study on implicit tutorials. Heliyon **8**(11) (2022)

12. Chazette, L., Brunotte, W., Speith, T.: Exploring explainability: a definition, a model, and a knowledge catalogue. In: 2021 IEEE 29th International Requirements Engineering Conference (RE). IEEE (2021)

13. Chazette, L., Brunotte, W., Speith, T.: Explainable software systems: from requirements analysis to system evaluation. Requir. Eng. **27**(4) (2022)

14. Cohen, J.: Statistical Power Analysis for the Behavioral Sciences. Routledge, Abingdon (2013)

15. Csikszentmihalyi, M., Csikzentmihaly, M.: Flow: The Psychology of Optimal Experience, vol. 1990. Harper & Row, New York (1990)

16. Daneva, M.: Striving for balance: a look at gameplay requirements of massively multiplayer online role-playing games. J. Syst. Softw. **134**, 54–75 (2017)

17. Das, A., Rad, P.: Opportunities and challenges in explainable artificial intelligence (XAI): a survey. CoRR arxiv:2006.11371 (2020)

18. Denisova, A., Cairns, P., Guckelsberger, C., Zendle, D.: Measuring perceived challenge in digital games: development & validation of the challenge originating from recent gameplay interaction scale (corgis). Int. J. Hum.-Comput. Stud. **137** (2020)

19. Deters, H., Droste, J., Fechner, M., Klünder, J.: Explanations on demand - a technique for eliciting the actual need for explanations. In: 2023 IEEE 31st International Requirements Engineering Conference Workshops (REW) (2023)

20. Deters, H., et al.: The x factor: on the relationship between user experience and explainability. In: Proceedings of the 13th Nordic Conference on Human-Computer Interaction (2024)

21. Droste, J., Deters, H., Obaidi, M., Klünder, J., Schneider, K.: Framing what can be explained-an operational taxonomy for explainability needs. Requir. Eng. **30**, 195–217 (2025)

22. Droste, J., Deters, H., Obaidi, M., Schneider, K.: Explanations in everyday software systems: towards a taxonomy for explainability needs. In: 2024 IEEE 32nd International Requirements Engineering Conference (RE), pp. 55–66. IEEE (2024)

23. Droste, J., Fuchs, R., Deters, H., Obaidi, M., Dockhorn, A., Schneider, K.: Supplementary Material - "Immersive and Enjoyable Explanations - On Distinct Explainability Requirements in Games" (REFSQ'26) (2026). https://doi.org/10.5281/zenodo.18244158

24. Dupree, J.L., Devries, R., Berry, D.M., Lank, E.: Privacy personas: clustering users via attitudes and behaviors toward security practices. In: Proceedings of the 2016 CHI Conference on Human Factors in Computing Systems, pp. 5228–5239 (2016)

25. El Ali, A., Venkatraj, K.P., Morosoli, S., Naudts, L., Helberger, N., Cesar, P.: Transparent ai disclosure obligations: who, what, when, where, why, how. In: Extended Abstracts of the CHI Conference on Human Factors in Computing Systems. CHI EA '24. ACM (2024)
26. Ferreira, J.J., Monteiro, M.S.: What are people doing about XAI user experience? A survey on AI explainability research and practice. In: Marcus, A., Rosenzweig, E. (eds.) HCII 2020. LNCS, vol. 12201, pp. 56–73. Springer, Cham (2020). https://doi.org/10.1007/978-3-030-49760-6_4
27. Fleiss, J.L.: Measuring nominal scale agreement among many raters. Psychol. Bull. **76**(5), 378–382 (1971)
28. Forward, A., Lethbridge, T.C.: A taxonomy of software types to facilitate search and evidence-based software engineering. In: Proceedings of the 2008 Conference of the Center for Advanced Studies on Collaborative Research: Meeting of Minds (2008)
29. Green, M., Khalifa, A., Barros, G., Togellius, J.: "press space to fire": automatic video game tutorial generation. In: Proceedings of the AAAI Conference on Artificial Intelligence and Interactive Digital Entertainment, vol. 13, pp. 75–80 (2017)
30. Harrison, G.W., Rutström, E.E.: Chapter 81 experimental evidence on the existence of hypothetical bias in value elicitation methods. In: Handbook of Experimental Economics Results, vol. 1, pp. 752–767. Elsevier, Amsterdam (2008)
31. Hassenzahl, M.: User experience and experience design. In: The Encyclopedia of Human-Computer Interaction (2nd Edition). The Interaction Design Foundation, Aarhus, Denmark (2014)
32. Hassenzahl, M., Tractinsky, N.: User experience-a research agenda. Behav. Inf. Technol. **25**(2), 91–97 (2006)
33. Ibrahim, M., Sweetser, P., Ozdowska, A.: Tutorial level design guidelines for 2d fighting games. In: Proceedings of the 18th International Conference on the Foundations of Digital Games, pp. 1–11 (2023)
34. IJsselsteijn, W.A., De Kort, Y.A., Poels, K.: The game experience questionnaire. Technical Report at Technische Universiteit Eindhoven (published version) (2013)
35. Ip, B.: Narrative structures in computer and video games: part 1: context, definitions, and initial findings. Games Cult. **6**(2), 103–134 (2011)
36. Jennett, C., et al.: Measuring and defining the experience of immersion in games. Int. J. Hum. Comput. Stud. **66**(9), 641–661 (2008)
37. Kasurinen, J., Maglyas, A., Smolander, K.: Is requirements engineering useless in game development? In: Salinesi, C., van de Weerd, I. (eds.) REFSQ 2014. LNCS, vol. 8396, pp. 1–16. Springer, Cham (2014). https://doi.org/10.1007/978-3-319-05843-6_1
38. Killingsworth, S.S., Clark, D.B., Adams, D.M.: Self-explanation and explanatory feedback in games: individual differences, gameplay, and learning. Int. J. Educ. Math. Sci. Technol. **3**(3), 162–186 (2015)
39. Köhl, M.A., Baum, K., Langer, M., Oster, D., Speith, T., Bohlender, D.: Explainability as a non-functional requirement. In: 2019 IEEE 27th International Requirements Engineering Conference (RE). IEEE (2019)
40. Landis, J.R., Koch, G.G.: The measurement of observer agreement for categorical data. Biometrics **33**(1), 159–174 (1977)
41. Martinez, J.J., Froehlich, J.E., Fogarty, J.: Playing on hard mode: accessibility, difficulty and joy in video game adoption for gamers with disabilities. In: Proceedings of the 2024 CHI Conference on Human Factors in Computing Systems (2024)
42. Meakin, E.: Video game structural layers for narrative design and articulation. Digital Creat. **35**(4), 321–340 (2024)

43. Molineaux, M., Dannenhauer, D., Aha, D.W.: Towards explainable npcs: a relational exploration learning agent. In: AAAI Workshops (2018)
44. Nacke, L., Drachen, A.: Towards a framework of player experience research. In: Proceedings of the 2nd International Workshop on Evaluating Player Experience in Games at FDG, vol. 11 (2011)
45. Nielsen, J.: The definition of user experience (ux) (1998). https://www.nngroup.com/articles/definition-user-experience/. Accessed 19 May 2025
46. Obaidi, M., et al.: Automating explanation need management in app reviews: a case study from the navigation app industry. In: 2025 IEEE/ACM 47th International Conference on Software Engineering: Software Engineering in Practice (ICSE-SEIP). IEEE (2025)
47. Obaidi, M., et al.: How to elicit explainability requirements? A comparison of interviews, focus groups, and surveys. In: 2025 IEEE 33rd International Requirements Engineering Conference (RE). IEEE (2025)
48. Obaidi, M., et al.: How does users' app knowledge influence the preferred level of detail and format of software explanations? In: Requirements Engineering: Foundation for Software Quality. pp. 106–122. Springer, Cham (2025). https://doi.org/10.1007/978-3-031-88531-0_8
49. Orzikulova, A., et al.: Time2stop: adaptive and explainable human-ai loop for smartphone overuse intervention. In: Proceedings of the 2024 CHI Conference on Human Factors in Computing Systems. CHI '24. ACM (2024)
50. Pagulayan, R.J., Keeker, K., Wixon, D., Romero, R.L., Fuller, T.: User-centered design in games. In: The Human-Computer Interaction Handbook. CRC Press (2002)
51. Pedersen, C., Togelius, J., Yannakakis, G.N.: Modeling player experience for content creation. IEEE Trans. Comput. Intell. AI Games (2010)
52. Petralito, S., Brühlmann, F., Iten, G., Mekler, E.D., Opwis, K.: A good reason to die: how avatar death and high challenges enable positive experiences. In: Proceedings of the 2017 CHI Conference on Human Factors in Computing Systems (2017)
53. Pfau, J.: The real mvp: quantifying individual performances in multiplayer online games. In: 2024 IEEE Conference on Games (CoG), pp. 1–8. IEEE (2024)
54. Rajanen, M., Tapani, J.: A survey of game usability practices in North American game companies. In: ISD2018 Proceedings (2018)
55. Rienzo, A., Cubillos, C.: Playability and player experience in digital games for elderly: a systematic literature review. Sensors **20**(14), 3958 (2020)
56. Saldaña, J.: The Coding Manual for Qualitative Researchers, 2nd edn. SAGE Publications Inc., Thousand Oaks (2013)
57. Suranto, B.: Software prototypes: enhancing the quality of requirements engineering process. In: 2015 International Symposium on Technology Management and Emerging Technologies (ISTMET), pp. 148–153 (2015)
58. Tintarev, N., Masthoff, J.: Designing and evaluating explanations for recommender systems. In: Ricci, F., Rokach, L., Shapira, B., Kantor, P.B. (eds.) Recommender Systems Handbook, pp. 479–510. Springer, Boston, MA (2011). https://doi.org/10.1007/978-0-387-85820-3_15
59. Unterbusch, M., Sadeghi, M., Fischbach, J., Obaidi, M., Vogelsang, A.: Explanation needs in app reviews: taxonomy and automated detection. In: 2023 IEEE 31st International Requirements Engineering Conference Workshops (REW) (2023)

60. Väkevä, J., Hämäläinen, P., Lindqvist, J.: "don't you dare go hollow": How dark souls helps players cope with depression, a thematic analysis of reddit discussions. In: Proceedings of the 2025 CHI Conference on Human Factors in Computing Systems (2025)
61. Vigano, L., Magazzeni, D.: Explainable security. In: 2020 IEEE European Symposium on Security and Privacy Workshops (EuroS&PW). IEEE (2020)
62. Watson, D., Clark, L.A., Tellegen, A.: Development and validation of brief measures of positive and negative affect: the panas scales. J. Pers. Soc. Psychol. **54**(6), 1063 (1988)
63. Wohlin, C., Runeson, P., Höst, M., Ohlsson, M.C., Regnell, B., Wesslén, A.: Experimentation in Software Engineering. Springer, Heidelberg (2012). https://doi.org/10.1007/978-3-662-69306-3

Misunderstandings by Design: Using Erroneous Tutorials to Induce Mental Model Conflicts and the Need for Explanations

Jakob Droste[✉][iD], Hannah Deters[iD], Carolin Kirchhoff, Lukas Nagel[iD], Martin Obaidi[iD], and Kurt Schneider[iD]

Software Engineering Group, Leibniz University Hannover, Hannover, Germany
`jakob.droste@inf.uni-hannover.de`

Abstract. **[Context and motivation]** Empirical research on software explainability is challenging, as users' needs for explanations are inherently subjective. In requirements engineering, these needs are often studied through hypothetical scenarios that assume users require certain explanations. **[Question/problem]** However, such scenarios rely on tacit knowledge and risk introducing hypothetical bias. This reduces the methodological robustness of the research and threatens the validity of its findings. **[Principal ideas/results]** To address this issue, we designed and conducted an experiment that induces genuine explanation needs by deliberately creating flawed mental models through erroneous tutorial material. Participant behavior during the experiment indicates that this approach successfully triggered authentic needs for explanations. **[Contribution]** Our methodology contributes to requirements engineering for explainable systems, by providing a way to systematically observe and examine users' explanation needs under realistic conditions.

Keywords: Requirements Engineering · Mental Models · Software Understandability · Explainability Needs · User Experience

1 Introduction

A user's ability to navigate and operate a system depends on the accuracy of their mental model [18,22]. The more accurate this model is, the more efficiently a user can interact with the system [27,29]. Conversely, whenever a mental model does not align with the system's actual behavior, conflicts arise, obstructing the user's strategies to achieve their goals [9,25]. One way to aid users in developing an accurate mental model is enhancing their understanding of the system through explainability [27,30]. A common method for implementing explainability is to provide explanations through the software itself [16]. These explanations can increase system transparency and understandability, leading to more trustworthiness [1,21]. Furthermore, explaining how to operate and navigate a system can increase the usability of the software and improve user experience [11,16].

R. Guizzardi and J. Araújo (Eds.): REFSQ 2026, LNCS 16497, pp. 20–35, 2026.
https://doi.org/10.1007/978-3-032-21423-2_2

Eliciting explainability requirements is challenging, as the need for explanations is highly subjective and context-dependent [6,27]. To examine whether the timing or design of an explanation is appropriate, the user must show a genuine need. However, explainability research often relies on hypothetical scenarios, which involve tacit knowledge and hypothetical bias [7,12]. Understanding the users' mental models could help to identify conflicts that occur when user expectations and system behavior do not match, thus causing a need for explanations. However, extracting mental models in a comprehensible manner has proven to be a challenging – if not infeasible – task [2,25,27]. Systematically inducing flawed mental models could address this issue, providing a controlled way to create authentic explanation needs.

In this work, we present an experiment that examines induced mental model conflicts and how they relate to an observable need for explanations. We use the term *observable need for explanation* to refer to externally visible indicators suggesting that users may experience a subjective need for clarification. Although we cannot directly access users' internal states, behaviors such as rewatching tutorial material or expressing confusion serve as proxies for an underlying subjective need. In our experiment, we used a purposefully incorrect tutorial video for the literature management software *Citavi* to induce flawed mental models in 30 novice users. We observed our participants as they solved tasks within *Citavi*, and we deduced whether and why mental model conflicts occurred, based on their behavior and by means of a questionnaire. Our results indicate that erroneous tutorial material is an effective means of inducing flawed mental models. Furthermore, our findings confirm that conflicts arising from such flawed models lead to an observable need for explanations. The main contribution of this paper is methodological in nature. Specifically, our methodology serves as a practical framework for researching requirements engineering for explainable systems, as it provides the necessary setup for experiments where a genuine need for explanations is required. This enables the assessment of users' reactions to explanations they genuinely need, and helps identify behavioral cues that could serve as triggers for providing explanations.

From hereon, this paper is structured as follow: Sect. 2 discusses related work. Our research questions and design are detailed in Sect. 3. Section 4 lays out the findings of this work, which are then discussed in Sect. 5. Finally, we conclude this paper and discuss future work in Sect. 6.

2   Related Work

2.1   Explainability Needs and User Experience

In human-computer interaction, an explainability need – or the need for explanations – describes a user's need for explanations while they interact with a software [16]. These needs may not only appear during different contexts of use, but also concern different software aspects [6]. One widely researched topic is the explainability of a software's inner workings, especially when it comes to black-box systems that incorporate artificial intelligence (AI). In this context, research into explainable AI has identified explanations as a promising tool to make these opaque systems more understandable and trustworthy [21].

However, making software comprehensible to the average user goes beyond the explanation of AI components [14]. In fact, numerous software research areas have used explanations as a means to make systems more stakeholder-friendly. In the context of privacy needs, Brunotte et al. [5] found that privacy explanations have the potential to increase software transparency and foster user trust. Similarly, recent research has applied explainability concepts to make software security [31] and hardware requirements [28] more understandable. Regarding everyday software systems, Droste et al. [16] found that explanations may also be used to guide users through interactions during runtime, or to detail domain-specific aspects of a software.

Deters at al. [11] researched the potential effects of explanations on user experience. They state that appropriate explanations can guide interactions and further understanding, improving ease of use and learnability. However, they also find that explanations may have negative effects, such as making the software less immersive and fun to use. Similarly, Chazette et al. [8] conclude that providing too many or too detailed explanations may lead to a *double-edged sword* effect, impairing user experience. This is underlined by the research of Nunes and Jannach [26], who find that abundant or needlessly complex explanations increase the mental load on the user.

2.2 Explanations and Mental Models

In 1980, Johnson-Laird [20] introduced the term *mental model* in cognitive science, building upon Craik's [10] idea that humans have internal, cognitive models of the real world, by which they can predict events before they occur. In the context of human-computer interaction, a mental model could therefore describe how a user believes a system would behave, or how it needs to be operated [25]. Staggers and Norcio [29] conclude that mental models are more easily formed when they are induced by a third party, rather than through self-inference. Furthermore, they suggest that individuals with more accurate mental models are more efficient at predicting system behavior and solving tasks. In the context of forming mental models, we define *explaining* as the act of providing information that either 1) helps users understand unexpected system behavior or 2) guides them through interactions they struggle with (cf. Droste et al. [16]).

Kieras and Bovair [22] report on three studies concerned with the relationship between users' mental models and their ability to learn how to operate a device. Their findings suggest that more accurate mental models help users learn to operate devices more quickly and proficiently. Furthermore, users with more accurate mental models were able to infer procedures with the device more easily. The authors conclude that training material should address specific information regarding procedures, rather than general principles, descriptions or analogies.

Kulesza et al. [23] examined how explaining intelligent agents influences their users' mental models. Their findings suggest that the explanation properties *soundness* and *completeness* play a major role when trying to support a user's mental model through explanations. Explanation completeness was the most impactful factor, as complete explanations resulted in the lowest cognitive cost and the highest perceived benefit. However, only explanations that were complete and sound – meaning that they contained no inaccurate or wrong information – resulted in the most accurate mental models, and in the highest perceived understanding of and trust in the software.

Chi [9] addresses flawed mental models and mental model conflicts in the context of self-explaining. According to Chi, a mental model can be internally consistent but still incorrect. In mental models, conflicts occur whenever the holder of the model recognizes that their knowledge disagrees with what is happening in reality. Holders of flawed mental models are often unaware of the gaps in their knowledge, and conflicts between their flawed model and real-world events are frequently dismissed or explained away. In order to resolve these mental model conflict, their holders must be explicitly informed about the flaws in their mental model, e.g. through explanations that address their misunderstandings.

Blömacher et al. [3] researched the induction of flawed mental models by means of incorrect system descriptions. They provided study participants with correct and incorrect descriptions of an autonomous driving system and observed their reactions during simulated driving. Their results indicate that the successful induction of a flawed mental model may lead to an increased mental load and to performance deficits during runtime. We suspect that these findings are at least partially transferable to the research context of this work, although we examine software tutorials for mental model induction, rather than system descriptions, and examine its correlation with the need for explanations.

3 Research Design

3.1 Research Questions

The goal of this research was to induce flawed mental models and the need for explanations, using erroneous tutorial material. To this end, we conducted an experiment that was framed by the following two research questions:

RQ1: To what extent can flawed mental models be induced using erroneous tutorial material?

RQ2: How do the induced mental model conflicts correlate with an observable need for explanations?

3.2 Participants' Demography

We used an e-mail distribution system of Leibniz University Hannover to contact students that signed up to participate in empirical research studies. Out of the more than 2,000 students we contacted, 30 agreed to participate in our study. Each participant received 12€ as compensation. At the beginning of the study, they were informed that they could withdraw at any point and still receive full compensation. All participants chose to complete the entire study.

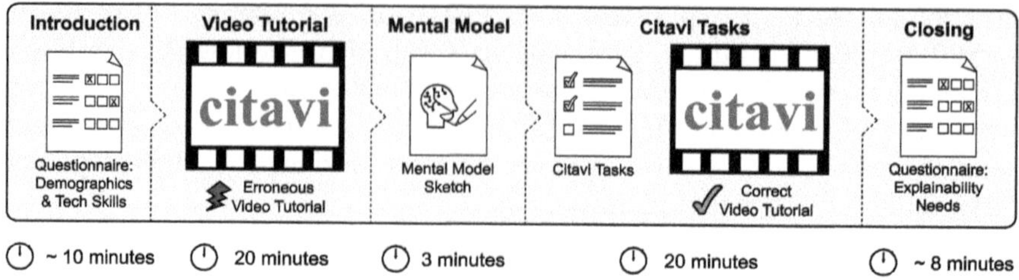

Fig. 1. Overview of the Experiment Procedure.

We chose *Citavi* as the test object, because one of its main stakeholder groups was easily accessible to us. University students are a major stakeholder group of *Citavi*, as they may use the literature management software for their own seminars, essays and theses. All participants had no prior experience with *Citavi*, which was a requirement to participate in the study. This way, we could ensure that they would not get suspicious when watching the erroneous tutorial video and could engage with the intended mental model conflicts as planned.

The ages of the participants ranged from 19 to 32. The average age was 25.3 and the median age was 25. 63.3% identified as female and 36.7% identified as male. 33.3% rated their own tech skills as above average, 60% as approximately average and only 6.7% as below average.

3.3   Material

To ensure the replicability of our experiment, we carefully prepared guidelines for experimenters. This material includes an experimenter guide detailing all steps required to prepare, conduct and conclude the experiment. Additionally, instructions for the participants were created to ensure that all participants received the exact same information. Further handouts included a data consent form and an information sheet outlining the goals of our experiment. We designed two questionnaires: one to collect information on the demographics and tech skills of our participants and a second to gather participants' feedback on their experiences during the experiment. Additionally, an observation sheet was prepared, on which experimenters noted down any questions or comments from the participants. Lastly, the computer system used for the experiment was set up with a *Citavi* project containing 38 titles, a folder of PDF files, a literature list in a Word file and two versions of the tutorial video. The first version included intentionally erroneous information to induce mental model conflicts. The second version described the correct steps. To avoid language barriers, we conducted the experiment and provided all materials in German language.

3.4   Experiment Procedure

An overview of our experiment procedure is provided in Fig. 1. The experiment started with participants reading the informed consent sheet as well as information on the processing and saving of data. Participants were also informed about the experiment structure and the fact that a screen recording was used to determine their strategies to solve the tasks. Then, they were asked to fill out the first questionnaire regarding demographic and tech skill information. Following this introductory phase, participants watched the erroneous video tutorial on how to use *Citavi*. Meanwhile, they were allowed to take notes. Participants were given a total of 20 min to familiarize themselves with the tutorial, but those who completed this task earlier could proceed at their own pace.

By initially watching the erroneous video tutorial, participants were supposed to form a flawed mental model of how to operate *Citavi* in the later stages of the experiment. We placed the correct video tutorial on the desktop, so that it could help participants when they encountered the intended errors during the later experiment. If participants chose to open the correct tutorial, we interpreted this as a need for explanation, as detailed in Sect. 3.6.

In a break of 3 min after the video tutorial phase, the video player was closed by the experimenter. This meant that only the correct video tutorial was now available for the remainder of the study. During this break, we asked participants to sketch their mental model of *Citavi* to the best of their ability on a piece of paper provided on a separate desk. In particular, we told them to "sketch how they think *Citavi* works, after having watched the tutorial".

After completing their sketch, participants returned to the lab computer. They received a set of instructions and a time frame of 20 min to work on them. The instructions consisted of tasks that participants were asked to fulfill by operating *Citavi* based on the information they had gathered from the video tutorial. They were informed that the video tutorial was available on the desktop, should they wish to rewatch it. During this period, the experimenters did not answer any questions that participants raised. Instead, any questions or comments were recorded on the observation sheet.

Once the participant had finished the tasks or the 20 min had expired, the screen recording was stopped and they were asked to fill out the feedback questionnaire. Experimenters collected all handwritten notes and mental model sketches. Lastly, an information sheet on the true purpose of the study - namely the induction of mental model conflicts - were handed out.

3.5 Experiment Tasks

As a literature management software, *Citavi* offers a number of different features to find, collect, organize and filter literature. In the context of our experiment, we had participants attempt tasks concerning two of *Citavi*'s main features: (1) adding literature to an existing project and (2) filtering literature by using the quick search feature. For both use cases, participants were faced with two tasks each, one that was correctly explained in the tutorial video and another containing an intended error. All participants started the experiment with the same existing *Citavi* project, which already contained some literature files, while all other necessary files (PDF and Word) were available on the lab computer's desktop. The tasks were structured as follows:

T1.1 PDF file drag & drop: We asked participants to add multiple PDF files to the existing *Citavi* project, which was possible using drag & drop. This was correctly explained in the video tutorial.

T1.2 Word file drag & drop (intended error task): We asked participants to add a Word file, which contained identifiers (e.g. DOI) for multiple scientific works, to the existing *Citavi* project. If done correctly (via the file browser), this adds all identified literature to the project. However, the erroneous tutorial falsely indicated that this could be done using drag & drop.

T2.1 Full-text search (intended error task): We asked participants to perform a full-text search that required wildcards (words starting with "un" and ending with "ing" can be found via "un*ing"). In reality, *Citavi* does not support wildcards in its full-text search, but the erroneous tutorial incorrectly stated that it does.

T2.2 Title search: We asked participants to search the *Citavi* project for literature using a specific term in the title. Furthermore, the publication dates had to be limited to a specified time frame. This is entirely possible and was correctly explained by the tutorial.

3.6   Data Analysis Procedures

Four different types of data were collected throughout the study: video recordings, audio recordings, mental model sketches and text data. Firstly, the participants' screens were recorded while they completed the task. Audio was recorded to capture any questions posed to the experimenters. The sketches of the mental models were drawn on blank white paper with a pen or pencil. Lastly, text data was collected from participants' answers in the feedback questionnaire, where they stated at which points they had problems solving the tasks.

To answer our research questions, we first analyzed whether the flawed mental models were successfully induced and then analyzed if there was a need for explanations due to the incorrect mental models. Figure 2 shows an overview of these two steps. Two measures were taken to determine whether the mental model was successfully induced. Firstly, the sketches of the mental models were examined by two authors to identify whether the two incorrect pieces of information - namely the drag & drop function and the search in full-texts - appeared in the sketches. While a sketch not containing an intended error does not proof that the mental model is entirely accurate, a sketch explicitly containing an error is a certain indicator of the mental model being flawed, and was treated as such. Secondly, we analyzed the screen recordings to check whether the participants followed the instructions from the erroneous tutorial when completing each task. For each task, we recorded whether participants followed the tutorial (y), did not follow it (n) or whether they did not attempt to work on the task at all (n.a.). Whenever the tutorial was followed despite being wrong, we concluded that the flawed mental model was successfully induced.

Next, we examined if the participants had a need for explanation when they were confronted with the mental model conflicts (RQ2). We defined five indica-

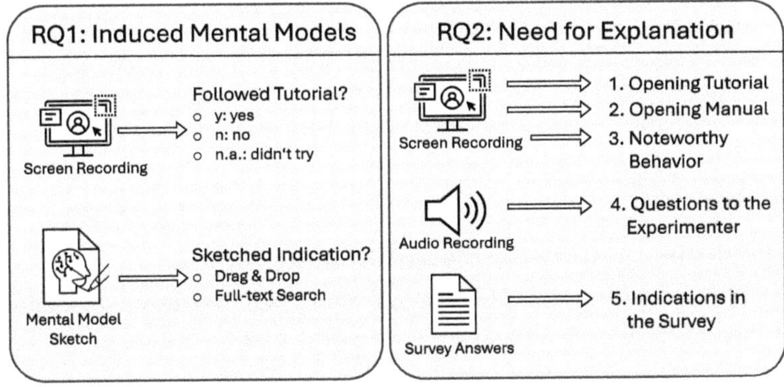

Fig. 2. Overview of the Data Analysis Practices.

tors that constituted a need for explanation after participants failed an intended error task:

1. **Opening the tutorial video:** Accessing the tutorial video indicates that the participant sought an explanation (identified in screen recordings).
2. **Opening the manual:** Consulting the manual also indicates an active search for an explanation (identified through screen recordings).
3. **Noteworthy behavior:** Behavior such as frantic clicking or repeated attempts at completing a task indicates a need for explanation, as found by Deters et al. [13] (identified through screen recordings).
4. **Questions to the experimenter about the software:** Some participants asked questions like"Are you sure it works this way?", indicating that they sought assistance (identified through audio recordings).
5. **Indications in the survey:** If participants mentioned difficulties with solving an intended error task in the survey, it indicates that they could have used an explanation (identified through survey responses).

Two authors individually reviewed the all screen recordings, including audio, and analyzed the survey responses. To report the inter-rater agreement, we calculate Cohen's κ [4] as well as its chance-corrected variant Brennan & Prediger κ [4]. After the inter-rater agreement was calculated, all remaining conflicts were discussed and resolved.

3.7 Data Availability Statement

To enable the verification and replication of our experiment, we provide a replication package [15]. Within the package, we provide a step-by-step protocol to prepare and conduct the experiment, as well as the instructions provided to participants throughout the experiment. This includes instructions for the deception and debriefing of the participants, as well as definitions for what qualifies as a need for explanations. We also provide both the erroneous and correct tutorial videos. The narrative audio tracks have been removed to address anonymity concerns on behalf of the narrator. To compensate for the removal of audio, we include the corresponding closed captions and text scripts, enabling researchers to reproduce the audio tracks in German or English language.

4   Results

4.1   RQ1: Induction of the Flawed Mental Models

Mental Model Sketches. The participants each produced a mental model sketch, resulting in 30 overall sketches. As described in Sect. 3.6, we filtered the sketches for contents related to the intended error tasks. Furthermore, to show differences between different kinds of sketches, we decided to categorize them according to their form of visualization. The summarized findings can be found in Table 1. Each mental model sketch could contain either both, only one or none of the intended errors.

Table 1. Mental Model Sketches and Induced Mental Model Flaws

Type of Sketch	Count	Error 1.2 (Drag & Drop)	Error 2.1 (FT Search)
User interface	12	4	3
Mindmap	6	3	4
Descriptive text	5	1	1
Functional diagram	4	1	1
Casual drawing	3	/	/
Overall	30	9	9

Overall, only every third sketch contained each error respectively. Errors appeared more often in drawings of the user interface and in mindmaps – which are rather casual forms of visualization – compared to more complex descriptive texts and functional diagrams. While this could indicate that the presence of intended errors relates to the complexity of the sketch, no errors appeared in the casual drawings, which contradicts this interpretation. In order to draw more confident conclusions concerning these observations, a larger sample size would be required. Furthermore, both intended errors appeared to be evenly split for every type of mental model sketch. As such, we cannot draw conclusions regarding the relationship between the type of mental model error and the form of visualization.

Following the Erroneous Tutorial. When analyzing the screen recordings of our participants attempting the tasks, we noted whether or not they attempted the task. If they did, we also noted whether or not they followed the erroneous tutorial, leading them to encounter the intended errors. A summary of these findings is shown in Table 2.

Table 2. Experiment Task Resolution and Tutorial Following

Task Resolution	Task 1.1	Task 1.2 (Error)	Task 2.1 (Error)	Task 2.2
Did follow tutorial	28	23	18	22
Did not follow tutorial	2	6	10	4
Did not attempt task	/	1	2	4

All 30 participants attempted task 1.1 (PDF file drag & drop), which contained no intended errors. Out of the 30 participants, 28 (93.3%) followed the steps described in the tutorial. The related intended error task 1.2 (Word file drag & drop) was attempted by 29 participants, 23 of whom (79.3%) followed the erroneous tutorial. Task 2.1 (full-text search), which was an intended error task, was attempted by 28 participants, 18 of whom (64.3%) followed the erroneous tutorial. Lastly, the related task 2.2 (title search), with no intended errors, was attempted by 26 participants, 22 of whom (84.6%) followed the tutorial.

These findings suggest that the flawed mental model was successfully induced in at least 79.3% of participants for the first intended error and in at least 64.3% for the second intended error. A chi-square test showed no significant association ($\chi^2 = 1.59$, $p = .207$) between task and intended error commitment. However, the ratios being much higher than the ones identified through the mental model sketches underlines the notion that the explicit extraction of mental models alone does not provide sufficient grounds for the investigation of mental model flaws.

In light of this observation, we analyzed the relationship between participants who included intended errors in their sketches and those who ultimately committed the errors during the tasks. The findings are summarized in Table 3.

Table 3. Intended Errors in Mental Model Sketches and their Committing during Task Attempts

Error 1.2	sketched	not sketched	Error 2.1	sketched	not sketched
Committed	6	17	Committed	5	13
No commit	2	4	No commit	3	7
No attempt	1	/	No attempt	1	1

In both cases (1.2 and 2.1), the majority of participants committed the intended errors. This was true in all cases, independent of whether the participant had included the error in their previously provided mental model sketch. As intended error 2.1 (64.3%) was committed less often than intended error 1.2 (79.3%), we hypothesize that the successful induction of the flawed mental model depends on the complexity of the conveyed information – the (incorrect) tutorial for task 2.1 (full-text search) being more complex than for task 1.2 (drag & drop) and also being followed less often.

Notably, some participants whose sketches contained the induced mental model flaws did not commit the intended errors during their attempts at solving the tasks, but instead committed different types of unintended errors. This indicates that even if the flaws were successfully induced initially, some participants forgot how they were supposed to (incorrectly) attempt the tasks. As the phenomenon was more prevalent for intended error task 2.1 (37.5%) than for 1.2 (25%), we deduce that the loss of the flawed mental model is also connected to the complexity of the conveyed information, similar to our previous observations.

4.2   RQ2: Mental Model Conflicts and Explanation Needs

Whenever participants followed the erroneous tutorial while attempting an intended error task, we deduced whether they showed a need for explanations based on the behavior they displayed and the survey answers they provided. We applied the criteria described in Sect. 3.6 and report the inter-rater agreement accordingly. The summarized findings can be found in Table 4. Mean occurrence $\bar{x}$ applies to all participants for whom the indicator occurred at least once. $\bar{x}$ reflects how often these participants showed the respective behavior on average.

Table 4. Observed Indicators for Explanation Needs – Percentage of Participants who commited the Error (%) and Mean Occurrence per Participant ($\bar{x}$)

Observed Indicators	Error 1.2 (Drag & Drop)		Error 2.1 (FT Search)	
Opening tutorial	50%	$\bar{x} = 1.3$	27%	$\bar{x} = 2.4$
Opening manual	7%	$\bar{x} = 2.5$	0%	$\bar{x} = 0.0$
Noteworthy behavior	30%	$\bar{x} = 1.3$	10%	$\bar{x} = 1.0$
Asking question	20%	$\bar{x} = 1.0$	3%	$\bar{x} = 1.0$
Survey indication	53%	$\bar{x} = 2.0$	37%	$\bar{x} = 1.7$
Need for explanation	87.0%	$\bar{x} = 3.7$	66.7%	$\bar{x} = 3.5$

The proportional agreement between the raters was 91.3% for intended error task 1.2, and 88.9% for intended error task 2.1. This describes the percentage of cases in which both researchers reached the same conclusions. Cohen's κ [4] was determined at 69.7% and 77.5%. The chance-corrected Brennan & Prediger κ [4] values were 82.6% and 77.8%. In accordance with Landis and Koch [24], these values reflect substantial to almost perfect inter-rater agreement.

The induction of the flawed mental models for both intended error tasks resulted in an observable need for explanations in the majority of participants. We identified a need for explanation in 87.0% of participants whenever the intended error for task 1.2 was committed. For task 2.1, 66.7% of participants encountering the intended error showed a need for explanation. A chi-square test showed no significant association ($\chi^2 = 2.43$, $p = .119$) between task and explanation need. Similar to our previous observations, we attribute the observed divergence in success to the higher complexity of intended error task 2.1. In particular, we observed that some participants, who had the flawed mental model successfully induced, did not realize that they had not successfully solved the task, due to its complexity, and thus did not display an explicit need for explanations.

5 Discussion

5.1 RQ1: The Potential of Inducing Mental Model Conflicts

Our results show that it is possible to induce mental model conflicts in a targeted manner, using erroneous tutorial material. Notably, whether a flawed mental model is successfully induced in a participant, and how easily they lose this incorrect knowledge, seems to depend on the complexity of the information. This is a valuable insight, as it can support future explainability research, specifically in the context of explanation contents and design.

Research into explanation content and design is concerned with what information a stakeholder requires from an explanation and how that information should be presented. A common method to address these questions are explainability scenarios [7], in which subjects are asked what explanation content and design they might prefer in a specific scenario. This kind of research is commonly subject to hypothetical bias [19] and relies on participants' tacit knowledge [17], as the scenario in question might not be a familiar use case for the subject. Consequently, researchers cannot ensure that a study participant genuinely needs the explanations that they are showing them. Inducing mental model conflicts has the potential to address this issue, as the explanations are known to be actually needed when they are shown to the subjects.

5.2 RQ2: The Relationship Between Mental Models and Explainability Needs

Our findings indicate that conflicts between a user's mental model and the system often lead to explainability needs, which in turn cause confusion and frustration. Conversely, this means that a more accurate mental model should reduce the need for explanations. Since reading and understanding explanations can be time-consuming and puts a cognitive load on the user, the goal should be to develop systems that provide only as many explanations as necessary. Minimizing explanation needs could be achieved by providing appropriate tutorial material when introducing users to a new software, helping them form a more accurate mental model and avoiding conflicts with the system.

In some cases, participants did not notice that they had failed to complete a task. Following Chi [9], these cases still constitute flawed mental models, even if the user is unaware. If a user is not aware of the flaws in their mental model, they are unlikely to request help on their own initiative, even though an explanation might be helpful to them. This serves as further motivation for future research into alternative triggers for explanations, such as physiological data or telemetry, to detect when a user may need assistance without explicitly asking for it.

5.3   How to Use in RE

The practical application of our methodology requires a minimum setup of two researchers, one lab computer with the test software (e.g. *Citavi*) installed, video viewing and task instructions, sketching materials and the pre- and post-experiment questionnaires. During the experiment only one researcher is required as supervisor. However, the coding procedure should be conducted by two researchers as data analysts, to ensure strong internal validity. Examples of the experiment materials can be found in our replication package [15].

5.4   Threats to Validity

We discuss the limitations of the validity of this work in accordance with Wohlin et al. [32]:

Construct Validity. Our experiment was conducted within-subjects, as all participants attempted the same set of two correctly explained and two incorrectly explained tasks. Furthermore, we had no participants attempting the tasks without viewing any tutorial at all. A between-subjects design, using two control groups, could have increased the validity of our findings. Future work should include the treatment group, watching the erroneous tutorial, and two control groups – one without a tutorial and one with a correct tutorial. Since the ability to form a mental model depends on the time available to engage with the tutorial, our experiment relies on participants' ability to learn and retain information quickly. More time to view the tutorial might have led to a higher success rate in inducing the flawed mental models.

Internal Validity. The experiment was conducted by one of three researchers each, in individual sessions. Given the duration of each session and the verbal communication with participants, differences between the researchers might have introduced bias. We mitigated this by preparing and following a thorough experiment guide, and by piloting the experiment with multiple researchers present. The piloting itself was done in three iterations, with a total of 8 pilots. We refined the study material according to the feedback of the pilots. As discussed in our findings, the results of our study are likely biased by task complexity. Different tasks might have led to a different success rate, which highlights the importance of identifying a suitable task complexity before inducing the erroneous mental model. What can be considered a suitable complexity depends on the participants' backgrounds, as more tech-affine users would likely be able to understand more complex instructions. As the erroneous instructions were followed less often for task 2.1 than for task 1.2, we can reasonably assume that the complexity of task 2.1 was too high for at least some of our participants' level of tech skills.

Conclusion Validity. We conducted our experiment with a total of 30 individual participants. As the main contributions of this work is methodological, we consider this to be a sufficient sample size. Thus, we are confident in the validity of our conclusions within the context of our experimental setting (*Citavi* used by students). Furthermore, we followed a rigorous protocol to ensure that all participants were subjected to identical test conditions, avoiding bias that may arise from varied test conditions. Although none of our participants had previously used *Citavi*, we cannot ensure that had no pre-existing mental model of a similar software before the experiment. As such, we cannot guarantee that the tutorial really was responsible for the observed effects in all participants.

External Validity. The experiment was conducted using *Citavi*, which may limit the generalizability of our findings to similar types of software. In particular, other types of software might differentiate in the ways that mental model conflicts manifest and explainability needs arise. All participants of our study were university students or recently graduated. Their median age was 25 and all of them were living in Germany. Therefore, the findings of this work may not be generalizable to a broader population. Our findings might also be confounded by participants' memory retention, as the successful induction of the flawed mental models relied on their ability to remember the erroneous tutorial. As our participants were young students, they were likely able to remember the tutorial better, limiting the generalizability to other demographics.

6 Conclusion

Forming an accurate mental model is a key factor in interacting with systems in an effective manner. In particular, knowing how to operate a system and understanding its behavior enables high levels of user experience and efficiency. Whenever users encounter unexpected system behavior or misunderstand an interaction, their mental model conflicts with the actual software behavior, leading to confusion and frustration. Explanations provided within the software have the potential to resolve these conflicts by providing transparency and increasing the users' understanding of the software.

In this work, we reported on an experiment that investigated the relationship between induced mental model conflicts and observable explanation needs. Our research results in two key observations: (1) it is possible to induce mental model conflicts in users by providing them with erroneous tutorial material, and (2) the majority of these mental model conflicts result in an explicit need for explanations. These findings have important implications for research on explainability, as our methodology enables researchers to induce an authentic need for explanation in system users. This enables observations in realistic user scenarios, which are a prerequisite for methodologically robust explainability research.

Acknowledgments. This work was funded by the Deutsche Forschungsgemeinschaft (DFG, German Research Foundation) under Grant No.: 470146331, project softXplain (2022–2026). We sincerely thank Michael Rohs for his thorough feedback concerning the research procedure and written manuscript.

References

1. Adadi, A., Berrada, M.: Peeking inside the black-box: a survey on explainable artificial intelligence (xai). IEEE Access **6**, 52138–52160 (2018)
2. Anders, M., Obaidi, M., Paech, B., Schneider, K.: A study on the mental models of users concerning existing software. In: Gervasi, V., Vogelsang, A. (eds.) REFSQ 2022. LNCS, vol. 13216, pp. 235–250. Springer, Cham (2022). https://doi.org/10.1007/978-3-030-98464-9_18
3. Blömacher, K., Nöcker, G., Huff, M.: The evolution of mental models in relation to initial information while driving automated. Transport. Res. F: Traffic Psychol. Behav. **68**, 198–217 (2020)
4. Brennan, R.L., Prediger, D.J.: Coefficient kappa: some uses, misuses, and alternatives. Educ. Psychol. Measur. **41**(3), 687–699 (1981)
5. Brunotte, W., Specht, A., Chazette, L., Schneider, K.: Privacy explanations-a means to end-user trust. J. Syst. Softw. **195**, 111545 (2023)
6. Chazette, L., Brunotte, W., Speith, T.: Exploring explainability: a definition, a model, and a knowledge catalogue. In: 2021 IEEE 29th International Requirements Engineering Conference (RE), pp. 197–208. IEEE (2021)
7. Chazette, L., Klünder, J., Balci, M., Schneider, K.: How can we develop explainable systems? Insights from a literature review and an interview study. In: Proceedings of the International Conference on Software and System Processes and International Conference on Global Software Engineering, pp. 1–12 (2022)
8. Chazette, L., Schneider, K.: Explainability as a non-functional requirement: challenges and recommendations. Requir. Eng. **25**(4), 493–514 (2020). https://doi.org/10.1007/s00766-020-00333-1
9. Chi, M.T.: Self-explaining expository texts: the dual processes of generating inferences and repairing mental models. In: Advances in Instructional Psychology, vol. 5, pp. 161–238. Routledge (2013)
10. Craik, K.J.W.: The Nature of Explanation. Cambridge University Press, Cambridge (1943)
11. Deters, H., Droste, J., Hess, A., Klös, V., Schneider, K., Speith, T., Vogelsang, A.: The x factor: on the relationship between user experience and explainability. In: Proceedings of the 13th Nordic Conference on Human-Computer Interaction, pp. 1–12 (2024)
12. Deters, H., Droste, J., Schneider, K.: On the pulse of requirements elicitation: physiological triggers and explainability needs. In: CreaRE Workshop at the 2024 International Working Conference on Requirements Engineering: Foundation for Software Quality (2024)
13. Deters, H., Reinhardt, L., Droste, J., Obaidi, M., Schneider, K.: Identifying explanation needs: towards a catalog of user-based indicators. In: 2025 IEEE 33rd International Requirements Engineering Conference (RE), pp. 31–42. IEEE (2025)
14. Droste, J., Deters, H., Fuchs, R., Schneider, K.: Peeking outside the black-box: AI explainability requirements beyond interpretability. In: RE4AI Workshop at the 2024 International Working Conference on Requirements Engineering: Foundation for Software Quality (2024)
15. Droste, J., Deters, H., Kirchhoff, C., Nagel, L., Obaidi, M., Schneider, K.: Supplementary Material - "Misunderstandings by Design: Using Erroneous Tutorials to Induce Mental Model Conflicts and the Need for Explanations" (REFSQ'26) (2026). https://doi.org/10.5281/zenodo.18300484

16. Droste, J., Deters, H., Obaidi, M., Klünder, J., Schneider, K.: Framing what can be explained-an operational taxonomy for explainability needs. Requir. Eng. 1–23 (2025)
17. Ferrari, A., Spoletini, P., Gnesi, S.: Ambiguity and tacit knowledge in requirements elicitation interviews. Requir. Eng. **21**(3), 333–355 (2016). https://doi.org/10.1007/s00766-016-0249-3
18. Halasz, F.G., Moran, T.P.: Mental models and problem solving in using a calculator. In: Proceedings of the SIGCHI Conference on Human Factors in Computing Systems, pp. 212–216 (1983)
19. Harrison, G.W., Rutström, E.E.: Experimental evidence on the existence of hypothetical bias in value elicitation methods. Handb. Exp. Econ. Results **1**, 752–767 (2008)
20. Johnson-Laird, P.N.: Mental models in cognitive science. Cogn. Sci. **4**(1), 71–115 (1980)
21. Kästner, L., Langer, M., Lazar, V., Schomäcker, A., Speith, T., Sterz, S.: On the relation of trust and explainability: why to engineer for trustworthiness. In: 2021 IEEE 29th International Requirements Engineering Conference Workshops (REW), pp. 169–175. IEEE (2021)
22. Kieras, D.E., Bovair, S.: The role of a mental model in learning to operate a device. Cogn. Sci. **8**(3), 255–273 (1984)
23. Kulesza, T., Stumpf, S., Burnett, M., Yang, S., Kwan, I., Wong, W.K.: Too much, too little, or just right? Ways explanations impact end users' mental models. In: 2013 IEEE Symposium on Visual Languages and Human Centric Computing, pp. 3–10. IEEE (2013)
24. Landis, J.R., Koch, G.G.: The measurement of observer agreement for categorical data. Biometrics **33**(1), 159–174 (1977)
25. Norman, D.A.: Some observations on mental models. In: Mental Models, pp. 15–22. Psychology Press (2014)
26. Nunes, I., Jannach, D.: A systematic review and taxonomy of explanations in decision support and recommender systems. User Model. User-Adapt. Interact. **27**, 393–444 (2017)
27. Sokol, K., Flach, P.: One explanation does not fit all: the promise of interactive explanations for machine learning transparency. KI-Künstliche Intelligenz **34**(2), 235–250 (2020)
28. Speith, T., Speith, J., Becker, S., Zou, Y., Biega, A., Paar, C.: Explainability as a requirement for hardware: introducing explainable hardware (xhw). In: 2024 IEEE 32nd International Requirements Engineering Conference (RE). IEEE (2024)
29. Staggers, N., Norcio, A.F.: Mental models: concepts for human-computer interaction research. Int. J. Man Mach. Stud. **38**(4), 587–605 (1993)
30. Tankelevitch, L., et al.: The metacognitive demands and opportunities of generative ai. In: Proceedings of the CHI Conference on Human Factors in Computing Systems, pp. 1–24 (2024)
31. Vigano, L., Magazzeni, D.: Explainable security. In: 2020 IEEE European Symposium on Security and Privacy Workshops (EuroS&PW), pp. 293–300. IEEE (2020)
32. Wohlin, C., Runeson, P., Höst, M., Ohlsson, M.C., Regnell, B., Wesslén, A.: Experimentation in Software Engineering. Springer, Heidelberg (2012). https://doi.org/10.1007/978-3-662-69306-3

All Eyes on User Needs: Using Gaze and Pupillometric Measures to Identify Explanation Needs

Laura Reinhardt(✉)[iD], Hannah Deters(✉)[iD], Jakob Droste[iD],
and Kurt Schneider[iD]

Software Engineering Group, Leibniz Universität Hannover, Hannover, Germany
{laura.reinhardt,hannah.deters,jakob.droste,
kurt.schneider}@inf.uni-hannover.de

Abstract. **[Context and motivation]** Due to the increasing complexity of software systems, explainability has become a relevant quality aspect. Since the need for explanation is highly user- and context-dependent, the requirements engineering process of explainability is particularly important. **[Question/problem]** The elicitation of explanation needs is time-consuming and may be subject to several biases. To mitigate these biases, explanation needs are often elicited by observing users while using the respective system. However, this process is not trivial and depends on detailed insights into user behavior. **[Principal ideas/results]** Eye tracking data provides precise eye movement visualizations and indicates how long specific points on the screen are focused on, allowing for deeper insights into user behavior. Eye trackers can also provide indications of stress and mental load by monitoring pupil diameter. These insights might support the elicitation of explanation needs. **[Contribution]** In this paper, we aim to take the first step towards identifying explanation needs using eye tracking data. We provide three key contributions: (1) We demonstrate that eye tracking data supports the manual detection of explanation needs. (2) We identify four gaze patterns that occur during the need for explanation. (3) We determine the amplitude of saccades in combination with gaze patterns as a promising indicator of the need for explanation, paving the way for future research.

Keywords: Eye Tracking · Explainability · Requirements Engineering

1 Introduction

Nowadays, software systems are becoming increasingly extensive and therefore more complicated for users to understand. The emergence of artificially

---

L. Reinhardt and H. Deters—These authors contributed equally to this research and share the first authorship.

R. Guizzardi and J. Araújo (Eds.): REFSQ 2026, LNCS 16497, pp. 36–52, 2026.
https://doi.org/10.1007/978-3-032-21423-2_3

intelligent (AI) systems further contributes to the complexity of system outputs [1]. Therefore, software-sided explanations have become an important part of quality-oriented software development [5,10].

The elicitation of explanation needs is challenging as it can be affected by hypothetical and confirmation bias [11,15,18]. When users are asked if they want a specific explanation, they tend to agree because they do not see any downsides [15]. However, explanations do have downsides, such as time or mental effort [12,21]. On the other hand, if no specific suggestions are made, users find it difficult to put themselves in the situation and imagine what possible explanations they might need. [18].

For this reason, an effective method is to identify the need for explanation by observing users as they use the system [9,11]. To this end, Deters et al. [12] established indicators that point to explanation needs. They revealed that physical reactions can indicate a need for explanation. An explanation need may trigger emotional reactions, such as anger or stress. Furthermore, behavior within the system also proved to be a promising indicator of a need for explanation [12].

Eye tracking offers a way to monitor the exact gaze of users and to track how long they focus on specific points on the screen [2]. This makes it useful for gaining deeper insight into user behavior. Furthermore, eye trackers are able to monitor pupil diameter, which is an established indicator of mental load and stress [23]. Due to these two features, it appears reasonable that eye trackers can also assist in identifying the need for explanation.

In this paper, we conduct an exploratory study that investigates in which way eye tracking data can help to identify the need for explanation. In particular, we aim to establish a starting point for research in this area. To this end, we manually analyze the visualizations of the eye tracking data from 14 participants in order to extract eye movement patterns and create an initial approach for identifying explanation needs. In this process, we identified four gaze patterns that occurred more frequently when explanations were needed. We then mapped these gaze patterns to common eye tracking metrics such as saccade amplitude and fixation time and investigated whether these are able to detect the need for explanations. Thus, we are taking the first step toward automated detection of explanation needs, considerably facilitating the requirements elicitation process.

The remainder of this paper is structured as follows: In Chap. 2, we provide background information on explainability and eye tracking. In Chap. 3, we outline the research questions and present the study design. In Chap. 4, we present the results of the study, and in Chap. 5, we discuss the implications. We conclude in Chap. 6 and outline future research.

2 Background and Related Work

2.1 Explainability

Explainability has become a key quality aspect and non-functional requirement of many modern software systems [5,10]. In essence, explainability describes the ability of a system to explain any aspect of itself to its stakeholders [5,

14]. In the context of AI, these explanations often concern the reasoning for system behavior and decision-making, to increase transparency and trust [1, 13]. However, explanation requirements may address a number of other system aspects as well [13] and are not limited to AI software [14]. In the context of human-computer interaction, explanations are a prominent method to guide user interactions and improve learnability [9,14]. Software-sided explanations may also be used to improve the users' domain knowledge [13,14] or convey privacy information [3,13].

With regard to end-users' explainability needs, traditional empirical methods such as workshops [14,22], interviews [6,22] and questionnaires [6,15] have proven to be effective means of requirements elicitation. However, in some cases it is important to minimize potential bias in order to achieve particularly reliable results, or to conduct the elicitation during the runtime in order to trigger explanations at the right time. In these cases, the evaluation of user behavior is a suitable method for identifying explanation needs [9,11]. Note that a need for explanation does not necessarily mean that an explanation must be embedded in the system, but rather expresses a desire for change or clarification, which may also be implemented with UI changes [12].

2.2 Eye Tracking

Non-intrusive eye trackers are devices that measure eye movements in real time as participants perform a task involving looking at a stimulus on a screen [16]. They have the capability of externalizing internal processes and the visual attention of the user, including unconscious gazes, without distracting or interrupting the user's task [2]. A critical component of analyzing emotional processes, such as frustration or stress, is the measurement of pupil diameter. Pupillometric measures, such as pupil diameter, change according to cognitive load [25], mental effort [7] and informational or emotional processes [17]. Specifically pupil dilation serves as an indicator of stress factors, including mental and cognitive load [25], or general changes in the user's mood [27].

Furthermore, there are multiple metrics to analyze different eye movements of users. The most important metrics can be divided in metrics based on scan paths, metrics based on fixations and metrics based on saccades [27]. Scan paths are defined as sequences of eye movements, created by combining both fixations and saccades [24]. They can visualize complete gaze patterns over a longer period of time. Most of the cognitive processing takes place during the fixations [27,28]. Fixations are the stabilization of the eyes on a specific part of a stimulus for around $200 - 300$ ms and can last up to a few seconds [27,28]. Chen et al. [7] demonstrated that increased fixation duration correlates with heightened attention allocated to more complex tasks. Saccades are voluntary eye movements that occur between fixations within $40 - 50$ ms [27]. Amplitude of saccade, also referred to as saccade magnitude or saccade size, is defined as the angular distance traversed by the eye across the screen [27].

2.3 Related Work

Deters et al. [11] examined whether biometric data, such as electrodermal activity, could serve as an indicator of needs for explanation. This investigation was predicated on the assumption that such needs would correlate with increased stress levels. Participants were assigned tasks designed to trigger explanation needs, while biometric data was recorded as a byproduct using a biometric watch. The researchers concluded that electrodermal activity might serve as a useful indicator for the need for explanation.

Jyotsna et al. [4] attempted to measure students' stress levels using an eye tracker. Test subjects were confronted with various stimuli, including mathematical tasks and videos. In order to examine the effects of cognitive load and fatigue on stress, the researchers analyzed pupil diameter and blink frequency. The findings revealed that eye trackers can accurately measure stress levels, and that there is a correlation between pupil dilation or blink frequency, and stress experienced by test subjects.

Li et al. [20] present a framework for evaluating the level of satisfaction of non-functional requirements (NFR). This framework utilizes four initial levels of eye tracking metrics, including fixations and saccades to detect events in users. Moreover, the researchers extracted three distinct gaze patterns: Learning, Searching and Processing. These patterns, when combined with eye tracking metrics, can be used to identify needs in implicit user feedback regarding consistency and ease of use. To this date, there are no known gaze patterns or eye tracking metrics to identify explanation needs in the context of explainability requirements.

3 Research Design

3.1 Research Questions

RQ1: Do the visualizations of gaze paths help to manually determine the time intervals when a need for explanation arises?
RQ2: What gaze patterns do users exhibit when they need an explanation in a software system?
RQ3: Which eye tracking metrics provide indications of a need for explanation?

RQ1 aims to determine whether visualizations of gaze paths help to pinpoint exactly when a need for explanation arises. To this end, we want to examine whether the time intervals of two coders are more consistent when they have access to the gaze paths. A higher degree of consistency would indicate that subjectivity in recognizing the need for explanation would be reduced. With RQ2, we manually examine which gaze patterns users exhibit when they need an explanation. By manually analyzing gaze patterns, we want to establish a starting point that will facilitate automated recognition at a later stage. With RQ3, we take one further step to the automatic detection by investigating suitable eye tracking metrics. To this end, we examine common eye tracking metrics that correspond to the gaze patterns from RQ2 and assess whether these change measurably during the need for explanation. In addition, we also examine whether pupil diameter changes during the need for explanation.

3.2   Study Design

We conducted a controlled experiment to answer the two research questions. During the experiment, we asked participants to interact with a test software which was designed to trigger needs for explanation. The experiment took approximately 9 min on average. Throughout the study, participants' eyes were tracked via the screen-based Tobii X3-120 eye tracker mounted to the monitor the participants were working on. The Eye Tracker recorded the users' eye movements and pupil diameter during their interaction with the test software. At the end of the experiment, we conducted a semi-structured interview in which participants described their needs for explanations regarding the software.

Test Software. The test software was a tool for students to plan their courses for the next semester. In the first step, users registered with their name, email address, and date of birth. In the second step, they selected the courses they had already taken. In step three, they are asked to rate three modules to help subsequent users choose their courses. In step four, the user receives five suggestions for courses. In step five, the user can view details and ratings for the suggested courses. We provide screenshots of the tool in our supplementary material [26].

Table 1. Intended needs for explanation

Needs	Description	Type of need [14]
E1	The user does not know how to enter the date of birth in the correct format	Interaction
E2	The user does not know how to select the modules they have already passed	Interaction
E3	The user does not know that they must enter at least 90 characters and therefore cannot proceed	Interaction
E4	The user is unfamiliar with the term "erudite" (an unusual German term for "lecturer")	Domain Knowledge
E5	The user is confused about a course recommendation, that does not fit their field of study	System Behavior
E6	The user does not know how to return to the previous page, because there is no back button	Interaction

The test software we used for our experiment was specifically designed to trigger different types of explanation needs. Six parts of the software intended to trigger a need for explanation (see Table 1). The first three needs (E1 − E3) were intended to trigger explanation needs concerning the interaction with the system. In need E4, the user was confronted with a specific term, that was intended to trigger an explanation need regarding domain knowledge. After selecting their modules in E2, the user gets shown an unsuitable module recommendation(E5), triggering a need for an explanation regarding system behavior. For the last intended explanation need (E6), the software does not include a back button on one page, so that the user must find another way to return to the previous page.

Demographics. A total of 14 participants were included in the study through convenience sampling. The participant pool included 8 males and 6 females, between 21 and 36 years old. All of them were Computer Science Students.

Data Collection. We collected three types of data (see Fig. 1). First, we collected eye tracking data and screen recordings using the Tobii X3-120 Eye Tracker, including the Tobii Pro Lab software. Tobii Pro Lab enables collecting multiple eye tracking metrics (e.g. pupil diameter). The eye tracking data can be visualized on the screen recordings, allowing us to see the exact scan paths of each participant while using the software. Furthermore, we conducted a semi-structured interview, in which the participants specified their demographics, their needs for explanation and whether they had felt stressed at any point during interaction with the test software. Participants also stated on which page of the test software the explanation needs occurred and which task they were trying to perform. The obtained information of the interviews enabled our subsequent data analysis.

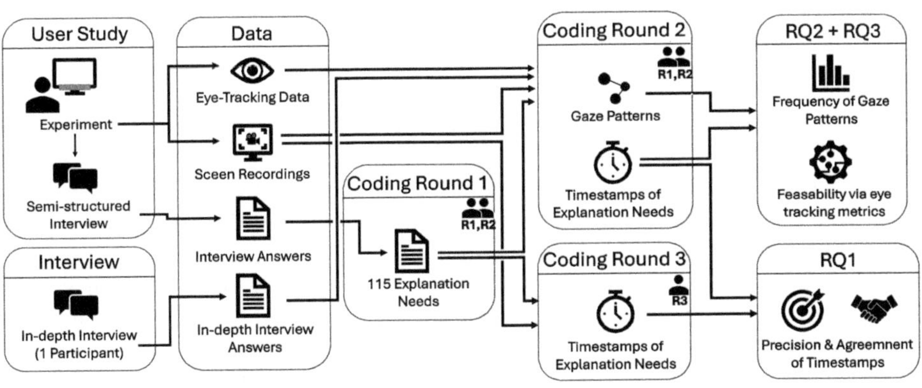

Fig. 1. Data Collection and Analysis.

Data Analysis. Our data analysis involved multiple steps (see Fig. 1). In the first labeling round, we coded the participants' descriptions of their explanation needs from the semi-structured interview answers according to the taxonomy of Droste et al. [14]. After the first labeling round, we compared our codes and subsequently resolved any conflicts.

The second round began with two coders watching the first eye tracking recording and looking for anomalies in the gaze patterns, by analyzing the visualized scan paths in the recording. We noted a brief description of each anomaly identified during an explanation need, along with the time interval. After finishing the first eye tracking recording, we conducted an in-depth interview with one of the participants to verify if the explanation needs and time intervals matched the participants' actual needs for explanation. Following the disclosure of the participant's thoughts, major disagreements between the raters could be eliminated. Based on the results of the first eye tracking recording, we developed four codes for gaze patterns by comparing our anomaly descriptions. We used these four codes for the subsequent coding process of the remaining 13 participants, with the option of adding further codes if further anomalies were noticed that did not fit the previous four codes. For all 14 eye tracking recordings, we determined the exact time intervals at which a need for explanation arose. The allocation of time intervals was facilitated by the interview descriptions of the page and task on which the participants' explanation needs occurred. We also labeled the gaze patterns for each time interval. If a need for explanation has occurred, but no gaze pattern was identified, no code was assigned. At the end of this labeling round, we compared all gaze pattern codes and time intervals. In the subsequent analyses, we only used the intersections of our time intervals and gaze pattern codes for each explanation need, because these were the time intervals where a need for explanation was agreed upon by both coders.

In order to compare whether the distance between time intervals changes without viewing the participants' gaze paths, a third coder conducted a third labeling round. This coder watched the screen recordings without the visualization of the gaze paths and also coded the time intervals with explanation needs.

To answer RQ1, the timecodes of the three coders were compared and the degree of agreement between the coders was examined. Our hypothesis was that the timecodes would be more accurate with the help of gaze path visualizations. This would mean that the agreement between the coders in round 2 would be higher than with the coder who did not have the visualizations at hand. To answer RQ2, we examine which gaze patterns frequently occur during certain explanation needs. To do this, we evaluate the manually coded gaze patterns. To answer RQ3, we examine whether the gaze patterns are also automatically recognizable with established eye tracking metrics. To do this, we check whether these metrics show an increase in the time intervals when an explanation is needed compared to time intervals when no explanation was needed.

4   Results

We were able to extract a total of 115 explanation needs from the interview responses. According to Landis and Koch [19], we achieved an almost perfect agreement during this labeling round (Cohen's kappa $\kappa = 0.88$). Overall, all 14 participants reported the needs E1 − E3. The needs E4 and E6 were reported by 13 participants each, and the need E2 was reported by only 2 participants. In addition to these 70 reported needs that were intended, a further 45 needs were reported (resulting in a total of 115 needs).

4.1 Manual Detection of Explanation Needs

The two raters R1 and R2 who had access to the gaze paths were able to agree on time intervals for 73 needs (through intersections of the respective time intervals). With the third rater R3, who only had access to the screen recordings without gaze paths, it was only possible to agree on time intervals for 66 needs with R1 and 64 needs with R2.

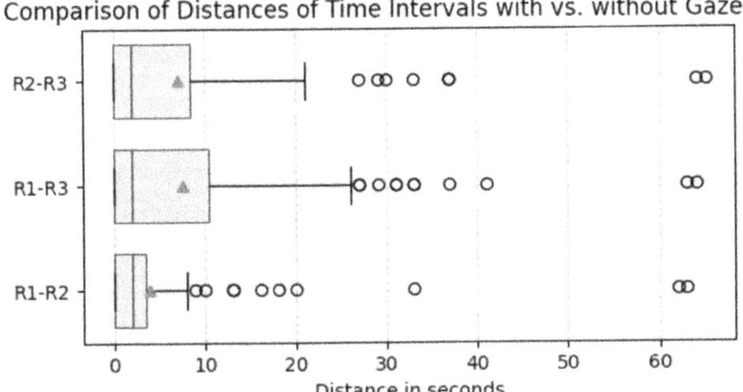

Fig. 2. Distance between time intervals of pairs of coders who coded with and without gaze paths.

Figure 2 shows the distance between the coded time intervals per need. By distance, we mean the number of seconds by which the intervals differ. For the time intervals (07:31 − 07:57) and (07:29 − 07:54), for example, the distance would be 5 s and the agreed time interval would be the intersection, i.e. (07:31 − 07:54). The bottom box plot shows the distances of raters R1 and R2, both of whom had access to the gaze path. The top two box plots show the distances with rater R3, who did not have access to the gaze paths. The box plots illustrate that the time intervals of raters R1 and R2 were significantly more consistent than those with rater R3. These significant differences are also evident in the corresponding statistical tests. We used Wilcoxon to test significance and Cohen's d to test effect sizes. The difference between the distances of Rater 1 with R2 and R3 (dist(R1,R2) vs. dist(R1,R3)) is statistically significant with a p-value of $p = 0.0019$, and shows a small effect size with a value of Cohen's d = 0.328. The difference between the distances of Rater 2 with R1 and R3 is also statistically significant with a p-value of $p = 0.0006$, and also has a small effect size with Cohen's d = 0.292.

> **Finding 1:** Visualizations of gaze paths help to consistently identify time intervals in which a need for explanation arose.

4.2 Types of Gaze Patterns

The coding process yielded a total of four different gaze patterns. The occurrence of these patterns was more prevalent in instances where a participant indicated a need for explanation. **Long Fixation (FX)** is employed to denote a participant's sustained focus on an object for one or more seconds, extending the typical fixation duration. The second gaze pattern, **Circling Element (CE)**, involves the rapid execution of small saccades directed towards a specific object. The **Glance Jump (GJ)** gaze pattern was characterized by participants' rapid, widespread eye movements across the screen. Ultimately, we identified **Back-and-Forth Glances (BF)** referring to a participant's alternating gaze between two objects.

Interrater Agreement. Since the coding process involved two coders and the data was labeled on a nominal scale, we report the interrater agreement using Cohen's Kappa κ [8]. It was possible that multiple gaze patterns occurred in a single time interval, so some items were assigned multiple codes. Therefore, we calculated the interrater agreement for each code individually. These values can be seen in Table 2. According to Landis and Koch [19], we reached substantial agreement on the codes for FX and BF. For the CE pattern, we only reached moderate agreement, whereas for the GJ pattern, we reached almost perfect agreement. Overall, we have thus reached a substantial agreement.

Table 2. Interrater Agreement (Cohen's Kappa κ) for the Gaze Patterns

	FX	CE	GJ	BF	Overall
κ	0.66	0.58	0.92	0.68	0.71

> **Finding 2:** We identified four gaze patterns that occur more frequently during the need for explanation: Long fixations (FX), circling an element (CE), glance jumps (GJ) and back-and-forth glances (BF).

4.3 Gaze Patterns per Type of Need

We were able to identify gaze pattern in 68 of the 73 explanation need time intervals. Table 3 shows the occurrence of each pattern for the explanation needs

E1 − E4 and E6. The column "#" indicates the number of participants for whom the pattern was identified during the respective need. The column "%" puts this number in relation to the number of participants. For example, need E1 was identified for 14 participants, of whom 11 showed the pattern FX âĂŞ that is 11/14 = 79%.

Table 3. Occurrences of Gaze Patterns

Need	#Participants with need	Detected Gaze Patterns			
		FX	CE	GJ	BF
		# %	# %	# %	# %
E1	14	11 **79%**	10 71%	2 14%	9 64%
E2	10	3 30%	2 20%	9 **90%**	2 20%
E3	12	4 33%	5 42%	9 **75%**	3 25%
E4	12	11 **92%**	6 50%	3 25%	3 25%
E6	12	0 0%	1 8%	12 **100%**	0 0%

The results of the manual coding process reveal that long fixations (FX) and glance jumps (GJ) occur most frequently when explanations are required. 92% of participants fixed their gaze on a technical term (E4) for a longer period of time when they needed an explanation. For 90% of participants, their eyes jumped around on the screen when they didn't know how to proceed to the next step (E2). Similarly, all participants showed glance jumps when searching for the back button (E6).

Finding 3: The longer fixation on an object (FX) and glance jumps (GJ) occur most frequently during a need for explanation.

4.4 Eye Tracking Metrics

The following results present various eye tracking metrics analyzed for E1 − E4 and E6. We examined pupil dilation in order to determine whether the need for explanations induced stress in participants. Based on the Li et al. [20] metrics and our identified gaze patterns, we decided to focus on three basic eye-tracking metrics, such as average fixation duration and amplitude of saccades to provide a preliminary overview of the suitability of these metrics for identifying the need for explanation. All metrics were analyzed for the time intervals with vs. without explanation need to determine whether the metrics change when users have a need for explanation.

Pupil Dilation. Table 4 presents the results regarding the differences in pupil diameter. The table presents how many participants with a need showed a physical pupil dilation and their average increase in pupil diameter. Pupil dilation occurred for most participants during the need E1 with ten out of fourteen participants. The highest pupil dilation was also recognized during need E1 with an average increase of 0.156 mm. In eight out of twelve explanation needs for E3, the pupils dilated by an average of 0.088 mm. Participants with detected needs E2, E4 and E6 only showed a pupil dilation in less than 8 cases.

Table 4. Pupil Dilation

Need	#Participants with need	Detected Pupil Dilations (mm)	
		#	avg. (max, min, sd)
E1	14	**10**	**0.156 (max: 0.437; min: 0.027; sd: 0.155)**
E2	10	5	0.092 (max: 0.195; min: 0.028; sd: 0.063)
E3	12	8	0.088 (max: 0.233; min: 0.007; sd: 0.079)
E4	12	4	0.129 (max: 0.319; min: 0.001; sd: 0.139)
E6	12	3	0.099 (max: 0.124; min: 0.053; sd: 0.041)

> **Finding 4:** Pupil dilation was most apparent in need E1, but varies greatly for each need and participant.

Fixation Duration. The results for fixation duration, as presented in Table 5, indicate that the majority of participants exhibited an increased average fixation duration when need E1 occurred. Nine participants with need E4 also showed an increase in fixation duration. On average, the fixation duration increased by 142.035 ms, with a maximum increase of 575.25 ms. Moreover, the fixation duration increased for seven participants with need E3, which is notably three more participants than we manually identified the FX pattern. Three participants also showed a longer fixation duration when need E2 arose. However, none of the participants' fixation durations increased in response to need E6.

Table 5. Fixation Duration

Need	#Participants with need	Manual Coding		Detected increase in Fixation Duration (ms)	
		# FX	#	avg. (max, min, sd)	
E1	14	11	12	84.183 (max: 194.833; min: 0.5; sd: 51.536)	
E2	10	3	3	25.563 (max: 52.5; min: 9.357; sd: 23.488)	
E3	12	4	7	29.515 (max: 76.25; min: 10.545; sd: 23.359)	
E4	12	11	9	142.035 (max: 575.250; min: 9.524; sd: 174.774)	
E6	12	0	0	–	

Amplitude of Saccades. Table 6 describes the results for the increase in saccadic amplitudes. Need E2 had the highest number of detected increases in amplitude, with ten out of ten participants. The three largest increases in average saccadic amplitude were observed for needs E2, E3 and E6. The latter also had the maximum increase, at 13.118 $°/s$ and the highest standard deviation, at 4.362. Needs E1 and E4 show the lowest number of detected increases and the smallest averages in saccadic amplitude increases.

Table 6. Amplitude of saccades

Need	#Participants with need	Manual Coding		Detected increase in saccadic amplitude ($°/s$)	
		#GJ	#	avg. (max, min, sd)	
E1	14	2	3	0.105 (max: 0.166; min: 0.034; sd: 0.067)	
E2	10	9	10	1,636 (max: 5,308; min: 0,138; sd: 1,467)	
E3	12	9	8	1,329 (max: 3,795; min: 0,269; sd: 1,097)	
E4	11*	3	2	0,225 (max: 0,294; min: 0,157; sd: 0,097)	
E6	11*	12	8	**3,105 (max: 13,118; min: 0,004; sd: 4,362)**	

*Number of participants, excluding those participants with missing measurements

---

Finding 5: The highest increases in average saccadic amplitudes were observed in those needs, in whom the glance jump (GJ) gaze pattern was most frequently identified.

---

5 Discussion

5.1 Answering the Research Questions

RQ1: Do the Visualizations of Gaze Paths Help to Manually Determine the Time intervals When a Need for Explanation Arises? The consistency of the time intervals was significantly better for the raters who had access to the gaze visualizations than for the rater who did not use the gaze visualizations. This indicates that the accuracy of the time intervals is higher with gaze visualizations. The raters with gaze visualizations were also able to identify more explanation needs (on average 10% more needs).

RQ2: What Gaze Patterns Do Users Exhibit When They Need an Explanation in a Software System? We were able to identify four gaze patterns that occurred more frequently among users when they needed an explanation. The four gaze patterns are Long fixations (FX), circling an element (CE), glance jumps (GJ) and back-and-forth glances (BF).

RQ3: Which Eye Tracking Metrics Provide Indications of a Need for Explanation? Pupil dilation was observed in all cases where an explanation need occurred. However, the number of participants with pupil dilation varied greatly depending on the need for explanation. Therefore, pupil dilation may indicate the need for explanation, but not automatically. Rather, it can serve to further analyze manually detected needs for explanation by checking whether certain needs trigger more cognitive load in users than others.

An increase in amplitude of saccade may indicate the need for an explanation when using the glance jump gaze pattern. However, since users behave differently depending on the software and their level of understanding, saccadic amplitudes alone are not a reliable indicator of the need for explanation. Nevertheless, when combined with gaze patterns, amplitude of saccades can indicate how users respond to different needs for explanation. Higher saccadic amplitudes combined with glance jumps indicate a global search, in which users scan a larger area. Conversely, the needs that resulted mostly in the long fixation gaze pattern showed an increase in fixation duration, implying that users were concentrating on a small, fixed area.

5.2   Threats to Validity

We report the threats to validity of our research according to Wohlin et al. [29].

Construct Validity. Eye tracking data is easily influenced by lighting conditions or user distractions. To minimize these influences, we conducted the experiment in a quiet environment, where we ensured that lighting conditions remained as consistent as possible. However, we cannot guarantee that we have eliminated all influences on the eye tracking data, which might threaten the construct validity. The setup was identical for each participant to avoid differences between participants.

Internal Validity. The behavior of participants may be influenced by the feeling of being observed, known as the *Hawthorne Effect*. This might be a confounding factor, especially in eye tracking studies. To minimize this effect, we assured participants that the study was about testing the software, not them. Internal validity may also be affected by varying eye-tracker calibration values for different participants. Our fixation duration results may be influenced by the size of the UI elements. To mitigate this factor, we analyzed the experimental group (time intervals including needs for explanation) against a control group (time intervals without explanation needs). Since fixation duration only increased on the UI elements within the explanation needs, we can assume that in this study, the UI element size has no significant influence on the results of fixation duration.

Conclusion Validity. Due to the small number of participants (n=14), we are unable to draw any conclusions about statistical significance regarding gaze patterns and eye tracking metrics. However, as this study was exploratory in nature and aimed to identify future directions in this field of research, we decided to conduct a comprehensive qualitative analysis of the data rather than include a larger number of participants. Furthermore, although we were able to find statistical significance in the evaluation of the manual coding of the intervals, it should be noted that these results depend on the quality of the raters. Since there were only three raters, the results could easily be influenced if one of the raters was significantly better or worse at coding the need for explanation. However, all three raters are experienced in labeling explanation needs, which is why we believe that the results were not influenced by the quality of the raters.

External Validity. Due to the limited demographics, the study results cannot be directly generalized to the entire population. For example, it is conceivable that computer science students generally approach the use of software systems differently. However, since the study focused on gaze patterns rather than general usage, and we validated through interviews that the participants had a need for explanation, it is reasonable to assume that similar gaze patterns would occur in other demographic groups.

6   Conclusion and Future Work

In this paper, we examined the extent to which eye tracking data can support the identification of explanation needs. We found that the manual identification of explanation needs from screen recordings is significantly more consistent when using gaze visualizations. In addition, we laid the groundwork for future research by identifying four gaze patterns that occur more frequently when there is a need for explanation and by preliminary investigating whether these gaze patterns can be detected using standard eye tracking metrics. The gaze pattern *glance jump (GJ)* was found to be particularly concurrent when the user was looking for information or an object on the screen. This was also reflected in the eye tracking metric *amplitude of saccade*. When explanation was needed, the amplitude (length) of the saccade increased markedly in most participants. In contrast, the pupil diameter metric was found to provide no reliable conclusions about the need for explanation. Our findings have implications for future research on both explainability and eye tracking. In explainability research, eye tracking can be used when it is important to determine exact time intervals in which explanation needs arise. Furthermore, the results provide a basis for research into automated detection of explanation needs, which would simplify the time-consuming process of requirements elicitation. For eye tracking research, the identified gaze patterns may be applied to general confusion. Our research confirms that search patterns result in longer and more frequent saccades and that complex words result in increased fixation duration. Our findings also imply that eye tracking metrics are dependent on the context information available.

In future work, we plan to incorporate areas of interest into the evaluation of eye tracking metrics. It is conceivable that the metrics will be more meaningful if the areas are defined. This could be a promising approach, especially for complex objects or words, to trigger explanations individually for users when they look at the area for a longer period of time. We also plan to explore the possibility of automated detection of explanation needs by combining the patterns found and appropriate eye tracking metrics. To do this, we intend to create a model that predicts explanation needs based on eye tracking data and then evaluate it using precision and recall values.

Acknowledgments. This work was funded by the Deutsche Forschungsgemeinschaft (DFG, German Research Foundation) under Grant No.: 470146331, project softXplain (2022–2026) and Grant No.: 560847561, project EyeGuide (2025–2028).

Data Availability Statement. We provide the following data in our supplementary material [26]: We provide the abridged interview responses from all participants. We also provide the coded time intervals and gaze pattern codes from all coders. The eye tracking recordings cannot be published due to data protection regulations for the participants. However, we provide the eye tracking data in pseudonymized form by making the evaluation tables of the metrics available.

References

1. Adadi, A., Berrada, M.: Peeking inside the black-box: a survey on explainable artificial intelligence (xai). IEEE Access **6**, 52138–52160 (2018)
2. Ahrens, M., Schneider, K., Kiesling, S.: How do we read specifications? Experiences from an eye tracking study. In: Daneva, M., Pastor, O. (eds.) REFSQ 2016. LNCS, vol. 9619, pp. 301–317. Springer, Cham (2016). https://doi.org/10.1007/978-3-319-30282-9_21
3. Brunotte, W., Specht, A., Chazette, L., Schneider, K.: Privacy explanations-a means to end-user trust. J. Syst. Softw. **195**, 111545 (2023)
4. Chandrasekharan, J., Joseph, A.: Eye gaze as an indicator for stress level analysis in students. In: 2018 International Conference on Advances in Computing, Communications and Informatics (ICACCI), pp. 1588–1593 (2018)
5. Chazette, L., Brunotte, W., Speith, T.: Exploring explainability: a definition, a model, and a knowledge catalogue. In: 2021 IEEE 29th international requirements engineering conference (RE), pp. 197–208. IEEE (2021)
6. Chazette, L., Klünder, J., Balci, M., Schneider, K.: How can we develop explainable systems? Insights from a literature review and an interview study. In: Proceedings of the International Conference on Software and System Processes and International Conference on Global Software Engineering. ICSSP '22. ACM (2022)

7. Chen, S., Epps, J., Ruiz, N., Chen, F.: Eye activity as a measure of human mental effort in hci. In: Proceedings of the 16th International Conference on Intelligent User Interfaces. ACM (2011). https://doi.org/10.1145/1943403.1943454

8. Cohen, J.: A coefficient of agreement for nominal scales. Educ. Psychol. Meas. **20**(1), 37–46 (1960). https://doi.org/10.1177/001316446002000104

9. Deters, H., Droste, J., Fechner, M., Klünder, J.: Explanations on demand - a technique for eliciting the actual need for explanations. In: 2023 IEEE 31st International Requirements Engineering Conference Workshops (REW), pp. 345–351 (2023)

10. Deters, H., Droste, J., Obaidi, M., Schneider, K.: Exploring the means to measure explainability: metrics, heuristics and questionnaires. Inf. Softw. Technol. 107682 (2025)

11. Deters, H., Droste, J., Schneider, K.: On the pulse of requirements elicitation: physiological triggers and explainability needs. In: REFSQ Workshops (2024)

12. Deters, H., Reinhardt, L., Droste, J., Obaidi, M., Schneider, K.: Identifying explanation needs: towards a catalog of user-based indicators. In: 2025 IEEE 33rd International Requirements Engineering Conference (RE), pp. 31–42 (2025)

13. Droste, J., Deters, H., Fuchs, R., Schneider, K.: Peeking outside the black-box: AI explainability requirements beyond interpretability. In: REFSQ Workshops. CEUR Workshop Proceedings (2024)

14. Droste, J., Deters, H., Obaidi, M., Schneider, K.: Explanations in everyday software systems: towards a taxonomy for explainability needs. In: 2024 IEEE 32nd International Requirements Engineering Conference (RE), pp. 55–66 (2024). https://doi.org/10.1109/RE59067.2024.00016

15. Droste, J., Deters, H., Puglisi, J., Klünder, J.: Designing end-user personas for explainability requirements using mixed methods research. In: 2023 IEEE 31st International Requirements Engineering Conference Workshops (REW)

16. Duchowski, A.T., Duchowski, A.T.: Eye Tracking Methodology: Theory and Practice. Springer, Heidelberg (2017). https://doi.org/10.1007/978-1-84628-609-4

17. Granholm, E., Steinhauer, S.R.: Pupillometric measures of cognitive and emotional processes. Int. J. Psychophysiol. **52**(1), 1–6 (2004). https://doi.org/10.1016/j.ijpsycho.2003.12.001

18. Harrison, G.W., Rutström, E.E.: Chapter 81 experimental evidence on the existence of hypothetical bias in value elicitation methods. In: Handbook of Experimental Economics Results, vol. 1, pp. 752–767. Elsevier, Amsterdam (2008). https://doi.org/10.1016/S1574-0722(07)00081-9

19. Landis, J.R., Koch, G.G.: The measurement of observer agreement for categorical data. Biometrics **33**(1), 159–174 (1977). https://doi.org/10.2307/2529310

20. Li, R., Li, T.: Telling us your needs with your eyes. In: 2022 IEEE 30th International Requirements Engineering Conference (RE), pp. 323–329 (2022). https://doi.org/10.1109/RE54965.2022.00048

21. Nunes, I., Jannach, D.: A systematic review and taxonomy of explanations in decision support and recommender systems. User Model. User-Adapt. Interact. **27**, 393–444 (2017)

22. Obaidi, M., et al.: How to elicit explainability requirements? A comparison of interviews, focus groups, and surveys. In: 2025 IEEE 33rd International Requirements Engineering Conference (RE) (2025). https://doi.org/10.1109/RE63999.2025.00025

23. Pfleging, B., Fekety, D.K., Schmidt, A., Kun, A.L.: A model relating pupil diameter to mental workload and lighting conditions. In: Proceedings of the 2016 CHI Conference on Human Factors in Computing Systems, pp. 5776–5788 (2016)

24. Poole, A., Ball, L.: Eye tracking in human-computer interaction and usability research: current status and future prospects. In: Encyclopedia of Human Computer Interaction, pp. 211–219 (01 2006)
25. Rafiqi, S., Wangwiwattana, C., Kim, J., Fernandez, E., Nair, S., Larson, E.C.: Pupilware: towards pervasive cognitive load measurement using commodity devices. In: Proceedings of the 8th ACM International Conference on PErvasive Technologies Related to Assistive Environments. PETRA '15. ACM (2015)
26. Reinhardt, L., Deters, H., Droste, J., Schneider, K.: Supplementary material for All Eyes on User Needs: Using Gaze and Pupillometric Measures to Identify Explanation Needs (2026). https://doi.org/10.5281/zenodo.18302021
27. Sharafi, Z., Shaffer, T., Sharif, B., Guéhéneuc, Y.G.: Eye-tracking metrics in software engineering. In: 2015 Asia-Pacific Software Engineering Conference (APSEC). pp. 96–103 (2015). https://doi.org/10.1109/APSEC.2015.53
28. Sharafi, Z., Soh, Z., Guéhéneuc, Y.G.: A systematic literature review on the usage of eye-tracking in software engineering. Inf. Softw. Technol. **67**, 79–107 (2015). https://doi.org/10.1016/j.infsof.2015.06.008
29. Wohlin, C., Runeson, P., Höst, M., Ohlsson, M.C., Regnell, B., Wesslén, A.: Experimentation in Software Engineering. Springer, Heidelberg (2012). https://doi.org/10.1007/978-3-662-69306-3

Simulation and Visual Formalism

Extending iStar for Synthetic Data Generation and Simulation Modeling for Industry 5.0

Vânia Sousa[1,2], Ana Lavalle[3(✉)], Alejandro Maté[3], António Vieira[1,2], and Maribel Yasmina Santos[1,2]

[1] ALGORITMI Research Centre, University of Minho, Guimarães, Portugal
{avieira,maribel}@dsi.uminho.pt
[2] CCG/ZGDV ICT Innovation Institute, Campus de Azurém, Guimarães, Portugal
vania.sousa@ccg.pt
[3] Lucentia Research Group, University of Alicante, San Vicent del Raspeig, Spain
{alavalle,amate}@dlsi.ua.es

Abstract. *Context and motivation:* Industry 5.0 emphasizes human-centric, resilient, and sustainable practices, but sustainability assessment is challenging due to limited organizational data. Discrete-Event Simulation can generate synthetic data reflecting business dynamics in virtual environments. *Question/problem:* While frameworks for simulation exist, there is no structured method to define what to simulate in alternative scenarios, especially regarding relevant data attributes for decision-making. *Principal ideas/results:* This paper extends the iStar modeling language to support scenario definition and synthetic data generation for "what-if" analysis. Applied to an order management process, the extension helps evaluate different packaging policies. Results show that combining simulation with goal-oriented modeling improves sustainability assessment. *Contribution:* The main contribution is a framework linking simulation and goal modeling to enable data-driven decisions in Industry 5.0, adding practical value for sustainability-focused analysis. Limitations include the need for testing in more cases and contexts, as different environments may pose unforeseen challenges.

Keywords: Industry 5.0 · Synthetic Data Generation · iStar · Simulation Modeling · Sustainability

1 Introduction

Industry 5.0 promotes human-machine collaboration and sustainable, resilient industrial practices [5]. Evaluating sustainability requires indicators capturing environmental, social, and economic impacts. However, operational data such as energy use or carbon footprint is often missing [12,13], hindering alignment with sustainable goals. Analytical systems must integrate business, process, and sustainability perspectives, yet sustainability indicators are frequently overlooked [7] due to lack of structured methodologies and data.

© The Author(s), under exclusive license to Springer Nature Switzerland AG 2026
R. Guizzardi and J. Araújo (Eds.): REFSQ 2026, LNCS 16497, pp. 55–64, 2026.
https://doi.org/10.1007/978-3-032-21423-2_4

Discrete-Event Simulation (DES) addresses this gap by modeling processes and generating synthetic data, including unavailable indicators, while capturing uncertainty [14,28]. To avoid inconsistencies, effective use of DES requires defining what to simulate, relevant variables, and their impact on performance.

Goal-oriented models help reason about how process elements affect sustainability. Although iStar supports goals and dependencies [6], it lacks constructs for simulation elements such as entities and variables. This paper proposes an iStar extension, developed with PRISE [9], to model simulation scenarios aligned with organizational goals. Following a problem-driven approach [23], we apply the proposed metamodel in an order management case study to illustrate its usefulness. By integrating goal modeling into simulation design, the approach improves scenario relevance for Industry 5.0 decision-making.

2   Related Work

Organizations increasingly recognize the need for data-driven decision-making in Industry 5.0, aligning technology with human-centered, resilient, and sustainable operations. Analyzing operational and sustainability data is essential for optimizing performance and fostering human-machine collaboration [5].

The European Union (EU) highlights six transformative technologies: (1) human-machine interaction, (2) bio-inspired materials, (3) digital twins and simulation, (4) data transmission and analytics, (5) Artificial Intelligence (AI), and (6) energy efficiency and autonomy [21]. Among these, simulation is critical for design optimization and sustainability assessment, enabling synthetic data generation when real data is missing and supporting scenario analysis [17,19,21].

Simulation has been combined with life-cycle assessment [18], event-log analysis [24], and scenario-based analysis [4]. But, using simulation to generate synthetic data for sustainability decisions remains unexplored. Literature highlights simulation's potential for resource allocation and planning [14], yet no structured approach exists for defining requirements aligned with sustainability goals.

Goal-Oriented Requirements Engineering (GORE), particularly iStar, is well-suited for modeling such scenarios, yet lacks constructs for simulation elements. Recent iStar extensions demonstrate adaptability for human-centered aspects, visualization, and machine learning [3,16,26]. Building on these, we propose an iStar extension to formalize simulation requirements, ensuring alignment with sustainability-oriented decision-making and enabling scenario evaluation.

3   Sustainability Indicators for Industry 5.0

For a human-centered, resilient, and sustainable industry, business and process indicators must be complemented with sustainability metrics. Sustainability is assessed across economic, social, and environmental dimensions [8]. In manufacturing, it aligns competitiveness with environmental and social responsibility, requiring processes that minimize impact, optimize resources, and ensure safety while remaining economically viable [8,22]. Measuring sustainability is key to improving performance across these dimensions [2,25].

Manufacturers face growing pressure to integrate sustainability into operations while balancing profitability [13]. One key framework to Industry 5.0 is the National Institute of Standards and Technology (NIST) indicators [13,25]. NIST organizes 212 indicators into five dimensions. Three of them, Environmental Stewardship, Economic Growth, and Social Well-Being, include metrics on emissions, resource use, costs, safety, and community impact, offering a structured basis for industrial sustainability assessment.

4   Requirements Framework for Simulation

To address the lack of a structured approach for defining what to simulate in alternative scenarios, we propose an iStar extension (Fig. 1). By linking goals with simulation scenarios, each scenario is explicitly tied to decision-makers' objectives, enabling trade-off analysis. iStar provides traceability to understand how scenario changes impact goal achievement, reducing the risk of isolated improvements that harm overall performance. The extension follows the PRISE methodology [9]. Next, each step and its role in this work is summarized.

Step 1 - Analyze the Need for Extension: We reviewed existing iStar extensions, focusing on the closest perspectives (iStar for BIM [10] and iStar for DW [20]). Although these extensions share goal-oriented concepts, they principally support strategic and tactical business planning at a higher abstraction level, rather than process simulation. They do not provide specific simulation elements required in our context, which motivated our extension. Section 3 provides an overview of sustainability indicators for Industry 5.0.

Steps 2 & 3 - Describe Concepts of the iStar Extension & Develop iStar extension: Sect. 4 presents the metamodel of the proposed iStar extension for simulation, describing the introduced concepts and its development using the Eclipse Ecore Tool. It is also publicly available in our repository [27].

Step 4 - Validate and Evaluate the iStar Extension: It was made iteratively through expert reviews by the five international experts authors: two in requirements engineering and goal modeling and three in business process modeling, simulation, and with experience in research in industrial projects. Moreover, a metamodel instantiation is presented in Sect. 5.

Step 5 - Check other New Constructs to be Introduced: This step was performed iteratively by identifying, documenting, refining, and integrating new elements identified during Steps 2, 3 and 4 into successive metamodel versions. Only the final version is presented in this paper.

Step 6 - Publicize the iStar Extension: To publicize the iStar extension, after publication, it will be included in the iStar extension catalog (https://istarextensions.cin.ufpe.br/catalogue/).

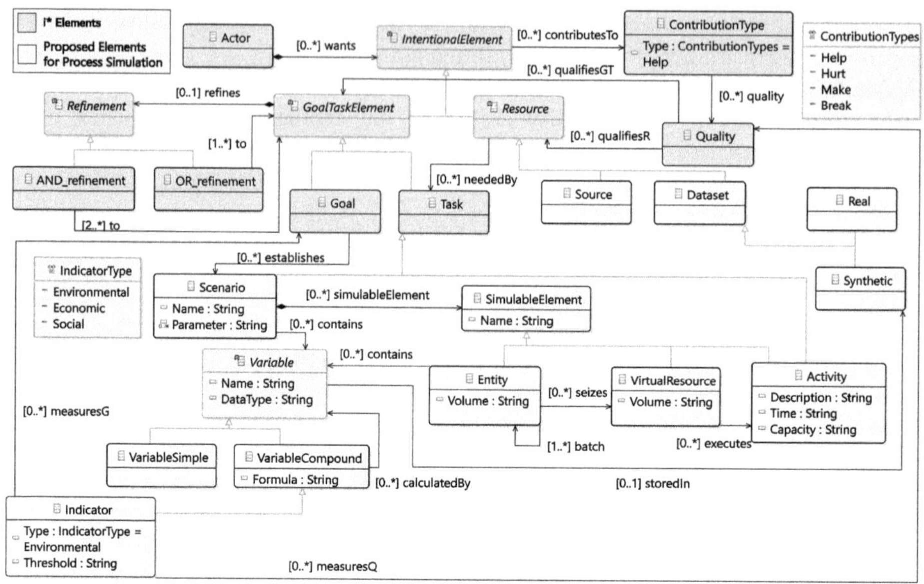

Fig. 1. iStar Extension for Simulation.

In our extension (Fig. 1), existing iStar elements appear in green, while new concepts introduced in our proposal are highlighted in yellow. `Goals` defined by `Actors` establish the `Scenarios` to be simulated. Each `Scenario` includes `SimulableElements`: `Entity`, `Virtual Resource` (distinct from iStar's `Resource`), and `Activity`. These common simulation elements model business rules and may use external resources, such as datasets. An `Entity` represents the token whose actions are modeled, while a `Virtual Resource` is something the token seizes to perform an `Activity`. For example, in bank service, the customer is the `Entity`, and the teller is the `Virtual Resource`. These elements must be specified as they vary across scenarios.

`Scenario` and `Activity` inherit `Task`, representing process steps and influencing non-functional requirements (`Quality`). `Variables`, defined in `Scenarios` or `Entities`, produce values for `Indicators`. Variables can be simple or compound and characterize system or entity states (e.g., waiting time). In particular, `Scenario` is defined as a specialization of `Task` that inherits from `GoalTaskElement` and it inherits from `IntentionalElement`. Since `IntentionalElement` can contribute to a `Quality` through the iStar `ContributionTypes`, a `Scenario` can also contribute to `Quality` element.

`Indicators` are compound variables linked to functional (`Goals`) and non-functional requirements (`Quality`), classified by domain: *Business*, *Process*, and *Sustainability* (`Economic`, `Environmental`, `Social`). This categorization supports trade-off analysis between sustainability and process efficiency. A `Dataset` can be `Real`, existing real-world dataset used as an input to run or parameterize a scenario, or `Synthetic`, those produced by the simulation runs. Moreover, the `Source` element represents the origin or producer of data.

5   Demonstration Case: Orders Process Model

5.1   Applying the Requirements Framework to Simulation

This case simulates a customer order management process [15] covering registration, payment, packaging, and shipping, involving sales, warehousing, and shipment staff. Customers place orders, assigned to a salesperson for registration and payment. A warehouser checks stock, reorders if needed, prepares items, and creates packages for delivery, which may fail until successful. Unlike the original model, where picking or reordering occurred before payment, our simulation makes all activities dependent on *Pay Order* (Fig. 2). The process, specified in OCEL 2.0 [1], includes six object types (*Customer, Order, Item, Product, Package, Employee*) and 11 activities from *Place Order* to *Package Delivered*. We also adopt dynamic human resource allocation and real-time stock checks, replacing probability-based stockouts. Simulation results, models, and data are publicly available for reproducibility [27], along with the iStar extension metamodel.

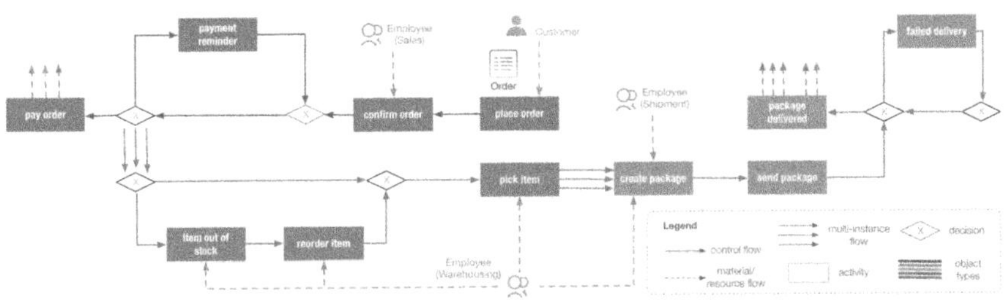

Fig. 2. Orders Process Model. Adapted from: [15].

We apply the proposed iStar extension (Fig. 1) to define simulation scenarios for the process in Fig. 2, aligning with Industry 5.0 principles and enabling sustainability evaluation through integrated indicators. The resulting model is shown in Fig. 3. The main goal is *Achieve sustainable operations*, refined into *Reducing shipping costs* and *Decreasing CO_2 emissions*, supported by *Optimize packaging*. Two scenarios are simulated: S1 packages each order separately; S2 consolidates orders from the same customer within five days.

Indicators measure economic (*Ownership, Packaging Costs*), environmental (*Carbon Emissions per Package*), and social (*Lateness, Waiting Time*) dimensions, linked to *Customer Satisfaction*. S1 supports satisfaction, while S2 negatively impacts it. Relevant simulation elements include *Package* (Entity), *Warehouser* and *Shipper* (Virtual Resources), and activities *Create Package* and *Send Package*, whose behavior varies by scenario.

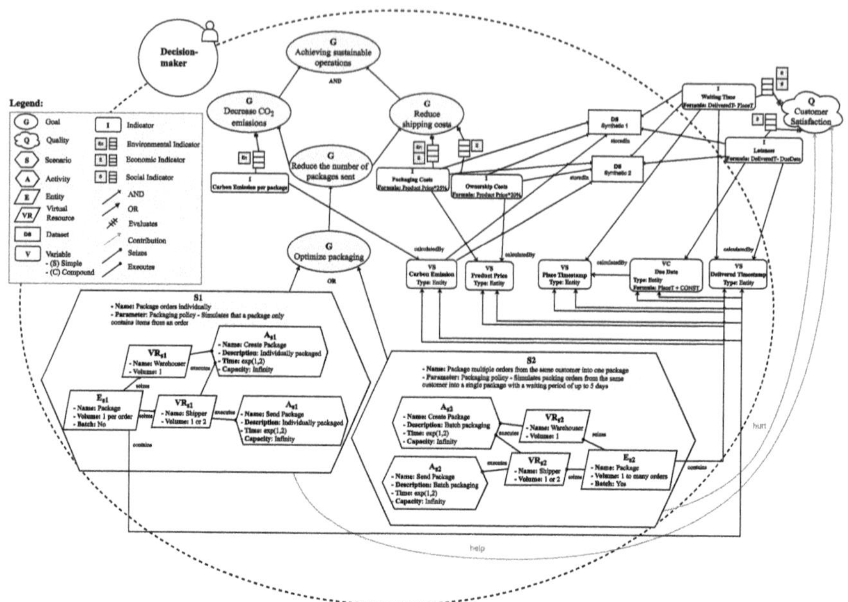

Fig. 3. Applying the Proposed Requirements Framework to the Orders Process Model.

Each simulation tracks Variables to evaluate performance: *Carbon Emission, Product Price, Place Timestamp, Due Date,* and *Delivered Timestamp. Due Date* is calculated by adding an x value to *Place Timestamp.* In this case, all variables belong to entities, though system-level variables (e.g., number of packages delivered) could also be used. These values feed indicator calculations and are stored in synthetic datasets, either as raw or computed values.

Indicators include *Waiting Time* (difference between delivery and placement), *Lateness* (due date vs. placement), *Ownership Costs* (20% of product price), *Packaging Costs* (25%), and *Carbon Emission* (taken directly from variable). Understanding variable-indicator relationships improves traceability and enables precise scenario adjustments.

At this stage, scenarios can be implemented in a simulation tool. Here, the model was developed using SIMIO® (Simulation with Intelligent Objects) [11,29]. The modeling process is technology-independent and replicable with other tools, as all relevant information is publicly available [27]. The proposed framework provides a structured approach to modeling scenarios by linking goals, non-functional requirements, and simulation elements. To validate the simulated process, we analyzed data from S1, our base scenario. We first checked interarrival times for orders, payments, and deliveries. Figure 4-A compares weekly trends of these events to confirm expected behavior. Figure 4-B shows time-to-payment distribution, matching the case description. Figure 4-C validates event intervals by analyzing dispersion, with medians consistent with specified distributions. Finally, Fig. 4-D confirms item demand per order aligns with expectations. These checks ensure the simulation accurately represents the intended process.

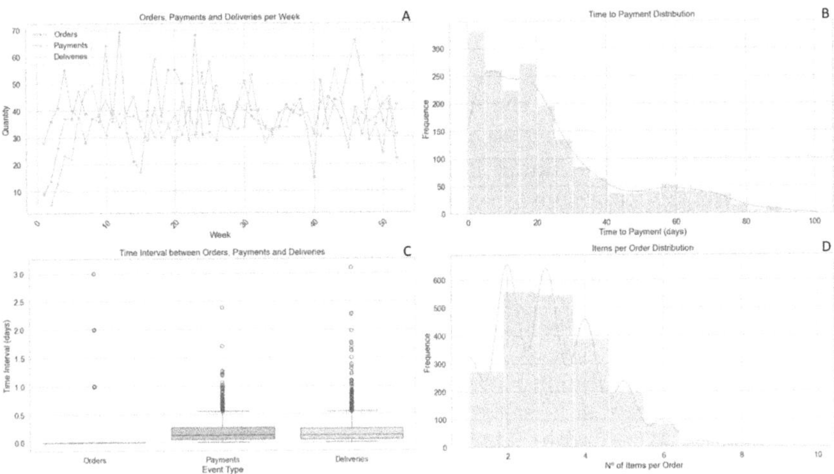

Fig. 4. Validation of the Simulation Process.

5.2   Evaluation and Discussion of Results

Data from both scenarios were analyzed to assess the impact of packaging strategies on CO_2 emissions and other indicators. The goal of *Achieving sustainable operations* depends on reducing emissions per package and shipping costs, which include packaging and ownership costs (especially in S2, where items are stored longer). *Customer Satisfaction* is evaluated through waiting time and lateness, balancing environmental, economic, and social indicators.

One year of simulated data enabled comparison of emissions, costs (packaging and ownership), waiting time, and lateness. In per-package and annual results: S1 had lower emissions and costs per package, while S2 cut annual emissions by 19% and costs by 17%, but increased lateness by 53% and waiting time by 55%. Overall, S2 offers economic and environmental gains but may negatively impacts customer satisfaction. Sustainability efforts often fail due to gaps between goals and actions [7], caused by weak governance, inadequate metrics, and poor integration. Our iStar extension addresses these gaps by embedding sustainability metrics into requirements, linking goals and quality attributes with measurable indicators for more accountable decision-making.

6   Conclusions

This paper introduced an iStar extension for simulation to address the lack of a structured method for defining what to simulate in alternative scenarios, supporting data-driven decisions that integrate sustainability concerns. We applied the approach to an order management process to assess packaging policies' impact on CO_2 emissions, costs, and customer satisfaction. "What-if" scenarios and synthetic data showed that aggregating orders reduced emissions and costs but increased delivery delays, potentially affecting customer satisfaction. This highlights the need to integrate diverse metrics to analyze trade-offs.

Threats to validity include scenarios that alter process behavior without affecting the iStar model and the limitation of iStar supporting only one active scenario at a time, requiring post-execution comparison. Future work will test additional contexts and evaluate usability with practitioners. We also plan to propose an Industry 5.0-aligned taxonomy of indicators to guide systematic selection and strengthen sustainability-focused decision-making.

Acknowledgments. This work has been co-funded by the KOSMOS-UA project (PID2024-155363OB-C43), funded by Spanish Ministry of Science and Innovation; the BALIDA-AA project (CIPROM/2024/13), funded by Conselleria de Educación, Cultura, Universidades y Empleo (Generalitat Valenciana); and has been supported by FCT, *Fundação para a Ciência e e Tecnologia*, within the R&D Unit Project Scope UID/00319/2025, Centro ALGORITMI (ALGORITMI/UM)(https://doi.org/10.54499/UID/00319/2025). Grammarly and CoPilot and were used for text summarisation, sentence polishing and rephrasing. This paper uses icons made available by www.flaticon.com.

Data Availability Statement. Data and other materials are available at https://zenodo.org/records/15552512.

References

1. Adams, J.N., Van Der Aalst, W.M.: Precision and fitness in object-centric process mining. In: 2021 3rd International Conference on Process Mining (ICPM), pp. 128–135 (2021)
2. Ahmad, S., Wong, K.Y., Rajoo, S.: Sustainability indicators for manufacturing sectors: a literature survey and maturity analysis from the triple-bottom line perspective. J. Manufact. Technol. Manag. **30**, 312–334 (2019)
3. Barrera, J.M., Reina-Reina, A., Lavalle, A., Maté, A., Trujillo, J.: An extension of iSTAR for machine learning requirements by following the prise methodology. Comput. Stand. Int. **88**, 103806 (2024)
4. Borbolla, A., Aboujarra, M.N., Ramanujan, D.: Investigating sustainable production planning of an industrial progressive die stamping process using discrete event simulation. In: 29th Design for Manufacturing and the Life Cycle Conference (DFMLC), vol. 5 (2024)
5. Breque, M., Nul, L.D., Petridis, A.: Industry 5.0 – towards a sustainable, human-centric and resilient European industry. Publications Office of the EU (2021)
6. Dalpiaz, F., Franch, X., Horkoff, J.: istar 2.0 language guide. CoRR **abs/1605.07767** (2016)
7. Farri, E., Cervini, P., Rosani, G.: How sustainability efforts fall apart. Harvard Business Review (2022)

8. Feng, S.C., Joung, C.B.: An overview of a proposed measurement infrastructure for sustainable manufacturing. In: The 7th Global Conference on Sustainable Manufacturing, pp. 1–6 (2009)
9. Gonçalves, E., Araujo, J., Castro, J.: Prise: a process to support iSTAR extensions. J. Syst. Softw. **88** (2020)
10. Horkoff, J., et al.: Strategic business modeling: representation and reasoning. Softw. Syst. Model. **13**(3), 1015–1041 (2014)
11. Houck, D., Whitehead, C.: Introduction to Simio. Proc. Winter Simul. Conf., 3802–3811 (2025)
12. Hristov, I., Chirico, A.: The role of sustainability key performance indicators (KPIS) in implementing sustainable strategies. Sustainability (Switzerland) **11** (2019)
13. Joung, C.B., Carrell, J., Sarkar, P., Feng, S.C.: Categorization of indicators for sustainable manufacturing. Ecolog. Indicators **24**, 148–157 (2012)
14. Chan, K.C., Rabaev, M., Pratama, H.: Generation of synthetic manufacturing datasets for machine learning using discrete-event simulation. Prod. Manufact. Res. **10**(1), 337–353 (2022)
15. Knopp, B., van der Aalst, W.M.: Order management object-centric event log in ocel 2.0 standard. [Data set] (2023). https://doi.org/10.5281/zenodo.8428112
16. Lavalle, A., Maté, A., Trujillo, J., Teruel, M.A., Rizzi, S.: A methodology to automatically translate user requirements into visualizations: experimental validation. Inf. Softw. Technol. **136**, 106592 (2021)
17. Leng, J., et al.: Industry 5.0: prospect and retrospect. J. Manufact. Syst. **65**, 279–295 (2022)
18. Löfgren, B., Tillman, A.M.: Relating manufacturing system configuration to lifecycle environmental performance: discrete-event simulation supplemented with lca. J. Clean. Prod. **19**(17), 2015–2024 (2011)
19. Maddikunta, P.K.R., et al.: Industry 5.0: a survey on enabling technologies and potential applications. J. Industr. Inf. Integration **26**, 1–19 (2022)
20. Maté, A., Trujillo, J., Franch, X.: Adding semantic modules to improve goal-oriented analysis of data warehouses using i-star. J. Syst. Softw. **88**, 102–111 (2014). https://doi.org/10.1016/j.jss.2013.10.011
21. Müller, J.: Enabling Technologies for Industry 5.0. [Publications Office of the European Union] (2020)
22. Paju, M., et al.: Framework and indicators for a sustainable manufacturing mapping methodology. In: Proc. of the 2010 Winter Simulation Conference, pp. 3411–3422 (2010)
23. Peffers, K., Tuunanen, T., Rothenberger, M.A., Chatterjee, S.: A design science research methodology for information systems research. J. Manag. Inf. Syst. **24**(3), 45–77 (2007)
24. Rai, S., Daniels, M.: An event-log analysis and simulation-based approach for quantifying sustainability metrics in production facilities. In: 2015 Winter Simulation Conference (WSC), pp. 1033–1043 (2015)
25. Sarkar, P., Carrell, J., Joung, C.B., Feng, S.C.: Sustainable manufacturing indicator repository. In: Proc. of the ASME 2011 Design Engineering Technical Conferences & Computers and Information in Engineering Conference, vol. 2, pp. 943–950 (2011)
26. Singh, H., Khalajzadeh, H., Paktinat, S., Graetsch, U.M., Grundy, J.: Modelling human-centric aspects of end-users with iSTAR. J. Comput. Lang. **68**, 101091 (2022)

27. Sousa, V., Lavalle, A., Maté, A., Vieira, A., Santos, M.Y.: Synthetic datasets of different packaging strategies from an order management process with sustainability indicators (2025). https://zenodo.org/records/15552512
28. Turner, C.J., Garn, W.: Next generation des simulation: a research agenda for human centric manufacturing systems. J. Ind. Inf. Integr. **28**, 100354 (2022)
29. Vieira, A.A.C., Figueira, J.R., Fragoso, R.: A multi-objective simulation-based decision support tool for wine supply chain design and risk management under sustainability goals. Expert Syst. Appl. **232** (2023)

The Software Engineering Simulations Lab: Agentic AI for RE Quality Simulations

Henning Femmer[(✉)][iD] and Ivan Esau

South Westphalia University of Applied Sciences (FH SWF), Haldener Straße 182, 58095 Hagen, Germany
`{femmer.henning,esau.ivan}@fh-swf.de`

Abstract. Context and motivation. Requirements Engineering (RE) quality still lacks empirical evidence on how specific requirement defects affect downstream activities. **Problem:** However, empirical data on the detailed effects of requirements quality defects is scarce, since it is costly to obtain. Furthermore, with the advent of AI-based development, the requirements quality factors may change: Requirements are no longer only consumed by humans, but increasingly also by AI agents, which might lead to a different efficient and effective requirements style. **Principal ideas:** We propose to extend the RE research toolbox with *Agentic AI simulations*, in which software engineering (SE) processes are replicated by standardized agents in qualitative simulations. We argue that their speed and simplicity makes them a valuable addition to RE research, although limitations in replicating human behavior need to be studied and understood. **Contribution:** This paper contributes a first concept, a research roadmap, a prototype, and a first feasibility study for RE simulations with agentic AI. Study results indicate that even a naïve implementation leads to executable simulations, encouraging technical improvements along with broader application in RE research.

Keywords: Simulations · Requirements Engineering Quality · Agentic AI

1 Motivation

Most researchers in requirements engineering (RE) agree that *"requirements are a means to an end rather than an end in themselves"* [3, p.14], emphasizing that requirements quality is context-dependent and defined by how and by whom requirements are used. Formalizing this paradigm, the activity-based RE artifact quality model (ABRE-QM) allows us to precisely define quality in a falsifiable way as measurable and observable factors that have measurable consequences on requirements-affected activities [6,8]. Theoretically, this allows to systematically evaluate in which contexts quality factors matter. However, looking at the state of the art [13], the vast number of factors and possible impacts exposes a

R. Guizzardi and J. Araújo (Eds.): REFSQ 2026, LNCS 16497, pp. 65–74, 2026.
https://doi.org/10.1007/978-3-032-21423-2_5

fundamental problem: **Problem 1:** There is currently no solid and economically viable way to understand the impact of requirements quality and we have limited evidence to extrapolate from [13].

In addition, we see a new usage of requirements (in ABRE-QM terms): generative AI may change quality factors and impacts; we need to understand which requirements quality factors improve the output quality of AI-based tools (e.g. code-generators). Initial studies indicate that requirements quality matters [7], though perhaps differently than in human interaction [21]. Finally, the rapid evolution of AI models increases the problem further. **Problem 2:** Generative AI introduces new quality factors, since requirements now affect both human and automated consumers. And as AI models evolve, we need fast, cost-effective ways to study how requirement quality influences downstream processes.

General Idea: We argue for adding Agentic-AI-based Simulations to the toolbox of empirical RE researchers: For this, we define a software development lifecycle (SDLC) and replace the participating humans with a set of AI agents such as agentic developers or testers, who simulate typical project behavior. Since this is purely automatic, we can replicate the experiment multiple times and feed a subset of the replications with requirements that differ in quality. After several repetitions, we can compare the outcomes and thus understand the impact of the requirements quality factors on the AI agents.

We argue that, while surely coming with limitations that need to be studied in this stream of research, this method could be a fitting tool for the aforementioned problems due to its low cost and quick execution. Given that the limitations of such simulations are understood, we argue that researchers could build a more complete model of RE quality for both AI-centric and human-centric SE processes enabling better-informed decisions in the context of RE.

Scope of this Work: The focus of this paper is to describe the general idea and evaluate whether the approach is computationally feasible at the current state of agentic AI. Therefore, for this first feasibility study we operationalized requirements quality through a broad list of observable quality factors (i.e. complex sentence structure, incorrect legal binding, inconsistent terminology, passive voice, missing coherence, and technical density) and assessed whether we can see any impact on the produced output, here operationalized by merge success, unit test coverage and unit test passing, calculation time and resource usage. Given that feasibility can be shown, future studies can use the methodology to assess other quality factors and/or to assess the impact of these quality factors in detail.

2 Background and Related Work

Due to space constraints we cannot give an in-depth review into the various fields that converge in this work. Instead, this section summarizes the key conceptual foundations that informed our study.

Requirements Quality has been defined from multiple perspectives in the past. Standards such as ISO 29148 or the IREB CPRE Syllabus have postulated quality as a set of defined quality factors. The differences of quality factors in IREB and ISO 29148, e.g. as analyzed in [6], indicates that such a selection is subjective and requires a different theoretical approach if we want to systematically evaluate and empirically falsify them.

Formalizing this modern paradigm, the activity-based RE artifact quality model (ABRE-QM) [6,8] defines quality factors as *facts* of the *requirements entity* that have *impacts* on effectiveness or efficiency of *requirements-affected activities* executed by (typically human) *agents*. For example in a use case document (entity), the presence of a complex sentence structure (entity fact) increases (impact) the time needed (activity fact) to understand the requirement (activity) for a tester (agent) under certain contexts [8]. In theory, this defines quality as falsifiable statements which can be validated and refined, leading to a holistic, empirically grounded quality model. But despite individual studies on the impact of selected quality factors, such as ambiguity [2,15] or passive voice [5,9,11], systematic analysis [13] shows that, overall, we lack empirical evidence on the detailed impact of individual RE quality factors.

Simulations have long been used i.a. to analyze dynamic, complex systems [14]. Therefore, we rely on established guidelines and processes [14].

LLMs now play a major **role in RE and SE** [4,10], producing useful artifacts for elicitation [18], quality assurance [12], modeling [7], code [23] and test generation [20], usability testing [16], and traceability [21]. However, to the best of our knowledge the existing research examines only activities in isolation and lacks an integrated view of the overall process.

Other works focus on **evaluating the impact of requirements quality on automated development.** Recent studies suggest that the linguistic and structural quality of requirements influences performance of automated development tools and agents [21]. High-quality requirements appear to lead to more consistent and complete outcomes in downstream tasks, whereas ambiguity and complexity can reduce reliability. Despite these first indications, systematic research remains scarce, and existing studies usually focus on one isolated activity.

3   Agentic Simulations in Requirements Engineering with DevOps Pipelines

3.1   Vision

As we envision the process, (1) the experimenter begins by setting up template (*baseline*) projects in the DevOps environment, for example, one baseline project describing requirements as tickets in active voice and one baseline project describing the same requirements as tickets in passive voice. (2) The experimenter opens the simulation system and defines, i.a., the number of project replications (*clones*) per baseline. (3) The simulation system then creates the requested number of identical clones of the baseline projects in the DevOps system and (4) starts a number of AI *agents* according to the defined parameters, which now take up different tasks, such as planning, developing, testing or reviewing. (5.1) These agents simulate the behaviors of actual project members and work directly on the DevOps platform. (5.2) Modern DevOps platforms contain automated quality checks through a CI/CD pipeline mechanism, which is run on any change of the codebase. Typical pipelines contain compiler checks, unit tests, and static code analysis but can be extended to any type of automated analysis. (5.3) The feedback from these pipelines now flows back to the agents, which helps them to iteratively solve their individual tasks (continues with step 5.1 until the feature is approved by the review agent). (6) After all features are implemented or certain exit criteria are fulfilled, experimenters can check the outcomes (e.g. the created code) and compare the clones, e.g., did the active voice requirements have a higher success rate, faster code generation with less agentic iterations, or less defects according to unit tests?

This would provide researchers with data on the question whether passive voice requirements are a relevant requirements quality factor for agentic SE projects. And in a second step, given that a deeper understanding of similarities and differences between human and agentic SE agents behavior allows us to extrapolate from agentic to human behavior, it might even provide first insights for improving human-driven SE projects.

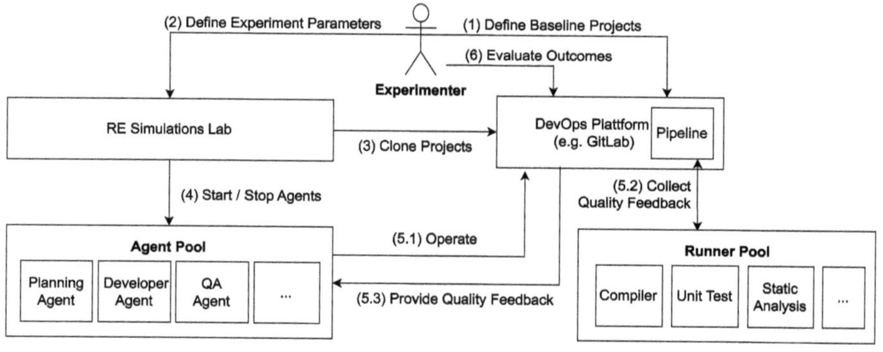

Fig. 1. The Process Behind A Pipeline-based Agentic Simulation

3.2   Research Roadmap

The usage of agentic simulations in RE has two research objectives (RO): First, to understand how to do RE effectively and efficiently for agentic AI. Second, to understand to what degree these results can be generalized to human-centric SE processes. Together, this provides practitioners with a more complete and evidence-based RE quality model and researchers with a novel research method to study certain RE phenomena in a simulated environment. The following roadmap describes our long-term research agenda.

3.3   RO 1: Define a RE Quality Model for AI-Coding Agents

The first objective is to design and implement a technical infrastructure that replicates realistic SE processes on a DevOps platform such as GitLab. For this process, we need to define actors, artifacts and actions. For actors, we need to elicit a set of agent roles (such as developer or testers) and envision to use docker as a standardized interface to agents. For agent actions the Model Context Protocol (MCP) could form a standardized interface to the DevOps system.

Research Method: Since the quality model is a continuous endeavor, we should design the research accordingly. Therefore, we propose to apply a design-science approach with agentic simulations as validation methods. In each cycle, researchers will extend the quality model with further stakeholders, activities, quality factors, impacts and context.

RQs: RQ 1.1: Can agentic AI cooperatively implement requirements in a DevOps process simulation? RQ 1.2: What is the impact of known quality factors onto agents' activities? RQ 1.3: What is the cost (financial & environmental) of the simulations?

Data Collection: To answer these, we proceed as discussed in the previous section. The approach allows to collect various performance metrics for each clone from the DevOps environment, such as the number of successful merge requests, automated unit test metrics, manual assessment of requirements fulfillment, static QA assessments about the code output, and dynamic QA assessments such as usability tests. Both are elicited for the simulation results in general (RQ 1.1) and per quality factor (i.e. project A vs. B, RQ 1.2). Furthermore, we elicit token consumption, cost, and runtime metrics for the used LLMs (RQ 1.3).

Data Analysis: We calculate success percentage for RQ 1.1, comparative analysis for RQ 1.2 and average costs per replication for RQ 1.3.

3.4   RO 2: Understand Agentic Simulation's Abilities and Limitations in Generalization to Human Behavior

The second RO investigates how well simulated processes represent human work.

Research Method: Comparative analysis of human and agentic AI behavior in controlled environments must be conducted in which human engineers replace one of the agents while the rest of the process remains automated.

RQs: RQ 2.1: How does the context taken into account by the humans differ from the agents? RQ 2.2: How does the process executed by the humans differ? RQ 2.3: How do the artifacts created by humans differ?

Data Collection: Quantitative and qualitative metrics as in RO1 as well as interview and observation data from the experiment.

Data Analysis: By comparing process metrics and output quality, differences in reasoning, error patterns, and decision strategies can be identified. This enables systematic assessment of where simulations produce representative results and where human-specific factors (such as interpretation, ambiguity resolution, or creativity) play a decisive role. This data will help determine under which conditions simulations are a valid proxy for human-driven software processes.

3.5 Risks

Any research involving LLMs risks evolving model behavior affecting reproducibility, data leaks, and varying outputs. We suggest mitigating this by using open-weights models (allowing version pinning) and publishing complete interaction logs as proposed in [19]. Besides these standard risks, this roadmap faces two specific risks:

R_1: **Limited abilities of individual agents.** The agents used in this study might not yet be able to handle complex or dependent tasks reliably, which would limit how realistic the simulations can be.

R_2: **Scalability problems due to high computing, financial or environmental costs.** Running many simulations could require substantial resources, which could call into question whether the results justify these costs.

4 Software Engineering Simulations Lab (SESL)

To understand the risks specified and get first insights into RO1 of this research agenda, we set up a feasibility study with a limited scope as defined in the introduction. Following the methodology of [14], the **purpose** of this work focuses on *process improvement* of RE processes by *understanding* the impact of quality factors in RE artifacts on subsequent manual and automated SE activities. The **scope** of the simulations is a single project or a single iteration thereof. The **reference behavior** is the real-world behavior of iterative SE projects in a DevOps/Git Flow context, working with or without agentic AI systems. In these iterations, automated CI/CD pipelines provide quality feedback. Our **model concepts** can be found in Fig. 1. The subsequent sections describe the remaining two steps of the simulation process according to [14].

4.1 Executable Model: SESL Architecture

To evaluate the risks and to evaluate feasibility, we developed a prototype of SESL, including a naïve baseline implementation of all relevant components.

For our prototype, we used our GitLab instance with four GitLab pipeline runners. As a pipeline, we employed Java compilation and JUnit testing with JaCoCo for coverage. Feedback from static analysis was not included in our feasibility study to shorten iterations. The SDLC was operationalized through a simplification of an agile project in a typical Git Flow [17] style, defining agents by their I/O behavior (see Table 1). Agents were run in sequential orchestration in the form of the supervisor pattern [22]. In addition, each agent was instructed to create a textual report as a markdown file in a dedicated folder at the end of their action, which was read by the subsequent agents to reduce hallucinations by setting the context and enable human validation (as proposed by [1]). All further design details, such as applied prompts, source code etc. can be found in the supplementary material.

Table 1. Employed AI agents in feasibility study

Agent	Responsibilities	➡Inputs & ↪Outputs
Planning Agent	Order work items and define plan	➡Work items ↪Prioritized plan, Architecture file
Coding Agent	Create code for a work item	➡Work items, Existing code, Architecture ↪Branches, Code commits
Testing Agent	Create test cases for a work item	➡Work items, Existing code, Architecture ➡Branches, Commits with unit test code
Review Agent	Check pipeline and unit tests for success and code against requirements implementation	➡Pipeline results ↪Merge request

4.2 Simulation Results: First Risk Insights from a Feasibility Study

As a first feasibility study, we ran a simulation using the aforementioned prototype architecture, looking into RQ 1.1-1.3.

Data Collection and Analysis: To evaluate and/or mitigate the aforementioned risks, we follow existing guidelines [1, 19] by recording model version and date, publishing all prompts and configurations (available in our repository), saving results in Git, and using DeepSeek as an open weights model. Future work will include comparing output consistency and validating results with human reviewers as recommended in [1].

As a baseline, we created two projects in GitLab with five requirements each for implementing a battleships game. One baseline (A) contains five work items which could be considered high quality requirements, the other (B) contains the same work items, but we injected six requirements quality defects: Complex sentence structure, incorrect legal binding, inconsistent terminology, passive voice, missing coherence, and technical density. We intentionally combined multiple defects to increase the effect for the feasibility study. Each work item was described using a title, a user story, a detailed description and three acceptance criteria each, with an average of 162.4 words in total for the whole description.

The SESL platform replicated both baselines 10 times each, leading to a total of 20 simulations. Of these, 6 simulations needed to be repeated a second time due to GitLab getting stuck. The agents were run using the DeepSeek-V3.2-Exp model on Oct. 10th-22nd 2025 at a temperature of 0.2 to reduce variance.

First Results RQ 1.1&1.2: The overall results are promising: With just a naïve baseline implementation, 34% of the requirements (A:38%, B:30%) were automatically implemented and merged, 23% (A:26%, B:20%) passed all unit tests provided by testing agents. The average line coverage in unit tests was 40% (A:44%, B:37%). A first inspection of the details indicates that the agents struggled particularly with the defects injected into requirement#2 (e.g. on average 18.5 points worse line coverage for agents working with defective requirements vs. defect-free requirements, 2.5 times more timeouts and errors during pipeline execution). Overall this provides first evidence for a higher success rate and higher quality for agents working with the high quality requirements (A).

First Results RQ 1.3: The simulation for these 20 successful projects took 110 h or 5.5 h per clone (A: 5.3h, B: 5.7h) with GitLab pipelines being the main bottleneck. Required tokens per clone averaged at 94.2 mio. input and 269.6k output tokens, leading to costs of $3.27 per simulation clone. According to a carbon calculation tool (https://llmemissions.com) the LLM component of the experiment had an environmental footprint of approx. 0.6 kg CO2 overall.

5   Discussion, Summary and Outlook

This work proposes understanding RE quality by simulating human behavior with agentic AI. These agents work directly on clones of DevOps projects and get feedback from CI/CD pipelines. The work furthermore contributes a prototypical architecture as well as first results from a feasibility study with 20 projects on a total of 100 requirements run sequentially over a period of 110 h.

Our results indicate that running simulations with LLM-based agents is fast and cost-effective, and it can produce working software (RQ 1.1). Moreover, the early results suggest that lower requirements quality has a negative impact on the agents' output (RQ 1.2). We furthermore present first data on environmental and financial cost and execution time, supporting our claim that simulations could provide a cost- and time-effective method (RQ 1.3). Future work will analyze the results in detail, looking at various assumed quality factors, such as passive voice, complex language, structure, etc. To which degree the created results generalize to human behavior (RO2) is also out of scope of this preview.

Threats to Validity: As this work presents an early research preview, threats to validity are many-fold. Results are constrained by the prototype setup, the selected AI model and instructions. Therefore, future work must include state-of-the-art agents and look deeper into addressing risks of overfitting. A qualitative analysis into the actions of the agents and a comparison against human participants is furthermore necessary. This includes also an analysis on the consistency and hallucinations of the agentic behavior within a model, over time and across models. The chosen requirements reflect a well-known game and are therefore probably part of the training set, which might lead to a lesser effect of the requirements quality, since the ambiguity can be compensated by the model. It is furthermore a small set of requirements, scalability beyond that remains unclear at this early point. The reported execution times are mostly constrained by the GitHub setup and our approach of sequential execution and are more of an upper bound for the given project. A follow-up detailed analysis will also report on the specific impact of other quality factors on other activity facts, such as manual assessment of the correctness of requirements implementation or test quality.

Data Availability Statement. The code of our implementation can be found at https://github.com/FH-SWF-SSQL/SESL. The template projects as well as the resulting executed projects with all pipeline logs from the simulations are available on GitLab https://gitlab.nibbler.fh-swf.de/publications/sesl-feasibility.

References

1. Baltes, S., et al.: Guidelines for empirical studies in software engineering involving large language models. arXiv preprint arXiv:2508.15503 (2025)
2. de Bruijn, F., Dekkers, H.L.: Ambiguity in natural language software requirements: a case study. In: REFSQ (2010)
3. Bühne, S., et al.: CPRE Foundation Level - Syllabus – v.3.2.0 (2024)
4. Dabrowski, J., Cai, W., Bennaceur, A., Nuseibeh, B., Alrimawi, F.: Intelligent agents for requirements engineering: use, feasibility and evaluation. In: RE (2025)
5. Femmer, H., Kučera, J., Vetrò, A.: On the impact of passive voice requirements on domain modelling. In: ESEM (2014)
6. Femmer, H., Vogelsang, A.: Requirements quality is quality in use. IEEE Softw. **36**(3) (2018)
7. Ferrari, A., Abualhaija, S., Arora, C.: Model generation with LLMs: from requirements to UML sequence diagrams. In: RE Workshops (REW). IEEE (2024)
8. Frattini, J., Montgomery, L., Fischbach, J., Mendez, D., Fucci, D., Unterkalmsteiner, M.: Requirements quality research: a harmonized theory, evaluation, and roadmap. Requirements Eng. **28**(4) (2023)
9. Frattini, J., et al.: A second look at the impact of passive voice requirements on domain modeling: Bayesian reanalysis of an experiment. In: WSESE (2024)
10. Hou, X., et al.: Large language models for software engineering: a systematic literature review. Trans. Softw. Eng. Methodol. **33**(8) (2024)
11. Krisch, J., Houdek, F.: The myth of bad passive voice and weak words an empirical investigation in the automotive industry. In: RE (2015)
12. Lubos, S., et al.: Leveraging LLMs for the quality assurance of software requirements. In: RE (2024)
13. Montgomery, L., et al.: Empirical research on requirements quality: a systematic mapping study. Requirements Eng. **27**(2) (2022)
14. Müller, M., Pfahl, D.: Simulation methods. In: Guide to Advanced Empirical Software Engineering. Springer (2008)
15. Philippo, E.J., et al.: Requirement ambiguity not as important as expected - results of an empirical evaluation. In: REFSQ (2013)
16. Pourasad, A.E., Maalej, W.: Does GenAI make usability testing obsolete? In: ICSE (2025)

17. Ríos, J.C.C., Embury, S.M., Eraslan, S.: A unifying framework for the systematic analysis of git workflows. Inf. Softw. Technol. **145** (2022)
18. Ronanki, K., Berger, C., Horkoff, J.: Investigating chatgpt's potential to assist in requirements elicitation processes. In: SEAA (2023)
19. Sallou, J., Durieux, T., Panichella, A.: Breaking the silence: the threats of using LLMs in software engineering. In: ICSE NIER (2024)
20. Steenhoek, B., et al.: Reinforcement learning from automatic feedback for high-quality unit test generation. In: DeepTest (2025)
21. Vogelsang, A., Korn, A., Broccia, G., Ferrari, A., Fischbach, J., Arora, C.: On the impact of requirements smells in prompts: the case of automated traceability. In: ICSE-NIER (2025)
22. Wang, Y., et al.: Agents in software engineering: survey, landscape, and vision. Autom. Softw. Eng. **32**(2) (2025)
23. Wei, B.: Requirements are all you need: from requirements to code with LLMs. In: RE (2024)

A Visual Formalism for the Specification of Maritime Traffic Scenarios

Anna Austel[(✉)], Georg Hake, and Nina Wetzig

Institute of Systems Engineering for Future Mobility, German Aerospace Center (DLR), Oldenburg, Germany
`{anna.austel,georg.hake,nina.wetzig}@dlr.de`

Abstract. Context and Motivation: The advent of automated vessels or Maritime Autonomous Surface Ships (MASS) brings new challenges for requirements engineering. In addition to classical, more technical requirements, now a vessel's behaviour, including its interactions with infrastructure and other traffic participants, has to be taken into account. Relevant requirements can be described in terms of traffic scenarios.

Problem: Formal specification of these traffic scenarios provides the basis for clear communication and objective evaluation of behavioural requirements, which is crucial to ensure trustworthiness of MASS. However, there currently is no domain-specific language suitable for this task.

Principal Ideas/Results: Initially presented for the automotive domain, Traffic Sequence Charts (TSCs) are a domain-specific visual modelling language for the formal specification of traffic scenarios. In this paper, we present Maritime TSCs, an extension of classical TSCs to the maritime domain, and show that they are suitable for the formal specification of important maritime traffic rules.

Contribution: With Maritime TSCs we provide a visual formal language for the specification of maritime traffic scenarios. This language enables clear communication of requirements between stakeholders and automatic, objective evaluation of vessel behaviour.

Keywords: Visual Formalism · Requirement Formalisation · Maritime Autonomous Surface Ships · Domain Specific Modelling Language

1 Introduction

Maritime shipping is responsible for the transportation of over 80% of goods in the global economy [28]. There is an ever increasing traffic flow not only by volume of goods but also in number of vessels in domestic, regional, and international shipping that need to be operated safely in ports, locks, and the high seas. To support the efficient and safe operation, there is a growing interest in automated and autonomous ships. The International Maritime Organization (IMO) defines Maritime Autonomous Surface Ships (MASS) as ships which operate independently of human operators to a certain degree, ranging from automated processes and decision support, over remote control, to fully autonomous ships [9, 19, 20].

R. Guizzardi and J. Araújo (Eds.): REFSQ 2026, LNCS 16497, pp. 75–90, 2026.
https://doi.org/10.1007/978-3-032-21423-2_6

A key issue according to the IMO is to address the functional and operational requirements of automated systems. These include classical safety requirements for cyber physical systems (such as reliability and timing of communication in remote control) but also a new class of requirements on *how automated ships are supposed to drive,* i.e., how they should conduct manoeuvres such as collision avoidance on the high seas, approaching and leaving ports, or mooring. To ensure that MASS are trustworthy and ethical, they need to be objectively evaluated for compliance with rules and safety requirements, such as the "International Regulations for Preventing Collisions at Sea" (COLREG) [15]. Objective evaluation necessitates formal specifications of these rules to avoid ambiguity. To increase trustworthiness, the specification should be comprehensible to and take into account knowledge of different stakeholders like certification and port authorities, vessel traffic service providers, vessel operators, shipbuilders and suppliers.

While efforts towards formalisation of maritime scenarios have been made before, there exists no domain-specific language for scenario specification in the maritime domain that enables formal specification of complex traffic scenarios [22].

The scenario specification language Traffic Sequence Charts (TSCs) [5–7] has been developed as a formal, visual specification language for abstract traffic scenarios and scenario-based requirements. Originally tailored to the needs of the automotive domain, the language has seen application in the railway domain [30]. TSCs as used for automotive and railway cannot immediately be used for scenarios in the maritime domain because ship dynamics, variety of operating environments and infrastructure, and impact of environmental conditions are very different in this domain and cannot be adequately represented. Initial attempts at a TSC-based formalisation of individual maritime traffic scenarios have previously been presented in the context of research on potential applications of an extended TSC language in the maritime domain [1–3,13].

In this work we now discuss extensions to TSCs, necessary for their general application in the maritime domain, and present the resulting language we call Maritime Traffic Sequence Charts (MTSCs). We evaluate the formalism to answer the following:

Research Question: Are MTSCs as introduced in this work suitable for the visual formal specification of maritime traffic rules?

The paper is structured as follows. After a discussion of related work in Sect. 2, we give a brief introduction to the original TSC language in Sect. 3. We present our extensions to the formalism in Sect. 4 and our evaluation in Sect. 5. In Sect. 6 we conclude and outline future work.

2   Related Work

So far, no dedicated language for the specification of abstract maritime traffic scenarios exists.

There is some previous work on building knowledge databases of historic traffic data which is semantically annotated [8, 23, 24, 29]. This allows to query for occurrences of traffic situations or concrete scenarios matching specific criteria, including combinations of spatial relations. These works use general purpose topological relation frameworks which define relations like containment or overlap of geometries.

Previous approaches to the specification of maritime traffic rules and scenarios rely on purely formula-based temporal logics without visualisation or a focus on spatial relations: Krasowski and Althoff [17] provide a formalisation of parts of the Convention on the International Regulations for Preventing Collisions at Sea (COLREG) in metric temporal logic (MTL). They evaluate their formalised rule set on historical AIS data and report that the observed behaviour matches their specification in 98% of the recorded encounters. They further adapt and extend their formalisation for the synthesis of rule compliant behaviour in safe reinforcement learning for MASS [18]. Torben et al. [26, 27] propose the use of signal temporal logic (STL) in the test design for MASS, including formalisation of COLREG requirements. Johansen et al. [16] use this framework for risk assessment of an autonomous ship.

Popular domain-specific languages for automotive scenarios such as Open-SCENARIO [21] and SCENIC [11] clearly focus on simulation and testing. Greenyer et al. [12] as well as Fockel et al. [10] evaluate methods for scenario-based requirements specification and analysis. They propose to specify requirements in a scenario language that is based on live sequence charts [4].

While MTSCs have not previously been presented as a language, there is some previous work on different applications of prototypical extensions of TSCs in the maritime domain. This includes the specification of experiment conduction for evaluation of maritime assistance systems [2], generation of online monitors for runtime assessment of vessel behaviour with respect to predefined scenarios [1] and the specification of relevant test scenarios and requirements in scenario-based testing of MASS [3, 13].

3 Preliminaries: Traffic Sequence Charts

Traffic Sequence Charts (TSCs) are an object-oriented, spatio-temporal, visual formalism for the specification of traffic scenarios. TSCs are used to specify *abstract scenarios*, i.e., characteristic properties of *concrete scenarios*. A concrete scenario maps each point in time to a scene, which gives a concrete valuation of attributes of traffic objects. In the following subsections, we introduce the concepts and components of the TSC language in more detail. For a complete description of the TSC language we refer to Damm et al. [5–7].

3.1 Object Model

Traffic objects, like vehicles, infrastructure elements, etc. are modelled by an *object model*. An object model consists of a finite set $\mathcal{T}$ of *basic types* and a finite set $\mathcal{C}$ of *object types*. Each object type $C \in \mathcal{C}$ has a finite set of attributes $Attr(C) = \{a_1 : \tau_1, \ldots, a_n : \tau_n\}$ of basic type, that is, each attribute $a_i \in Attr(C)$ has a basic type $\tau_i \in \mathcal{T}$. Each basic type $\tau \in \mathcal{T}$ is associated with a set $\mathcal{D}(\tau)$ which is called the *domain* of τ. An *instance* of object type C with attributes $\{a_1 : \tau_1, \ldots, a_n : \tau_n\}$ is a function σ that assigns to each attribute a type consistent domain value, i.e., $\sigma(a_i) \in \mathcal{D}(\tau_i)$ for $i \in \{1, \ldots, n\}$. For each object type C, $\mathcal{D}(C)$ are pairwise disjoint, infinite sets of *object identities* that can be compared for equality. A *scene* over an object model $(\mathcal{T}, \mathcal{C})$ is a function Σ that maps a finite set of object identities to type consistent objects, that is, for each object identity $id \in \mathcal{D}(C)$ in the domain of Σ, $\Sigma(id)$ is an instance of C. Generally, basic types represent physical quantities while object types and their attributes model physical objects and their relevant, observable properties. As spatial properties and relations are of particular interest in the specification of traffic scenarios, $\mathcal{T}$ includes dedicated basic types **position** and **distance** with domains $\mathcal{D}(\textbf{position}) = \mathbb{R}^2$ and $\mathcal{D}(\textbf{distance}) = \mathbb{R}$.

A simple object model for the specification of a braking manoeuvre could for example have basic types **velocity, acceleration, position** and **distance** with $\mathcal{D}(\textbf{velocity}) = \mathcal{D}(\textbf{acceleration}) = \mathbb{R}$ and object types *Car*, *Obstacle* and *Lane* with attributes

$$Attr(Car) = \{v : \textbf{velocity}, a : \textbf{acceleration}, pos : \textbf{position}\}, \tag{1}$$

$$Attr(Obstacle) = \{pos : \textbf{position}\}, \tag{2}$$

$$Attr(Lane) = \{pos_{min} : \textbf{position}, pos_{max} : \textbf{position}\}. \tag{3}$$

3.2   Spatial Views and Symbol Dictionary

A spatial view is a rectangular canvas on which *object symbols* from a *symbol dictionary* are placed, possibly annotated with *distance lines* and *predicate connectors*. It allows us to graphically model constraints on spatial relations and attribute values.

Given an object model, the symbol dictionary introduces graphical symbols that represent objects in the specification, and the visual appearance of these model elements can be freely chosen. In the automotive domain, it is common to choose car-shaped symbols for object types that model vehicles, box-shaped symbols for obstacles on the road, and stylised lane markings to represent road segments. *Point-anchors*, annotated as $\otimes$ can be used in the symbol definition to represent attributes of type **position**. The relative placement of point-anchors along the axes of a spatial view signify a corresponding order on the position attributes the anchors represent along two reference directions, typically along and perpendicular to a road the scenario takes place on. Distance lines can be annotated between a pair of point-anchors and are labelled with a constraint on the dedicated variable d that may contain constant symbols and attribute references. A predicate connector is connected to a symbol on one end and a boolean expression over the attributes associated with the symbol, constants and further attribute references on the other end.

As an example, Fig. 1 shows a simple TSC from the automotive domain with three spatial views. The leftmost spatial view uses three object symbols, one distance line, and two predicate connectors.

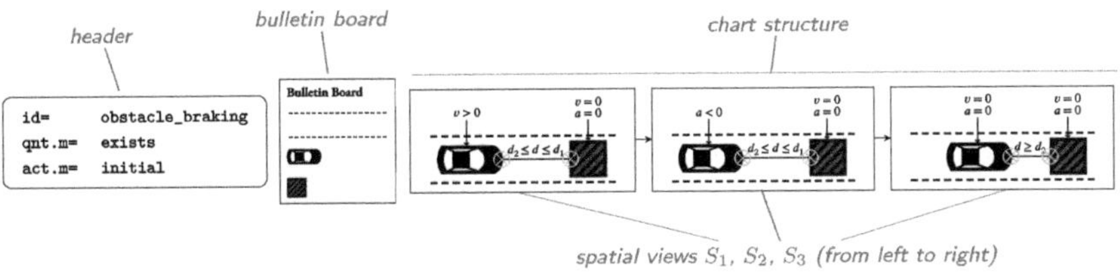

Fig. 1. Simple automotive scenario specification: stopping in front of an obstacle [14].

The semantics of a spatial view S is algorithmically defined in [6] as a formula $\phi(S)$ of a many-sorted first-order logic where the set of sorts consists of the basic types and object types from the object model. That is, there is an algorithm that takes a well-formed spatial view and yields a formula according to the presence of object symbols and their relative placement in the spatial view, in addition to an integration of the expressions of predicate connectors and distance constraints. Given a scene Σ over the object model then we say Σ satisfies spatial view S if and only if $\Sigma \models \phi(S)$.

3.3   Header, Bulletin Board and Chart

A complete TSC consists of a *header*, a *bulletin board*, and a *chart*. The chart consists of nodes that are related by operations like sequential composition, concurrency, or choice. The example TSC in Fig. 1 has three nodes related by sequential composition. Each node in the chart structure is labelled with a spatial view. The bulletin board serves as a declaration of logical object variables that are global to the chart. In the example this means each car symbol represents the same car throughout the scenario and will be referenced by the same logical variable in the constraints obtained for the three spatial views. The header provides a name for the TSC, the quantification mode (**exists** or **forall**), and the activation mode (**initial** or **always**). The semantics of a complete TSC with header, bulletin board, and chart structure is algorithmically defined as a temporal logic formula over logical variables that are quantified for branching and activation (cf. [6]). These formulae have a satisfaction relation to sets of concrete scenarios, i.e., temporal evolutions of scenes over the object model. Intuitively, the TSC in Fig. 1 is satisfied if there is at least one (since the quantification mode is **exists**) concrete scenario with a car and an obstacle for which, starting from the beginning (since the activation is **initial**), there is a phase where the car's position is in braking distance in front of the stationary object, then a phase of deceleration ($a < 0$), and then a standstill at a safe distance in front of the obstacle.

4   Maritime TSCs

In this section we present extensions to the TSC formalism with the goal of allowing a comprehensible and concise formalisation of abstract maritime traffic scenarios like traffic rules and test scenarios.

The general idea of TSCs is to subdivide traffic scenarios into phases with invariant conditions and represent the temporal and logical structure of these phases as a chart. A key feature is the visual specification of the invariant conditions, including the graphical representation of involved objects and their spatial relations. This concept lends itself to the specification of traffic scenarios independently of the domain. As the temporal structure of all maritime scenarios we have considered this far could sufficiently be expressed using the existing chart operators, we leave the chart structure as is. However, the provided tools for specifying spatial properties and relations and the underlying model of space of the spatial view formalism is heavily geared towards automotive scenarios on roads. Our extensions thus adapt this underlying model of space and introduce additional model elements to adequately capture spatial relations relevant in maritime traffic.

4.1   Direction Attributes

An important aspect of describing the state, movement, and interaction of ships is the concept of directions. The most apparent examples of relevant directions are heading, i.e., the direction the bow of the ship is facing, and course (over ground), i.e., the direction in which the vessel is moving. Other than in the automotive domain, a ship's course can deviate significantly from its heading, due to influences of current and wind.

To integrate directions into the TSC formalism, we introduce an additional dedicated basic type **direction** (like the **position** type) and a visual syntax for the representation of attributes of this type similar to the point-anchors used for attributes of type **position**. In navigation, directions like the heading or course of a ship are typically given in degrees with values in $[0, 360)$, increasing clockwise. That is, $0°$ refers to a direction towards true north, $90°$ to a direction towards true east, and so on. We accordingly choose $\mathcal{D}(\textbf{direction}) = \{a° | a \in [0, 360)\}$. To model a ship, its position, heading and course over ground, we may then for example define an object type *Ship* with attributes $\{pos : \textbf{position}, hdg : \textbf{direction}, cog : \textbf{direction}\}$. For an intuitive visual representation of attributes of type **direction** we use straight arrows ($\longrightarrow$) that we call *direction-anchors*. Like point-anchors ($\otimes$ cf. Sect. 3), direction-anchors can then be used in symbols, for instance as shown in Fig. 2a for the object type *Ship*. To avoid ambiguity regarding which direction-anchor represents which attribute, the position of each direction-anchor within an object symbol is fixed by the symbol dictionary. In examples like ours above, the ship symbol is meant to resemble the shape of a ship from above and intuitively the direction-anchor representing the ships heading should point in the same direction as the part of the symbol resembling a ship's bow. The course of a ship on the other hand can vary relative to its orientation and the direction-anchor for the *cog* attribute should be allowed to be rotated within the ship symbol. Here, the rotation of symbol and anchors in the spatial view is not semantically relevant, i.e., does not introduce a constraint into the formula for the spatial view, but is graphical means to support readability.

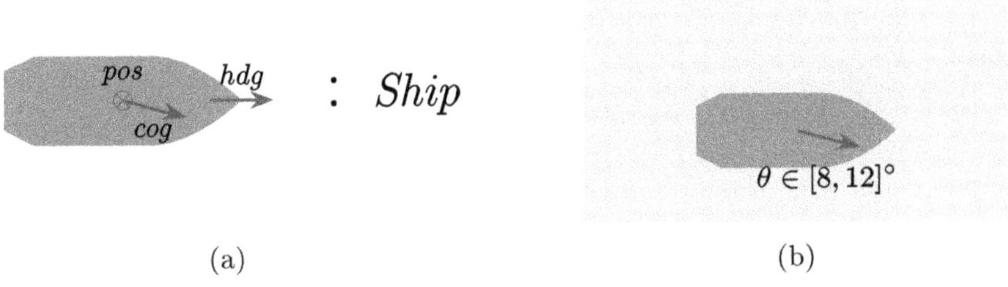

(a)   (b)

Fig. 2. (a) symbol dictionary for object type *Ship* with a point-anchor and two direction-anchors and (b) spatial view specifying a course over ground between 8° and 12° of a ship.

Similar to distance lines, direction anchors can be annotated with constraints over a dedicated variable θ referencing the represented direction. Beyond standard mathematical operations and relations we introduce notation for intervals of directions for this purpose. We write $[a, b]°$ to denote the set of directions $\{c°|c \in [a, b]\}$. To enable simple notation of direction intervals with 0 in the interior, a and b are allowed to take any values in $\mathbb{R}$. Values in the interval are simply normalized modulo 360. The ship symbol from the symbol dictionary in Fig. 2a can for example be used to specify a simple test-scenario regarding the capabilities of a system to approximately hold to a predefined course of 10° using the spatial view shown in Fig. 2b. The corresponding constraint is $s.cog \in [8, 12]°$.

The spatial view in Fig. 2b depicts only one of the three anchors declared in the symbol dictionary, the one referenced in the specification. This exemplifies another extension to the formalism. In MTSCs each anchor of an object symbol as defined in the symbol dictionary can be included in a spatial view individually. Only included anchors are depicted in the spatial view and can be referenced.

4.2 Spatial Relations

Different directions are also the basis for relevant spatial relations in the maritime domain. For example, there could be a temporary requirement that heading and course should not differ by more than a certain amount or the *bearing* of an object O from a ship S should be in a specific range. Maritime scenarios frequently contain constraints on directions and angles. For instance a ship is required to orient itself parallel to a quay wall in a mooring manoeuvre and to pass specific markers on its port side.

For attributes of type **position** represented via point-anchors, automotive TSCs provide tools for the graphical specification of distances as well as orders

along two axes. This is quite useful for scenarios on roads or in similarly structured environments such as fairways. The order relations are, however, not a
good fit for scenarios on the open sea. There, spatial relations on directions, like
the relative bearing of a target ship viewed from the own ship, i.e., the angle
between the own ships heading and the direction from the own ship's position to
the target ship's position, are frequently referenced, while maritime (functional)
scenarios outside restricted waterways rarely refer to relevant axes along which
to order positions.

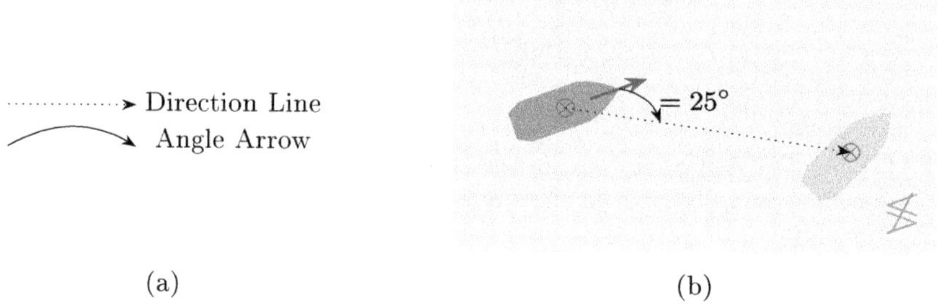

Fig. 3. Graphical notation for directions and angles. (a) new model elements (b) used
in a spatial view to formalise a relative bearing of 25°.

To support the specification of spatial relations in terms of directions, we
extend the collection of model elements that can be used in spatial views by
two additional fixed model elements, *direction lines* and *angle arrows* for an
intuitive graphical representation of the direction between a pair of positions
and the angle between a pair of directions. An angle arrow has a start and an
end. Both are connected to either a direction-anchor or a direction line. Similar
to a distance line, an angle arrow is annotated with a constraint on a dedicated
variable α. Direction lines also have a start and an end and both are connected
to point-anchors. Like direction anchors they can be annotated with constraints
on θ. The symbol for an angle arrow is a curved black arrow and the symbol for
a direction line is a straight, dotted, black arrow, as shown in Fig. 3a.

Using direction lines and angle arrows, we can visually formalise properties
like "a ship is at a relative bearing of 25° from a second ship" using the object
type *Ship* from Fig. 2a as shown in Fig. 3b. Note that, to avoid visual clutter in
spatial views, we allow to omit d, θ and α from annotated distance, direction and
angle constraints. Additionally we allow the implicit specification of equality of
directions and positions by annotating them at the same place within a spatial
view.

Since in this scene, as in many maritime scenes, we do not need or want to
specify any order on the positions represented using point anchors, we relax the
original model of space to make the order on positions optional. We mark the
spatial view with "⋧" to indicate that the relative placement of point-anchors
within this spatial view has no semantical relevance. The semantics of Fig. 3b

includes a constraint $ang(o.hdg, dir(o.pos, y.pos)) = 25$ on two object variables o and y of type *Ship* for the orange and yellow ship symbol respectively, which uses the function $ang()$ that yields the (clockwise) angle between two directions, and $dir()$ that yields the direction from one position to another one.

4.3   Environmental Conditions

Another aspect that is neglected in classical TSCs are properties of the environment. As nautical navigation is sensitive to environmental conditions like wind and current these have to be taken into account in maritime traffic scenarios. Wind and current can be modelled as regular object types. For example, to model wind with its direction and speed, we might define an object type *Wind* with attributes dir : **direction** and *speed* : **velocity**. We present a symbol definition for the object type *Wind* in Fig. 4a. We can use this object type and symbol, e.g., to specify a scenario for testing the ability to hold to a course perpendicular to the wind direction, using the spatial view shown in Fig. 4b.

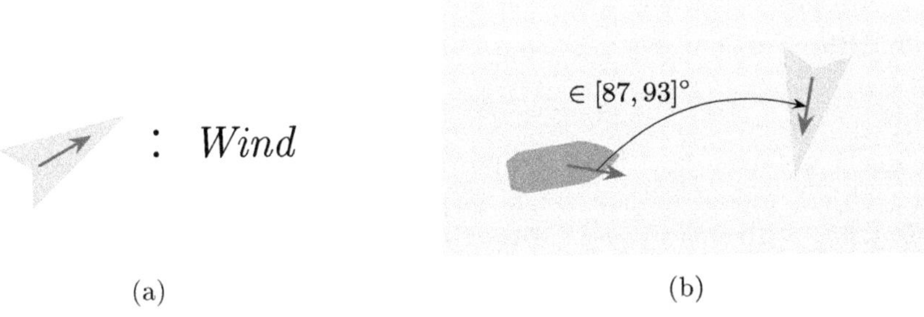

(a)   (b)

Fig. 4. Example specification of an environmental condition: (a) a symbol definition for object type *Wind* and (b) spatial view specifying a ship's course approximately perpendicular to the wind direction.

5   Evaluation

To evaluate our language with respect to its suitability for the formal specification of maritime traffic rules, we take a look at the International Regulations for Preventing Collisions at Sea (COLREG) [15], as adhering to COLREG is a necessary prerequisite for operating MASS on the open sea. We restrict ourselves to requirements regarding encounters of two power-driven vessels on the open sea with no restrictions on manoeuvrability. Rules 13, 14 and 15 describe 3 different types of such encounters and regulate corresponding reactions. Additionally, rules 3, 7, 8, 11, 16 and 17 further detail some aspects of the required behaviour and have to be taken into account for a complete specification. We identified the traffic properties referenced by these rules to define the type of encounter and corresponding required reaction and list them in Table 1.

Table 1. Traffic properties mentioned in COLREG rules regarding encounters of power-driven vessels on the open sea

ID	Property	relevant rules
A	Vessels within sight of each other	3, 11
B	Approaching with risk of collision	7, 14, 15
C	Approaching another vessel from behind	13
D	Keeping out of the way of another vessel	8, 13, 15, 16, 17
D1	Taking action early on	8, 16
D2	Changing course significantly	8, 16
D3	Resulting in passing at a safe distance	8, 16
D4	Until past and clear of other vessel	8
E	Altering course to starboard	14
F	Observing bow aspect of another vessel nearly ahead	14
G	Other vessel on own starboard side	15
H	Other vessel on own port side	14
I	Keeping course and speed roughly constant	17
J	Other vessel unable to avoid collision on its own	17

In Fig. 5 we show how these properties can be formalised as spatial views over an object model with a single object type *Ship* with attributes $\{pos :$ **position**$, hdg :$ **direction**$, cog :$ **direction**$, rot :$ **velocity**$_{\mathbf{ang}}, sog :$ **velocity**$\}$, (where $\mathcal{D}(\mathbf{velocity_{ang}}) = \{r°/\min|r \in \mathbb{R}\}$, $\mathcal{D}(\mathbf{velocity}) = \{r\mathrm{kn}|r \in \mathbb{R}\}$) and the symbol dictionary from Fig. 2a. Property H is symmetrical to G and E can be expressed with a single annotated predicate '$rot > 0$' similar to D2, so we omit the spatial views. D1 is a temporal property and is specified as part of the chart instead of a spatial view in MTSCs. Within the spatial views we reference some parameters for which appropriate values have to be chosen depending on the specific vessel and the intended application of the specification:

- $d_{\mathbf{sight}}$: max distance at which another vessel can be visually perceived
- $d_{\mathbf{safe}}$: min distance two vessels must keep for safe passage
- $d_{\mathbf{clear}}$: min distance for a vessel to be considered clear of another
- $d_{\mathbf{crit}}$: max distance for a vessel to be considered critically close
- rot_{l}: min absolute rate of turn considered significant and clearly noticeable
- $rot_{\mathbf{s}}$: max absolute rate of turn, at which the course is still nearly constant
- $\dot{sog}_{\mathbf{s}}$: max absolute change in sog still considered nearly constant sog
- $\dot{\beta}_{\mathbf{s}}$: max absolute change of bearing still considered insignificant
- $\alpha_{\mathbf{s}}$: max angle between directions still considered nearly identical.

Where appropriate values for these parameters cannot be found in the literature, one has to rely on expert knowledge, evaluation of historical traffic data and potentially finetuning in simulation and real world experiments to establish them.

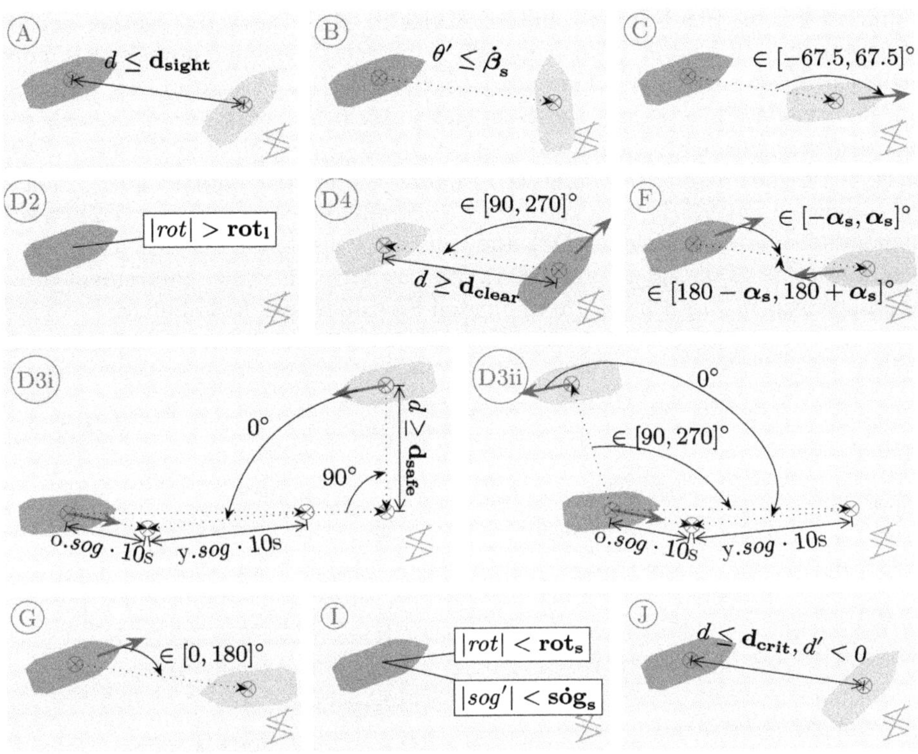

Fig. 5. Spatial views formalising properties from Table 1 as indicated by green labels. In D3 the yellow and orange ship symbols are referenced as y and o.

Some of our formalisations require additional context.
(B): Rule 7 states that a risk of collision should be assumed in case the compass bearing of an approaching vessel does not appreciably change for some time.
(C): Rule 13 specifies overtaking as approaching at an angle of more than 112.5 degrees of another vessels heading.
(D): Rule 8 specifies that adequately keeping out of the way requires (D1)-(D4).
(D1): We consider early action to be action within a certain time from the beginning of the encounter.
(D3): We consider a manoeuvre to result in passing at a safe distance if it results in (i) a projected distance at closest point of approach (DCPA) larger than the minimum safe passing distance until (ii) the time to closest point of approach (TCPA) falls (and stays) below 0.
(J): We consider the distance between the vessels falling below a critical threshold as an indication that the other vessel cannot avoid a collision by its action alone.

Given a formalisation of the properties from Table 1 as spatial views, we can formalise all requirements for encounters of power-driven vessels given by COLREG as MTSCs. To see how to do this, consider for example COLREG requirements on Head-On encounters. Rules 8, 11, 14 and 16 together specify what encounters should be considered to be Head-On and how vessels must behave in these encounters. They state that two vessels *in sight of each other*(A) can be considered to be in a Head-On encounter if *one observes the other's bow aspect nearly ahead*(F). In that case each *shall alter her course to starboard*(E) to *pass on the port side of the other*(H). Finally, the *evasive manoeuvre*(D) should be *conducted early*(D1) and *consist of a significant course change*(D2), result in *passing at a safe distance*(D3) and only be considered finished once one is *past and clear of the other vessel*(D4). We can formalise this requirement as an MTSC shown in Fig. 6 using the indicated Spatial Views from before.

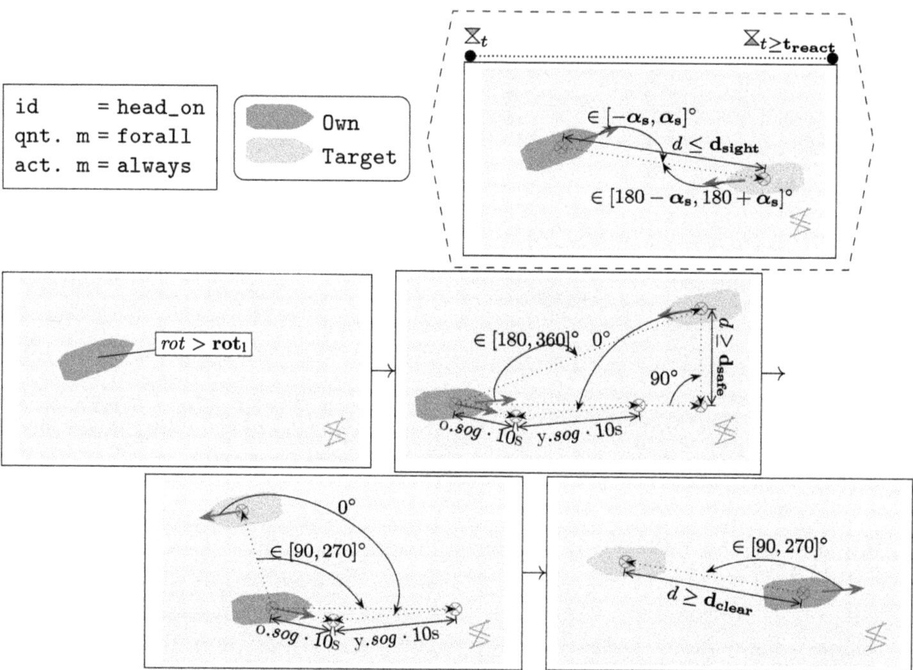

Fig. 6. Formalisation of COLREG requirement for Head-On encounters constructed by combining spatial views A, F, D2, E, D3i, D3ii, H and D4 from Fig. 5. $\mathbf{t_{react}}$ is a parameter for the maximum reaction time for which a Head-On situation may persist until the evasive manoeuvre must be started (D1).

The chart in Fig. 6 has a so-called "History-implies-Consequence" pattern where the consequence is a sequence of three invariant nodes and the History is a single invariant node annotated with a duration constraint (cf. [5–7]). The chart specifies that whenever the first spatial view consistently holds for a duration of at least $\mathbf{t_{react}}$, immediately afterwards there have to be consecutive intervals of time in which the second, third and fourth spatial views are satisfied respectively.

Rules for other types of encounters can be formalised in the same way. Using the object type *Wind* and corresponding symbol introduced in Sect. 4.3 the formalisation can similarly be extended to Rule 12 on encounters of sailing vessels. We conclude that MTSCs are generally suitable for the formal specification of relevant maritime traffic rules.

Our primary goal for MTSCs is to provide a language that enables formal specification of maritime traffic scenarios, so that scenario-based requirements can be clearly and objectively communicated between stakeholders with varying backgrounds. We consider the main problem of previous formalisations (mainly using temporal logics) for this purpose to be the complexity of mathematical formulae that require previous knowledge of mathematical notation for interpretation. Additionally, previous formalisations typically rely on supplementary visualisation with non-standardised and informal notation to clarify and in some cases define spatial relations referenced in the specification. We consider this to be a potential threat to clarity of communication and objectivity of the specification. Our formalisation of COLREG rules does not contain complex formulae that require mathematical background knowledge for interpretation and does not rely on informal supplementary visualisation to provide clarification of spatial constraints. At the same time, its underlying semantics does allow objective and automated evaluation of vessel behaviour relative to our specification.

For practical application, e.g. in monitoring vessel behaviour for compliance with COLREG, parameter values need to be set and the formalisation needs to be validated based on traffic data and expert knowledge. This would ensure that the specification of requirements adequately matches the intentions of COLREG and expectations of nautical practitioners. We have already shown, however, that relevant spatial and temporal aspects of maritime traffic rules can be captured by MTSCs in a visual and formal manner. This can effectively support the elicitation and validation of formal specifications. Evaluation of a given MTSC against historical traffic data can be automated using established monitoring methods [1,25].

6   Conclusion

In this work we present Maritime Traffic Sequence Charts (MTSCs), a visual formalism for the specification of abstract maritime traffic scenarios and scenario-based requirements. The formalism is an extension of Traffic Sequence Charts (TSCs), that were originally developed for the automotive domain. We propose extensions to the TSC language which provide appropriate modelling tools and corresponding visual syntax for the specification of requirements on how automated ships are supposed to drive. This is a new class of requirements that has only emerged with increasing automation of vessels. Specifically, we provide tools for the visual formalisation of directions, complex spatial relations, and environmental conditions. We evaluate whether MTSCs are suitable for the visual formalisation of maritime traffic rules and find that important traffic rules for collision avoidance on the open sea can be adequately formalised.

It has previously been shown that TSC-based formalisation of maritime traffic scenarios has the added potential to support experimental evaluation [2], runtime monitoring [1] and scenario-based testing [3,13] of autonomous vessels, all of which are crucial for the development of trustworthy and ethical MASS.

For practical application of the formalism, existing methods and tools for TSC applications have to be further adapted for the maritime context. Further evaluation of expressivity and comprehensibility of the formalism in additional settings such as further application contexts, different stakeholders and scenarios in other environments (like the port or waterways) is future work.

Data Availability Statement. No new data was created or analysed in this work. Data sharing is not applicable to this article.

Disclosure of Interests. The authors have no competing interests to declare that are relevant to the content of this article.

References

1. Austel, A., Panneke, L., Piotrowski, J., Wetzig, N., Steidel, M., Westphal, B.: Using monitoring of maritime traffic scenarios in the validation of maritime systems. In: 2025 Symposium on Maritime Informatics and Robotics (MARIS), pp. 1–8 (2025). https://doi.org/10.1109/MARIS64137.2025.11139541
2. Austel, A., Steidel, M., Westphal, B.: Formal specification of traffic scenarios in scenario-based testing of maritime assistance systems. In: 4th European Workshop on Maritime Systems, Resilience and Security 2024 (MARESEC 2024), Bremerhaven, Germany (2024). https://doi.org/10.5281/zenodo.14214762
3. Bogner, M., Steidel, M., Austel, A.: Leveraging maritime automation for efficient and sustainable port maintenance. J. Phys. Conf. Ser. **3123**, 012033 (2025). https://doi.org/10.1088/1742-6596/3123/1/012033
4. Damm, W., Harel, D.: LSCs: breathing life into message sequence charts. Formal Methods Syst. Des. **19**, 45–80 (2001). https://doi.org/10.1023/A:1011227529550
5. Damm, W., Kemper, S., Möhlmann, E., Peikenkamp, T., Rakow, A.: Using traffic sequence charts for the development of HAVs. In: 9th European Congress on Embedded Real Time Software and Systems (ERTS 2018), pp. 1–11. SEE and 3AF associations, Toulouse, France (2018). https://hal.science/hal-01714060
6. Damm, W., Kemper, S., Möhlmann, E., Peikenkamp, T., Rakow, A.: Traffic sequence charts – from visualization to semantics. Technical report, SFB/TR 14 AVACS (2017). https://doi.org/10.13140/RG.2.2.15190.42563
7. Damm, W., Möhlmann, E., Peikenkamp, T., Rakow, A.: A formal semantics for traffic sequence charts. In: Lohstroh, M., Derler, P., Sirjani, M. (eds.) Principles of Modeling, pp. 182–205. Springer, Cham (2018). https://doi.org/10.1007/978-3-319-95246-8_11
8. Del Mondo, G., Peng, P., Gensel, J., Claramunt, C., Lu, F.: Leveraging spatio-temporal graphs and knowledge graphs: perspectives in the field of maritime transportation. ISPRS Int. J. Geo Inf. **10**(8), 541 (2021). https://doi.org/10.3390/ijgi10080541
9. DNV: Class guideline DNV-CG-0264 - Autonomous and remotely operated ships (2021)

10. Fockel, M., Holtmann, J., Koch, T., Schmelter, D.: Formal, model- and scenario-based requirement patterns. In: Proceedings of the 6th International Conference on Model-Driven Engineering and Software Development (MODELSWARD 2018), pp. 311–318. SCITEPRESS - Science and Technology Publications, Lda (2018). https://doi.org/10.5220/0006554103110318
11. Fremont, D.J., et al.: Scenic: a language for scenario specification and data generation. Mach. Learn. **112**(10), 3805–3849 (2023). https://doi.org/10.1007/s10994-021-06120-5
12. Greenyer, J., et al.: ScenarioTools – a tool suite for the scenario-based modeling and analysis of reactive systems. Sci. Comput. Program. **149**, 15–27 (2017). https://doi.org/10.1016/j.scico.2017.07.004
13. Hake, G., Austel, A., Becker, J.S., Putze, L., Wetzig, N.: Safety assessment of maritime autonomous surface ships: a scenario-based approach. J. Phys: Conf. Ser. **3123**(1), 012022 (2025). https://doi.org/10.1088/1742-6596/3123/1/012022
14. Hakemann, J.: Automated monitoring of traffic sequence chart specifications for simulated driving scenarios. Master's thesis, Carl von Ossietzky Universität Oldenburg (2022)
15. International Maritime Organization: COLREG: Convention on the International Regulations for Preventing Collisions at Sea, 1972. IMO Publication, International Maritime Organization, London (2003)
16. Johansen, T., Blindheim, S., Torben, T.R., Utne, I.B., Johansen, T.A., Sørensen, A.J.: Development and testing of a risk-based control system for autonomous ships. Reliab. Eng. Syst. Saf. **234**, 109195 (2023). https://doi.org/10.1016/j.ress.2023.109195
17. Krasowski, H., Althoff, M.: Temporal logic formalization of marine traffic rules. In: 2021 IEEE Intelligent Vehicles Symposium (IV), pp. 186–192. IEEE, Nagoya, Japan (2021). https://doi.org/10.1109/IV48863.2021.9575685
18. Krasowski, H., Althoff, M.: Provable traffic rule compliance in safe reinforcement learning on the open sea. IEEE Trans. Intell. Veh. **9**(12), 7617–7634 (2024). https://doi.org/10.1109/tiv.2024.3400597
19. Maritime Safety Committee: Outcome of the regulatory scoping exercise for the use of maritime autonomous surface ships (MASS). Technical Report MSC.1/Circ.1638, International Maritime Organization (2021)
20. Martelli, M., Virdis, A., Gotta, A., Cassarà, P., Di Summa, M.: An outlook on the future marine traffic management system for autonomous ships. IEEE Access **9**, 157316–157328 (2021). https://doi.org/10.1109/ACCESS.2021.3130741
21. Rauschert, A., Amid, G.: ASAM OpenSCENARIO XML 1.3.0: release presentation. Presentation (2024). https://www.asam.net/standards/detail/openscenario-xml/older/. Accessed 15 Jan 2026
22. Reiher, D., Hahn, A.: Review on the current state of scenario- and simulation-based V&V in application for maritime traffic systems. In: OCEANS 2021: San Diego – Porto, pp. 1–9. IEEE, New York (2021). https://doi.org/10.23919/OCEANS44145.2021.9705781
23. Santipantakis, G., Kotis, K.I., Vouros, G.A.: Ontology-based data integration for event recognition in the maritime domain. In: Proceedings of the 5th International Conference on Web Intelligence, Mining and Semantics, WIMS 2015, pp. 1–11. Association for Computing Machinery, New York, NY, USA (2015). https://doi.org/10.1145/2797115.2797133
24. Song, R., et al.: Semantic modeling of ship behavior in cognitive space. J. Mar. Sci. Eng. **10**(10), 1347 (2022). https://doi.org/10.3390/jmse10101347

25. Stemmer, R., et al.: Runtime monitoring of complex scenario-based requirements for autonomous driving functions. Sci. Comput. Program. **244**, 103301 (2025). https://doi.org/10.1016/j.scico.2025.103301
26. Torben, T.R., Glomsrud, J.A., Pedersen, T.A., Utne, I.B., Sørensen, A.J.: Automatic simulation-based testing of autonomous ships using gaussian processes and temporal logic. Proc. Inst. Mech. Eng. Part O J. Risk Reliab. **237**(2), 293–313 (2023). https://doi.org/10.1177/1748006X211069277
27. Torben, T.R., Smogeli, Ø., Utne, I.B., Sørensen, A.J.: On formal methods for design and verification of maritime autonomous surface ships. In: Proceedings of the World Maritime Technology Conference, vol. 1, pp. 251–261 (2022). https://ntnuopen.ntnu.no/ntnu-xmlui/handle/11250/3058210
28. UN Trade and Development (UNCTAD): Review of Maritime Transport 2024: Navigating Maritime Chokepoints. United Nations (2024)
29. Vandecasteele, A., Napoli, A.: Spatial ontologies for detecting abnormal maritime behaviour. In: 2012 Oceans - Yeosu, pp. 1–7. IEEE, Yeosu, Korea (South) (2012). https://doi.org/10.1109/OCEANS-Yeosu.2012.6263532
30. Wild, M., Becker, J.S., Ehmen, G., Möhlmann, E.: Towards scenario-based certification of highly automated railway systems. In: Milius, B., Dutilleul, S.C., Lecomte, T. (eds.) Reliability, Safety, and Security of Railway Systems. Modelling, Analysis, Verification, and Certification.RSSRail2023. Lecture Notes in Computer Science, vol. 14198, pp. 78–97. Springer, Berlin (2023). https://doi.org/10.1007/978-3-031-43366-5_5

Software Development

A Context-Aware Multi-agent Approach to Enhancing User Story Management in Agile Software Development

Khoa Nguyen, Malik Abdul Sami(✉), Zheying Zhang,
and Pekka Abrahamsson

Software Engineering Research Center (TASE), Tampere University,
Tampere, Finland
`{khoa.h.nguyen,malik.sami,zheying.zhang,pekka.abrahamsson}@tuni.fi`

Abstract. [**Context and motivation**] User stories are central in agile software development, yet creating and managing high-quality ones remains challenging. Existing tools for user story quality enhancement often lack semantic analysis or project-specific context alignment. [**Questions**] This paper investigates how multi-agent systems (MAS) based on large language models (LLMs) can refine user story quality and strengthen traceability by linking them to project artifacts, while preserving human oversight. [**Results**] We present a context-aware system that integrates LLMs with retrieval-augmented generation (RAG) to refine, group, and link user stories to Jira tickets. Implemented using LangGraph, the system distributes reasoning across designed agents and allows feedback loops for oversight. The implementation was evaluated on three projects comprising ten user stories each, with project members participating as experts in the assessment. Results show notable improvements in user story quality in completeness (mean $+2.32$) and testability (mean $+2.01$), and overall quality (mean $+0.84$), while inter-rater agreement indicated high reliability for user story grouping ($\alpha = 0.771$) and modest agreement in linking stories with Jira tickets ($\alpha = 0.491$). [**Contribution**] The study contributes an LLM-based architecture for AI-assisted requirements refinement and management. It demonstrates how modular agent roles, RAG-based contextual information, and human-in-the-loop evaluation enhance the performance. It illustrates evidence of both the opportunities and current limitations of AI-driven requirements management.

Keywords: Large language model · multi-agent system · Retrieval-augmented generation · user story

1 Introduction

User stories are central in agile software development, providing lightweight, user-centered descriptions of product functionality that facilitate communication between stakeholders and developers, guide story elaboration and prioritization, and ensure traceability from requirements to implementation [1]. However, their

R. Guizzardi and J. Araújo (Eds.): REFSQ 2026, LNCS 16497, pp. 93–109, 2026.
https://doi.org/10.1007/978-3-032-21423-2_7

quality in real-world projects is often inconsistent [2,3]. Many stories are vague, incomplete, untestable, or poorly aligned with project goals, which undermines agile planning, causes miscommunication, and results in costly rework.

Beyond individual story quality issues, agile teams also face challenges in backlog management. Large collections of user stories frequently overlap or describe related features without clear dependencies [4]. Furthermore, traceability between user stories and other project artifacts such as Jira issues or bug reports are often missing or inconsistently maintained [5]. These issues hinder effective requirements management and complicate project progress monitoring.

Existing tools for automated user story improvement and management remain limited. Tools such as AQUSA [3] perform mainly syntactic checks, while frameworks like ALAS [6] present large language model (LLM)-based agent environment for iterative story refinement. Yet, current solutions either focus narrowly on linguistic quality, rely on rigid prompts, or lack integration with industrial agile platforms. Although retrieval-augmented generation (RAG) and multi-agent system (MAS) architectures have recently improved contextual reasoning and LLM collaboration [7], few works combine these advances to enhance the quality, contextual alignment, and traceability of user stories within agile workflows.

This study addresses this gap by designing and evaluating a context-aware MAS that leverages LLMs, RAG [7], and prompt engineering [20] to refine, group, and link newly added user stories with existing ones in issue tracking tools. The goal is to support agile teams in improving user story clarity, maintaining contextual consistency, and strengthening traceability between evolving requirements and project artifacts. The research is guided by the following three research questions (RQs).

1. **RQ1:** To what extent does the proposed context-aware multi-agent system improve the semantic quality of user stories?
2. **RQ2:** How reliably does the proposed system support contextual alignment and traceability of user stories through grouping refined user stories and linking them to issue-tracking artifacts, compared to expert judgment?
3. **RQ3:** What are experts' perceived usefulness, usability, and limitations of the system when applying it to user story refinement and management tasks?

Following the design science research (DSR) methodology [17,18], this study iteratively identifies the problem, defines objectives, designs and implements the MAS, and evaluates it through both quantitative and qualitative analysis. The overall research process and the corresponding sections reporting each activity are presented in Fig. 1.

The paper extends the first author's master's thesis research [9]. The main contributions are threefold: (1) a novel MAS architecture that integrates LLMs, RAG, and prompt engineering for automated user story refinement and organization; (2) an evaluation framework combining semantic quality criteria with inter-rater agreement metrics; and (3) empirical evidence on user story quality improvements, usability, and current limitations of AI-driven requirements management.

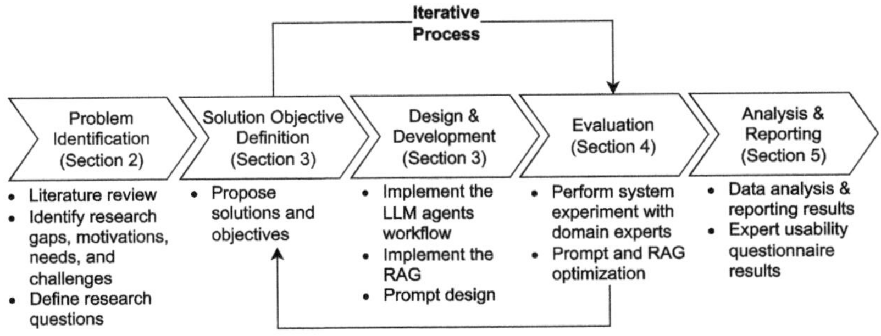

Fig. 1. Research process following the Design Science Research (DSR) methodology.

2   Related Work

In agile software engineering, user stories are the main means of capturing product requirements, emphasizing the *who* (role), *what* (requirement), and *why* (benefit) of a feature [2]. Well-written stories improve communication, traceability, and alignment with business goals [8], yet, achieving high-quality user stories is challenging: they are often ambiguous, incomplete, or lack dependency links [10]. Quality frameworks such as ISO/IEC/IEEE 29148-2018 [11], INVEST [12], and QUS [3] offer structured criteria but remain largely manual and inconsistently applied.

Several tools addressed requirement analysis challenges. Early tools like AQUSA [3] checks pragmatic and syntactic quality issues in user stories, while Yang et al. [13] apply clustering to capture semantic similarities between user stories. Recent frameworks integrate LLMs: MARE [14] offers a pipeline to automate requirement specification, ALAS [6] employs agents for iterative story refinement, and Goal2Story [15] decomposes high-level goals into structured stories. These approaches show the potential of LLMs to reduce manual effort, though they often depend on rigid prompts, lack robust human feedback mechanisms, and provide limited integration with agile tools like Jira.

The effectiveness of multi-agent frameworks depends on agent coordination and prompt design. Role-based prompting, reasoning traces, and structured output formats [20,21,29] reduce hallucination and improve collaboration between agents. However, even advanced MAS struggle with domain-specific reasoning that requires access to factual context [7,16]. Without grounding in project documentation, refined user stories may remain generic or deviate from organizational context. The use of RAG mitigates this by combining LLMs with retrieval from documents such as roadmaps, minimum viable product (MVP) description, or backlogs, improving factual accuracy and contextual grounding, while keeping the response concise.

In summary, existing tools [3,6,13–15] do not fully integrate MAS, prompt engineering, and RAG to jointly improve user-story quality, contextual alignment, and traceability within industrial tools. This study addresses that gap by

Table 1. Comparison of automated RE tools: features, limitations, and contributions of this study

Tool	Features	Limitations	Contribution of This Study
AQUSA [3]	NLP for syntactic & structural checks	Rule-based checks, no context-awareness	LLMs provide semantic & contextual feedback
ML-Based User Story Grouping [13]	ML-based embedding & clustering	Pre-defined templates, poor for large stories, no human judgment	LLMs handle semantics of coarser stories, allow human feedback
ALAS [6]	Multi-agent for automated story enhancement	limited context, lack in-loop feedback	RAG adds context-relevant feedback, human feedback, dynamic story grouping
MARE [14]	Multi-agent for eliciting, modeling, verifying & specifying req.	prompt-dependency, limited human oversight	Flexible prompting, human validation, story grouping with Jira ticket linkage
Goal2Story [15]	Multi-agent user story generation via goal-driven Impact Mapping	predefined context, prompt-dependency	Flexible prompting, human validation, story grouping with Jira ticket linkage

proposing a scalable MAS framework that refines, groups, and links user stories in Jira using contextual knowledge through RAG. Table 1 summarizes prior tools, their limitations, and how this work advances beyond them.

3   Approach

The central artifact of this study is a multi-agent system (MAS) that integrates LLMs with RAG. The MAS is designed to serve two purposes: (1) to improve the quality of user stories, and (2) to strengthen contextual alignment and traceability within agile workflows by linking refined user stories to project artifacts.

The system consists of six specialized agents, each with a distinct role, which collaborate iteratively to refine user stories using project-specific knowledge retrieved through the RAG component. This architecture supports both the semantic enhancement of user stories and their seamless integration with industrial tools such as Jira, forming a scalable, context-aware framework for AI-assisted requirements management.

3.1   Multi-agent Architecture Implementation

The artifact was implemented using *LangGraph* [19], a framework for building stateful multi-agent applications with LLMs. With its graph-based workflow, LangGraph enables structured collaboration between agents and supports iterative refinement through human-in-the-loop feedback, which increases trustworthiness in generated responses.

Figure 2 presents the system architecture, where six specialized agents, i.e. Planner, Supervisor, Requirement Engineer (RE), Product Owner (PO), User Story Grouper (USG), and Jira Ticket Linker (JTL), collaboratively refine, organize, and link user stories. Each agent plays a unique role within the workflow, and their interactions are represented through three types of flows. Blue arrows

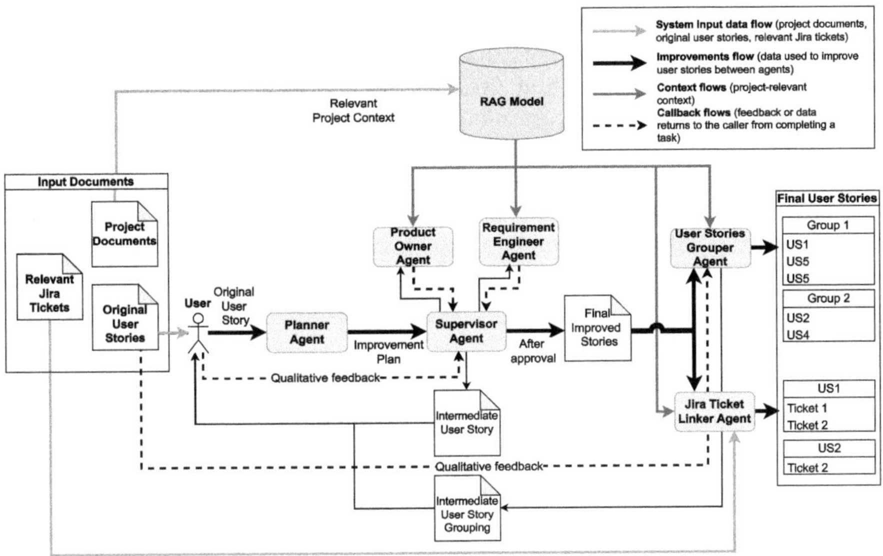

Fig. 2. System architecture for the proposed MAS.

denote system input data flows, including project documents, original user stories, and Jira tickets. Red and solid black arrows represent context and improvement flows, showing data exchange between agents and RAG-based retrieval processes. Dashed arrows indicate callback flows, where user feedback is incorporated into the refinement loop to ensure transparency, accountability, and human oversight over the MAS's outputs.

The **Planner Agent** initiates the process by analyzing the newly proposed user stories, identifying missing elements, and generating an improvement plan. This plan is passed to the **Supervisor Agent**, who acts as the central orchestrator, assigning tasks to the RE and PO agents and iteratively integrating their outputs. The **RE Agent** focuses on linguistic and technical quality—clarity, completeness, testability, and compliance with standards, e.g., INVEST, ISO/IEC 29148. It may query the RAG model to retrieve project-specific technical context. In parallel, the **PO Agent** ensures alignment with product scope, stakeholder goals, and organizational context, also supported by RAG-based retrieval of roadmap or MVP documentation.

Once both agents complete their refinements, the Supervisor integrates their outputs and presents the updated story to the user for review through the callback feedback loop. Users can approve or request further refinements, providing qualitative feedback that triggers new iterations. This mechanism reinforces transparency, controllability, and user trust in the refinement process. After approval, refined stories are sent to the **USG Agent**, which groups them based on functional or thematic similarity. This agent may query the RAG model to ensure contextual consistency and alignment with project goals. The grouping results can also be validated by the user via feedback callbacks, ensuring that human oversight governs the organization of requirements. Finally, the **JTL Agent** connects the refined and grouped user stories to relevant Jira tickets based on dependency and feature relationships, ensuring end-to-end traceability from refinement to implementation.

By distributing responsibilities across specialized agents, the MAS can minimize prompt complexity while maintaining explainability and modular scalability. The setup also uses LangGraph's flexibility, that is, new agents can be added whenever needed, without disrupting the workflow. With this modular agent setup, LangGraph ensures a streamlined, scalable framework that is open for modification and scalability.

3.2 RAG Integration and Prompt Engineering Strategies

RAG functions as the system's contextual layer, enabling agents to ground the generated refinements in organizational knowledge, avoiding over-wordiness and verbosity. For instance, the PO agent can query the latest product roadmap when validating scope, while the Grouper and Linker agents retrieve cross-references from project documentation to ensure accurate grouping and Jira integration. This mitigates the model's hallucination and ensures that story refinements, grouping, and linking with Jira tickets are contextually valid and reliable.

The agents are guided by structured prompts that define roles, tasks, and expected outputs. A modular prompt design was adopted, consisting of:

1. **System prompts** defining agent's roles and responsibilities: *"You are the <AGENT>, tasked with <TASK>... Your response must take the following <FORMAT>...".*
2. **Task prompts** specifying inputs and objectives: *"Here is the <INPUT DATA>... Based on the data, do <TASK> so that <CONDITIONS>...".*
3. **Iterative prompts** incorporating user or system feedback: *"Here is the <FEEDBACK>. Based on current <DATA STATE & WORK>, please complete <TASK>...".*

Different prompting strategies were applied: persona prompts [20] for role-specific behavior, ReAct [21] for reasoning–action coordination, and template [20] prompts for structured outputs in JSON format. ReAct prompts following a step-by-step structure were most beneficial for multi-step reasoning tasks such as expanding incomplete user stories or resolving inconsistencies, while persona prompts improved the interpretability and focus of agent responses by aligning outputs with specific roles, e.g., PO versus RE. The RAG integration ensured factual grounding and contextual coherence of the software product. These prompting techniques were adopted as complementary mechanisms to enable robust coordination within the MAS. The agents' responsibilities, their interaction with RAG, and applied prompting techniques are summarized in Table 2.

Table 2. Overview of agents in the MAS framework, their responsibilities, and examples of RAG and prompt usage.

Agent	Responsibilities	Use of RAG/Prompt Type/Example
Planner	Analyzes the initial user story and creates a refinement plan outlining tasks, objectives, and missing acceptance criteria.	Uses structured prompts aligned with INVEST and ISO-29148 standards: *"Create a concise plan that includes key tasks and objectives, identifying missing acceptance criteria."*
Supervisor	Orchestrates workflow, delegates tasks, integrates outputs, and coordinates iterative refinement.	Uses *Persona* and *ReAct* prompting for reasoning–action cycles: *"Based on <FEEDBACK>, please update the user story accordingly and request a new review."*
RE	Enhances linguistic and technical quality, ensuring feasibility, completeness, and alignment with INVEST/ISO criteria.	Employs RAG for retrieving technical context (e.g., stack, architecture). Uses RAG guided by *Persona* prompting for requirement elicitation rationale: *"Retrieve project architecture details to ensure the story's technical feasibility."*
PO	Ensures alignment with product goals, scope, and stakeholder needs. Prevents scope creep.	Uses RAG to retrieve roadmap and product vision; guided by *Persona* prompting for business rationale: *"Get related content from the company documentation to verify if the feature aligns with strategic objectives."*
User Story Grouper	Organizes refined stories into functional clusters for backlog management.	Uses RAG for contextual grouping and *Template* prompting for structured JSON output: *"Group stories based on shared functionality. Return output in JSON format."*
Jira Linker	Maps grouped user stories to Jira tickets to support traceability.	Uses RAG for ticket metadata and *Template* prompting for linking format: *"Your respond must take this JSON format."*

4 Evaluation

We evaluate the proposed MAS along three dimensions: (1) improvements in the semantic quality of user stories (RQ1), (2) the reliability of contextual alignment and traceability support via story grouping and Jira ticket linking (RQ2), and (3) practical usability and adaptation in agile workflow (RQ3). The evaluation follows a mixed-method design, combining quantitative quality ratings, inter-rater agreement analysis, and qualitative expert feedback.

4.1 Evaluation Setup

The evaluation used data from three software projects in diverse contexts. They are an open-source project on smart wearables for elderly people (DS1) [28], a university project on a note-taking application (DS2), and an ongoing industrial project from a partner company (DS3). These were chosen to span academic, open-source, and industrial settings with varying documentation quality and development practices. Each project provided at least one overview document (e.g., product vision or MVP statement), supplemented by additional materials such as user analysis, sprint reviews, etc. to support the RAG component.

From each project, ten user stories were selected, for a total of thirty stories in total. These stories described core product functionality, including key interactions, requirements, and constraints essential for system operation. They all have common issues such as missing acceptance criteria, vague or ambiguous wording, inconsistent structure, etc. The identified quality issues were present in the original user stories and were not artificially introduced for the purpose of this study. As an example, the story *"As an Older Person, I want to know exactly what the device does with my personal data, and share it only on my specific permission"* is a compound, contains vague terms like *exactly* and *specific permission*, and lacks an explicit statement of value.

To enable traceability analysis, Jira tickets were collected from past and upcoming sprints. For project DS1, where tickets were absent, we reconstructed 25 synthetic tickets including 5 epics and 20 issues, using OpenAI's GPT-4o [22] based on project documentation. These synthetic tickets were used solely to enable exploratory linking analysis for DS1 and to maintain methodological consistency across datasets. Consequently, DS1 is not used to draw strong conclusions regarding real-world traceability performance, which is primarily assessed through DS2 and DS3.

For DS1 and DS2, the authors selected the stories and tickets to evaluate. As for DS3, story selection was performed by a domain expert from the partner company, who identified ten representative user stories from their backlog.

The MAS was implemented in Python using GPT-4o [22] as the LLM backend with temperature $= 0$ and top-p $= 0$ for deterministic outputs. The system was allowed a maximum of four refinement iterations per story to balance quality against time consumption.

4.2 Subjects and Procedure

Four experts participated in the evaluation independently, and they are three software developers (E1, E2, E3) with 2-4 years' IT industrial experience and one director of technology (E4) with 10 years experience. E1–E3 were team members of the university project (DS2) and were already familiar with it. They evaluate the system outputs for both DS1 and DS2 individually, generating three sets of evaluation, which were used to assess DS1 and DS2. E4 contributed datasets for DS3 and, together with E1, assessed the corresponding system outputs for this dataset. All participants were experienced in agile software development and requirements engineering tasks such as sprint planning, backlog refinement, and defining acceptance criteria. Table 3 summarizes the available documentation for each project, along with the number of user stories, corresponding tickets, and experts involved in evaluation.

Table 3. Evaluation setup details of the selected dataset and experts.

Project	Documentation	#User Stories	#Tickets	Experts
DS1	Project Overview, Reqs, User Groups, Product Interaction	10	25	E1, E2, E3
DS2	Project Plan, Features, Impact Analysis, Scopes & Goals, Risk Assessment, Stakeholders, Sprint Planning & Review	10	26	E1, E2, E3
DS3	Product Vision & Scope	10	57	E1, E4

Each participant completed four tasks independently. They are (1) rating the semantics quality of both original and refined user stories; (2) grouping the refined stories based on features, similar to the grouping task of the *User Story Grouper* Agent; (3) linking refined stories to relevant issue tickets, similar to the linking task of the *Jira Ticket Linker* Agent; and (4) answering a brief questionnaire on performance, usability, and adaptability of the tool.

For participants E1-E3 interacting with the MAS directly, the time and number of user feedback rounds required per story were also recorded.

4.3   Data Analysis

After the tasks were completed, data generated by the MAS and collected from the experts were compared and analyzed. The analysis focused on three aspects: improvements in semantic quality, agreement on grouping and linking, and expert perceptions of system usability.

(1) Semantic Quality Evaluation. Each story was rated against 11 criteria derived from established frameworks for assessing the quality of user stories, listed in Table 4. Each criterion was provided a Likert scale from 1 (strong disagreement) to 5 (strong agreement). The criteria were synthesized from the Quality User Story (QUS) framework [3], the INVEST framework [2], and the ISO/IEC/IEEE 29148 standard [11]. Overlapping criteria were merged and redundant syntactic aspects were excluded to focus on semantic quality, that is, the extent to which a story's meaning, intent, and contextual relevance can be consistently interpreted and acted upon.

The resulting set of 11 criteria cover both syntactic and linguistic aspects like clarity and unambiguity (S1, S9) and contextual relevance such as alignment with project scope (S2, S5, S10), completeness (S3), testability (S6), consistency (S4), alignment with agile principles and values (S7, S8, S11), etc. It

Table 4. Statements on the user story semantics quality in the survey.

ID	Statement
S1	The user story is clear and easy to understand, with precise language and intent.
S2	The user story addresses a relevant need within the project, aligning with its objectives.
S3	The user story includes all necessary details, such as who, what, why, and acceptance criteria.
S4	The user story is free from contradictions (e.g., between description and acceptance criteria).
S5	The user story is appropriately scoped, aligning with product goals, neither too broad nor too narrow for implementation.
S6	The user story has clear, testable acceptance criteria that allow verification of completion.
S7	The user story can be implemented independently, with minimal dependencies on other stories.
S8	The user story delivers clear value to end-users or stakeholders, reflecting their needs.
S9	The user story is concise, avoiding unnecessary detail while remaining complete.
S10	The user story reflects project-specific goals, constraints, and technology stack.
S11	The user story is practical for use in an agile workflow, supporting prioritization, implementation, and tracking (e.g., in Jira).

is worth noting that syntactic and linguistic aspects inherently contribute to semantic clarity [3]. Hence, the criteria represent an integrated view ensuring comprehensive evaluation.

For this evaluation, experts were provided with both the original and refined versions of each user story as separate documents and evaluated them using the same set of quality criteria. The two versions were clearly labeled as original and refined, and were presented simultaneously rather than in a randomized or blinded order. This design choice was made to reduce cognitive load and allow direct comparison of improvements across criteria, reflecting a realistic review scenario in agile backlog refinement. However, we acknowledge that this may introduce a positive bias toward refined stories, which is addressed explicitly as a threat to validity in Sect. 6.

(2) Agreement on Grouping and Linking. To evaluate the alignment of story grouping and linking among the MAS and experts, we measured *interrater reliability* (IRR) using Krippendorff's α (K-α) [23]. Values of K-α range from -1 (systematic disagreement) to 1 (perfect agreement), with 0 indicating agreement no better than chance. Following Landis and Koch [24], a value of 0.75 or greater represents an excellent level of agreement, 0.40 or less is poor agreement, and between 0.40 and 0.75 is moderate agreement.

For user story grouping, the experts independently clustered the improved user stories. In DS1 and DS2, the manual grouping was done one month after the experiment with the MAS, while in DS3, it was done before using the tool, to reduce carry-over effects. Agreement among experts and between experts and the MAS was measured using K-α with a nominal distance metric [23], where $\delta_{ck} = 0$ if $c = k$ and $\delta_{ck} = 1$ otherwise. Thus, all label differences were treated as equally distinct.

For ticket linking, experts associated multiple tickets with corresponding user stories, resulting in set-valued annotations, where experts may select overlapping but not identical group of tickets to a story. Although thematic grouping similar to ticket grouping is viable, to capture the nuanced relationships between sets, the MASI distance metric [25] was used as the distance function δ_{ck} in K-α [23]. MASI extends Jaccard similarity [26] with a scaling factor $m(A, B)$ to reflect partial agreement in two sets A and B (in this case, the ticket IDs linked into each user story by experts). This makes MASI more sensitive to partial matches than basic overlap metrics.

(3) Expert Feedback. To address RQ3, participants completed an open-ended questionnaire, presented in Table 5, regarding the perceived strengths, weaknesses, and usefulness of the MAS. We analyzed the qualitative feedback using thematic grouping. Comments were independently reviewed and clustered into recurring themes (e.g., verbosity, clarity, traceability), which were then discussed and refined jointly.

Table 5. Questions on the participant perspective regarding the model.

ID	Question
Q1	What specific improvements did you notice in the user story compared to the original version?
Q2	What challenges or limitations, if any, did you observe in the improved user story?
Q3	How well does the improved user story support the project's goals and agile workflow (e.g., sprint planning, development, tracking)?
Q4	Do you have any suggestions for further improving the user story refinement process?
Q5	Did you find the tool intuitive to use? Do you have any suggestions regarding the usability of the tool?

5 Results and Discussion

Across all projects, refining a user story with the MAS took on average *3:02 min* and required *1.15 feedback rounds* (SD: *1:38 min* and *1.26 rounds*, respectively). While the average time and number of feedback rounds per user story were relatively low, the high standard deviations indicate substantial variance across stories. This variability can be attributed to the absence of a common template for the improvement process.

5.1 Semantic Quality Results (RQ1)

Experts rated each original and improved story on 11 quality criteria using a 5-point Likert scale. For each project, the mean values in Table 6 represent the average of expert ratings across ten user stories, which can provide a project-level view of quality changes. As shown in Table 6, the MAS substantially improved overall quality (mean +0.84). The strongest gains were observed in completeness (+2.32), testability (+2.01), and agile usability (+1.74). These improvements stem from the fact that many original stories lacked acceptance criteria and technical details, making them difficult to understand, test, and integrate into agile processes. The MAS addressed these gaps by enriching stories with missing contextual and functional information, ensuring clearer structure and verifiable conditions. Moderate improvements were in clarity (+1.41) and scope (+1.00), while smaller changes in relevance (+0.73) and conciseness (+0.18) indicate occasional verbosity in the refined outputs.

These results imply that the MAS effectively addressed linguistic and structural deficiencies in stories by enforcing standard formats of who, what, and why, and enriching context. However, some refinements introduced unnecessary detail or restated information already implied in the project scope.

Table 6. Mean quality scores (with Standard Deviation in parentheses) for original and refined user stories, and change in mean values after refinement.

Criterion	Original - Mean (SD)			Refined - Mean (SD)			Change in Mean values			
	DS1	DS2	DS3	DS1	DS2	DS3	DS1	DS2	DS3	Ave.
S1 – Clarity	3.33 (0.65)	3.10 (0.67)	2.25 (0.59)	4.23 (0.47)	4.17 (0.28)	4.50 (0.53)	+0.90	+1.07	+2.25	+1.41
S2 – Relevance	3.97 (0.58)	3.37 (0.81)	2.30 (0.82)	3.87 (0.61)	3.90 (0.69)	4.05 (0.69)	-0.10	+0.53	+1.75	+0.73
S3 – Completeness	1.67 (0.22)	2.97 (1.18)	1.95 (0.64)	4.43 (0.32)	4.57 (0.22)	4.55 (0.28)	+2.77	+1.60	+2.60	+2.32
S4 – Consistency	3.50 (0.24)	3.73 (0.49)	2.75 (0.49)	4.37 (0.25)	4.40 (0.31)	4.35 (0.34)	+0.87	+0.67	+1.60	+1.04
S5 – Scope	2.93 (0.62)	2.40 (0.54)	1.95 (0.28)	3.13 (0.48)	3.30 (0.73)	3.85 (0.41)	+0.20	+0.90	+1.90	+1.00
S6 – Testability	1.40 (0.34)	2.50 (1.07)	1.70 (0.59)	3.63 (0.64)	3.73 (0.49)	4.25 (0.54)	+2.23	+1.23	+2.55	+2.01
S7 – Independence	2.87 (0.59)	2.80 (0.97)	1.60 (0.66)	3.67 (0.57)	3.33 (0.35)	3.80 (0.54)	+0.80	+0.53	+2.20	+1.18
S8 – Value to Stakeholders	3.80 (0.67)	3.53 (0.74)	2.85 (0.58)	3.70 (0.69)	3.90 (0.63)	3.65 (0.91)	−0.10	+0.37	+0.80	+0.36
S9 – Conciseness	3.67 (0.38)	3.23 (0.55)	1.85 (0.71)	3.67 (0.27)	3.53 (0.48)	3.95 (0.69)	+0.00	+0.30	+2.10	+0.18
S10 – Alignment with Context	3.57 (0.74)	3.73 (0.99)	2.50 (0.53)	3.90 (0.61)	4.17 (0.39)	3.65 (0.71)	+0.33	+0.44	+1.15	+0.64
S11 – Agile Usability	1.53 (0.17)	3.40 (0.81)	1.95 (0.64)	3.80 (0.32)	4.07 (0.34)	4.25 (0.49)	+2.27	+0.67	+2.30	+1.74
Ave.	2.93	3.16	2.15	3.85	3.92	4.08	+0.92	+0.76	+1.93	+0.84

5.2 Grouping and Linking Results (RQ2)

Table 7 reports Krippendorff's α for grouping and linking. User story grouping achieved high agreement between the MAS and experts ($\alpha = 0.771$), whereas linking achieved only moderate agreement ($\alpha = 0.491$). The negative change in α values indicates that MAS introduced disagreement in the linking task, likely due to insufficient recognition of dependency relationships, over- or under-assignment of tickets, and the inherent complexity of multi-link mappings.

DS2 reached perfect grouping agreement ($\alpha = 1.000$) among experts and the MAS, which highlights that comprehensive documentation enables consistent grouping decisions for both experts and AI. In contrast, DS3 showed the lowest agreement in grouping ($\alpha = 0.045$ among humans, 0.262 with MAS inclusion), due to limited project documentation (only product vision and scope) and uneven domain familiarity of experts. only E4 was a project member, while E1 relied solely on extracted materials.

Table 7. Krippendorff's α for grouping and linking.

Dataset	Human α	(Human + MAS) α	Change
DS1 (grouping)	0.808	0.789	-0.018
DS2 (grouping)	1.000	1.000	+0.000
DS3 (grouping)	**0.045**	**0.262**	+0.217
DS1+DS2+DS3 (grouping)	0.693	0.771	+0.078
DS1 (linking)	0.865	0.697	-0.067
DS2 (linking)	0.331	0.264	-0.067
DS3 (linking)	0.502	0.484	-0.018
D1+D2+D3 (linking)	0.580	0.491	-0.090

Ticket linking, in contrast, reached only moderate agreement ($\alpha = 0.491$). The negative α shifts across projects imply that the MAS struggled with the nuanced relationships between user stories and tickets, constrained by the granularity of retrieved context in the RAG model. In DS3, even human–human agreement was low, highlighting that the linking task itself is subjective and context-sensitive. Improving retrieval quality through better chunking, embeddings, or iterative feedback could mitigate this limitation.

5.3 System Performance and Adaptability (RQ3)

All experts agreed that the MAS effectively enriched user stories by adding missing details and clarifying intent. E4 noted that *"...now they include technical steps and acceptance criteria, which make them easier to test and understand"* and that *"The stories now leave no confusion about how the feature should behave"*, while E2 highlighted that it *"...gives more information, and [is] somewhat useful for further understanding the US"*. Collectively, these remarks indicate that the MAS captures context and expands requirements meaningfully. Experts also agreed that the tool reduces time and effort by automating refinement, generating technical requirements, and outlining testing strategies, with E4 emphasizing that *"This makes testing easier since QA can directly check if the results match what is written"*.

However, both E2 and E3 observed that the system sometimes produced overly verbose outputs, *"...sometimes it offers too many irrelevant info..."*, which risked overwhelming rather than assisting developers. Another recurring issue was addressed by E1, E2, and E3 about the system's inability to decompose large "epic" stories, leaving them poorly scoped. E2 and E3 noted that the lack of an appropriate story refinement template led to inconsistent formatting. Consequently, the first story in each session took longer to refine as the experts had to establish and balance the necessary level of detail and eliminate redundancy from scratch every time.

Overall, across RQ1–RQ3, the MAS improved semantic quality and grouping performance but achieved only moderate reliability in linking. Experts valued its enrichment and time savings but pointed out verbosity, sensitivity to vague feedback, and limited usability of the current command-line interface. The system shows strong potential as a support tool for agile requirements management but requires refinement before practical deployment.

In summary, three implications emerge: (1) MAS-driven refinement can reduce manual effort in improving story quality and backlog organization but needs more concise outputs and stronger Jira integration. (2) Combining MAS with RAG highlights the value of contextual grounding for LLM-based refinement, addressing gaps in prior systems like AQUSA and ALAS. (3) Usability remains critical—GUI support, standardized templates, and iterative feedback loops are essential to balance automation with practitioner expectations.

6   Threats to Validity

This study acknowledges several potential limitations, following the validity framework by Wohlin et al. [27]. *Internal, construct,* and *conclusion validity* are interrelated in our evaluation. Experts followed written task instructions defining evaluation criteria, rating scales, and evaluation procedures; however, task framing may have influenced expert focus and introduced unintended bias. The study relied on a limited number of domain experts and datasets, and differences in domain familiarity, documentation quality, and user story complexity may have influenced the observed outcomes. For example, DS2's perfect agreement likely reflects shared project experience rather than the artifact's effect alone, while DS3's lower reliability highlights the strong dependence on contextual understanding. These factors complicate causal interpretation between the use of MAS with RAG and the measured improvements.

In addition, participants evaluated original and refined user stories concurrently, with versions clearly labeled and without randomization. While this setup reflects realistic backlog refinement practices and supports direct comparison, it may have introduced a positive bias toward refined stories. To mitigate this risk, future iterations would instruct participants to assess each version independently against predefined quality criteria rather than simultaneously. Nevertheless, evaluator bias cannot be fully excluded. Furthermore, some constructs, such as "agile usability", act as proxies for real-world effectiveness rather than direct measures of productivity or delivery outcomes, which may affect construct and conclusion validity.

External and *reliability validity* are also intertwined. DS1 relied on synthetic user stories and tickets to enable controlled analysis, which may reduce realism compared to industrial backlogs and limit generalization of those results. The evaluation involved three datasets and four experts, which limits generalisability across different domains, team structures, and tooling ecosystems. Moreover, the MAS's behaviour depends on prompt design, RAG configuration, and the availability and quality of project documentation, which may not be directly reproducible in other settings. Although code, prompts, and datasets are provided where possible, variability in context and configuration may affect replication outcomes. Future work should therefore include larger-scale industrial studies, diversified documentation conditions, and longitudinal evaluations to strengthen external confidence and reproducibility.

7 Conclusion

This study presents a MAS that integrates LLM agents with RAG and structured prompt engineering to improve the quality and management of user stories in agile projects. The MAS distributes reasoning across specialized agents and incorporates human-in-the-loop feedback to maintain transparency and control. Evaluation across three datasets showed substantial gains in completeness, usability for Agile, and testability, along with strong expert alignment in story grouping and moderate agreement in Jira linking. Together, these findings highlight the potential of context-aware MAS architectures to enhance user-story quality and reduce manual backlog effort.

At the same time, the moderate agreement observed in Jira linking indicates that traceability support remains limited, pointing to the need for improved contextual retrieval and tighter integration with issue tracking systems. Our future work will broaden the evaluation scope, introduce a graphical interface with unified templates, and refine orchestration and retrieval processes to improve reliability and conciseness.

Acknowledgments. This work has been supported by the Research Council of Finland through Synthetica, and by Business Finland through ANSE and 6GSoft.

Data Availability Statement. The dataset includes user stories and project documentation derived from (1) an open-source software project, (2) an academic dataset provided by the university's software engineering course, and (3) expert evaluation results. The source code for the MAS prototype, along with experiment scripts and evaluation data, is publicly accessible at: https://github.com/hkhoa-ng/musr under an MIT license. Sensitive or proprietary information from company-related material has been removed.

References

1. Cao, L., Ramesh, B.: Agile requirements engineering practices: an empirical study. IEEE Softw. **25**(1), 60–67 (2008)
2. Mike Cohn. User Stories Applied: For Agile Software Development. Addison-Wesley Professional (2004)
3. Lucassen, G., Dalpiaz, F., van der Werf, J.M.E., Brinkkemper, S.: Improving agile requirements: the quality user story framework and tool. Requirements Eng. **21**(3), 383–403 (2016)
4. Ruiz, M., Hu, J.Y., Dalpiaz, F.: Why don't we trace? A study on the barriers to software traceability in practice. Requirements Eng. **28**(4) (2023)
5. Pasuksmit, J., Thongtanunam, P., Karunasekera, S.: Towards just-enough documentation for agile effort estimation: what information should be documented?. In: 2021 IEEE International Conference on Software Maintenance and Evolution (ICSME), pp. 114–125. IEEE (2021)
6. Zhang, Z., Rayhan, M., Herda, T., Goisauf, M., Abrahamsson, P.: LLM-based agents for automating the enhancement of user story quality: an early report. In: International Conference on Agile Software Development, pp. 117–126. Springer, Cham (2024)
7. Shahade, A.K., Deshmukh, P.V.: Enhancing natural language processing: a comprehensive review of retrieval augmented generation. In: 2024 4th International Conference on Sustainable Expert Systems (ICSES), pp. 609–611. IEEE (2024)
8. Lucassen, G., Dalpiaz, F., Werf, J.M.E.V.D., Brinkkemper, S.: The use and effectiveness of user stories in practice. In: International Working Conference on Requirements Engineering: Foundation for Software Quality, pp. 205–222. Springer, Cham (2016)
9. Nguyen, K.: Context-based user story enhancement with LLM and RAG: a multi-agent system implementation, Master's thesis, Tampere University (2025)
10. Domínguez, F.A.M., Quintana, M.A., Cinco, R.R.P., Borrego, G., González-López, S.: User story automation in software engineering: insights from the literature. In: 2024 12th International Conference in Software Engineering Research and Innovation (CONISOFT), pp. 279–286. IEEE (2024)
11. Aware, T., Documentation, T.: ISO/IEC/IEEE international standard-systems and software engineering-life cycle processes-requirements engineering, pp. 1–104. ISO/IEC/IEEE 29148: 2018 (E) (2018)
12. INVEST in good stories, and smart tasks. https://xp123.com/articles/invest-in-good-stories-and-smart-tasks/. Accessed 10 Oct 2025
13. Yang, B., Guo, H., Liu, H.: Evaluation and assessment of machine learning based user story grouping: a framework and empirical studies. Sci. Comput. Program. **227**, 102943 (2023)
14. Jin, D., Jin, Z., Chen, X., Wang, C.: Mare: multi-agents collaboration framework for requirements engineering. arXiv preprint arXiv:2405.03256 (2024)
15. Zou, X., Liu, Y., Shi, X., Yang, C.: Goal2Story: A Multi-Agent Fleet based on Privately Enabled sLLMs for Impacting Mapping on Requirements Elicitation. arXiv preprint arXiv:2503.13279 (2025)
16. Chuang, C.C., Chen, K.C.: Retrieval augmented generation on hybrid cloud: a new architecture for knowledge base systems. In: 2024 16th IIAI International Congress on Advanced Applied Informatics (IIAI-AAI), pp. 68–71. IEEE (2024)
17. Hevner, A.R., March, S.T., Park, J., Ram, S.: Design science in information systems research. MIS Q. 75–105 (2004)

18. Peffers, K., Tuunanen, T., Rothenberger, M.A., Chatterjee, S.: A design science research methodology for information systems research. J. Manag. Inf. Syst. **24**(3), 45–77 (2007)
19. LangChain (n.d.). LangGraph. https://www.langchain.com/langgraph
20. White, J., et al.: A prompt pattern catalog to enhance prompt engineering with chatgpt. arXiv preprint arXiv:2302.11382 (2023)
21. Yao, S., et al.: React: synergizing reasoning and acting in language models. In: The Eleventh International Conference on Learning Representations (2022)
22. OpenAI. Hello GPT-4o. OpenAI (2024). https://openai.com/index/hello-gpt-4o/. Accessed 10 Oct 2025
23. Krippendorff, K.: Computing Krippendorff's Alpha-Reliability. Annenberg School for Communication, University of Pennsylvania, Philadelphia, PA (2011)
24. Landis, J.R., Koch, G.G.: The measurement of observer agreement for categorical data. Biometrics 159–174 (1977)
25. Passonneau, R.J.: Measuring agreement on set-valued items (MASI) for semantic and pragmatic annotation. In: Proceedings of the Fifth International Conference on Language Resources and Evaluation (LREC 2006), pp. 831–836, Genoa, Italy (2006)
26. Jaccard, P.: Nouvelles recherches sur la distribution florale. Bull. Soc. Vaud. Sci. Nat. **44**, 223–270 (1908)
27. Wohlin, C., Runeson, P., Höst, M., Ohlsson, M.C., Regnell, B., Wesslén, A.: Experimentation in Software Engineering, vol. 236. Springer, Berlin (2012)
28. ALFREDProject (n.d.). ALFREDProject. ALFRED. https://github.com/ALFREDProject
29. Sami, M.A., et al.: Bridging humans and LLMs: investigating human AI collaboration in multi agent requirements analysis for organizational AI adoption. e-Inf. Softw. Eng. J. **20**(1), 260103 (2026)

Security Under Pressure: How Agile Teams Experience and Manage Security Requirements

Dahlia Vingtoft Andreasen, Oksana Kulyk, and Elda Paja[✉]

IT University of Copenhagen, Copenhagen, Denmark
{dava,okku,elpa}@itu.dk

Abstract. Context and motivation. Agile development promotes flexibility and rapid delivery but often challenges the systematic treatment of non-functional requirements such as security. Ensuring security within fast-paced, iterative processes remains a persistent concern in both research and practice. **Question/problem.** This paper investigates how practitioners in agile settings experience and handle security requirements, which practices support their integration, and how responsibility for security is distributed across roles. **Principal ideas/results.** We report on a qualitative study with sixteen professionals across twelve Danish companies. Using reflexive thematic analysis, we found that security is widely acknowledged yet handled implicitly and often reactively. Teams rely on lightweight assurance practices such as testing, shared guidelines, and peer review, while prioritization typically increases only after incidents. **Contribution.** The study provides an empirically grounded view of how securit unfolds in everyday agile development, complementing prior work that focuses on frameworks, governance, or large-scale settings. It identifies routine practices that help make security more visible, actionable, and collectively owned within agile teams.

Keywords: agile development · requirements engineering · security requirements · security integration · qualitative study

1   Introduction

Security remains a persistent concern in agile software development. Agile methods emphasize adaptability, collaboration, and rapid delivery, but these principles often conflict with the planning and assurance activities required for robust security [1,2]. Despite increasing emphasis on "security by design", empirical studies show that security is still frequently addressed reactively or delegated to specialists in agile contexts [3,4]. As a result, agile teams continue to face challenges in translating security expectations into concrete requirements and everyday practices [5–7].

Research on non-functional requirements (NFRs) in agile development shows that qualities such as performance, usability, and maintainability often receive

R. Guizzardi and J. Araújo (Eds.): REFSQ 2026, LNCS 16497, pp. 110–125, 2026.
https://doi.org/10.1007/978-3-032-21423-2_8

less explicit attention than functional features [8,9]. Security shares many of these challenges but remains distinctive because it cuts across organizational boundaries and is subject to external compliance and risk management pressures [3,4,10]. These characteristics make security requirements particularly difficult to specify, prioritize, and coordinate within iterative, fast-paced development processes. A growing body of empirical work has examined security in agile settings from different perspectives. Early interview-based studies highlighted tensions between agile values and security concerns from practitioners' viewpoints [3,11]. More recent work has examined security challenges in large-scale agile organizations [12,13] and assessed the perceived impact of security activities on agile delivery through practitioner surveys [14]. Together, these studies demonstrate that security remains a recurring concern in agile development. However, it remains insufficiently understood how in particular security requirements are handled, supported, and taken responsibility for in everyday agile work across roles and organizational contexts, beyond formal processes, frameworks, or governance structures.

This study addresses this gap by examining how practitioners across different roles handle security requirements within agile projects. Drawing on semi-structured interviews with sixteen practitioners from twelve Danish software organizations, we explore how security requirements are handled, supported, and taken responsibility for in everyday agile work across roles and organizational contexts, addressing the following research questions:

RQ1. *How do practitioners in agile settings approach and experience the handling of security requirements in their daily work?*
RQ2. *What practices support the integration of security requirements in agile projects?*

RQ3. *How do practitioners describe the understanding and distribution of responsibility for security in agile development?*

The study provides an empirically grounded account of how agile teams manage security under delivery pressure, contributing to a more nuanced understanding of security requirements engineering in agile contexts.

The paper is structured as follows: Sect. 2 reviews related work, Sect. 3 presents the study design and analysis approach, Sect. 4 reports the findings, Sect. 5 discusses their implications, and Sect. 6 concludes.

2   Related Work

Research on security in agile software development spans three main strands: studies of non-functional requirements (NFRs) in agile contexts, frameworks for integrating security into agile methods, and empirical investigations of how practitioners experience security work. The following subsections summarize these areas and outline how our study builds upon and extends them.

Agile and Non-functional Requirements. Agile development promotes flexibility, collaboration, and early delivery of customer value, but systematic reviews show that these same principles complicate the elicitation, specification, and tracing of NFRs within short iterations [5]. Because qualities such as performance, safety, and security are difficult to capture in user stories or acceptance criteria, they are often handled informally or postponed [5,8]. Jarzębowicz and Weichbroth [8] confirm that practitioners lack guidance on how to operationalize NFRs in agile backlogs, while Ramesh et al. [11] observed that requirements not perceived to add immediate business value, such as security, are commonly deprioritized. Collectively, these studies frame NFRs as a persistent blind spot in agile projects and motivate closer empirical investigation of how such qualities, particularly security, are addressed in practice.

Secure Practices and Frameworks in Agile. To address this gap, researchers have proposed numerous frameworks for "securing agile." Examples include S-Scrum [15], Secure Scrum [16], XP Security [17], and SEAP [18]. Early systematic reviews synthesized these proposals. Villamizar et al. [19] analyzed 21 studies (2005âĂŞ2017), identifying three common strategies: modifying agile methods to include security-specific practices, introducing new artifacts such as abuser stories or security backlogs, and providing elicitation guidelines. More recently, Valdés-Rodríguez et al. [20] reviewed over 100 papers and found that most evidence remains conceptual rather than empirical. Beyond method extensions, Tøndel et al. [21] proposed a conceptual framework summarizing empirical insights into how security requirements are managed in agile projects, emphasizing organizational and cultural factors over specific tools. These frameworks provide theoretical grounding for our work, which empirically examines how such factors manifest in everyday development settings.

Empirical Studies on Security in Agile Contexts. Complementing secondary studies, a growing body of empirical work examines how security is enacted in agile environments. Early work by Bartsch [3] explored practitioners' perspectives on secure software development, highlighting tensions between agile values and security practices. Terpstra et al. [22] conducted a grounded-theory study of practitioners' discussions and found that security work is often driven by personal initiative rather than process prescriptions. Oyetoyan et al. [23] explored developers' security skills and training needs, reporting widespread reliance on external specialists and limited internal expertise. Quantitative and longitudinal studies show that while dedicated security roles can improve protection, they may also affect agility, and that security responsibility evolves dynamically across roles in agile teams [10,24]. A recent practitioner survey [14] similarly investigates security in agile development, focusing on the impact of security activities on agility and delivery outcomes. Together, these studies highlight the persistent tension between agile delivery and security assurance, yet few examine how practitioners themselves perceive and organize this work in their day to day routines, which our study addresses.

Work by van der Heijden et al. [12] also examines security in agile contexts using interviews, but specifically in large-scale agile settings where multiple teams must align objectives and roles across organizational boundaries, highlighting coordination and role clarity as key challenges. More recently, a mixed-method study combining a systematic literature review and interviews analyzed security governance and compliance in large-scale agile organizations, highlighting tensions between centralized control mechanisms and agile principles of autonomy and flexibility [13]. These studies show how scale intensifies the aforementioned tension between security and agility.

Overall, existing empirical studies on security in agile development have examined practitioner perceptions, security challenges, and governance mechanisms, including work focusing on large-scale agile contexts where coordination in distributed settings and compliance introduce additional complexity. In contrast, our study adopts a cross-organizational, practitioner-centered perspective, examining how security requirements are handled in everyday agile work across roles and company contexts, independent of scale. This design allows us to examine routine decision-making and responsibility allocation that may remain implicit in large-scale or governance-oriented analyses.

3   Methodology

We conducted a qualitative, exploratory study using semi-structured interviews with practitioners involved in agile software development. The goal was to characterize how security requirements are understood, managed, and shared across roles and routines. An overview of the study process is shown in Fig. 1.

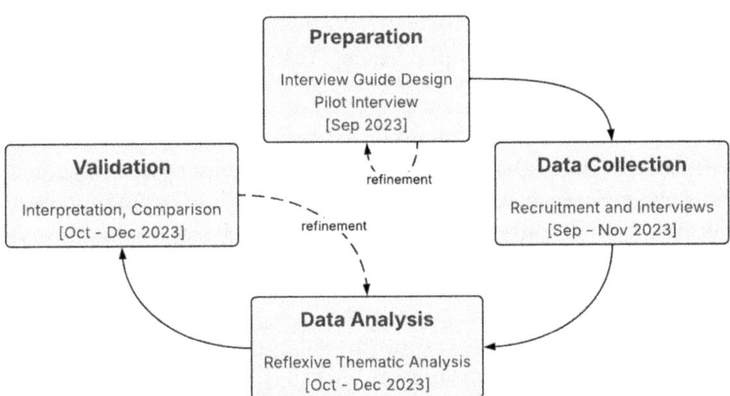

Fig. 1. Overview of the exploratory interview study.

Preparation. As part of our study design we started with the interview guide design, followed by a pilot interview.

Interview guide design. We developed two interview guides, one for developers and one for product owners, project managers, or Scrum Masters, covering four broad topics: (1) background, (2) agile processes, (3) security requirements engineering, and (4) awareness or organizational support. The purpose of the first topic was to establish rapport with the participant and to get the necessary background about the company and their role in it, as well as about the most current project they were involved in, to contextualize our findings. The rest of the topics included questions that covered diverse aspects of processes and practices in the participants' company related to all three of our research questions, such as asking the participant to elaborate on why security was considered as a part of the current project (RQ1), which specific practices were used for the elicitation, specification and assurance of security requirements relevant for the project (RQ2) and how various roles were involved in managing these requirements (RQ3). The guides were iteratively refined through research team discussions and a pilot interview. The final versions are available on Zenodo.[1]

Data Collection. We used purposive sampling through professional networks and social media to recruit practitioners with recent experience in agile projects. Participants held roles such as developer, product owner, Scrum Master, architect, or manager. The unit of our analysis was the individual practitioner's account of agile security practices.

Participants and context. Sixteen practitioners from twelve Danish organizations participated, representing both consultancies and product companies of varying sizes, ranging from startups to large enterprises. The participants worked in domains with varying degrees of security sensitivity, including finance, energy, public IT services, and digital platforms. Table 1 summarizes their roles and organizational contexts.

Interviews. Interviews were conducted between October and December 2023, lasting 45–60 min each. Eight interviews took place in person and eight online. All were conducted in English, with Danish allowed ad hoc if participants felt more comfortable with it. The first author conducted and transcribed the interviews, and led the analysis process.

Data Analysis. We analyzed the data using reflexive thematic analysis [25], supported by affinity diagramming in Miro. Coding proceeded inductively: quotes were clustered and refined into candidate themes, which were iteratively reviewed and named through research team discussions. Two researchers independently coded the first two transcripts to identify differing interpretations, followed by reflexive coding with regular peer debriefs. The analysis was informed by the authors' professional perspectives as a junior researcher with background

---

[1] Zenodo dataset link: https://doi.org/10.5281/zenodo.18224792.

Table 1. Overview of interview participants. Roles are anonymized; all worked in agile contexts (following Scrum, Kanban, XP, DX, Devops, SaFe, etc.)[a].

ID	Role	Domain	Size
P_0	Consultant Developer (Cloud Engineering)	Consultancy	Large
P_1	Developer (Custom Applications)	Consultancy / Software Development	Large
P_2	Consultant Developer (Cloud Engineering)	Consultancy	Large
P_3	Consultant Developer (Security)	Consultancy / Software Development	Large
P_4	Consultant Developer	Consultancy / Software Development	Large
P_5	Product Owner (Enterprise Resource Mgmt.)	Humanitarian / Non-profit	Medium
P_6	Scrum Master	E-commerce / Digital Services	Medium
P_7	Front-end Developer	Digital Solutions	Medium
P_8	Senior Software Engineer	Consumer Tech / Manufacturing	Large
P_9	Full-stack Developer	HR Technology	Small
P_{10}	Back-end Developer	FinTech	Medium
P_{11}	Back-end Developer	Software Development	Small
P_{12}	Back-end Developer	Software Development	Small
P_{13}	IT Architect / Product Owner	Public IT	Large
P_{14}	CTO	Energy / IoT	Medium
P_{15}	Developer	Energy / IoT	Medium

[a] Some organizations operate as both consultancies and software development companies. "Consultant Developer" denotes developers seconded to client projects; functionally they perform development work similar to in-house developers.

in software design, a senior researcher with background in software engineering and practical industrial experience, and a senior researcher with background in human aspects of cybersecurity. While this supported the interpretation of participants' accounts, we acknowledge that researchers with different backgrounds might emphasize other aspects and arrive at alternative interpretations. Consistent with the reflexive approach, we emphasized analytic transparency, maintaining an audit trail in Miro and prioritizing depth and coherence of themes over inter-coder reliability metrics.

Validation. To enhance credibility, we adopted multiple validation strategies. *Peer debriefing* was used throughout the analysis, findings and emerging themes were discussed regularly with the research group to challenge assumptions and ensure interpretative consistency. *Member reflections* were invited by sharing preliminary interpretations with the Pilot interview participant, confirming that the emerging themes resonated with their experiences.

Ethics. Participation in our study was voluntary, with no compensation. Before each interview, participants were informed about the study's purpose, data handling, and right to withdraw. All interviews were recorded with consent, anonymized during transcription, and stored securely.

4   Results

This section presents the study findings per research question. Our analysis revealed recurring themes that correspond to the three research questions: how practitioners experience and handle security requirements (RQ1), what practices support their integration (RQ2), and how responsibility for security is distributed across roles (RQ3). Figure 2 summarizes the themes and their relationships.

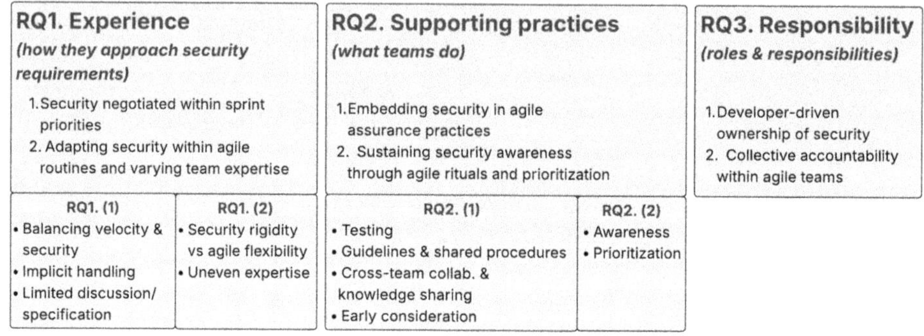

Fig. 2. Overview of themes mapped to research questions. Each research question is summarized by two higher-level clusters (1–2), with detailed subthemes below.

4.1   [RQ1] How Practitioners Approach and Experience the Handling of Security Requirements in Agile Settings

To address RQ1, we examined how practitioners describe their everyday engagement with security in agile development. Across interviews, security work appeared as interwoven with everyday agile routines rather than a distinct phase. Handling security was often described as a *balancing act between maintaining development velocity and safeguarding systems*. While participants valued security as part of "good development", they also revealed how time pressure, implicit expectations, and uneven expertise shaped its treatment in practice. The following themes summarize these experiences.

Balancing Velocity and Security. Practitioners described constant tension between sprint progress and attention to security tasks. Deadlines and the demand for visible functionality, frequently pushed security considerations to the margins. One participant reflected that *"it's a balancing act between security and moving forward, and developing some of the features, and getting some things done"* (P_{15}). Others said that even when security was recognized as important, it was rarely among the top sprint priorities: *"it's a priority on the list, but not among the top ones ... it's not like we're saying, what are the security requirements for it first."* (P_1).

Security as a Background Concern. Security was commonly treated as a meta-task or underlying premise rather than an explicit backlog item. As one practitioner noted, *"security ... is a very meta-task, and it's not always a top priority ... it quickly becomes a zero-sum game of what to prioritize"* (P_0). They added that there were *"no explicit security requirements ... it was often more of an underlying premise"* (P_0). Such implicit handling left developers to decide individually what "secure enough" meant within each sprint.

Limited Discussion and Specification. Security seldom appeared in routine agile conversations. One participant remarked that *"our developers do know about security, but it's just not in our everyday conversations at all"* (P_7). Without explicit tickets or acceptance criteria, requirements were inferred on the fly: *"they're not specified in the tickets ... just what we can think of to make it secure."* (P_{15}). When requirements existed, they were often vague or changing, creating uncertainty: *"if the security requirements were clearer from the beginning ... it would be easier to make sure whatever we develop follows them"* (P_{10}); *"there's nothing well-defined ... it's something we have to figure out from one day to the next."* (P_2).

Adapting Security Within Agile Flexibility. Rapid change was valued but also seen as undermining consistent treatment of security. As P_{15} put it, *"for security specific issues think it through to the end before creating a ticket ... but it's not very agile to think something through to the end ... then you lose the idea that you can change it when you need to."* Practitioners thus experienced security as something that must bend to agility, but as a result risks being weakened by it.

Uneven Expertise and Access to Support. Security knowledge was unevenly distributed across roles. Developers and product owners described relying on ad-hoc advice from specialists or colleagues. *"It might be nice to have someone deeply knowledgeable about security on each team ... but it's not something you just bring to your refinement meeting"* (P_4). When such expertise was absent, developers carried the burden: *"if all the responsibility lies with the developers ... and not all developers have had courses on security ... then all the responsibility is on the developers"* (P_1). Product owners' limited technical literacy also affected prioritization; one practitioner observed that *"our PO and PM were not technical ... they knew the basics of GDPR but not the concrete steps to meet these security requirements'* (P_0).

Summary RQ1 Findings. Practitioners handle security requirements as part of their everyday agile work, but typically in an implicit or informal manner. Their accounts reveal two broader patterns: (1) how teams negotiate security within sprint priorities and (2) how they adapt it to agile routines under varying expertise. Together, these experiences explain why explicit and visible practices are needed to sustain attention to security in everyday work (see RQ2).

4.2   [RQ2] Practices that Support the Integration of Security Requirements in Agile Projects

RQ2 explored which practices help practitioners integrate security into agile workflows without slowing down development or disrupting delivery. Our analysis revealed a mix of technical, procedural, and social mechanisms that together embed security across development routines.

Testing as Security Assurance. Testing was the most frequently cited mechanism to ensure that security measures work as intended and to catch problems early. *"Testing is highly emphasized ... we create detailed test plans, test scenarios, and test cases, with a focus on security aspects ... requiring more test cases and specific reaction tests we always need to run."* (P_4) Secure review processes reinforced this assurance: *"they have some pretty secure processes regarding pull requests ... at least two people have to review the pull request ... we go environment by environment to ensure that it works before we get to production."* (P_{11}) *"There are some safeguards ... prevent us from just putting things in and deploying them ... at least two of the others say this code is something we can accept ... so there are a lot of steps where we should ideally catch it."* (P_8)

Guidelines and Shared Procedures. Formal or team-defined guidelines offered a baseline for consistent security practices. *"We have a platform team ... who defines all the security guidelines. ... The team member that has to be in the company for a minimum six months has to review your code and approve it."* (P_{10}) *"Internally within the team, we also have some guidelines ... we document these in Confluence ... so we can go back and see what we agreed on as a team."* (P_8) Such procedures helped maintain a shared understanding of acceptable security behavior as teams evolved.

Cross-Team Collaboration and Knowledge Sharing. Dedicated departments or informal experts supported agile teams when specialized knowledge was needed. *"If I encountered something, I would have to reach out to our security department ... they probably have a better answer than I do."* (P_2) *"The access to the team managing the security is quite good because we're all located in the same building."* (P_{10}) Pair-programming further enabled learning-by-doing: *"If there's something I don't know how to do at all ... I'd like to pair program on this."* (P_{11}) These practices illustrate how distributed teams draw on nearby or embedded expertise rather than relying solely on external audits.

Considering Security Early. Several practitioners emphasized the importance of addressing security from the beginning of a project. *"It's easy to solve [security issues] if we address them from the start. ... We try to address them as early as possible."* (P_1) *"If you have security in mind from the beginning, the chance of building what's needed on time and with the agreed-upon quality* *is much higher than if you try to consider it retroactively."* (P_4) *"Already at the beginning of the process, we tell what it is we need to remember ... to be aware of."* (P_8) Early consideration was seen as reducing rework and ensuring compliance without slowing down sprints.

Fostering Security Awareness. Daily discussions and organizational initiatives kept security visible and relevant. *"It's often during our DSUs ... we discuss our projects, which have some security issues. ... Security is a big part of our everyday life."* (P_{13}) *"When we have ... a security flaw, then we would talk about it in the code inspection."* (P_7) *"There's an initiative ... called Secure Code Warrior. We're trained to be good at incorporating security issues ... and how we can code defensively."* (P_8) *"One got a bit annoyed at first because one was bombarded so much with security. But maybe that just created an awareness ... I'm so aware of it now."* (P_{13}) Such routines help sustain attention to security as a shared team value rather than a compliance afterthought.

Prioritizing by Criticality. Finally, teams managed trade-offs by adjusting priority according to risk. *"If we discovered that there was a security breach, we would create a story for it ... If it's a serious one, then it would be 100% high."* (P_9) *"Our process was to assess the situation and see what the most critical security issues were ... ensuring we had an SSL certificate ... and not storing sensitive data unencrypted."* (P_0) *"If the customer says there's a production error or a security flaw ... then he had to prioritize together with the customer ... one called Fast Track ... throw everything else out and focus on this."* (P_{12}) Although reactive, these mechanisms ensured that severe vulnerabilities were treated with urgency, keeping the backlog aligned with security risk.

Summary RQ2 Findings. Teams sustain security in agile contexts through layered practices that combine technical checks (testing, reviews), procedural consistency (guidelines), and social mechanisms (expert access, awareness, and ongoing prioritization, emerging from team discussions and shared judgments about risks and delivery trade-offs). These cluster into two broader patterns: embedding security in agile assurance activities and sustaining security awareness through agile rituals and prioritization (see Fig. 2). While they do not eliminate all challenges, these practices make security a recurring, collective concern and pave the way for how responsibility is shared in practice (see RQ3).

4.3   [RQ3] Understanding and Distribution of Responsibility for Security

RQ3 explored how teams understand and distribute responsibility for security within agile development. Practitioners described security responsibility as both individual and collective. While developers were often seen as the primary actors ensuring secure implementation, many also emphasized their teams' shared accountability for outcomes. Responsibility was thus distributed across roles but unevenly enacted in practice.

Developers as the Main Security Owners. Across most cases, developers perceived themselves as directly responsible for implementing secure solutions and integrating security into everyday tasks. *"We are transitioning to me assisting in crafting some user stories ... How they get it integrated into the existing codebase. What security scanning should be included as well. What automated tests should be included."* (P_1)

Several practitioners explained that security requirements were incorporated in acceptance criteria or embedded within coding practices: *"we would incorporate these security requirements into our acceptance criteria, and it was the developers who were responsible for this."* (P_0) *"Well, you're responsible for your own security, so to speak. If I'm the one creating a user service, it's my responsibility to ensure its security ... it's easier to keep track of security because I know exactly what's being accessed within the code."* (P_{15})

Developers also felt responsible for communicating sound practices to others: *"technical team members also have a responsibility to communicate the importance of using HTTPS instead of HTTP and ensuring the right security measures are in place."* (P_0)

Even when not explicitly required by customers, developers treated security as part of software development professional good practice: *"Unless the client has insight into security and a specific focus on it ... it's probably something that will remain unsaid. ... It just needs to be secure. And then it's up to us to choose the implementation."* (P_1)

Shared and Collective Responsibility. Alongside individual accountability, several practitioners described security as a collective concern embedded in team culture. When teams shared ownership of features, they also shared the consequences of security outcomes. *"If something goes wrong, it's us as a team who will face the consequences. So, it also fosters a sense of responsibility."* (P_8)

Collaboration during development reinforced this shared understanding: *"On my project, we share a lot of responsibility for it. We naturally work together on the requirements ... It's my responsibility to ensure that the approach I've chosen is secure. But it's naturally the responsibility of the business specialists to double-check and see if what I'm doing makes sense. Is it secure?"* (P_4)

The examples suggest that team ownership in agile can naturally extend to security when collaboration and mutual verification (e.g., through peer reviews) are part of the process.

Summary RQ3 Findings. Security responsibility in agile development is distributed but uneven. Developers carry much of the operational burden, often acting as de facto security owners, while shared accountability emerges through collaboration and peer review. These two complementary forms, developer-driven ownership and collective accountability within agile teams, summarize how security responsibility is shared in practice (see Fig. 2). This distribution reflects both agile values of collective ownership and the practical reality that explicit security roles are rare. Together, these experiences suggest that sustaining security in agile work depends less on formal role definitions and more on how teams enact shared responsibility in their daily collaboration.

5   Discussion

This study examined how practitioners in agile settings handle security requirements, what practices support their integration, and how responsibility for security is understood and distributed. The results extend prior work on secure agile development (e.g., [10,19,24]) by providing an empirically grounded account of how security is managed in day-to-day development work rather than prescribed through frameworks or roles.

5.1   Security as a Balancing Act in Everyday Work

Practitioners described handling security as a constant negotiation between iteration speed and safeguarding systems. Our findings extend and nuance earlier work by Bartsch [3], which identified persistent tensions between agility and security, by showing that security is not simply neglected but often handled implicitly as part of everyday work. Some participants reported more formalised approaches to security requirements, while others described security as emerging from an ongoing judgement process integrated into ordinary tasks. This perspective reframes problem-centred accounts of a "lack of security focus" (e.g., [5]) by showing that attention to security exists even in companies without formal and clearly defined processes, but is shaped by agile priorities of iteration speed and customer value and often remains under-discussed in everyday work. The framing of security as a "balancing act" (P_{15}) emphasizes that practitioners might experience security not as resistance to agility but as part of routine trade-offs negotiated during development. This finding aligns with Tøndel et al. [10], who emphasize the contextual nature of security priorities, while our interviews reveal the reasoning behind those day-to-day trade-offs.

5.2   Everyday Practices that Keep Attention to Security

Whenever security was formalized among our participants' teams, it was done through lightweight, recurring practices to sustain attention to security, including testing, peer reviews, adherence to guidelines, early consideration of risks, and ongoing awareness initiatives. These are not formal extensions of agile but adaptive routines that make security visible without undermining agility.

This complements prior proposals for dedicated new security artifacts or process extensions (e.g., S-Scrum, SEAP, or abuser stories) [15,16,18], by showing how teams achieve similar aims through team routines and shared procedures. Security awareness programs and peer-based review mechanisms have the potential to help transform security from a compliance requirement into a shared, everyday reflex, supporting calls to strengthen security culture within agile teams rather than relying solely on external audits.

5.3 Distributed and Hybrid Ownership of Security

Responsibility for security in our participants' companies tended to be distributed but uneven. Developers bore much of the operational responsibility for implementing secure solutions, while product owners and managers engaged mainly through prioritization decisions. This reflects a hybrid ownership structure that combines individual accountability with collective responsibility, where teams share both the work and the consequences of security outcomes.

These findings extend earlier work [3] moving from unclear responsibility towards a more nuanced categorization of centralized versus distributed responsibility (e.g., [21]) showing how hybrid, practice-driven forms of ownership operate in agile contexts. They also underline that formal roles might be less influential than everyday collaboration and mutual trust in sustaining security.

5.4 Implications for Requirements Engineering and Practice

For *requirements engineering research*, these results highlight the need to study how security requirements are handled as part of everyday decision-making in agile routines rather than as missing or incomplete artifacts. Understanding how practitioners interpret, adapt, and negotiate security expectations can inform more lightweight approaches to specification and validation that fit agile processes. For *requirements engineers*, this points to the importance of embedding security considerations directly into agile artifacts, such as user stories, acceptance criteria, or definition-of-done, rather than maintaining them in separate documentation. For *practice*, the results suggest that teams can strengthen security integration by: (a) making security criteria explicit within backlog items and acceptance criteria definitions, (b) embedding security discussions into existing ceremonies such as sprint planning and retrospectives, and (c) ensuring accessible expertise, e.g., through security champions, pair programming, or local advisory roles, instead of depending mainly on external compliance checks.

Summary. Overall, this study shows that security in agile development is not entirely an afterthought compared to prior work [3] but a recurring concern embedded, to varying degrees, in everyday work. Viewing security as a collective, iterative practice rather than a discrete requirement provides a more realistic foundation for secure agile development and contributes to a more nuanced understanding of how agile teams translate security expectations into everyday work, practices, and shared responsibility, complementing work that focuses on scale or process-level structures [12, 13].

5.5 Limitations and Threats to Validity

As with all qualitative studies, the findings are shaped by the participants, context, and interpretive process. The study is based on interviews with sixteen practitioners from different organizations in Denmark and related contexts; while this diversity supports breadth, the results do not aim for statistical generalization. Instead, they provide an analytical generalization illustrating how security work is experienced across agile environments. The interviews were conducted in SeptemberâĂŞNovember 2023; therefore, the findings do not reflect more recent changes in available software engineering and security testing tools. This time gap is particularly relevant given the rapid proliferation of AI-assisted tools such as ChatGPT and Copilot since the interviews were conducted. At the same time, our findings primarily concern attitudes and everyday practices, such as the perception of security as a background concern. While these may be influenced by new tools, we expect them to be relatively stable over time, as changes in attitudes, behavior, and organizational culture typically occur more slowly than technical practices as shown by work in organizational change [26]. Therefore, we expect the reported attitudes and behaviors to remain relevant despite evolution in tooling. However, the potential impact of emerging tools on these practices remains an important direction for future work.

Researcher interpretation is an inherent aspect of reflexive thematic analysis. To enhance credibility, coding and theme development were iteratively discussed among the authors, and representative participant quotations are presented to ground interpretations in the data. However, other researchers might cluster or label themes differently. The interview format also means that the study captures reported rather than observed practices. Although participants offered rich accounts, complementary data sources, such as backlog items, user stories, or other project artifacts, could further clarify how security requirements are represented and tracked in practice.

Finally, while the interviews covered multiple sectors, organizational culture and maturity may influence security practices. Since most Danish software organizations now adopt agile methods, recruiting teams using more plan-driven or hybrid processes proved difficult. Comparative research across different development models could help distinguish which of the identified challenges are specific to agile contexts and which reflect broader requirements engineering concerns.

6   Conclusions and Future Work

This study provides an empirical view of how agile practitioners handle, integrate, and take responsibility for security requirements. Our findings show that in many cases, security is not a separate activity but a continuous concern embedded in daily agile work. Practitioners navigate tensions between agility and protection, relying on lightweight practices, such as testing, peer reviews, shared guidelines, early consideration, and awareness routines, that make security visible and actionable within agile workflows.

The findings extend prior research by showing how security work can be coordinated and shared in practice, highlighting hybrid ownership patterns that emerge through collaboration rather than formal role definitions. For requirements engineering, this emphasizes the importance of understanding how practitioners interpret and negotiate security expectations as part of ongoing decision-making, informing lightweight approaches to specification and validation that fit agile processes. For practitioners, the results suggest that improving everyday visibility and shared responsibility for security may be more effective than adding new process artifacts or roles. By recognizing security as a collaborative, evolving aspect of agile development, teams can move toward more sustainable and collectively owned approaches to secure software (requirements) engineering.

Future research could investigate how these patterns evolve across organizational scales, domains, and over time, and how they differ in non-agile settings. Complementary access to project artifacts, such as backlogs or user stories, could also clarify how security requirements are represented, prioritized, and operationalized in practice.

Data Availability Statement. The interview guides and the code book used for analysis are made available on Zenodo.

References

1. Beznosov, K., Kruchten, P.: Towards agile security assurance. In: Proc. of the 2004 workshop on New security paradigms, pp. 47–54
2. Goertzel, K.M., et al.: Software security assurance: a state-of-art report (sar). Tech. Rep, IATAC HERNDON VA (2007)
3. Bartsch, S.: Practitioners' perspectives on security in agile development. In: 6th Intl Conference on Availability, Reliability and Security. IEEE , pp. 479–484 (2011)
4. Daneva, M., Wang, C.: Security requirements engineering in the agile era: how does it work in practice? In: IEEE 1st International Workshop On Quality Requirements In Agile Projects (QuaRAP). IEEE 2018, pp. 10–13 (2018)
5. Inayat, I., Salim, S. S., Marczak, S., Daneva, M., Shamshirband, S.: A systematic literature review on agile requirements engineering practices and challenges. Comput. Human Behav, 915–929 (2015)
6. Türpe, S.: The trouble with security requirements. In: IEEE 25th International Requirements Engineering Conference (RE). IEEE 2017, pp. 122–133 (2017)
7. Rindell, K., Ruohonen, J., Holvitie, J., Hyrynsalmi, S., Leppänen, V.: Security in agile software development: a practitioner survey. Inf. Softw. Technol. **131**, 106488 (2021)
8. Jarzębowicz, A., Weichbroth, P.: A qualitative study on non-functional requirements in agile software development. IEEE Access, vol. 9, pp. 40 458–40 475 (2021)
9. Behutiye, W., et al.: Management of quality requirements in agile and rapid software development: a systematic mapping study. Inf. Softw. Technol. **123**, 106225 (2020)
10. Tøndel, I.A., Cruzes, D.S., Jaatun, M.G., Sindre, G.: Influencing the security prioritisation of an agile software development project. Comput. Secur. **118**, 102744 (2022)
11. Ramesh, B., Cao, L., Baskerville, R.: Agile requirements engineering practices and challenges: an empirical study. Inf. Syst. J. **20**(5), 449–480 (2010)
12. van der Heijden, A., Broasca, C., Serebrenik, A.: An empirical perspective on security challenges in large-scale agile software development In: Proceedings of the 12th ACM/IEEE International Symposium on Empirical Software Engineering and Measurement , pp. 1–4 (2018)

13. Nägele, S., Schenk, N., Matthes, F.: The current state of security governance and compliance in large-scale agile development: a systematic literature review and interview study. In: CBI. IEEE, pp. 1–10 (2023)
14. Thool, A., Brown, C.: Securing agile: assessing the impact of security activities on agile development. In: Proceedings of the 28th International Conference on Evaluation and Assessment in Software Engineering, pp. 668–678 (2024)
15. Mougouei, D., Sani, N.F.M., Almasi, M.M.: S-scrum: a secure methodology for agile development of web services. World Comput. Sci. Inf. Tech. J. (WCSIT) **3**(1), 15–19 (2013)
16. Pohl, C., Hof, H.-J.: Secure scrum: development of secure software with scrum. arXiv preprint arXiv:1507.02992 (2015)
17. Boström, G., Wäyrynen, J., Bodén, M., Beznosov, K., P. Kruchten.: Extending xp practices to support security requirements engineering. In: Proc. of the International Workshop on Software Engineering For Secure Systems, pp. 11–18 (2006)
18. Baca, D., Boldt, M., Carlsson, B., Jacobsson, A.: A novel security-enhanced agile software development process applied in an industrial setting. In: 10th Intnl Conference on Availability, Reliability and Security. IEEE, pp. 11–19 (2015)
19. Villamizar, H., Kalinowski, M., Viana, M., Fernández, D. M.: A systematic mapping study on security in agile requirements engineering. In: 44th Euromicro conf on software engineering and advanced applications. IEEE, pp. 454–461 (2018)
20. Valdés-Rodríguez, Y., Hochstetter-Diez, J., Díaz-Arancibia, J., Cadena-Martínez, R.: Towards the integration of security practices in agile software development: a systematic mapping review. Appl. Sci. **13**(7), 4578 (2023)
21. Tøndel, I. A., Jaatun, M. G.: Towards a conceptual framework for security requirements work in agile software development. In: Research Anthology on Agile Software, Software Development, and Testing. IGI Global, pp. 247–279 (2022)
22. Terpstra, E., Daneva, M., Wang, C.: Agile practitioners' understanding of security requirements: insights from a grounded theory analysis. In: 25th international requirements engineering conference workshops (REW). IEEE, pp. 439–442 (2017)
23. Oyetoyan, T. D., Cruzes, D. S., Jaatun, M. G.: An empirical study on the relationship between software security skills, usage and training needs in agile settings. In: 2016 11th International Conference on Availability, Reliability and Security (ARES). IEEE, pp. 548–555 (2016)
24. Mihelič, A., Vrhovec, S., Hovelja, T.: Agile development of secure software for small and medium-sized enterprises. Sustainability **15**(1), 801 (2023)
25. Clarke, V., Braun, V.: Thematic analysis. J. Posit. Psychol. **12**(3), 297–298 (2017)
26. Armenakis, A., Bedeian, A.: Organizational change: a review of theory and research in the 1990s. J. Manag. **25**(3), 293–315 (1999)

Understanding Usefulness in Developer Explanations on Stack Overflow

Martin Obaidi[1]([✉])[iD], Kushtrim Qengaj[1], Hannah Deters[1][iD], Jakob Droste[1][iD], Marc Herrmann[1][iD], Kurt Schneider[1][iD], and Jil Klünder[2][iD]

[1] Leibniz Universität Hannover, Software Engineering Group, Hannover, Germany
{martin.obaidi,hannah.deters,jakob.droste,marc.herrmann,
kurt.schneider}@inf.uni-hannover.de, kushtrim.qengaj@stud.uni-hannover.de
[2] University of Applied Sciences|FHDW Hannover, Hannover, Germany
jil.kluender@fhdw.de

Abstract. [Context and motivation]. Explanations are essential in software engineering (SE) and requirements communication, helping stakeholders clarify ambiguities, justify design choices, and build shared understanding. Online Q&A forums such as *Stack Overflow* provide large-scale settings where such explanations are produced and evaluated, offering valuable insights into what makes them effective.

[Question/problem]. While prior work has explored answer acceptance and voting behavior, little is known about which specific features make explanations genuinely useful. The relative influence of structural, contextual, and linguistic factors, such as content richness, timing, and sentiment, remains unclear.

[Principal ideas/results]. We analyzed 3,323 questions and 59,398 answers from *Stack Overflow*, combining text analysis and statistical modeling to examine how explanation attributes relate to perceived usefulness (normalized upvotes). Structural and contextual factors, especially explanation length, code inclusion, timing, and author reputation, show small to moderate positive effects. Sentiment polarity has negligible influence, suggesting that clarity and substance outweigh tone in technical communication.

[Contribution]. This study provides an empirical account of what drives perceived usefulness in developer explanations. It contributes methodological transparency through open data and replication materials, and conceptual insight by relating observed communication patterns to principles of requirements communication. The findings offer evidence-based implications for how developers and RE practitioners can craft clearer and more effective explanations, potentially supporting fairer communication in both open and organizational contexts. From an RE perspective, these determinants can be interpreted as practical signals for ambiguity reduction and rationale articulation in day-to-day requirements communication.

Keywords: explainability · software engineering · developer communication · data mining · empirical study

1   Introduction

With the rising complexity of software systems, particularly in data-driven and requirements-intensive domains, clear and comprehensible explanations are becoming ever more essential [1,12]. In requirements engineering (RE), explanations help clarify requirements, resolve ambiguities, and support shared understanding among stakeholders [11,18]. Clarity and shared understanding have long been linked to successful RE practice [24]. Yet, producing high-quality, context-sensitive explanations remains difficult as artifacts, tools, and teams scale. In practice, breakdowns in RE often stem from missing or weakly communicated rationale and delayed clarification, which can propagate ambiguity into implementation and validation. Thus, understanding which explanation attributes developers perceive as useful provides an empirical basis for improving RE communication practices that aim at shared understanding and ambiguity reduction.

Building on the definition of explainability by Chazette et al. [11], we focus on *developer explainability*—how developers explain software behaviour, code, or design decisions to peers. Such explanations act as coordination mechanisms that align mental models and reduce uncertainty [9]. Recent work further shows that context-proximate explanations embedded in development workflows can improve comprehension and confidence [56]. In software projects, the ability to explain and understand technical or design rationales directly affects how requirements are interpreted and implemented. Satisfying explanatory needs among developers therefore helps preserve requirement intent and ensures that implementation aligns with stakeholder expectations. In RE terms, these explainability practices parallel activities such as rationale articulation and clarification during elicitation and validation, where stakeholders exchange explanations to achieve mutual understanding.

Online Q&A platforms such as *Stack Overflow* provide large-scale evidence of this explanatory behaviour. Prior work has characterized *Stack Overflow* as particularly effective for conceptual questions and code-review-like exchanges, noting that review-oriented questions are often concrete and include code snippets that facilitate explanation and assessment [49]. Building on this foundation, our study quantifies how specific structural, contextual, and linguistic attributes of explanations relate to *perceived usefulness* at scale. Engagement signals like upvotes reflect community judgments of usefulness, albeit biased by visibility, timing, and author reputation [3,26]. Prior studies have explored factors influencing answer quality, such as code inclusion, length, and response time [6,42], yet little is known about which structural, contextual, or linguistic features make explanations themselves *useful* in RE-related discussions.

To address this gap, we empirically analyze 3,323 questions and 59,398 answers from *Stack Overflow* to examine how structural (e.g., content richness), contextual (e.g., timing, reputation), and linguistic (e.g., sentiment) factors relate to perceived usefulness. Specifically, we investigate which characteristics distinguish explanations that developers perceive as more useful in technical and RE-oriented communication. We conceptualize developer explainability as a communicative competence that supports rationale sharing and ambiguity reduction, which are key qualities of effective RE communication. By identifying key drivers of perceived usefulness, this study contributes to a better understanding of how developers communicate explanations effectively. The insights aim to inform RE communication practices and the design of tools that foster clear, fair, and context-aware explanations. The remainder of this paper presents related work (Sect. 2), the study design (Sect. 3), results (Sect. 4), discussion (Sect. 5), and conclusion (Sect. 6).

2   Background and Related Work

2.1   Background

Explainability is a software quality aspect aimed at making systems and their behavior understandable to humans [11]. Beyond its roots in AI transparency [1], explainability has become relevant across software engineering (SE), where understanding and rationale exchange are essential for effective collaboration [18]. Following Chazette et al. [11], we view explainability as a non-functional requirement (NFR) closely linked to transparency, trust, and usability.

We extend this concept toward *developer explainability*—how developers explain technical artifacts such as code, APIs, or design decisions to peers. Explanations in this sense facilitate understanding, reduce ambiguity, and support shared reasoning, making them critical for both development and requirements communication. When well designed, they enhance clarity and trust; when poor or excessive, they may hinder comprehension [12]. On-demand environments such as *Stack Overflow* exemplify this dynamic by enabling developers to request and evaluate explanations in real time [20].

2.2   Related Work

Explainability in Software Engineering. Recent work increasingly investigates explainability as a NFR beyond XAI [13–15,17,30,31,33,41,51]. Chazette et al. [11] conceptualized explainability as an NFR and highlighted its context-dependent and potentially conflicting effects. Building on this, Chandra et al. [9] and Yan et al. [56] showed that embedded, in-situ explanations improve comprehension and help align developers' mental models. Research on developer communication [2,10] further indicates that a large share of developer dialogue involves rationale sharing and explanation construction, suggesting that explainability is not confined to user-facing AI but pervades everyday collaboration.

Explanation Usefulness on Q&A Platforms. Online Q&A platforms such as *Stack Overflow* provide large-scale data on peer-generated explanations. Prior work links explanation quality to structural and contextual factors: code inclusion, textual length, and timing [4,6,27,42]. User reputation and engagement also correlate with perceived quality [43,53]. However, popularity does not always align with accuracy or clarity [26]. Few studies explicitly interpret these determinants as facets of *developer explainability*—how explanations convey rationale and foster understanding within technical discussions.

Our study extends this perspective by analyzing structural, temporal, and social factors as predictors of explanation usefulness, linking insights from Q&A research to explainability and requirements communication.

Sentiment Analysis. Sentiment analysis in SE has gained significant attention over the past decade as a means to assess affective tone in developer communication such as discussions or and Q&A posts [8,21–23,35,37,38,45,57]. Calefato et al. [5] introduced *Senti4SD*, a supervised classifier trained on over 4,400 *Stack Overflow* posts, demonstrating that SE-specific sentiment models outperform generic social-media tools. Novielli et al. [29] released a manually annotated gold-standard dataset of 4,800 Stack Overflow posts, enabling benchmarking and reproducibility across sentiment studies. Swillus and Zaidman [48] applied sentiment analysis to testing-related Stack Overflow posts, uncovering affective dimensions such as insecurity or aspiration that influence attitudes toward testing practice. Complementarily, Uddin et al. [50] focused on opinion mining in API discussions, automatically classifying sentiments toward API usability and performance aspects. Recent work [34,36,57] further demonstrates that fine-tuned transformer models (e.g., BERT, RoBERTa) achieve state-of-the-art performance for polarity detection in software-related text.

However, prior work primarily associates sentiment with emotional or experiential factors—such as developer satisfaction, motivation, or team climate—rather than with the perceived usefulness of content. Our study addresses this gap by examining whether the affective tone of explanations has any measurable effect on their perceived usefulness within technical discussions.

3   Study Design

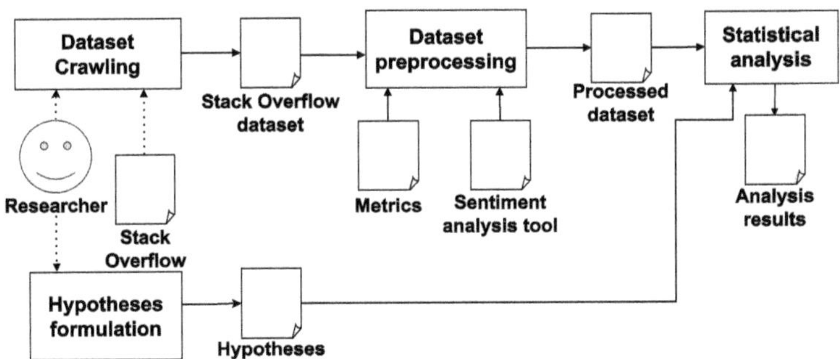

Fig. 1. Overview of the study workflow following FLOW notation [47]. The symbols are chosen accordingly to the notation [47].

This study investigates which structural, contextual, and social factors contribute to the perceived usefulness of developer explanations on *Stack Overflow*. Following the workflow shown in Fig. 1, we collected and preprocessed data, derived explanatory metrics, and applied correlation analyses to identify significant associations.

Methodologically, our metadata-driven, hypothesis-based correlation approach is in line with prior explainability research that linked explanation-related constructs to platform metadata in other domains (e.g., app reviews) [40].

3.1   Research Questions

The goal is to identify what makes explanations in developer discussions useful and how this relates to *developer explainability*. We address four research questions:

- **RQ1:** How does *perceived usefulness* relate to the sentiment polarity of an explanation?
- **RQ2:** How does *perceived usefulness* relate to content features (e.g., text length or readability)?
- **RQ3:** How does *perceived usefulness* relate to timing and visibility factors (e.g., posting delay and response order)?
- **RQ4:** How does *perceived usefulness* relate to author characteristics (e.g., reputation and badges)?

These questions capture linguistic, structural, temporal, and social determinants of explanation usefulness, extending prior Q&A research toward RE-related communication.

3.2   Dataset and Forum Selection

Stack Overflow was selected for its structured Q&A format and rich metadata (scores, timestamps, user reputation). We focused on posts tagged `[android]` because it is a long-running and high-volume tag with comparatively stable usage over time, and it contains a balanced mix of conceptual questions (e.g., design and API usage) and code-level debugging discussions, providing sufficient variation and sample size for robust statistical estimation. To ensure high-quality data, only questions with at least 50 upvotes and at least one positively rated answer were included. This yielded 3,323 questions and 59,398 answers posted between 2009 and 2024. Duplicate and incomplete entries from API exports were removed manually. We treat this dataset as a case study of a large developer community. Replication across additional tags and platforms is needed to assess generalizability.

These thresholds were chosen to ensure representativeness and linguistic substance: highly upvoted questions better reflect community consensus, while a minimum word count of 100 (see Sect. 3.4) ensures textual completeness for reliable linguistic analysis.

3.3   Metrics and Operationalization

Perceived usefulness was approximated through an answer's *relative score*, i.e., its score normalized by the total score of all answers to the same question. This allows comparisons across threads of differing popularity. Importantly, votes and scores should be interpreted as a noisy signal of *perceived* usefulness in a specific platform context: they may reflect explanatory value, but are also influenced by visibility, timing, author reputation, and community norms, and therefore do not directly measure correctness or understanding.

Independent variables were grouped as follows:

- **Sentiment:** sentiment polarity (negative, neutral, positive) obtained via a fine-tuned transformer model [16] applied to the cleaned answer text.
- **Content:** number of code blocks, links, paragraphs, sentences, and words; readability (Flesch Reading Ease); lexical diversity; and textual similarity to the question and other answers (Jaccard coefficient over lemmatized tokens).
- **Timing:** creation date, time since the corresponding question, and posting order.
- **Author:** reputation and badge counts (bronze, silver, gold) of the answer owner and last editor.

All variables were scaled or log-transformed where appropriate to ensure comparability. Quantitative metrics were computed automatically using *textstat* and *LexicalRichness*; code and link counts were extracted via regular expressions.

3.4   Data Preprocessing

For each answer, raw and processed text versions were retained. Preprocessing involved removing code blocks and HTML, decoding entities, eliminating stop words, and lemmatizing tokens [46]. Answers shorter than 100 words were excluded from linguistic analyses (e.g., readability, similarity) to maintain statistical reliability [19]. All preprocessing was performed using *BeautifulSoup 4.12*, *NLTK 3.9*, and *spaCy 3.7* (*en_core_web_sm* model), ensuring consistent tokenization and stopword handling.

3.5   Analysis Procedure

We conducted correlation analyses to test associations between variables and usefulness, selecting the coefficient according to the measurement scale of each predictor: Spearman's ρ for ordinal/continuous variables, point-biserial r_{pb} for binary variables, and eta η for nominal groupings. These coefficients are used as descriptive association measures and are not contingent on normally distributed variables. Accordingly, we focus on effect sizes with Bonferroni-corrected thresholds for multiple testing. This design follows the same general rationale as metadata-based explainability studies that relate observable platform signals to explanation phenomena [40].

3.6   Data Analysis

All analyses were conducted using established scientific libraries (*pandas, numpy, scipy, pingouin, statsmodels*). This ensured reproducibility and statistical comparability across all analytical steps.

Sentiment Analysis. To estimate the emotional tone of explanations, we applied a fine-tuned *BERT*-based sentiment classifier [16], trained and validated on the annotated *Stack Overflow* corpus by Novielli et al. [29] using 10-fold cross-validation. Posts were classified into negative, neutral, or positive polarity following the emotion mapping in [28]. The model achieved an average F1-macro score of 0.89 and an F1-micro score of 0.89. Implementation used *Transformers 4.44* with default parameters and the *BERT-base-uncased* model.

Table 1. Variables and abbreviations used in the analysis.

Variable (Abbreviation)	Scale/Range
Usefulness Metric	
Usefulness score (U_{ps})	Interval $\mathbb{R}$
Content Features	
Sentiment polarity (E_{pol})	Nominal $\{-1, 0, 1\}$
Code blocks/links (E_{cb}, E_{ln})	Ratio $\mathbb{N}_0$
Has code/links ($E_{\mathrm{has\_cb}}$, $E_{\mathrm{has\_ln}}$)	Nominal $\{0, 1\}$
Paragraphs/words/sentences (E_{pg}, E_{wd}, E_{st})	Ratio $\mathbb{N}_0$
Words per sentence (E_{wps})	Ratio $\mathbb{Q}_0^+$
Readability (E_{read})	Interval $(-\infty, 206.8]$
Lexical diversity (E_{lex})	Ratio $\mathbb{Q}_0^+$
Relevance Features	
Similarity to question/peers (E_{simQ}, E_{simE})	Ratio $[0, 1]$
Temporal Features	
Time since question (E_{time})	Ratio (sec)
Time of day (E_{tod})	Interval $[0, 24)$
Creation date (E_{cd})	Interval (timestamp)
Answers after ($E_{\mathrm{ans\_after}}$)	Ratio $\mathbb{N}_0$
Explainer Features	
Author reputation (E_{rep})	Ratio $\mathbb{N}_0$
Author badges (bronze/silver/gold) (E_{badges})	Ratio $\mathbb{N}_0$
Editor reputation/badges ($E_{\mathrm{rep\_edit}}$, $E_{\mathrm{badges\_edit}}$)	Ratio $\mathbb{N}_0$

Variables. We distinguished between *raw variables* (directly retrieved from the Stack Overflow API) and *computed variables* (derived from text processing and metadata). Raw variables include votes, timestamps, and user reputation; computed variables capture readability, lexical diversity, and textual similarity. Table 1 summarizes the analyzed variable groups.

U_{ps} quantifies normalized usefulness (relative score). $E\mathrm{pol}$ represents sentiment polarity detected by a fine-tuned BERT model. Content measures ($E\mathrm{cb}$–$E\mathrm{lex}$) capture structure and readability. Relevance metrics ($E\mathrm{simQ}$, $E\mathrm{simE}$) assess textual overlap. Temporal variables ($E\mathrm{time}$–$E\mathrm{ans\_after}$) model posting dynamics. Explainer features ($E\mathrm{rep}$–$E\mathrm{badges\_edit}$) reflect author reputation and expertise.

Collectively, these variables operationalize structural, temporal, and social facets of *developer explainability*.

Hypotheses and Statistical Testing. For each research question, we formulated corresponding null hypotheses (H_0) assuming no relationship between usefulness and the investigated feature group (sentiment, content, timing, author). Table 2 summarizes all hypotheses and their associated variables. Type I error inflation from multiple testing was mitigated using Bonferroni correction ($\alpha_{\mathrm{adj}} = \alpha/k$), with a base significance level of $\alpha = 0.05$.

Table 2. Overview of tested hypotheses and associated variables.

Hypo.	Description (There is no relation...)	Used Variables
$H1_0$	...between usefulness and sentiment polarity of the explanation.	U_{ps}, E_{pol}
$H2_0$	...between usefulness and the structural content of the explanation.	
$H2.1_0$	...and the presence or number of embedded resources (code or links).	E_{cb}, E_{ln}, $E_{\mathrm{has\_cb}}$, $E_{\mathrm{has\_ln}}$
$H2.2_0$	...and textual length or density measures.	E_{pg}, E_{wd}, E_{st}, E_{wps}
$H2.3_0$	...and textual complexity and expressiveness.	E_{read}, E_{lex}
$H2.4_0$	...and similarity to the question or peer explanations.	E_{simQ}, E_{simE}
$H3_0$	...between usefulness and the timing of the explanation.	E_{tod}, E_{time}, $E_{\mathrm{ans\_after}}$, E_{cd}
$H4_0$	...between usefulness and characteristics of the explainer.	E_{rep}, E_{badges}, $E_{\mathrm{rep\_edit}}$, $E_{\mathrm{badges\_edit}}$

Correlation Analysis. Non-parametric correlations were used to identify associations between explanation features and usefulness:

- **Spearman's** ρ for ordinal and ratio variables (e.g., length, reputation).
- **Point-biserial** r_{pb} for binary variables (e.g., code or link presence).
- **Eta coefficient** η for nominal variables (e.g., sentiment polarity).

All coefficients were calculated with two-tailed significance testing and Bonferroni correction at the hypothesis level. Results were interpreted in terms of communicative effectiveness, whether structural, contextual, or author-related features consistently aligned with higher perceived usefulness in developer explanations.

4   Results

4.1   Data Overview

We analyzed 3,323 *Stack Overflow* questions and 59,398 answers ($\sim$17.9 answers/question on average) across 2,348 tags, contributed by 9,146 unique users (85,733 including commenters). The average relative usefulness score per answer was 0.0559. Activity peaked mid-week (most on Wednesdays, fewest on Saturdays).

4.2   Correlation Analysis

We examined associations between explanation features and their relative usefulness using non-parametric correlations (Spearman's ρ, Point-biserial r_{pb}, and Eta η; see replication package for details). All coefficients were computed two-tailed with Bonferroni correction per hypothesis group.

Table 3 summarizes the results for continuous and ordinal predictors, while Table 4 reports correlations for binary and nominal variables. Together, these tables provide a comprehensive overview of how structural, temporal, and author-related features relate to perceived usefulness.

Overall Trends. Content-related features, such as the number of code blocks, links, and textual length, show small but consistent positive correlations with usefulness. In contrast, readability and lexical diversity exhibit negligible effects, indicating that linguistic complexity has little influence on perceived helpfulness. Timing variables show the strongest relationships: earlier answers (shorter delay since question) correlate clearly with higher usefulness. Among author-related attributes, reputation and badge counts correlate moderately positively, whereas last-editor metrics are negligible. Finally, sentiment polarity (negative/neutral/positive) shows virtually no association with usefulness, underscoring that emotional tone is irrelevant in this task-oriented setting.

> **Finding:** Usefulness increases with the inclusion of code and links, longer and earlier answers, and higher author reputation. Linguistic complexity, post-editing, and sentiment show no meaningful association.

4.3   Hypotheses Evaluation

Table 5 summarizes the hypothesis testing outcomes. Bonferroni correction [54] was applied to mitigate Type I error inflation. Due to the large sample size, even weak correlations reached statistical significance; thus, interpretation focuses on effect strength rather than p-values alone.

Table 3. Spearman correlation results (dependent variable: relative usefulness score U_{ps}).

Hyp.	Variable	ρ	Effect	Sig.	N
$H2.1.1.1_0$	*num code blocks*	0.26	Small	$< .0001$	59,398
$H2.1.2.1_0$	*num links*	0.23	Small	$< .0001$	59,398
$H2.2.1_0$	*num paragraphs*	0.24	Small	$< .0001$	59,398
$H2.2.2_0$	*num words*	0.19	Small	$< .0001$	59,398
$H2.2.3_0$	*num sentences*	0.17	Small	$< .0001$	59,398
$H2.2.4_0$	*words per sentence*	0.10	None	$< .0001$	59,398
$H2.3.1_0$	*readability*	-0.06	None	$< .0001$	11,700
$H2.3.2_0$	*lexical diversity*	0.03	None	$< .0001$	11,700
$H2.4.1_0$	*sim. to question*	0.09	None	$< .0001$	59,398
$H2.4.2_0$	*sim. to peers*	0.16	Small	0.0058	59,321
$H3.1_0$	*time of day*	0.01	None	$< .0001$	59,398
$H3.2_0$	*time since question*	-0.50	Strong	$< .0001$	59,398
$H3.3_0$	*answers after*	0.12	Small	0.0046	59,398
$H3.4_0$	*creation date*	-0.26	Small	$< .0001$	59,398
$H4.1.1_0$	*owner reputation*	0.41	Moderate	$< .0001$	58,979
$H4.1.2_0$	*owner badges (bronze)*	0.27	Small	$< .0001$	58,979
$H4.1.3_0$	*owner badges (silver)*	0.34	Moderate	$< .0001$	58,979
$H4.1.4_0$	*owner badges (gold)*	0.31	Moderate	$< .0001$	58,979
$H4.2.1_0$	*editor reputation*	0.05	None	$< .0001$	31,315
$H4.2.2_0$	*editor badges (bronze)*	0.04	None	$< .0001$	31,315
$H4.2.3_0$	*editor badges (silver)*	0.04	None	$< .0001$	31,315
$H4.2.4_0$	*editor badges (gold)*	0.00	None	0.47	31,315

Table 4. Binary/nominal features vs. usefulness (U_{ps}): point-biserial and eta results.

Hyp.	Method	Independent variable	Coef.	Effect	Sig.	N
$H2.1.1.2_0$	Point-biserial	has code blocks	0.08	None	$< .0001$	59,398
$H2.1.2.2_0$	Point-biserial	has links	0.19	Small	$< .0001$	59,398
$H1_0$	Eta (η)	sentiment polarity	0.0009	None	$< .0001$	59,398

Table 5. Hypothesis testing with Bonferroni-adjusted thresholds.

H_0	# Sub-Hyp.	Threshold	Rejected Sub-Hypotheses	Result
$H1_0$	1	0.05	–	rejected
$H2_0$	12	0.0042	$H2.1_0$–$H2.4_0$	Rejected
$H3_0$	4	0.0125	$H3.1_0$–$H3.4_0$	Rejected
$H4_0$	8	0.0063	$H4.1_0$, $H4.2_0$	Rejected

$H1_0$ (sentiment polarity) was rejected, but the effect size is negligible, confirming that emotional tone does not affect perceived usefulness. $H2_0$ (content), $H3_0$ (timing), and $H4_0$ (author) were also rejected, indicating that structural richness, timeliness, and contributor reputation significantly influence perceived usefulness. These findings reinforce that structural and contextual features are stronger predictors of communicative effectiveness than linguistic tone or post-editing metadata.

5   Discussion

This section interprets the results and answers the research questions.

5.1   Answering the Research Questions

RQ1: How does the usefulness of an explanation relate to its sentiment polarity? Sentiment showed no meaningful association with usefulness. The negligible effect supports the view that developer communication is primarily functional and goal-oriented, where clarity and factual accuracy outweigh emotional tone.

RQ2: How does usefulness relate to content features such as code inclusion, text length, and readability? Content-related factors, particularly the number of code blocks, links, and explanation length, showed small but consistent positive correlations with usefulness. This suggests that richer, example-driven explanations tend to be perceived as more helpful, consistent with prior findings on answer quality and with principles of clarity and completeness in requirements communication.

RQ3: How does timing (e.g., response order and posting delay) influence usefulness perception? Temporal factors show the strongest effects. Earlier answers receive higher usefulness scores, reflecting visibility advantages and the importance of timely feedback. In RE terms, this parallels how early clarification reduces uncertainty and guides subsequent discussion.

RQ4: How do author characteristics (e.g., reputation, badges) affect perceived usefulness? Author reputation and badge counts are moderately correlated with usefulness, while editor attributes have negligible influence. This suggests that perceived credibility affects evaluations independently of content, pointing to a potential reputation bias similar to authority effects in collaborative RE activities.

Overall, structural and contextual factors best explain perceived usefulness. Timely, detailed, and reputable explanations tend to be valued more, suggesting that in developer-to-developer and RE-like communication, usefulness is driven by informational quality and context rather than affective tone.

5.2   Reflection on Findings and Implications

Our findings show that in developer communication, and by extension in requirements engineering (RE), perceived usefulness is primarily shaped by structural and contextual factors rather than linguistic tone. Content richness, timing, and author reputation are associated with higher perceived usefulness, whereas emotional style contributes little.

This challenges assumptions that sentiment meaningfully affects quality perceptions. In task-oriented contexts such as RE, communication serves knowledge transfer, and clarity, completeness, and evidence matter most.

Content-related attributes such as code blocks, links, and explanation length were associated with modest but consistent increases in usefulness, supporting prior work showing that detailed, example-based explanations improve comprehension [7, 42]. At the same time, such structural richness can also amplify fluency or verbosity effects, where well-written and confidently phrased explanations may be perceived as helpful even when their technical grounding is weak. This aligns with recent evidence that LLM-generated answers can be verbose and well-articulated, and that user study participants may still prefer such answers even when they contain incorrect information, indicating a fluency-driven trust risk [25]. Complementing this concern, [32] reports that users can often recognize LLM-formulated explanations and tend to prefer manually written ones when LLM outputs appear less correct or less aligned with the underlying facts, underscoring that perceived clarity should not be conflated with correctness. Timing was the strongest predictor: earlier answers were rated more useful, reflecting both visibility effects and the value of prompt clarification, paralleling how early feedback in RE reduces ambiguity and supports shared understanding.

Author reputation showed moderate positive effects, indicating possible credibility bias [53]. In RE practice, this underlines the need for transparent authorship and balanced peer review to avoid overreliance on perceived expertise when judging rationale quality.

From a practical perspective, the results suggest two complementary implications. For developers and RE practitioners, useful explanations tend to be detailed, contextually grounded, and supported by concrete artifacts (e.g., code, links, measurable acceptance criteria, scenarios). Accordingly, RE communication and documentation should capture clarification and rationale early and in an example-based form, while reviews and tools should reduce visibility and authority bias by prioritizing well-structured content over popularity or posting time.

For teaching explainable AI, the findings motivate training students to ground explanations in evidence and traceable assumptions (e.g., examples or snippets) and to explicitly reflect on fluency and reputation cues, so that well-written explanations are not automatically treated as correct or trustworthy.

In sum, effective explainability emerges as a communicative competence grounded in structure and context, not style. Developers who explain early and substantively contribute most to collective understanding and decision quality in software projects.

5.3 Threats to Validity

We discuss threats to validity following Wohlin et al. [55].

Construct Validity. Usefulness was approximated through normalized engagement metrics (relative score), which mitigate but do not eliminate visibility or popularity effects [3,53]. Upvotes were chosen as the most widely used proxy in prior Q&A research, balancing availability and comparability across threads. However, votes do not measure correctness, comprehension, or ambiguity reduction directly; they primarily capture perceived usefulness under platform-specific biases. Sentiment was derived via automated classification and may misinterpret neutral or technical phrasing. Jaccard similarity, being surface-based, cannot fully capture semantic relatedness.

Internal Validity. As the analysis is correlational, causal inferences cannot be made [44]. Uncontrolled confounders such as topic difficulty [52], author expertise, or community norms may influence results. Reputation might also act both as cause and effect of perceived usefulness.

Conclusion Validity. Skewed sentiment class distributions could attenuate effects. Bonferroni correction reduced false positives but increased the chance of false negatives. Most significant effects were small, indicating limited practical impact despite statistical significance. Given the large sample size, even small effects reached statistical significance, emphasizing the need to interpret effect strength rather than p-values.

External Validity. The dataset covers highly upvoted, English-language *Stack Overflow* posts and may not generalize to other communities or less technical audiences. Platform dynamics may also affect applicability over time. Post-2022 shifts in developer workflows, including increased LLM use, can change answer style and user preferences and may therefore influence voting-based signals [25]. The dataset focuses on high-quality Android-tagged questions (≥ 50 upvotes), which may bias the sample toward established topics and may not reflect other domains such as security or ML. Stack Overflow captures developer-to-developer Q&A rather than stakeholder-facing RE communication, but similar mechanisms such as visibility effects, authority cues, and timing can shape which explanations receive attention in RE discussions. Finally, generalizability across replications may be sensitive to analytic choices, including preprocessing, sentiment models, and the use of bivariate correlations without controlling for confounders.

6 Conclusion and Future Work

This study analyzed 59,398 *Stack Overflow* explanations to identify which factors shape their perceived usefulness. Results indicate that usefulness depends primarily on structural and contextual qualities: explanations that are timely, detailed, and supported by code or links are rated most helpful. In contrast, sentiment has no meaningful influence, suggesting that clarity and substance outweigh linguistic tone in developer communication. Explainer reputation shows a moderate effect, implying that credibility cues partially drive perceived quality—a potential source of reputation bias also relevant for requirements evaluation. Overall, the findings underline that effective explainability in both online and RE contexts is grounded in structure and context rather than affective style. Clear, complete, and well-timed explanations strengthen shared understanding and decision quality in software projects.

Future work should examine the generalizability of these results across platforms with different audiences (e.g., *Reddit, Quora*) and complement quantitative analyses with qualitative studies to better understand why certain explanations are perceived as useful. Further studies should test explicit mappings from explanation features to RE practices, e.g., linking code-supported explanations to requirements-by-example (acceptance criteria) and timely explanations to early clarification in elicitation and validation. In addition, refining textual features (e.g., specificity, factual accuracy, confidence) and running controlled experiments (e.g., anonymized authorship) could clarify whether reputation effects reflect actual quality or perception bias and support fairer surfacing of useful explanations.

Acknowledgment. This work was funded by the Deutsche Forschungsgemeinschaft (DFG, German Research Foundation) under Grant No.: 470146331, project softXplain (2022–2025).

Data Availability Statement. All data of our study is publicly available at Zenodo [39].

References

1. Adadi, A., Berrada, M.: Peeking inside the black-box: a survey on explainable artificial intelligence (xai). IEEE Access **6**, 52138–52160 (2018)
2. Alkadhi, R., Lata, T., Guzman, E., Bruegge, B.: Rationale in development chat messages: an exploratory study. In: 2017 IEEE/ACM 14th International Conference on Mining Software Repositories (MSR), pp. 436–446 (2017)
3. Anderson, A., Huttenlocher, D., Kleinberg, J., Leskovec, J.: Discovering value from community activity on focused question answering sites: a case study of stack overflow. In: Proceedings of the 18th ACM SIGKDD International Conference on Knowledge Discovery and Data Mining, KDD '12, pp. 850–858 (2012)
4. Bhat, V., Gokhale, A., Jadhav, R., Pudipeddi, J., Akoglu, L.: Effects of tag usage on question response time. Soc. Netw. Anal. Min. **5**(1), 1–13 (2015). https://doi.org/10.1007/s13278-015-0263-3
5. Calefato, F., Lanubile, F., Maiorano, F., Novielli, N.: Sentiment polarity detection for software development. Empirical Softw. Eng. **23** (2018)
6. Calefato, F., Lanubile, F., Marasciulo, M.C., Novielli, N.: Mining successful answers in stack overflow. In: 2015 IEEE/ACM 12th Working Conference on Mining Software Repositories, pp. 430–433 (2015)
7. Calefato, F., Lanubile, F., Novielli, N.: Moving to stack overflow: Best-answer prediction in legacy developer forums. In: 10th ACM/IEEE International Symposium on Empirical Software Engineering and Measurement. ESEM 2016 (2016)

8. Cassee, N., Agaronian, A., Constantinou, E., Novielli, N., Serebrenik, A.: Transformers and meta-tokenization in sentiment analysis for software engineering. Empir. Softw. Eng. **29**(4), 77 (2024)

9. Chandra, K., et al.: Watchat: explaining perplexing programs by debugging mental models (2024). https://arxiv.org/abs/2403.05334

10. Chatterjee, P., Damevski, K., Kraft, N.A., Pollock, L.: Automatically identifying the quality of developer chats for post hoc use. ACM Trans. Softw. Eng. Methodol. **30**(4) (2021)

11. Chazette, L., Brunotte, W., Speith, T.: Exploring explainability: a definition, a model, and a knowledge catalogue. In: RE. IEEE (2021)

12. Deters, H., et al.: The x factor: on the relationship between user experience and explainability. In: NordiCHI 2024. ACM (2024)

13. Deters, H., Droste, J., Obaidi, M., Schneider, K.: How explainable is your system? towards a quality model for explainability. In: REFSQ 2024 (2024)

14. Deters, H., Droste, J., Obaidi, M., Schneider, K.: Exploring the means to measure explainability: metrics, heuristics and questionnaires. IST **181**, 107682 (2025)

15. Deters, H., Reinhardt, L., Droste, J., Obaidi, M., Schneider, K.: Identifying explanation needs: towards a catalog of user-based indicators. In: RE 2025, pp. 31–42

16. Devlin, J., Chang, M.W., Lee, K., Toutanova, K.: Bert: pre-training of deep bidirectional transformers for language understanding (2019)

17. Droste, J., Deters, H., Obaidi, M., Klünder, J., Schneider, K.: Framing what can be explained – an operational taxonomy for explainability needs. Requirements Engineering (2025)

18. Droste, J., Deters, H., Obaidi, M., Schneider, K.: Explanations in everyday software systems: towards a taxonomy for explainability needs. In: RE 2024 (2024)

19. Graesser, A.C., McNamara, D.S., Louwerse, M.M., Cai, Z.: Coh-metrix: analysis of text on cohesion and language. Behav. Res. Methods Instruments Comput. **36**(2), 193–202 (2004)

20. Gupta, R., Reddy, P.K.: Learning from gurus: analysis and modeling of reopened questions on stack overflow. In: Proceedings of the 3rd IKDD Conference on Data Science, 2016. CODS 2016 (2016)

21. Herrmann, M., Obaidi, M., Chazette, L., Klünder, J.: On the subjectivity of emotions in software projects: how reliable are pre-labeled data sets for sentiment analysis? JSS **193** (2022)

22. Herrmann, M., Obaidi, M., Klünder, J.: Modeling communication perception in development teams using Monte Carlo methods. In: EASE 2025. Association for Computing Machinery (2025)

23. Herrmann, M., Obaidi, M., Klünder, J.: Different and similar perceptions of communication among software developers. IST **181**, 107698 (2025)

24. Hofmann, H.F., Lehner, F.: Requirements engineering as a success factor in software projects. IEEE Softw. **18**(4), 58 (2001)

25. Kabir, S., Udo-Imeh, D.N., Kou, B., Zhang, T.: Is stack overflow obsolete? an empirical study of the characteristics of chatgpt answers to stack overflow questions. In: CHI 2024 (2024)

26. Mondal, S., Rahman, M.M., Roy, C.K.: Do subjectivity and objectivity always agree? a case study with stack overflow questions. In: 2023 IEEE/ACM 20th International Conference on Mining Software Repositories (MSR), pp. 389–401 (2023)

27. Nasehi, S.M., Sillito, J., Maurer, F., Burns, C.: What makes a good code example?: a study of programming q&a in stackoverflow. In: ICSM, pp. 25–34 (2012)

28. Novielli, N., Calefato, F., Dongiovanni, D., Girardi, D., Lanubile, F.: Can we use se-specific sentiment analysis tools in a cross-platform setting? In: MSR 2020 (2020)

29. Novielli, N., Calefato, F., Lanubile, F.: A gold standard for emotion annotation in stack overflow. In: MSR 2018 (2018)
30. Obaidi, M., Droste, J., Deters, H., Herrmann, M., Klünder, J., Schneider, K.: Do users' explainability needs in software change with mood? In: REFSQ (2025)
31. Obaidi, M., et al.: How to elicit explainability requirements? a comparison of interviews, focus groups, and surveys. In: RE 2025, pp. 167–178 (2025)
32. Obaidi, M., et al.: Automatic generation of explainability requirements and software explanations from user reviews. In: REW (2025)
33. Obaidi, M., et al.: How does users' app knowledge influence the preferred level of detail and format of software explanations? In: REFSQ (2025)
34. Obaidi, M., Herrmann, M., Klünder, J., Schneider, K.: Towards trustworthy sentiment analysis in software engineering: Dataset characteristics and tool selection. In: REW (2025)
35. Obaidi, M., Herrmann, M., Schmid, E., Ochsner, R., Schneider, K., Klünder, J.: A German gold-standard dataset for sentiment analysis in software engineering. In: REW (2025)
36. Obaidi, M., Holm, H., Schneider, K., Klünder, J.: On the limitations of combining sentiment analysis tools in a cross-platform setting. In: Product-Focused Software Process Improvement. Springer International Publishing (2022)
37. Obaidi, M., Klünder, J.: Development and application of sentiment analysis tools in software engineering: a systematic literature review. In: EASE 2021 (2021)
38. Obaidi, M., Nagel, L., Specht, A., Klünder, J.: Sentiment analysis tools in software engineering: a systematic mapping study. IST **151** (2022)
39. Obaidi, M., et al.: Dataset: understanding usefulness in developer explanations on stack overflow. https://doi.org/10.5281/zenodo.17988272
40. Obaidi, M., et al.: From app features to explanation needs: analyzing correlations and predictive potential. In: REW (2025)
41. Obaidi, M., et al.: Automating explanation need management in app reviews: a case study from the navigation app industry. In: ICSE-SEIP'25 (2025)
42. Omondiagbe, O.P., Licorish, S.A., MacDonell, S.G.: Features that predict the acceptability of Java and Javascript answers on stack overflow. In: EASE '19, pp. 101–110 (2019)
43. Procaci, T.B., Siqueira, S.W.M., Braz, M.H.L.B., Vasconcelos de Andrade, L.C.: How to find people who can help to answer a question? – analyses of metrics and machine learning in online communities. Comput. Hum. Behav. **51**, 664–673 (2015), computing for Human Learning, Behaviour and Collaboration in the Social and Mobile Networks Era
44. Randolph, K.A., Myers, L.L.: 35Inferential statistics. In: Basic Statistics in Multivariate Analysis. Oxford University Press, February 2013
45. Schroth, L., Obaidi, M., Specht, A., Klünder, J.: On the potentials of realtime sentiment analysis on text-based communication in software projects. In: Human-Centered Software Engineering. Springer, Cham (2022)
46. Schütze, H., Manning, C.D., Raghavan, P.: Introduction to information retrieval, vol. 39. Cambridge University Press Cambridge (2008)
47. Stapel, K., Knauss, E., Schneider, K.: Using flow to improve communication of requirements in globally distributed software projects. In: CIRCUS 2009, pp. 5–14 (2009)
48. Swillus, M., Zaidman, A.: Sentiment overflow in the testing stack: analyzing software testing posts on stack overflow. JSS **205**, 111804 (2023)
49. Treude, C., Barzilay, O., Storey, M.A.: How do programmers ask and answer questions on the web? (nier track). In: ICSE 2011, p. 804–807 (2011)

50. Uddin, G., Khomh, F.: Automatic mining of opinions expressed about apis in stack overflow. IEEE Trans. Softw. Eng. **47**(3) (2021)
51. Unterbusch, M., Sadeghi, M., Fischbach, J., Obaidi, M., Vogelsang, A.: Explanation needs in app reviews: taxonomy and automated detection. In: REW. IEEE (2023)
52. Vasilescu, B., Filkov, V., Serebrenik, A.: Stackoverflow and github: Associations between software development and crowdsourced knowledge. In: 2013 International Conference on Social Computing, pp. 188–195 (2013)
53. Wang, S., German, D.M., Chen, T.H., Tian, Y., Hassan, A.E.: Is reputation on stack overflow always a good indicator for users' expertise? no! In: ICSME, pp. 614–618 (2021)
54. Weisstein, E.W.: Bonferroni correction. Wolfram Research, Inc. (2004). Accessed 03.27.2024, 03:50 AM
55. Wohlin, C., Runeson, P., Höst, M., Ohlsson, M.C., Regnell, B., Wesslén, A.: Experimentation in Software Engineering. Springer, Heidelberg (2024)
56. Yan, L., Hwang, A., Wu, Z., Head, A.: Ivie: lightweight anchored explanations of just-generated code. In: Proceedings of the 2024 CHI Conference on Human Factors in Computing Systems (2024)
57. Zhang, T., Irsan, I.C., Thung, F., Lo, D.: Revisiting sentiment analysis for software engineering in the era of large language models. ACM Trans. Softw. Eng. Methodol. **34**(3) (Feb 2025)

User Feedback

FeClustRE: Hierarchical Clustering and Semantic Tagging of App Features from User Reviews

Max Tiessler[iD] and Quim Motger[(✉)][iD]

Department of Service and Information System Engineering, Universitat Politècnica de Catalunya, Barcelona, Spain
{max.tiessler,joaquim.motger}@upc.edu

Abstract. **[Context and motivation.]** Extracting features from mobile app reviews is important for multiple requirements engineering (RE) tasks, but noisy and ambiguous feedback makes it difficult to obtain interpretable insights. **[Question/problem.]** Syntactic approaches often miss semantic context, while LLM-based methods may miss fine-grained features and typically output flat, weakly organized feature lists, limiting interpretation and comparability. **[Principal ideas/results.]** We propose FeClustRE, a framework that combines hybrid feature extraction with auto-tuned hierarchical clustering and LLM-based semantic labeling to produce structured feature taxonomies. FeClustRE is evaluated through benchmarking on two annotated app review datasets, one expert-annotated and one crowdsourced, and through a sample study on reviews of generative AI assistant apps. The evaluation indicates that the hybrid extraction approach reduces missed features and achieves a stronger overall balance between precision and recall than single-method baselines. For feature structuring, the auto-tuned hierarchical clustering produces coherent multi-level taxonomies that remain stable under varying data volumes, and the LLM-generated cluster labels are generally semantically consistent and align with official app descriptions. **[Contribution.]** This paper contributes (1) FeClustRE, an open-source framework for feature extraction and taxonomy generation, (2) an auto-tuning clustering and labeling pipeline with a reproducible evaluation methodology, and (3) empirical evidence that combining syntactic and LLM-based extraction generates more complete and interpretable feature representations from app reviews.

Keywords: app stores · feature extraction · hierarchical clustering · large language models · semantic tagging · app reviews · requirements engineering

1 Introduction

Feature extraction (i.e., identifying user-visible functional attributes of a mobile app [5]) has gained significant attention over the past decade in the context of

R. Guizzardi and J. Araújo (Eds.): REFSQ 2026, LNCS 16497, pp. 145–160, 2026.
https://doi.org/10.1007/978-3-032-21423-2_10

app review mining. Requirements engineering (RE) has explored extended use cases derived from analysis of feature mentions, such as feature prioritization [16], competition analysis [4], and software evolution [1]. The state of the art in feature extraction is predominantly represented by syntactic-based approaches [5], which rely on syntactic structures and pattern-matching techniques to extract subsets of tokens within a user review referring to a particular app feature [8,10,14]. While efficient, replication studies have showcased several limitations in their correctness, such as overlap and ambiguity in syntactic patterns, limited precision and recall, and inability to capture contextual meaning [5,22,24]. These limitations motivate approaches that can better capture semantic context and remain robust to linguistic variability in reviews.

Meanwhile, large language models (LLMs) offer new opportunities to overcome the limited performance of traditional NLP tasks for RE practices [12]. Consequently, several studies have explored leveraging encoder-only LLMs like BERT [7] to improve feature extraction from app reviews [3,18,27]. In contrast to syntactic-based challenges, LLM-based feature extraction dynamically adapts to varied linguistic structures and leverages word embeddings that capture semantic nuances, excelling in context-based understanding through transformer architectures. More recently, generative LLMs such as GPT-4 and Llama-2 have also been investigated [23], demonstrating performance comparable to (or in some cases worse than) encoder-only LLMs such as BERT. However, even when extraction correctness improves, the resulting outputs are often still presented as flat feature lists, leaving open the question of how to organize features into interpretable structures.

In addition to correctness, the adoption of feature extraction tools in practice presents further challenges. Concerning interpretability, previous work output flat lists of features, potentially limiting their utility for developers seeking aggregated insights or inter-feature relationships to inform design decisions. This lack of structure is precisely a key limitation. The outputs remain flat and sometimes redundant, hiding semantic relationships between the features. To illustrate this, Fig. 1 shows how traditional methods generate unstructured feature lists, whereas organizing features into a structured, semantically coherent taxonomy with meaningful labels makes relationships clearer and easier to interpret.

Existing approaches either improve extraction correctness *or* provide limited grouping, but they typically do not offer an end-to-end, reproducible pipeline that jointly improves feature extraction and produces interpretable hierarchical taxonomies from noisy reviews.

To bridge this gap, we present *FeClustRE*, a framework for feature clustering and semantic tagging of mobile app review features via hierarchical taxonomies. The framework addresses this gap through an end-to-end solution, integrating multiple components into a unified workflow. Our contribution is three-fold. First, we design and implement a hybrid feature extraction pipeline that integrates syntactic and LLM-based state-of-the-art methods, and show that this combination reduces missed features while maintaining competitive

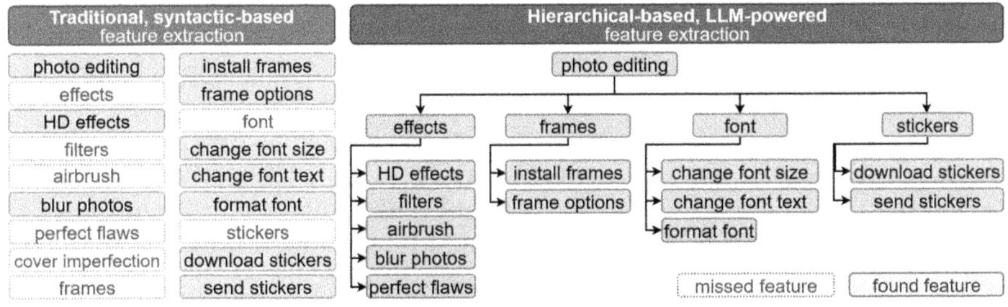

Fig. 1. Motivational example of FeClustRE

precision. Second, we develop an auto-tuning hierarchical clustering framework that automatically identifies optimal clustering parameters, creates semantically coherent taxonomies through automatic merging mechanisms, and generates meaningful cluster labels with an LLM-based semantic tagging; we further find that generated labels are generally semantically consistent and align with official app descriptions. Third, we provide an open-source implementation and a reproducible evaluation methodology to support replication and adoption in RE research.

Finally, our evaluation combines public datasets to benchmark the hybrid feature extraction correctness and a sample study on generative AI assistant app reviews to assess clustering quality, semantic coherence, and interpretability. All materials (code, data, prompts, and results) are publicly available in our replication package [25] (see also the *Data Availability Statement*). While we motivate interpretability as relevant for practitioners, validating developer utility through a user study is left as future work.

2 Related Work

Syntactic-based feature extraction methods rely on linguistic patterns such as part-of-speech (POS) structures [8–10,14]. However, replication studies reveal several performance limitations [5,22]. These methods are highly sensitive to dataset-specific syntactic patterns and often require extensive customization for different app categories, which limits their adaptability across domains [5]. They also lack the ability to capture semantic and contextual knowledge [22], leading to many false positives (e.g., *nice app*) and missed feature mentions (e.g., *synchronization*) [5]. Ambiguous or overlapping POS patterns often yield redundant or inaccurate extractions (e.g., *download stuff*) [22]. Performance also degrades in noisy text with typos, abbreviations, or slang (e.g., *focus functn*) [14]. Finally, syntactic methods frequently miss single-word (e.g., *note-taking*) and multi-noun features (e.g., *in-app purchases*), lowering overall recall [5].

To address some of these issues, solutions have turned to encoder-only LLMs, leveraging contextual embeddings to identify features based on semantic understanding [3,18,27]. While they overcome certain syntactic limitations, they introduce new challenges. LLM-based methods typically depend on domain-specific fine-tuning, as generic models underperform when applied to specialized app categories without adaptation [3]. Their performance also degrades on noisy data, where abbreviations or misspellings interfere with embeddings [27]. Moreover, they struggle with fine-grained features (e.g., *take off unwanted bits captured in the photo*), leading to low precision under exact or partial matching [18]. Rare or emerging features (e.g., *GPX track*) are also difficult to capture because they appear infrequently in training data [27]. Finally, encoder-only models often favor frequent patterns, biasing results toward common features while overlooking less frequent but important ones [18].

In addition, both syntactic and LLM-based approaches share limitations. They generally produce flat feature lists without meaningful organization. This makes it difficult for developers to identify user needs or to understand the feature set of an application as a whole. While some approaches either apply [10] or envision [2] topic modelling, these efforts are limited to grouping fine-grained features without providing semantic structure or hierarchical relationships. More recently, Jin et al. introduced a framework that automatically constructs multi-level feature trees from software artifact libraries by combining clustering algorithms with LLM-based summarization [13]. Unlike prior work, their contribution builds hierarchical structures, providing semantic organization and demonstrating improvements in artifact recommendation. However, its evaluation is centred on software artifacts rather than user-generated reviews, where input is noisier, domain-specific, and highly informal. Overall, prior work has problems handling noisy reviews, transferring across different app categories, capturing rare and detailed features, and producing structured outputs that are easy to interpret and compare across apps.

Despite advances, the practical application of feature extraction remains limited. Most methods are still evaluated in controlled settings [3, 8–10, 14, 18, 23, 27], with little focus on real-world use cases that turn extracted features into actionable insights. This gap is most evident beyond feature-based sentiment analysis, which remains the dominant application [5]. Promising alternatives such as app benchmarking [15] and competition analysis [6] require structured, interpretable feature insights. Yet current tools lack integrated visualization, cross-application comparison, and scalable architectures for large-scale data. Without frameworks that combine extraction, semantic organization, and interactive exploration, adoption remains limited, as practitioners need comprehensive solutions rather than isolated prototypes.

We address these gaps with FeClustRE by combining hybrid feature extraction with auto-tuned hierarchical clustering and LLM-based semantic labeling to produce interpretable taxonomies from noisy reviews in a reproducible, end-to-end pipeline.

3   System Design and Architecture

3.1   Research Goal

The goal of *FeClustRE* is to advance the state-of-the-art in feature extraction from app reviews by addressing two aspects: improving (1) the correctness of feature extraction methods, and (2) the structuring and interpretability of extracted features. To achieve these goals, and based on the challenges identified in Sect. 2, we propose the following research questions:

RQ₁. How does combining syntactic and LLM-based methods affect feature extraction correctness in app reviews?

RQ₂. How does hierarchical clustering help organize and interpret features extracted from app reviews?

To address **RQ₁**, we built on previous work to design a hybrid pipeline integrating a syntactic-based method and an LLM-based feature extraction method under a pre-processing stage. Given that feature extraction is a well-established task with publicly available benchmarks, we conducted a quantitative analysis on two annotated app review datasets. The specific evaluation settings and baselines are detailed in Sect. 4.

To address **RQ₂**, we designed and evaluated the performance of an auto-tuning hierarchical clustering framework combined with LLM semantic tagging over extracted features that are organized in interpretable taxonomies. This evaluation follows a two-fold strategy. First, we conducted a quantitative evaluation of our auto-tuning approach using clustering internal quality metrics [11]. Second, we qualitatively evaluated the semantic quality of LLM-generated taxonomy labels by computing semantic coherence scores for clusters and comparing top-ranked clusters against official Google Play store application descriptions [26].

3.2 System Architecture

In order to explore both research questions, we designed a three-stage pipeline within the FeClustRE framework. Figure 2 illustrates the pipeline design.

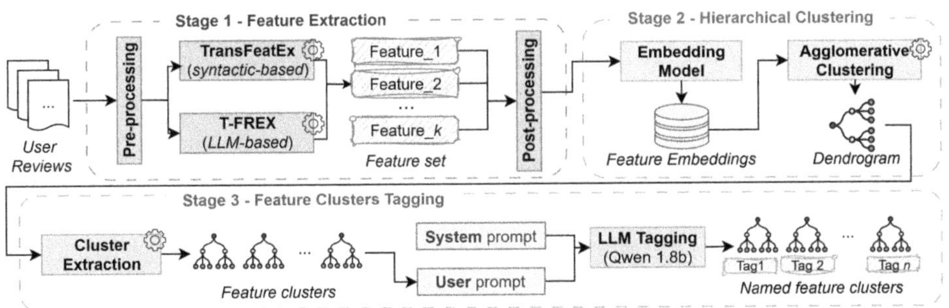

Fig. 2. FeClustRE three-stage pipeline.

Stage 1 Feature Extraction. Given a review set $\mathcal{R}$ as input, we extract features from the reviews using an ensemble of feature extraction methods. Based on the context of this research, we apply a hybrid approach that combines syntactic and LLM-based extraction, using two representative methods from our

---

Algorithm 1. Hierarchical Clustering with Auto-Tuning

Require:

    Feature set $\mathcal{F} = \{f_1, f_2, \ldots, f_n\}$, Embedding function e, Distance metric d, Linkage method λ

Ensure:

    Clustering candidates $\mathcal{C}$ with quality metrics

1: **(1) Compute Embeddings:** $\mathcal{E} \leftarrow e(\mathcal{F})$
2: **(2) Compute Affinity Matrix:** $\mathbf{A} \leftarrow \text{Affinity}(\mathcal{E}, d)$
3: **(3) Generate Linkage Matrix** $\mathbf{L} \leftarrow \text{Linkage}(\mathbf{A}, \lambda)$
4: **(4) Construct dendrogram** $\mathcal{D} \leftarrow \text{Dendrogram}(\mathbf{L})$
5: **(5) Auto-tune clustering:**
6: **for** threshold t in $[0.1, 0.9]$ **do**
7:     $clusters \leftarrow \text{Cut}(\mathcal{D}, t)$
8:     $silhouette \leftarrow \text{SilhouetteScore}(\mathcal{E}, clusters)$
9:     $davies\_bouldin \leftarrow \text{DaviesBouldinScore}(\mathcal{E}, clusters)$
10:     $score \leftarrow \text{CompositeScore}(silhouette, davies\_bouldin, |clusters|)$
11:     $\mathcal{C} \leftarrow \mathcal{C} \cup \{(clusters, score, metrics)\}$
12: **end for**
13: **return** $\mathcal{C}$

---

previous work: (1) for the syntactic method, we use TransFeatEx [9], an open-source tool that applies syntactic strategies [5] enhanced with encoder-only LLMs to provide linguistic annotations such as POS tags, and (2) for the LLM-based method, we use T-FREX [18], a fine-tuned encoder-only model for token classification. Specifically, we employ the BERT-base version of T-FREX for its balance between correctness and efficiency. Before feature extraction, reviews are pre-processed by removing emojis, filtering URLs, and applying normalization, while keeping punctuation for feature boundary detection. After extraction, we apply a post-processing step to normalize and deduplicate features.

The processed review set $\mathcal{R}$ is finally transformed into a feature set $\mathcal{F} = \{f_1, f_2, \ldots, f_n\}$.

Stage 2 Hierarchical Clustering. The second stage applies Algorithm 1, which describes the hierarchical agglomerative clustering process carried out for the set of features $\mathcal{F}$ obtained in the previous stage. First, the features in $\mathcal{F}$ are embedded in a high-dimensional space using configurable embedding models (e.g., Sentence-BERT [21], Sentence-T5 [19]) to generate semantic embeddings $\mathcal{E}$. Second, an affinity matrix $\mathbf{A}$ is computed using cosine dissimilarity metric d, which measures the semantic distance between each pair of features. Third, average linkage method λ is applied to $\mathbf{A}$, which iteratively merges the closest clusters based on the average pairwise distance between their members, producing a linkage matrix $\mathbf{L}$ that encodes the hierarchical structure of $\mathcal{F}$. Fourth, $\mathbf{L}$ is used to construct a complete dendrogram $\mathcal{D}$ of the set of features $\mathcal{F}$. The system then applies an auto-tuning mechanism that evaluates multiple height thresholds to cut $\mathcal{D}$ into clustering candidates, assessing each configuration using silhou-

---

Algorithm 2. LLM Semantic Tagging and Taxonomy Merging

Require: Selected clustering $\mathcal{C} = \{C_1, C_2, \ldots, C_k\}$, feature set $\mathcal{F}$, large language model g, similarity threshold σ

Ensure: Consolidated taxonomies $\mathcal{T} = \{T_1, T_2, \ldots, T_m\}$

1: **(1) Semantic Labeling:**
2: **for** each cluster $C_j \in \mathcal{C}$ **do**
3:     Retrieve feature subset $\mathcal{F}_j \subset \mathcal{F}$ assigned to C_j
4:     Generate descriptive label $l_j \leftarrow g(\mathcal{F}_j)$ using few-shot prompting
5:     Create mini-taxonomy: $T_j \leftarrow \text{BuildHierarchy}(\mathcal{F}_j, l_j)$
6: **end for**
7: **(2) Taxonomy Merging:**
8: **for** each pair (T_i, T_j) of mini-taxonomies **do**
9:     $similarity \leftarrow \text{CosineSimilarity}(\text{embed}(l_i), \text{embed}(l_j))$
10:     **if** $similarity \geq \sigma$ **then**
11:         $T_{\text{merged}} \leftarrow \text{MergeTaxonomies}(T_i, T_j)$
12:         Remove T_i, T_j and add T_{merged} to $\mathcal{T}$
13:     **end if**
14: **end for**
15: **return** $\mathcal{T}$

---

ette score and Davies-Bouldin index [11] to identify optimal cluster arrangements through composite scoring. Higher silhouette scores indicate denser, well-separated clusters, while lower Davies-Bouldin index values reflect more cohesive and distinct feature groupings. The result of this stage is a set of clustering candidates $\mathcal{C}$.

Stage 3 Feature Clusters Tagging. In the third stage, the framework automatically selects the most suitable clustering configuration from the candidate set $\mathcal{C}$ generated in the previous stage. To accommodate different usage scenarios, *FeClustRE* provides three strategies that users can select from: (1) the *silhouette* strategy prioritizes internal cluster coherence by selecting candidates with the highest silhouette score; (2) the *balanced* strategy combines multiple quality metrics, including silhouette score, inverted Davies-Bouldin score, and penalties for cluster count and cluster size; and (3) the *conservative* strategy prioritizes stability by promoting fewer, larger clusters with strong cohesion. Once a clustering configuration is selected, the pipeline applies LLM semantic tagging and taxonomy merging to create feature taxonomies, as described in Algorithm 2.

First, the selected clustering configuration provides a set of clusters $\mathcal{C} = \{C_1, C_2, \ldots, C_k\}$, where each cluster C_j contains semantically related features from the feature set $\mathcal{F}$. Second, for each cluster C_j, the corresponding feature subset $\mathcal{F}_j$ is passed to a generative LLM g (e.g., Qwen 1.8b), which generates a descriptive label l_j representing the semantic category of the cluster using few-shot prompting[1] with domain-specific examples from related apps (see

---

[1] Prompt template and examples available in the replication package.

Sect. 4.2). We adopt few-shot prompting (rather than zero-shot or other prompt-only strategies) to improve label consistency and reduce sensitivity to wording and app-specific terminology without relying on expert annotation.

Third, the labelled clusters are converted into small taxonomies by building hierarchical tree structures that preserve internal feature relationships. Fourth, a merging mechanism evaluates semantic similarity between taxonomies, considering both structural alignment and label embeddings. Taxonomies that exceed a similarity threshold σ, which can be defined by domain experts, are automatically merged, with the larger taxonomy serving as the primary structure and smaller ones integrated as sub-branches.

The resulting output is a set of taxonomies $\mathcal{T} = \{T_1, T_2, \ldots, T_m\}$ with semantic labels and hierarchical relationships, stored in a graph database for efficient querying and visualization.

4   Evaluation Design

4.1   Experimental Setting

To address $\mathbf{RQ_1}$, we perform a controlled comparison to validate the effectiveness of our hybrid feature extraction approach across three configurations: (1) a syntactic-based baseline using TransFeatEx, (2) an LLM-based baseline using T-FREX, and (3) our hybrid approach integrating both methods. Each method is evaluated against the same feature extraction benchmarks (see Sect. 4.2) using a common preprocessing pipeline including text cleaning, normalization, and tokenization. Performance was measured through precision, recall, and F-score calculated using the weighting factor $\beta = 2.385$, as proposed for feature extraction tasks in previous work [18].

To address $\mathbf{RQ_2}$, we evaluate the full auto-tuning hierarchical clustering framework with LLM semantic tagging through a two-step process: (1) quantitative analysis of clustering quality using internal metrics (e.g., silhouette score and Davies-Bouldin index), together with an assessment of the auto-tuning behavior and (2) a qualitative semantic assessment of the LLM-generated taxonomy labels. Specifically, we compute semantic coherence scores for clusters based on cosine similarity between embeddings of LLM-generated cluster labels and their member features, and use this ranking to identify top-ranked clusters for comparison against the official Google Play application descriptions. Guided by this ranking, we inspected one top-ranked cluster per app (7 clusters in total). One author shared the cluster label and a small set of representative features with the other author, and both authors independently confirmed that the label was descriptive and consistent with the app's official Google Play description. We considered a cluster aligned if its label and example features described a function explicitly mentioned in the description or a clear paraphrase of it.

4.2   Data Collection and Datasets

For $\mathbf{RQ_1}$ we established feature extraction benchmarks from mobile app reviews to ensure a robust validation of our hybrid approach. The first dataset (*expert*) contains 2,062 reviews [5], annotated by developers through multiple iterations to establish a reliable ground truth for feature extraction. The second dataset (*crowdsourced*) consists of 27,780 app reviews [18], annotated via a label transfer mechanism that leverages crowdsourced feature annotations from real users in a mobile app recommender platform.

For $\mathbf{RQ_2}$, we conducted a sample study evaluation on *generative LLM-based chatbot* mobile apps to evaluate our framework on a contemporary, evolving domain. Generative LLM-based chatbots (e.g., ChatGPT) leverage LLMs to provide conversational support, task automation, and information retrieval [20]. The selection of mobile apps was guided by four criteria: (*i*) popularity, ensuring substantial review volumes [12]; (*ii*) disruptive market impact, as they redefine assistant capabilities; (*iii*) relevance for feature discovery, through frequent introduction of novel functionalities; and (*iv*) potential for market analysis, as this segment reflects emerging trends and user demands. Based on these criteria, we selected seven representative apps and collected their user reviews from Google Play over a one-month span: OpenAI's ChatGPT (119,892 reviews), Google's Gemini (26,883), Microsoft's Copilot (5,323), Perplexity by Sonar (3,818), DeepSeek AI Assistant (1,334), Claude by Anthropic (882), and Le Chat by Mistral (75). Reviews were gathered on July 17th, 2025 using an app review collection service integrating multiple mobile sources [17].

To evaluate the effect of data quantity on the quality of the framework's results, and to validate that both small and large samples can produce reliable results while also assessing how quality improves as more data are fed into the pipeline, we adopted two sampling strategies: (1) subsets of 2K and (2) 50K reviews. These subsets were generated at runtime from the full dataset using stratified sampling to preserve app-level proportions.

Finally, to perform semantic taxonomy tagging without relying on expert annotation, we used a few-shot prompting approach based on features extracted from official developer descriptions. These descriptions, defined by the app developers themselves, serve as a close approximation to a gold standard. The features were manually extracted from the application descriptions to build training examples for the few-shot prompts, and the validation was manually reviewed independently by both authors. The prompts included examples from multiple apps within the same market segment to guide the model in generating contextually appropriate and semantically consistent category names.

5   Results

5.1   Feature Extraction Correctness (RQ$_1$)

Table 1 reports the correctness metrics for our hybrid feature extraction approach compared to syntactic-based (TransFeatEx) and LLM-based (T-FREX) baselines. We used the feature matching method proposed by Dabrowski et al. [5], which considers features as matching if one is identical to or a subset of the other, with an allowed length difference of up to n words: $n = 0$ for exact matches, $n = 1$ for minor differences, and $n = 2$ for slightly larger variations.

Table 1. Correctness results for feature extraction

Dataset	Method	Exact (n = 0)			Partial 1 (n = 1)			Partial 2 (n = 2)		
		P	R	F_β	P	R	F_β	P	R	F_β
Expert	**Syntactic**	0.027	0.022	0.023	0.197	0.165	0.169	0.248	0.208	0.213
	LLM	**0.211**	0.078	0.086	**0.386**	0.142	0.157	**0.471**	0.174	0.192
	Hybrid	0.082	**0.099**	**0.096**	0.238	**0.286**	**0.278**	0.291	**0.348**	**0.338**
Crowd.	**Syntactic**	0.022	0.021	0.021	0.162	0.140	0.143	0.263	0.226	0.231
	LLM	**0.722**	0.661	0.669	**0.739**	0.676	0.685	**0.739**	0.677	0.685
	Hybrid	0.472	**0.746**	**0.686**	0.489	**0.774**	**0.712**	0.496	**0.787**	**0.724**
Avg.	**Syntactic**	0.025	0.022	0.022	0.180	0.153	0.156	0.256	0.217	0.222
	LLM	**0.467**	0.370	0.378	**0.563**	0.409	0.421	**0.605**	0.426	0.439
	Hybrid	0.277	**0.423**	**0.391**	0.364	**0.530**	**0.495**	0.394	**0.568**	**0.531**

Results demonstrate that our hybrid method consistently achieves the highest recall across all datasets and evaluation settings, confirming the hypothesis that combining syntactic and LLM-based approaches significantly reduces missed features (false negatives). While the LLM-based method in isolation achieves higher precision, the hybrid setting achieves the highest balanced F-measure across all settings. For partial matches, which represent practical feature extraction scenarios, the hybrid method achieves the best F-score performance on both datasets, leading to an average F-score of 0.495 (n = 1) and 0.531 (n = 2).

Takeaway 1. Hybrid feature extraction combining syntactic and LLM-based methods can potentially improve feature correctness, particularly by reducing the amount of false negatives.

5.2   Feature Clustering Interpretability (RQ$_2$)

Table 2 summarizes clustering quality and granularity for LLM-based chatbot apps across different feature extraction models and embeddings. The results reveal three complementary perspectives. TransFeatEx achieves the highest cohesion/separation (silhouette up to 0.28) but produces coarser taxonomies with fewer clusters (18 to 24 per application), making it suitable for high-level analysis. T-FREX strikes a balance, with larger numbers of clusters (60 to 227) and stable cohesion. The hybrid setting, while slightly below TransFeatEx in cohesion (silhouette $\sim$0.19), generates much richer taxonomies (80–301 clusters), making them particularly effective for practitioners needing fine-grained feature understanding. This aligns with the insights from RQ$_1$, where the hybrid approach offered the most balanced performance, achieving high recall and strong overall F-measure while maintaining competitive precision.

On the other hand, the auto-tuning mechanism is particularly valuable in eliminating manual parameter selection while maintaining clustering quality

Table 2. Clustering performance at 2K vs. 50K samples

Model	Embedding	Sample	Silhouette	Davies-B	Clusters
Hybrid	AllMiniLM	2K	0.19 ± 0.02	0.96	88
		50K	0.19 ± 0.03	0.79	273
Hybrid	Sentence-T5	2K	0.18 ± 0.01	1.01	80
		50K	0.19 ± 0.03	0.76	301
T-FREX	AllMiniLM	2K	0.18 ± 0.04	0.91	69
		50K	0.19 ± 0.05	0.87	227
T-FREX	Sentence-T5	2K	0.18 ± 0.04	0.92	60
		50K	0.19 ± 0.05	0.87	227
TransFeatEx	AllMiniLM	2K	0.20 ± 0.04	0.96	19
		50K	0.28 ± 0.14	0.82	24
TransFeatEx	Sentence-T5	2K	0.19 ± 0.04	0.96	19
		50K	0.28 ± 0.14	0.82	24

across different app categories and dataset sizes. In our experiments, it generated between 80 and 301 clusters while keeping silhouette scores stable (around 0.19). This indicates that the framework is robust to varying feature densities and semantic complexities across different applications.

Takeaway 2. Hierarchical clustering with hybrid feature extraction enabled with auto-tuning settings allows different feature-level clustering granularities, facilitating domain and use case adaptation.

Concerning data quantity, TransFeatEx strengthens cohesion with more data (silhouette 0.19 to 0.28) while maintaining compact taxonomies (19 to 24 clusters). T-FREX maintains stable cohesion but substantially increases granularity (69 to 227 clusters). Hybrid extraction show the largest growth in detail while holding cohesion steady (around 0.19), expanding from 80 to more than 270 clusters. This progression shows that scaling data improves both cohesion and granularity. However, results with a small subset of reviews (2K) produce comparable internal cohesion and cluster distinctiveness scores, showcasing that FeClustRE is also applicable in contexts with a small number of reviews.

Takeaway 3. Larger review datasets improve internal cluster cohesion and external distinctiveness. However, FeClustRE can still achieve comparable results with limited review data.

From a structural perspective, the taxonomies averaged a depth of 3.41 and 9.39 leaves, yielding hierarchies that extended well beyond simple flat lists. Most structures were shallow (2–5 levels), although a few reached greater depth. Broad domains produced larger taxonomies (e.g., *image generation*, depth 11 with 438 leaves; *language translation*, depth 10 with 241 leaves), whereas narrower domains resulted in more compact structures (e.g., *translation assistant*, depth 4 with 12 leaves). Notably, no empty taxonomies were produced, underscoring the robustness of the pipeline.

Takeaway 4. The framework generates interpretable multi-level taxonomies that adapt to domain scope, supporting both high-level overviews and fine-grained feature analysis, while ensuring robust outputs across applications.

Table 3. Qualitative analysis of top semantically ranked clusters per app.

App	#C	Cluster	#F	Features	Match
ChatGPT	2168	Advice	12	*advise, advice, guiding, guidance, ...*	Guidance and recommendations
Claude	517	AI-assisted writing support	8	*computer languages, software development, programming, code generation, coding, ...*	Programming and code assistance
DeepSeek	676	AI interface	18	*ai apps, ai interface, ai chat, coding, multi languages, learning, intelligence, ...*	AI interaction and learning
Google Gemini	1571	Activities meetings working	13	*trips, gym, meet, office, working, tasks, activities, meetings, ...*	Task and activity management
Le Chat	144	Bot	5	*prompt, confirmation, bot, chat, message*	Chat interaction
Microsoft Copilot	1115	AI applications	12	*ai support, ai companion, ai search, ai platform, ai chat, ai assistant, ...*	AI tool variety
Perplexity	936	Analysis and visualization	8	*chart, data, statistics, analysis, data analysis, ...*	Data analysis and charts

For qualitative validation, we first computed semantic coherence scores for all clusters by measuring cosine similarity between embeddings of LLM-generated cluster labels and their member features. We then compared the top-ranked clusters against the official Google Play App Store application descriptions. Table 3 presents one best-scoring cluster per app, showing: (1) the mean number of clusters generated when analyzing the full dataset with Hybrid feature extraction (combining T-FREX and TransFeatEx) and the balanced clustering strategy (2) the best-scoring cluster name, (3) a representative (non-exhaustive) list of features, and (4) the corresponding match from the official documentation. Due to space constraints, these examples are illustrative and not intended to represent the full distribution of cluster quality.

Figure 3 illustrates hierarchical structures for one of the high-scoring clusters. The *AI-Assisted Communication* taxonomy organizes AI interaction and

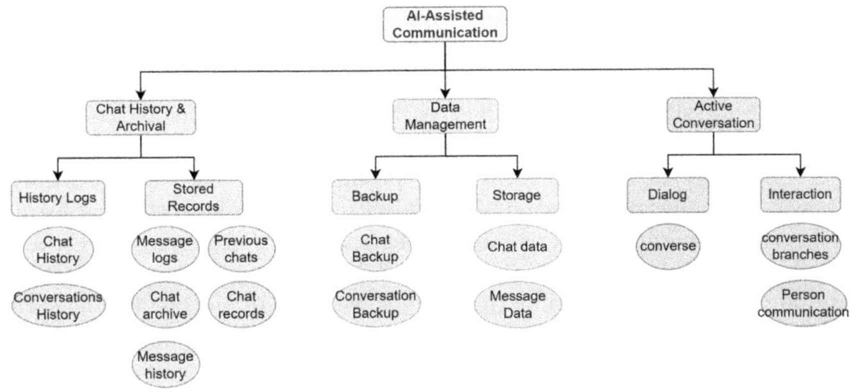

Fig. 3. Extracted generated taxonomy for a high semantic scoring cluster.

capability features, spanning from user-facing applications and communication tools to the underlying programming languages and intelligence technologies. The intermediate nodes represent subcategories automatically tagged by the LLM to capture thematic groupings, and the leaf nodes correspond to concrete features extracted from reviews.

While the resulting taxonomies in this example generally align well with intuitive semantic relations, minor inconsistencies appear. For example, *"message history"* might better fit under history logs, and the boundary between *"dialog"* and *"interaction"* is somewhat blurred. These small deviations reflect the inherent limitations of hierarchical clustering, but overall the taxonomy remains coherent and meaningful from a human–computer interaction perspective.

Takeaway 5. Structured feature taxonomies can be aligned with official mobile app documentation, demonstrating the applicability of *FeClustRE* in real-world scenarios and enabling better interpretation by RE practitioners.

Due to space constraints, the complete taxonomies and results are available in our replication package.

6   Discussion

Our results suggest that FeClustRE's main practical value is not only higher extraction recall (RQ1), but also producing hierarchical feature structures that support both overall benchmarking and fine-grained requirements exploration (RQ2). The hybrid pipeline trades some internal cohesion (i.e., silhouette score) for richer taxonomies (i.e., more leaves), which can be desirable when requirements engineers or product owners need detailed feature coverage rather than compact summaries. However, the approach may be less reliable when review volumes are very small, when domains contain highly specific terminology, or when feature mentions within user reviews are sparse. In such cases, clustering and labeling can become unstable or yield generic tags. While these hierarchical structures are intended to support RE tasks (e.g., feature prioritization and competitor analysis), validating their usefulness for real stakeholders requires a dedicated user study, left as future work. Exploring alternative prompting designs (e.g., zero-shot or reasoning-style prompts) is also left for future work.

Concerning construct and design validity, the framework's performance depends on the quality of initial feature extraction, with TransFeatEx and T-FREX chosen as representative syntactic- and LLM-based methods. The hybrid design may compound individual method errors, though our results suggest that the benefits outweigh these risks. Larger datasets increase computational cost but also return richer and more interpretable taxonomies, justifying this trade-off. For embeddings, we employed Sentence-BERT and T5-Sentence, and used silhouette score and Davies-Bouldin index for clustering evaluation; while standard, these do not capture all aspects of interpretability. Parameter sensitivity in hierarchical clustering (cut-off τ, sibling s_t) and few-shot prompt design are additional sources of variation. The few-shot strategy, while effective with 3–5 examples per domain, may benefit from more systematic optimization across categories.

Concerning external validity, annotation biases in expert and crowdsourced datasets for RQ_1 may affect evaluation outcomes, as annotation processes introduce artifacts. Manual cluster inspection by the authors also introduces evaluator bias, partially mitigated through alignment with official documentation; independent third-party evaluation would further strengthen objectivity. Our focus on generative LLM-based chatbot apps limits generalizability, as their technical terminology and evolving feature sets may differ from other domains.

Finally, concerning conclusion validity, our evaluation design introduces further limitations. The choice of correctness scores (P, R, F_β) and clustering metrics reflects our construct decisions and may emphasize certain aspects of performance. The 2K vs. 50K sampling strategies allowed us to examine data quantity effects, but results could vary under other schemes. The dataset's temporal scope (July 2025) and relatively small number of apps (seven) also restrict generalizability. Nevertheless, with 158,207 reviews, the dataset provides substantial evidence to support the robustness of our evaluation.

7   Conclusions

In this work, we proposed a hybrid method that combines syntactic feature extraction with LLM-based analysis and hierarchical clustering to improve correctness and interpretability in app review feature mining. Our contribution includes: (1) a hybrid framework combining syntactic precision with semantic understanding through automated clustering and LLM tagging, (2) an auto-tuning mechanism for optimal cluster configuration with a comprehensive evaluation methodology, and (3) an open-source implementation with graph-based storage.

Experimental validation confirms that our hybrid approach achieves the best balance of performance, with consistently higher recall and F_β scores compared to syntactic or LLM-only baselines. The auto-tuning component avoids manual parameter setting and adapts across app categories and dataset sizes, producing coherent structures from both small and large-scale datasets. Moreover, the hybrid configuration generated richer and more fine-grained taxonomies while maintaining stable clustering quality.

Our evaluation of LLM-based semantic tagging showed high distinctiveness and coherence of taxonomy labels, and qualitative validation against Google Play documentation indicated that cluster labels align with established feature descriptions. The resulting taxonomies capture semantically related features and exhibit multi-level structures, organizing concepts from general categories down to specific functionalities.

FeClustRE thus provides value for requirements engineering tasks through interpretable feature taxonomies and interactive usage. Current limitations include dependency on initial feature extraction quality, computational complexity for large-scale datasets, and sensitivity to clustering parameters. Future work will explore optimal configurations across app categories, domain-dependent thresholds for ranking clusters, and extending applicability to complex RE tasks such as competition and market analysis, further improving the utility and robust

Acknowledgments. This work was supported by Grant PID2024-156019OB-I00 funded by MICIU/AEI/10.13039/501100011033 and by ERDF, EU.

Data Availability Statement. Full source code, datasets, clusters, prompts, and evaluation reports are available in a replication package https://doi.org/10.5281/zenodo.17372435. Additionally, a GitHub repository is also available https://github.com/nlp4se/FeClustRE.

References

1. Al-Hawari, A., et al.: Classification of application reviews into software maintenance tasks using data mining techniques. Software Quality J. **29**(3) (2021)
2. Alam, K.A., et al.: A data-driven approach for mining software features based on similar app descriptions and user reviews analysis. In: Proceedings of the 39th IEEE/ACM International Conference on Automated Software Engineering (2024)
3. de Araújo, A.F., Marcacini, R.M.: Re-bert: automatic extraction of software requirements from app reviews using bert language model. In: Proceedings of the 36th Annual ACM Symposium on Applied Computing (2021)
4. Assi, M., et al.: Featcompare: Feature comparison for competing mobile apps leveraging user reviews. Empirical Softw. Eng. (2021)
5. Dabrowski, J., et al.: Mining and searching app reviews for requirements engineering: Evaluation and replication studies. Information Systems (2023)
6. Dalpiaz, F., et al.: Re-swot: From user feedback to requirements via competitor analysis. In: Requirements Engineering: Foundation for Software Quality (2019)
7. Devlin, J., et al.: BERT: pre-training of deep bidirectional transformers for language understanding. CoRR (2018). http://arxiv.org/abs/1810.04805

8. Dragoni, M., Federici, M., Rexha, A.: An unsupervised aspect extraction strategy for monitoring real-time reviews stream. Information Processing & Management (2019)
9. Gallego, A., Motger, Q., Franch, X., Marco, J.: TransFeatEx: a NLP pipeline for feature extraction. In: Joint Proceedings of REFSQ-2023 Workshops, Doctoral Symposium, Posters & Tools Track and Journal Early Feedback (2023)
10. Guzman, E., Maalej, W.: How do users like this feature? a fine grained sentiment analysis of app reviews. In: 2014 IEEE 22nd International Requirements Engineering Conference (RE) (2014)
11. Heumann, J., other: Reassessing taxonomy-based data clustering: Unveiling insights and guidelines for application. Decision Support Systems (2024)
12. Hou, X., et al.: Large language models for software engineering: A systematic literature review. ACM Trans. Softw. Eng, Methodol. (2024)
13. Jin, X., et al.: FTBUILDER: Automatic multi-level feature tree construction via clustering and large language models (2025), https://arxiv.org/abs/2506.03946
14. Johann, T., et al.: Safe: A simple approach for feature extraction from app descriptions and app reviews. In: International Requirements Engineering Conference (2017)
15. de Lima, V.M., de Araújo, A.F., Marcacini, R.M.: Temporal dynamics of requirements engineering from mobile app reviews. PeerJ Comput. Sci. (2022)
16. Malgaonkar, S., Licorish, S.A., Savarimuthu, B.T.R.: Prioritizing user concerns in app reviews – a study of requests for new features, enhancements and bug fixes. Inf. Softw. Technol. **144** (2022)
17. Motger, Q., et al.: MApp-KG: Mobile App Knowledge Graph for Document-Based Feature Knowledge Generation. In: Intelligent Information Systems (2024)
18. Motger, Q., et al.: Leveraging encoder-only large language models for mobile app review feature extraction. Empirical Softw, Engg (2025)
19. Ni, J., et al.: Sentence-t5: Scalable sentence encoders from pre-trained text-to-text models (2021). https://arxiv.org/abs/2108.08877
20. Ray, P.P.: Chatgpt: A comprehensive review on background, applications, key challenges, bias, ethics, limitations and future scope. Internet of Things and Cyber-Physical Systems (2023)
21. Reimers, N., Gurevych, I.: Sentence-bert: Sentence embeddings using siamese bert-networks (2019). https://arxiv.org/abs/1908.10084
22. Shah, F.A., Sirts, K., Pfahl, D.: Is the SAFE approach too simple for app feature extraction? a replication study. In: Knauss, E., Goedicke, M. (eds.) REFSQ 2019. LNCS, vol. 11412, pp. 21–36. Springer, Cham (2019). https://doi.org/10.1007/978-3-030-15538-4_2
23. Shah, F.A., et al.: How effectively do llms extract feature-sentiment pairs from app reviews? In: Requirements Engineering: Foundation for Software Quality (2025)
24. Sorathiya, A., Ginde, G.: Towards extracting software requirements from app reviews using seq2seq framework (2025). https://arxiv.org/abs/2507.09039
25. Tiessler, M., Motger, Q.: FeClustRE: Replication package (2025). https://doi.org/10.5281/zenodo.17372435, https://doi.org/10.5281/zenodo.17372435, code, datasets, prompts, and evaluation results
26. Unterkalmsteiner, M., Abdeen, W.: A compendium and evaluation of taxonomy quality attributes. Expert Systems (2023)
27. Wu, H., Deng, W., Niu, X., Nie, C.: Identifying key features from app user reviews. In: International Conference on Software Engineering (2021)

From Online User Feedback to Requirements: Evaluating Large Language Models for Classification and Specification Tasks

Manjeshwar Aniruddh Mallya[1], Alessio Ferrari[2] (iD),
Mohammad Amin Zadenoori[3] (iD), and Jacek Dąbrowski[1(✉)] (iD)

[1] Lero, The Research Ireland Centre for Software, University of Limerick, Limerick, Ireland
`jacek.dabrowski@lero.ie`
[2] University College Dublin (UCD), Dublin, Ireland
`alessio.ferrari@ucd.ie`
[3] University of Padova, Padova, Italy
`amin.zadenoori@unipd.it`

Abstract. **[Context and Motivation]** Online user feedback provides valuable information to support requirements engineering (RE). However, analysing online user feedback is challenging due to its large volume and noise. Large language models (LLMs) show strong potential to automate this process and outperform previous techniques. They can also enable new tasks, such as generating requirements specification. However, existing work largely focuses on large proprietary models. Consequently, lightweight open-source LLMs remain underexplored for feedback-driven RE. **[Question/Problem]** In particular, existing studies offer limited empirical evidence, lack thorough evaluation, and rarely provide replication packages, undermining validity and reproducibility. **[Principal Idea/Results]** We evaluate five lightweight open-source LLMs on three RE tasks: NFR classification, user request classification, and requirements specification generation. Classification performance was measured on two feedback datasets, and specification quality via human evaluation. LLMs achieved moderate-to-high classification accuracy (F1 $\approx$ 0.47–0.68) and moderately high specification quality (mean $\approx$ 3/5). **[Contributions]** We newly explore lightweight open-source LLMs for feedback-driven requirements development. Our contributions are: (i) an empirical evaluation of lightweight LLMs on three RE tasks, (ii) a replication package, and (iii) insights into their capabilities and limitations for RE.

Keywords: Requirements Engineering · User Feedback · Empirical Study · AI4RE · NLP · Mining Software Repositories · Large Language Models

1 Introduction

Online user feedback is a valuable source of information that supports various requirements engineering (RE) tasks [12,15]. Such feedback often provides

R. Guizzardi and J. Araújo (Eds.): REFSQ 2026, LNCS 16497, pp. 161–177, 2026.
https://doi.org/10.1007/978-3-032-21423-2_11

insights into bug reports, feature requests, and non-functional requirements (NFRs) [11]. However, manually analyzing this feedback is difficult because of its large volume and noisy nature [2,28]. Automating this analysis could help practitioners identify user needs and document requirements more effectively.

Numerous approaches have been proposed to analyze user feedback using natural language processing (NLP) and machine learning (ML) techniques for tasks such as classification and opinion mining [11,13]. However, these methods often overlook key RE tasks, such as generating software requirements specification (SRS); their effectiveness remains limited in tasks like NFR categorization, essential for addressing software quality attributes such as security and usability [17].

Recent advances in large language models (LLMs) create new opportunities to address these limitations [4,14,31]. LLMs perform well in classification [3], summarization, and text generation [8,19]. Their use in RE has been explored for tasks such as traceability and ambiguity detection but remains limited for leveraging user feedback, particularly for generating requirements specification [33].

Moreover, existing work has primarily focused on large proprietary language models [33]. Consequently, the potential of lightweight open-source models for feedback-driven RE remains insufficiently explored. Lightweight LLMs are particularly relevant in this context because they can be deployed locally, reducing privacy and compliance concerns, and require fewer computational resources [34]. This makes them more cost-effective and accessible to practitioners as well as better suited for integration into real-world RE workflows. Beyond model selection, a second major limitation is that most existing studies lack systematic evaluation or publicly available replication packages, which significantly limits reproducibility [1,11].

The goal of this research is to address prior limitations and explore lightweight open-source LLMs for automating online user feedback analysis in support of RE tasks. More specifically, we empirically evaluate five lightweight open-source LLMs (i.e., Llama 2, Llama 3, Mistral, Gemma 2, and Phi-3 Mini) using five prompting strategies on three RE tasks: classifying feedback by NFR type, classifying by user request type, and generating requirements specification. Classification uses two annotated user feedback datasets, while specification quality is assessed through human evaluation.

The main contributions are: (i) an empirical study of lightweight open-source LLMs on three RE tasks using user feedback, (ii) a replication package [26], and (iii) insights into the capabilities and limits of lightweight LLMs in RE. To our knowledge, this is the first empirical study of lightweight LLMs for feedback-driven requirements development, supported by a replication package [11,33].

The remainder of this paper is as follows. Section 2 introduces the terminology and problem, followed by an overview of the selected LLMs and prompting strategies. Section 3 presents the motivating scenarios, Sect. 4 details the study design, and Sect. 5 reports the results. Section 6 discusses the findings and, Sect. 7 details threats to validity. Section 8 reviews related work, and Sect. 9 concludes the paper.

2   Background

We now define key terms and formulate the problems of user feedback classification and requirements specification. We also provide a concise illustrative example and introduce background on the LLMs used in our study.

2.1   Terminology and Problem Formulation

Definition 1 (User Feedback). A user feedback instance is denoted as r, representing a textual message written by a user about an application. The set of all feedback messages for an application a is $R = \{r_1, r_2, ..., r_n\}$.

This study focuses on app reviews, a form of user feedback from mobile platforms (e.g., Google Play Store). Such feedback conveys diverse information useful for RE; in this work, we particularly focus on user requests and NFRs.

Definition 2 (User Request). A user request t_{UR} is an expressed intent in a feedback instance, which can be of a type *feature request*, or *bug report*.

Definition 3 (Non-functional Requirement). A non-functional requirement t_{NFR} is a reference in a feedback instance to one of the eight quality attributes of the application (e.g., *usability*) as defined in ISO/IEC 25010 [20].

Our study addresses two main problems: user feedback classification and requirements specification, as defined below.

Problem 1 (User Feedback Classification). Given a set of user feedback instances $R = \{r\}$ for an application a, find a multi-set $C = \{t\}$, where t is an information type assigned to a feedback instance $r \in R$. The type classification is performed either on user-request types t_{UR} or on NFR types t_{NFR}, each with an additional *other* category to capture feedback outside these types.

Problem 2 (Requirements Specification Generation). Given a set of user feedback instances $R = \{r\}$ for an application a and their associated information types $C = \{t\}$, generate a set of requirement statement $S = \{s\}$, where each s is a written statement that formalizes or summarizes the user needs expressed in one or more feedback instances $r \in R$.

Illustrative Example. Let $R = \{r_1, r_2, r_3\}$ be a set of user feedback instances for an application a, where r_1 states "The app crashes when saving a form", r_2 states "I want the app to automatically save my progress", and r_3 states "The app responds very slowly when opening large files". According to Problem 1, the resulting multi-set of information types is $C = \{t_1, t_2, t_3\}$, where $t_1 = $ *bug report*, as r_1 reports incorrect system behavior; $t_2 = $ *feature request*, as r_2 explicitly expresses a desired functionality; and $t_3 = $ *performance* NFR, as r_3 refers to system response time. Following Problem 2, a generated requirements specification in the form of a user story derived from r_2 is s: *"As a user, I want the app to automatically save my progress so that I do not lose data."*

Table 1. Lightweight open-source LLMs used in our study.

Model	Developer	Parameters	Context Window	Usage
Llama 2	Meta AI	7B	4K	Research
Llama 3	Meta AI	8B	8K	Research
Mistral	Mistral AI	7B	8K	Open
Gemma 2	Google DeepMind	9B	8K	Open
Phi-3 Mini	Microsoft	3.8B	4K	Open

2.2   Large Language Models

Large Language Models (LLMs) are neural networks trained on large text corpora [14,18]. They show strong performance in reasoning, summarization, and text generation [4,33]. Commercial models such as GPT-4, Claude, and Gemini are widely used in both industry and research. However, they are resource-intensive, provider-dependent, and difficult to customize. These characteristics limit their suitability for controlled research and small-scale SE projects.

Lightweight open-source LLMs provide a practical alternative. They contain fewer parameters and require less computational power. As a result, they can run efficiently on local machines. Their open and adaptable nature also makes them suitable for small-company projects and open-science research. Recent advances in such models have created new opportunities to explore their potential in RE.

In this study, we focus on five open-source lightweight LLMs: Llama 2, Llama 3, Mistral, Gemma 2, and Phi-3 Mini. For simplicity, we refer to these lightweight LLMs simply as LLMs throughout the paper. We selected these models from major AI developers as a representative set of open-source lightweight LLMs for RE experimentation. They differ in size and reasoning capability but can all be executed locally. The aim was to examine their performance and behavior rather than identify the best model. Table 1 summarises the LLMs used in our study. Model refers to the model name, and Developer to the releasing organisation. Parameters (in billions) indicate the number of trainable weights, reflecting each model's capacity and computational cost. The Context window shows how much text the model can process in one input, measured in tokens; larger windows support longer and more coherent inputs. Usage distinguishes models available for open access from those restricted to research.

Interaction with LLMs occurs through *prompts* [6], which are textual instructions that define the task and expected output [33]. The way a prompt is formulated, referred to as a *prompt strategy*, strongly influences the quality of the generated results [32]. Our study examines five representative strategies, as shown in Table 2. The Zero shot approach uses only task descriptions, while Few shot prompting provides a small set of labeled examples. Chain of thought prompts encourage step-by-step reasoning, which improves interpretability. Constraint based prompts introduce explicit rules to ensure structured and consistent outputs. Finally, Role based prompts assign the model a specific persona so that its responses align with relevant professional or contextual expectations.

3   Motivating Scenarios

We present three scenarios illustrating how feedback classification and requirements generation support RE, inspired by real cases [2], and prior studies [11].

Scenario 1 (Supporting Requirements Elicitation). App reviews often contain implicit requirements expressed as feature requests or bug reports [12]. Understanding these helps product teams capture evolving user needs, identify emerging issues, and plan product improvements. As an example, imagine that after releasing a new version of WhatsApp, the team wants to identify problems users mention in their reviews (e.g., "messages fail to send") and desired features (e.g., "add message scheduling"). Automatically classifying app reviews

Table 2. Overview of prompt strategies used in our study.

Prompt Strategy	Description and Example
Zero-shot	**Description:** A brief instruction describes the task, assuming the model can generalise from its pre-trained knowledge to perform it. **Example:** "Classify the following user feedback as a feature request, bug report, or usability issue."
Few-shot	**Description:** A few labelled examples show the desired pattern, assuming the model will apply it to new inputs. **Example:** "Example 1: 'Add dark mode' → Feature Request. Example 2: 'App crashes on login' → Bug Report. Now classify the next five items."
Chain-of-Thought	**Description:** The model is instructed to reason step by step and write intermediate steps before giving the final answer. **Example:** "Explain why this user comment indicates a performance issue, then label it as an NFR."
Constraint-based	**Description:** Prompts include explicit rules, templates, or conditions that the output must follow. **Example:** "Generate requirements that are testable, unambiguous, and measurable."
Role-based	**Description:** The model is assigned a specific role and responds using the perspective, tone, and knowledge expected from it. **Example:** "You are a requirements analyst. Rewrite the following user request as a formal functional requirement."

by request type helps teams quickly identify user needs, while quantifying the feedback shows their user-perceived importance.

Scenario 2 (Supporting Requirements Classification). Beyond identifying request types, the WhatsApp development team also wants to understand which non-functional qualities users discuss [11]. Feedback such as "too slow to open" or "confusing chat layout" reflects concerns about performance and usability. Automatically classifying feedback by referenced NFRs helps developers identify which quality attributes users value most, revealing whether users are more concerned with performance or usability. This supports task prioritization and helps balance new features with quality improvements.

Scenario 3 (Supporting Requirements Specification). After identifying and classifying requirements from WhatsApp user feedback, analysts may want to document them clearly and consistently. Translating informal comments into structured requirements is time-consuming and error-prone [2]. For example, feedback such as "add dark mode" can be reformulated as "The system shall provide a dark mode option". Although such documentation may not produce complete specification, automating it can provide initial drafts that accelerate refinement and maintain traceability with user feedback.

For these scenarios, a tool that classifies user feedback and generates requirements could help the team evolve their app more effectively.

4   Empirical Study Design

This section presents the empirical study conducted to evaluate the effectiveness of LLMs in analysing online user feedback to support RE.

4.1   Research Questions

The goal of this study is to evaluate LLMs in analysing online user feedback to support RE tasks. We specifically focus on three research questions:

- **RQ1**: How well do LLMs classify feedback by NFR type?
- **RQ2**: How well do LLMs classify feedback by user-request type?
- **RQ3**: How well do LLMs generate requirements specification?

In RQ1, we assess the models' ability to identify the NFR type mentioned in user reviews. RQ2 examines how accurately the models classify user feedback by request type. RQ3 evaluates their capability to generate requirements specification from the same feedback. All evaluations use human-annotated datasets (see Sect. 4.2). For RQ1–RQ2, model predictions are compared with annotations using precision, recall, and F1-score. For RQ3, SRSs generated from sampled reviews are assessed through human judgment based on predefined quality criteria.

4.2   Datasets

We use two annotated datasets of mobile app user feedback from prior studies [21,23]. The first dataset was originally labeled with NFR types [23] and is used to answer RQ1. The second dataset contains app reviews annotated with user request types [21] and is used to answer RQ2. In addition, a sample of annotated reviews from both datasets is used to answer RQ3. We selected these datasets for their relevance and availability in a public repository [11]. Each dataset contains thousands of reviews from approximately a dozen apps across diverse domains and both major app stores. This diversity mitigates the app sampling problem and supports validity [11].

Non-functional Requirements (NFR) Dataset. The first dataset, introduced by Lu and Liang [23], focuses on app reviews annotated with NFR types based on the software quality model [20]. The initial collected dataset comprised approximately 11,000 app reviews from two mobile applications in the books and communications categories. These reviews were drawn from both major app stores, the Apple App Store and Google Play Store. A subset of 4,000 review sentences was manually annotated according to five NFR categories.

User Request Dataset. The second dataset builds on previous studies [7,24] and includes additional user feedback collected for this study [21]. The initial collected dataset covered about 10 mobile applications across more than 10 categories from both the Apple App Store and Google Play Store. From an initial pool of the collected reviews, a curated subset of 2,912 was manually annotated into three user request types: feature requests, bug reports, and other. This dataset provides a diverse and representative sample of user feedback for evaluating automated classification approaches.

4.3   Evaluation Metrics and Criteria

We applied both quantitative and qualitative methods. Standard ML metrics [10] were used for RQ1 and RQ2, as feedback classification is a classification task [16]. Specification generation (RQ3) was evaluated via criteria-based assessment [22].

Evaluation Metrics for Classification (RQ1–RQ2). We compute precision, recall, and F1-score for two experiments: classifying user feedback by NFR type (RQ1) and by user request type (RQ2). Precision measures the proportion of correctly predicted labels among all predictions, while recall measures the proportion of correctly identified labels in the ground truth. Model performance is assessed by comparing each predicted label (user request or NFR type) with its annotated counterpart. Scores are calculated per class (e.g., feature request, bug report, other), along with macro averages. The macro average treats all classes equally.

Evaluation Criteria for Specification Generation (RQ3). For RQ3, the quality of generated requirement specification is evaluated qualitatively across five criteria derived from established specification attributes such as completeness, consistency, and clarity [30]. Each criterion was adapted to suit the characteristics of automatically generated specification. Table 3 outlines the evaluation rubric, which includes five criteria. These dimensions assess structural correctness, coverage of stakeholder input, factual grounding, semantic accuracy, and linguistic quality. Each criterion follows a defined scoring scheme combining quantitative (e.g., counts or coverage) and qualitative (e.g., 1–5 scale) measures, supporting systematic and replicable assessment of specification quality [22].

Table 3. Evaluation criteria and scoring used to assess generated specification (RQ3).

Criterion	Description and Scoring
Structural Adherence	**Description:** Evaluates how well the generated specification follows the expected structure, ensuring coverage of all sections.
	Scoring: Originally 1–8 points (one per correctly included section), linearly rescaled to 1–5 for consistency; higher is better.
Completeness	**Description:** Evaluates the coverage of requirements identified from user feedback.
	Scoring: Rated on a 1–5 scale, with higher scores reflecting greater completeness of identified requirements from user feedback.
Fidelity	**Description:** Evaluates how faithfully the generated specification reflects user feedback, identifying fabricated requirements.
	Scoring: Rated on a 1–5 scale; higher scores indicate greater fidelity (rescaled from the proportion of fabricated to valid requirements).
Conciseness	**Description:** Evaluates redundancy and verbosity in the generated text, indicating how efficiently information is conveyed.
	Scoring: Rated on a 1–5 scale, with higher scores reflecting greater conciseness and lower values indicate increased verbosity.
Clarity	**Description:** Evaluates the clarity of generated requirements in terms of unambiguity, specificity, and interpretability.
	Scoring: Rated on a 1–5 scale, with higher scores reflecting greater clarity and linguistic precision.

4.4   Experimental Setup and Procedure

We now describe the computational setup, prompting strategies, and evaluation procedures used in three experiments (RQ1–RQ3).

Computational Setup. All experiments were conducted under consistent hardware and parameter settings to ensure fairness and reproducibility. We evaluated five LLMs (see Sect. 2), running each model three times per task to reduce stochastic variance. Default parameters were used, with *temperature* set to 0 and a fixed *random seed* to minimise non-determinism. No hyperparameter tuning was applied to isolate the effects of prompting strategies. Experiments ran on a workstation with an NVIDIA RTX 4050 GPU (6 GB VRAM) and 16 GB RAM. Total runtime per model (3 runs) ranged from 20 min to 2 h for user request classification (512 reviews) and 2–5 h for NFR classification (1,278 reviews).

Prompting Strategies. We experiment with five prompting strategies (see Sect. 2). Prompting strategies are customised for each experiment (RQ1–RQ2).

Prompting Strategies for Classification (RQ1–RQ2). We apply three prompting strategies across two classification tasks (user request type and NFR type): *zero-shot*, *few-shot*, and *chain-of-thought (CoT)* prompting. These strategies capture increasing levels of reasoning and contextualization while remaining lightweight and reproducible. We omit more complex prompting (e.g., role-based or constraint-based), as classification primarily requires consistent label prediction rather than creative or constrained generation. Prompts are refined iteratively through a pilot study. Few-shot examples come from our dataset, and CoT prompts direct models to *"think step-by-step before giving the final category"*.

Prompting Strategies for Specification Generation (RQ3). We use all five prompting strategies for the specification generation task. Beyond the three classification strategies (*zero-shot, few-shot, CoT*), we add *constraint-based* and *role-based* prompting to improve structural coherence and contextual relevance. These strategies better suit generative tasks that require creativity and controlled output. In the constraint-based setup, prompts specify that outputs follow a defined structure (e.g., functional and non-functional sections) and include constraints such as *"avoid implementation details"* and *"ensure each requirement is unique"*.

Evaluation Procedures. We use quantitative evaluation for classification tasks (RQ1–RQ2) and qualitative evaluation for specification generation (RQ3).

Evaluation Procedure Classification (RQ1–RQ2). For RQ1 and RQ2, we evaluate models on the corresponding annotated dataset for each classification experiment (Sect. 4.2). Each review is processed by the LLM under each prompting setup (zero-shot, few-shot, CoT), and predicted labels are compared with the ground truth. We calculate precision, recall, and F1-score per class, along with macro- and weighted averages. We report mean values over three runs.

Evaluation Procedure for Specification Generation (RQ3). For RQ3, we use 90 annotated reviews randomly sampled from our collected data. Half are taken from the user request dataset, and the other half from the NFR dataset. The same input is provided to each LLM under every prompting setup. Each model generates requirements specification following the template, including Introduction, Functional Requirements, NFRs, and Glossary sections. The first author evaluates the outputs using the five criteria (see Table 3). The results are verified through manual examination of user feedback. The scores are averaged across all samples.

5   Results

RQ1: How Well Do LLMs Classify Feedback by NFR Type?

To answer RQ1, we evaluated how well LLMs classify user feedback by NFRs under three prompting strategies: zero-shot, few-shot, and chain-of-thought. Table 4 reports precision, recall, and F1 scores for each model, with the best results highlighted in bold. The effectiveness ranges from an F1 score of 0.40 to 0.55, with averages of 0.47, 0.49, and 0.51 for the zero-shot, few-shot, and chain-of-thought strategies, respectively. Across prompting strategies, performance improves steadily from zero-shot to few-shot to chain-of-thought, confirming that example-based and reasoning-enhanced prompts help LLMs better identify NFR types. Larger and newer models (Gemma, Llama 3, Mistral) generally outperform smaller or earlier ones (Llama 2, Phi-3 Mini). Gemma achieves the highest overall F1 score (0.55) and precision (0.53) under the chain-of-thought setting, while Llama 3 records the highest recall (0.59). Mistral performs most consistently across all prompting strategies, ranking near the top in zero-shot and few-shot modes. In contrast, Llama 2 yields the lowest scores across all metrics, while Phi-3 Mini remains stable but below the larger models.

> **Answer to RQ1:** LLMs achieve moderate accuracy (F1 ≈ 0.47–0.51) for classifying feedback by NFR type. Chain-of-thought prompting performs best, with Gemma leading overall (P = 0.53, R = 0.57, F1 = 0.55).

RQ2: How Well Do LLMs Classify Feedback by User Request Type?

To answer RQ2, we examined how LLMs classify user feedback by request type under three prompting strategies: zero-shot, few-shot, and chain-of-thought. Table 5 presents precision, recall, and F1 scores for each model, with the best results in bold. Model performance ranges from an F1 score of 0.32 to 0.74. The average F1 values are 0.59 for zero-shot, 0.68 for few-shot, and 0.64 for chain-of-thought prompting. Performance increases notably from zero-shot to few-shot prompting, while chain-of-thought yields moderate improvements. Larger and more recent models, such as Llama 3, Mistral, and Gemma, generally achieve higher accuracy than smaller or earlier ones, including Llama 2 and Phi-3 Mini. Llama 3 reaches the highest F1 score of 0.74 and recall of 0.75 under the few-shot setting. Mistral and Gemma perform consistently well across all strategies. Llama 2 produces the lowest scores, while Phi-3 Mini remains stable but below

Table 4. How well do LLMs classify feedback by NFR type? (RQ1)

Model	Zero-Shot			Few-Shot			Chain-of-Thought		
	P	R	F1	P	R	F1	P	R	F1
Llama 2	0.44	0.36	0.40	0.49	0.39	0.43	0.52	0.46	0.49
Llama 3	0.42	**0.54**	0.47	0.46	**0.57**	0.51	0.48	**0.59**	0.53
Mistral	0.49	0.51	**0.50**	**0.54**	0.51	**0.52**	0.47	**0.59**	0.52
Gemma	**0.51**	0.48	0.49	0.51	0.49	0.50	**0.53**	0.57	**0.55**
Phi-3 Mini	0.44	0.54	0.48	0.46	0.54	0.50	0.44	0.48	0.46
Average	0.46	0.49	0.47	0.49	0.50	0.49	0.49	0.54	0.51

the stronger models. Overall, few-shot prompting provides the best results (average F1 = 0.68); it suggests that including example-based context helps LLMs more accurately classify user feedback by request type.

> **Answer to RQ2:** LLMs achieve moderate-to-high average accuracy (F1 ≈ 0.59–0.68) for classifying feedback by user request type. Few-shot prompting performs best, with Llama 3 leading overall (P = 0.72, R = 0.75, F1 = 0.74).

Table 5. How well do LLMs classify user feedback by request type? (RQ2)

Model	Zero-Shot			Few-Shot			Chain-of-Thought		
	P	R	F1	P	R	F1	P	R	F1
Llama 2	0.28	0.36	0.32	0.57	0.56	0.57	0.60	0.42	0.49
Llama 3	**0.77**	0.67	**0.72**	0.72	0.75	**0.74**	0.71	0.70	0.71
Mistral	0.60	0.63	0.62	0.69	**0.74**	0.71	0.65	**0.72**	0.68
Gemma	0.66	**0.71**	0.68	0.68	0.67	0.68	0.65	0.60	0.63
Phi-3 Mini	0.69	0.51	0.59	0.68	0.67	0.68	0.67	0.70	**0.69**
Average	0.60	0.58	0.59	0.67	0.68	0.68	0.66	0.63	0.64

RQ3: How Well Do LLMs Generate Requirements Specification?

To answer RQ3, each model was evaluated on five criteria: structure (SA), completeness (CO), fidelity (FI), conciseness (CN), and clarity (CL), as defined in Table 3. Table 6 reports results across models and prompting strategies. Overall, the models produced moderate-quality specification (mean = 3.1; SD = 0.8). Llama 3 with chain-of-thought prompting and Mistral with few-shot prompting achieved the highest mean score (3.6), showing strong structure and clarity (SA = 4; CL = 5). Llama 2 followed with stable mid-range scores (mean = 3.2–3.4). Gemma produced the weakest but most consistent outputs (mean ≈ 2.9; SD = 0.4). Phi-3 Mini showed high fidelity and conciseness (FI ≈ 4; CN = 4–5) but low structure (SA = 1–2) and high variability. Across prompting strategies, few-shot and chain-of-thought improved structure and clarity, whereas constraint-based prompting offered limited gains. Most models scored highest in clarity (CL = 4–5) and completeness (CO = 4) but lagged with fidelity and conciseness (FI, CN = 2–3).

> **Answer to RQ3:** LLMs produced moderate-quality specification, with Llama 3 and Mistral performing best; model and prompt choice strongly influenced output quality.

Table 6. LLM performance on requirement specification (RQ3). SA – Structure; CO – Compl.; FI – Fidelity; CN – Conciseness; CL – Clarity. Scores are on a 1–5 scale (higher = better). **Bold** indicates the best overall performance across all models and prompt strategies, based on the highest Mean score (averaged over the five criteria) and the lowest SD.

Model	Prompt Strategy	SA (1–5)	CO (1–5)	FI (1–5)	CN (1–5)	CL (1–5)	Mean	SD
Llama 2	Zero-Shot	3	4	3	3	4	3.4	0.49
	Few-Shot	3	4	3	2	4	3.2	0.75
	Chain-of-Thought	3	4	3	2	4	3.2	0.75
	Constraint-based	3	4	3	2	4	3.2	0.75
	Role-based	3	4	3	2	4	3.2	0.75
Llama 3	Zero-Shot	3	4	3	2	4	3.2	0.75
	Few-Shot	3	4	3	2	4	3.2	0.75
	Chain-of-Thought	4	4	3	2	5	**3.6**	1.02
	Constraint-based	3	4	3	2	4	3.2	0.75
	Role-based	3	4	3	2	4	3.2	0.75
Mistral	Zero-Shot	3	3	3	2	4	3.0	0.63
	Few-Shot	4	4	3	2	5	**3.6**	1.02
	Chain-of-Thought	3	4	3	2	4	3.2	0.75
	Constraint-based	3	4	3	2	4	3.2	0.75
	Role-based	3	4	3	2	4	3.2	0.75
Gemma	Zero-Shot	2	3	3	3	3	2.8	**0.40**
	Few-Shot	3	3	3	2	4	3.0	0.63
	Chain-of-Thought	3	3	3	2	4	3.0	0.63
	Constraint-based	2	3	3	2	4	2.8	0.75
	Role-based	3	3	3	2	4	3.0	0.63
Phi-3 Mini	Zero-Shot	1	4	4	4	2	3.0	1.22
	Few-Shot	2	4	4	4	3	3.4	0.89
	Chain-of-Thought	1	3	4	4	3	3.0	1.10
	Constraint-based	1	3	4	5	2	3.0	1.22
	Role-based	2	4	3	4	3	3.2	0.75
Average	–	2.6	4.0	3.0	2.3	3.8	3.1	0.8

6   Discussion

Lightweight LLMs show promising potential for analysing user feedback in RE. Although more efficient and transparent than larger models, they are not yet suitable for reliable industrial use without further customization.

A) Feedback Classification. In feedback classification, Llama 3 and Mistral achieved F1-scores around 0.74 for identifying user request types. This shows that lightweight models can reliably detect explicit requests such as feature suggestions or bug reports. Their performance in NFR classification was weaker, with the best F1-score reaching 0.55. This result aligns with prior studies where models also struggled to capture implicit qualities like usability or reliability [23]. The limitation likely stems from two factors. Lightweight LLMs find it difficult to interpret subtle, context-dependent expressions. They also lack sufficient exposure to RE-specific terminology and training data. Structured prompting with few-shot or reasoning examples led to only minor improvements. These findings suggest that contextual examples and reasoning cues can enhance understanding. However, overall accuracy remains moderate. In practice, this may produce noisy classifications that mislead analysts. As a result, important feedback can be missed, while irrelevant comments may be misclassified as critical requirements.

B) Requirements Specification Generation. Lightweight LLMs produced requirement specification that were generally clear, coherent, and complete. They expressed user feedback readably but often failed to follow formal structures. Their outputs were sometimes verbose and required editing for conciseness and compliance with standards. Although the generated text was fluent, the models occasionally fabricated requirements, adding information absent from the original feedback. As a result, the content appeared plausible but not always accurate or grounded. In practice, these limitations mean lightweight LLMs can assist analysts by drafting initial requirement statements or summarising feedback. However, they still require human review to ensure accuracy and proper structure. With further refinement and adaptation, they could serve as drafting and documentation aids rather than autonomous specification generators.

C) Implications for Requirements Engineering. Lightweight LLMs can support RE tasks such as feedback filtering, classification, and initial specification drafting. However, they cannot yet replace human analysts. Their moderate precision and recall make them unreliable for use without supervision. These weaknesses may lead to missed insights or false positives that increase review effort. The generated outputs are clear and coherent but often lack factual grounding and formal consistency. This limits their value for downstream RE tasks, e.g., validation, and traceability. In several tasks, their performance is similar to earlier ML approaches [11,23]. Larger models alone do not guarantee better outcomes in RE. Future work should adapt models to RE contexts using prompt design, fine-tuning, and retrieval-based approaches. These methods can improve accuracy and help lightweight LLMs better support early RE tasks.

7   Threats to Validity

Internal Validity. The main threat lies in the manual evaluation of generated requirement specification by a single evaluator, without validating its reliability. This introduces potential subjectivity. To mitigate this, we applied a systematic rubric with clear criteria and examples of both high- and low-quality specification. The rubric was used consistently across all outputs. In addition, prompts and model parameters were standardised to ensure uniform conditions.

External Validity. We used two publicly available datasets from different domains to reduce domain bias. Their diverse vocabulary helps generalisability, though an app review represents only one feedback type. Results may not generalise to industrial datasets or other contexts such as issue trackers. Moreover, the study focused on lightweight LLMs; larger models may yield different results.

Construct Validity. We employed standard precision, recall, and F1-score metrics for classification and a rubric assessing completeness, consistency, and correctness for generation. As qualitative evaluation relied on one evaluator, some interpretation bias may persist. Prompt phrasing may also influence results; this was mitigated by systematically applying established prompting strategies.

Conclusion Validity. All models were tested under identical settings and prompts. However, the limited sample size for specification generation lowers statistical power, and no inferential tests were applied, making results exploratory. While precision and recall were key metrics, tasks may favour one over the other, and F1 may not always be optimal [5]. Our aim was to assess overall practical effectiveness rather than examine differences across RE-specific tasks.

8 Related Works

Online feedback analysis has long supported requirements and software engineering, with many automated methods proposed [2,11,27]. Earlier work relied on traditional ML and NLP methods for tasks such as feedback classification, topic detection, and opinion extraction [11,35]. Our study takes a new direction by applying LLMs to both established classification tasks and a novel one: generating requirements specification [31], a capability beyond earlier approaches [9]. Prior work also highlighted the lack of tools for automated requirements generation from user feedback [12]; we address this gap by evaluating lightweight LLMs across both classification and generation tasks [8].

Previous studies rarely ensured reproducibility or revisited results with newer AI methods [11]. We emphasise transparent experimentation by benchmarking lightweight models across RE tasks and releasing a full replication package for open, comparative research. While many recent works rely on proprietary models such as GPT [8,33], we focus on open, lightweight alternatives to improve transparency and reproducibility. Unlike prior LLM-based studies, our work applies lightweight LLMs to online feedback analysis [33]. To our knowledge, this is the first study to evaluate lightweight LLMs for feedback-driven requirements development, supported by a replication package for reproducible RE research.

9 Conclusion

Analysing online user feedback is important for RE tasks, yet automation remains challenging. This study presents the first systematic evaluation of open-source, lightweight LLMs for feedback-driven RE. Five models were evaluated with multiple prompting strategies on three RE tasks: classifying feedback by user request and NFR type, and generating requirement specification.

Lightweight LLMs classified user request types accurately (F1 $\approx$ 0.74) but performed moderately for NFRs (F1 $\approx$ 0.55). Structured prompting improved results slightly. Generated specification was generally complete and coherent but often verbose and sometimes included fabricated requirements. Lightweight LLMs can support early RE activities, but still require human oversight.

We release our evaluation framework and replication package to support further research [26]. Future work should explore fine-tuning lightweight open-source LLMs, developing retrieval-augmented pipelines, and creating domain-adapted benchmarks to improve their accuracy and reliability in RE. We also suggest that future studies should empirically benchmark the performance of lightweight LLMs against heavyweight language models (e.g., ChatGPT). This benchmarking would help determine whether the potential performance gains of heavyweight LLMs justify the trade-offs compared to lightweight models.

Acknowledgments. A major part of this work was conducted as part of the MSc thesis of M. A. Mallya, supervised by J. Dąbrowski [25]. The results contribute to the Prompt Me project [9]. This publication has emanated from research jointly funded by Taighde Éireann – Research Ireland under Grant Number 13/RC/2094_2, and co-funded by the European Union under the Systems, Methods, Context (SyMeCo) programme Grant Agreement Number 101081459. Views and opinions expressed are however those of the author(s) only and do not necessarily reflect those of the European Union or the European Research Executive Agency. Neither the European Union nor the granting authority can be held responsible for them.

Data Availability Statement. The artefacts supporting the findings of this study are publicly available in a GitHub repository [26]. The repository includes data, scripts, and supplementary materials. All artefacts are released under the MIT License. Documentation is provided to support use and reproduction.

Disclosure of Interests. The authors have no competing interests to declare that are relevant to the content of this article. ChatGPT-4 [29] was used to improve the readability, and the authors remain fully responsible for the final content.

References

1. Abualhaija, S., et al.: Replication in requirements engineering: for RE case. ACM Trans. Softw. Eng. Methodol. **33**(6) (2024)
2. Al-Subaihin, A.A., Sarro, F., Black, S., Capra, L., Harman, M.: App store effects on software engineering practices. IEEE Trans. Softw. Eng. **47**(2), 300–319 (2021)
3. Alhoshan, W., Ferrari, A., Zhao, L.: How effective are generative large language models in performing requirements classification? (2025). https://arxiv.org/abs/2504.16768

4. Arora, C., Grundy, J., Abdelrazek, M.: Advancing requirements engineering through generative AI: assessing the role of LLMs. In: Nguyen-Duc, A., Abrahamsson, P., Khomh, F. (eds.) Generative AI for Effective Software Development. Springer, Cham (2024). https://doi.org/10.1007/978-3-031-55642-5_6

5. Berry, D.M.: Requirements engineering for artificial intelligence: what is a requirements specification for an artificial intelligence? In: REFSQ, pp. 19–25 (2022)

6. Binkhonain, M., Alfayez, R.: Are prompts all you need? Evaluating prompt-based large language models (LLM)s for software requirements classification. Requirements Eng., 1–21 (2025)

7. Chen, N., Lin, J., Hoi, S.C.H., Xiao, X., Zhang, B.: AR-miner: mining informative reviews for developers from mobile app marketplace. In: Proceedings of the 36th International Conference on Software Engineering, ICSE 2014, Hyderabad, India, pp. 767–778. ACM (2014)

8. Cheng, H., et al.: Generative ai for requirements engineering: a systematic literature review. arXiv preprint arXiv:2409.06741 (2024)

9. Dąbrowski, J.: Prompt me: intelligent software agent for requirements engineering (2025). https://prompt-me.github.io/

10. Dąbrowski, J., Cai, W., Bennaceur, A., Nuseibeh, B., Alrimawi, F.: Intelligent agents for requirements engineering: use, feasibility and evaluation. In: 2025 IEEE 33rd International Requirements Engineering Conference (RE), pp. 535–543 (2025)

11. Dąbrowski, J., Letier, E., Perini, A., Susi, A.: Analysing app reviews for software engineering: a systematic literature review. Empirical Softw. Eng. **27**(2) (2022)

12. Dąbrowski, J., Letier, E., Perini, A., Susi, A.: Mining user feedback for software engineering: use cases and reference architecture. In: RE, pp. 114–126. IEEE (2022)

13. Dąbrowski, J., Letier, E., Perini, A., Susi, A.: Mining and searching app reviews for requirements engineering: evaluation and replication studies. Inf. Syst. **114** (2023)

14. Fan, A., et al.: Large language models for software engineering: survey and open problems. In: ICSE-FoSE, May 2023, pp. 31–53. IEEE Computer Society (2023)

15. Ferrari, A., Spoletini, P., Debnath, S.: How do requirements evolve during elicitation? An empirical study combining interviews and app store analysis. Requir. Eng. **27**(4), 489–519 (2022)

16. Géron, A.: Hands-On Machine Learning with Scikit-Learn, Keras, and TensorFlow, 3rd edn. O'Reilly Media (2022)

17. Glinz, M.: On non-functional requirements. In: 15th IEEE International Requirements Engineering Conference, RE 2007, pp. 21–26 (2007)

18. Hou, X., et al.: Large language models for software engineering: a systematic literature review. ACM Trans. Softw. Eng. Methodol. (2024)

19. Hou, X., et al.: Large language models for software engineering: a systematic literature review. ACM Trans. Softw. Eng. Methodol. **33**(8), 1–79 (2024)

20. ISO/IEC: Systems and software engineering – systems and software quality requirements and evaluation (square) – system and software quality models (2011). https://www.iso.org/standard/35733.html

21. Jha, N., Mahmoud, A.: Using frame semantics for classifying and summarizing application store reviews. Empir. Softw. Eng. **23**(6), 3734–3767 (2018). https://doi.org/10.1007/s10664-018-9605-x

22. Kuckartz, U.: Qualitative Text Analysis: A Guide to Methods, Practice & Using Software, 1st edn. SAGE Publications, London/Los Angeles (2014). https://doi.org/10.4135/9781446288719

23. Lu, M., Liang, P.: Automatic classification of non-functional requirements from augmented app user reviews. In: Proceedings of the 21st International Conference

on Evaluation and Assessment in Software Engineering, EASE 2017, Karlskrona, Sweden, June 2017, pp. 344–353. Association for Computing Machinery (ACM) (2017). https://doi.org/10.1145/3084226.3084241

24. Maalej, W., Kurtanovic, Z., Nabil, H., Stanik, C.: On the automatic classification of app reviews. In: Proceedings of the 2016 IEEE 23rd International Conference on Requirements Engineering (RE), Beijing, China, 2016, pp. 49–58. IEEE (2016). https://doi.org/10.1109/RE.2016.23

25. Mallya, M.A.: Developing software requirements using LLMs: a preliminary empirical study. Master of science in software engineering with data analytics (MSC), University of Limerick, Limerick, Ireland, August 2025. Supervised by Dr. Jacek Dabrowski. Student ID: 24124133

26. Mallya, M.A., Ferrari, A., Zadenoori, M.A., Dąbrowski, J.: From online user feedback to requirements: evaluating large language models for classification and specification tasks – replication package. GitHub repository, October 2025. https://github.com/jsdabrowski/REFSQ-2026/

27. Martin, W.J.: App store analysis for software engineering (2017). https://api.semanticscholar.org/CorpusID:67009007

28. Motger, Q., Oriol, M., Tiessler, M., Franch, X., Marco, J.: What about emotions? Guiding fine-grained emotion extraction from mobile app reviews. In: 2025 IEEE 33rd International Requirements Engineering Conference (RE), pp. 6–18 (2025)

29. OpenAI: ChatGPT-4: large language model (2024), version GPT-4. https://chat.openai.com/. Accessed Oct 2025

30. Porter, D., DeFranco, J.F., Laplante, P.: Requirements specification automated quality analysis: past, present, and future. Computer **58**(1), 101–104 (2025). https://doi.org/10.1109/MC.2024.3480629

31. Ullrich, J., Koch, M., Vogelsang, A.: From requirements to code: understanding developer practices in LLM-assisted software engineering. In: 2025 IEEE 33rd International Requirements Engineering Conference (RE), pp. 257–266 (2025)

32. Vogelsang, A., Fischbach, J.: Using large language models for natural language processing tasks in requirements engineering: a systematic guideline (2024). https://arxiv.org/abs/2402.13823

33. Zadenoori, M.A., Dąbrowski, J., Alhoshan, W., Zhao, L., Ferrari, A.: Large language models (LLMs) for requirements engineering (RE): a systematic literature review (2025). https://arxiv.org/abs/2509.11446

34. Zadenoori, M.A., Martino, V.D., Dąbrowski, J., Franch, X., Ferrari, A.: Does model size matter? A comparison of small and large language models for requirements classification. CoRR abs/2510.21443 (2025). https://doi.org/10.48550/ARXIV.2510.21443

35. Zhao, L., et al.: Natural language processing for requirements engineering: a systematic mapping study. ACM Comput. Surv. **54**(3) (2021). https://doi.org/10.1145/3444689

Requirements Specification and Privacy by Design

An Industry-Driven Template for the Documentation of Non-functional Requirements

Sabine Molenaar[(⊠)] and Fabiano Dalpiaz

Dept. of Information and Computing Sciences, Utrecht University,
Utrecht, The Netherlands
`{s.molenaar,f.dalpiaz}@uu.nl`

Abstract. **[Context]** In software development, the quality attributes that systems should exhibit are often expressed as non-functional requirements (NFRs). However, unlike functional requirements, there is no widely adopted writing format for NFRs. **[Problem]** This deficiency, and the more complex nature of NFRs due to their difficult quantification and architectural level of abstraction, poses obstacles for the specification of NFRs in practice. **[Results]** Following the design cycle methodology, we put forward a process for developing an NFR template based on meta-requirements from literature and gathered from practitioners in a focus group, and two existing templates. We validated the template through interviews with target users from three organizations, focusing on whether it could help practitioners overcome specific challenges in NFR writing. **[Contribution]** The interviewees appreciated the explicit documentation of measurable fit criteria the most, as it allows users to make the NFR quantifiable, and found the template easy to use. All expressed an intention to use the template again in the future.

Keywords: Non-functional requirement · Quality requirement · Requirements engineering · Design science

1 Introduction

Non-Functional Requirements (NFRs) are by nature more difficult to validate than functional requirements, as they are generally formulated in a way that is not measurable and they are usually subjectively evaluated [7]. NFRs are often not considered [13], and software at times fulfills NFRs in ad-hoc ways, as opposed to functional requirements, which are taken into account when software is designed [3]. In 2004, Paech and Kurkow stated that the understanding of NFRs is still limited and that they are barely discussed in prominent RE textbooks [26].

Glinz confirmed that quality requirements are described in a qualitative way such as *"we want an easy to use system"*, but this makes them subjective and difficult to measure [11]. In 2016, Eckhardt *et al.* still found some NFRs too vague to include in their study [8].

R. Guizzardi and J. Araújo (Eds.): REFSQ 2026, LNCS 16497, pp. 181–197, 2026.
https://doi.org/10.1007/978-3-032-21423-2_12

In 2018, Kopczyńska *et al.* [16] found that NFRs are still described as *"too often neglected, especially those that are difficult to write and ostensibly obvious"*. They also found that using a template results in more complete NFRs, which increases their verifiability, when compared to ad-hoc approaches to NFRs. This study used a catalog of 400 templates, and found that about 20% of the templates were used for almost 80% of the NFRs across the 40 investigated projects. Also, each project used less than 10% of the templates on average [16].

For functional requirements, many popular templates exist, such as the User Story (US) template by Mike Cohn [5], EARS [20], and FRETish [9], to name a few. In addition, guidelines and instructions exist for functional requirements, such as the ISO/IEC/IEEE 29148:2018 standard [1], the Quality User Story framework [19] and INVEST [33]. NFRs are not afforded the same luxury: while quality characteristics for NFRs are available [16], they are not commonly used.

In a previous study, we found that practitioners are unsure of how to document NFRs and, in an attempt to document them in a consistent and familiar way, try to 'force' them into a US template [23]. We intend to tackle this difficulty and uncertainty in expressing NFRs with a design cycle [34]. Our process demonstrates how to develop an artifact that supports practitioners in documenting NFRs in their particular real-life context. We take a novel approach, by actively engaging practitioners through the elicitation of meta-requirements, based on challenges they encounter in practice and by evaluating the suitability of existing templates. This ensures a tailored artifact, rather than a one-size-fits-all solution, which is unlikely to suit the context optimally.

This paper makes the following contributions to the literature:

1. We present a process for developing a situational NFR template, tailored to a specific context;
2. Through meta-requirements from literature and practitioners, following our process, we construct an industry-aligned NFR template that we name *iNFR*;
3. We validate *iNFR* through interviews with seven practitioners who could use the template. They valued the fit criteria most, as they allow users to make NFRs more specific and quantifiable. They found the template easy to use and expressed intention to use in the future.

Paper organization. We discuss relevant terminology in Sect. 2. We present our research method in Sect. 3 and we discuss the problem and available NFR definition methods in Sect. 4. We describe the design of the treatment in Sect. 5, followed by the treatment validation in Sect. 6. Finally, we present a discussion and conclusion in Sect. 7 and Sect. 8, respectively.

2   Background

Lawrence *et al.* identified ignoring NFRs as one of the top ten risks of requirements engineering in 2001 [18]. NFRs help ensure constraints on the system architecture are considered during design, instead of requiring later refactoring [4]. Paech and Kerkow explain that the need for NFRs only grows as the IT market becomes more competitive, both because society as a whole becomes more dependent on IT, so the system and system components on which we rely should be of high quality, and because customers and suppliers need to negotiate on the quality they expect [26].

We also discuss the basic terminology for this paper. In a previous study [22], we found that the terms NFR and Quality Requirement (QR) are used interchangeably by some, while others assign them different meanings. We follow the latter and use Glinz's definitions [12]:

1. NFR: "*a quality requirement or a constraint*".
2. QR: "*a requirement that pertains to a quality concern that is not covered by functional requirements*".
3. Constraint: "*a requirement that limits the solution space beyond what is necessary for meeting the given functional requirements and quality requirements*".
4. Functional requirement: "*a requirement concerning a result of behavior that shall be provided by a function of a system (or of a component or service)*".

For the sake of brevity and legibility, we will use the term NFR, which covers both QRs and constraints. In addition, we will not discuss which terms other, related works used and if this was the correct term and how it was defined, we will simply use the term mentioned in the original work.

There is some discourse regarding what an NFR is and if, because most NFRs describe system behavior, they cannot be managed and assessed like functional requirements instead. According to Eckhardt *et al.*: "*Our results suggest that most "non-functional" requirements are not non-functional as they describe behavior of a system. Consequently, we argue that many so-called NFRs can be handled similarly to functional requirements.*" [8]. In our previous study, practitioners shared similar sentiments; they find it difficult to judge when NFRs become functional in a previous study [23].

However, NFRs should be considered at architecture level, rather than related to specific features or functionalities of a system or system component. Rozanski & Woods refer to quality goals as 'cross-cutting concerns' that are "*likely to impact all of the different structures that make up your architecture*" [31]. Cleland-Huang *et al.* confirm this, stating: "*Early detection of NFRs is useful because it enables system level constraints to be considered and incorporated into early architectural designs as opposed to being refactored in at a later time.*" [4].

3   Research Method

We address a design problem, namely: *how to design an industry-specific template for defining NFRs?* We employ a design cycle, which consists of three phases: (i) problem investigation, (ii) treatment design, and (iii) treatment validation [34]. This process is an example of how a situational NFR template can be developed for specific contexts, such as organizations or even departments. Supporting materials are made available through an online appendix [21]. For phases one and two we used both literature and input from practitioners. Phase three solely involves feedback from practitioners. The research design is shown in Fig. 1.

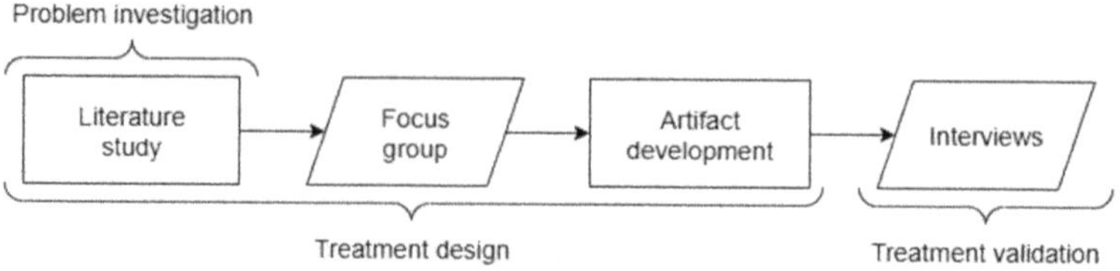

Fig. 1. Research design showing the three design science phases (parallelograms indicate activities involving practitioners).

Problem Investigation. We analyzed the literature and used findings from our previous work [22], for which data was gathered at the end of 2022. We focused on gathering information about the importance of NFRs, as well as difficulties practitioners may face in defining them, and available treatments in preparation for the treatment design phase. The relevant studies are discussed in Sect. 4.

Treatment Design. Our main focus is on the elicitation and specification of meta-requirements, the available treatments and, potentially, the development of a new treatment. We refer to requirements for the treatment as 'meta-requirements', to avoid confusion. We first consider the findings form our review study [22], we investigated the characteristics of definitions of the terms NFR and QR. We broaden this by gathering information from practitioners. From them, we wish to get answers to two questions: (i) how do they currently define NFRs and (ii) what are the advantages of and obstacles with available treatments? We used a focus group to obtain answers to these evaluative questions [32].

The focus group session included three participants, who discussed their process of defining and documenting NFRs. Afterwards, the participants were shown two NFR templates and asked to document an NFR using these templates. Benefits and limitations were discussed in the group, and the findings led to a set of meta-requirements. Both the meta-requirements gathered from the literature and the focus group are then used to either modify an existing treatment or create a new one; we refer to this activity as 'artifact development' in Fig. 1.

Treatment Validation. The modified or newly developed artifact from the previous phase is validated through expert opinion, as recommended by Wieringa [34]. Experts are asked to use the artifact and answer questions regarding the use through a one-on-one semi-structured interview. These questions are based on the input provided by the focus group participants, namely whether the treatment could help them overcome the challenges they described. In addition, participating experts are asked to answer questions regarding usefulness, ease of use, and intention to use.

Participants. Demographics of the participants are summarized in Table 1. All participants were selected through convenience sampling; willingness and availability to participate, although experience with definition and management of requirements was a prerequisite.

We present anonymized descriptions and data due to confidentiality agreements and to prevent information from being traced to a specific individual. 'Organization A' is a large organization based in the Netherlands, that develops and maintains a large number of applications. Development teams are organized in agile release trains and over 200 agile teams are active within the organization. In addition to the focus group participants, we also interviewed two IT specialists from the organization, who were uninvolved in the study until that point. To get an outside perspective, we invited two IT consultants from different consultancies to participate in the validation. Both IT consultancies are based in the Netherlands and have fewer than fifty employees.

Table 1. Demographics of participants in focus group and interviews.

	Focus group	Interviews	
	Org. A	Org. A	Consultants
Participants	3	5	2
Type of role(s)	Product owner, scrum master	Product owner, scrum master, IT specialist	IT consultant
Experience with reqs.	4–5 years	4–15 years	8 years

4   Problem Investigation

In a previous study, we found that practitioners experience difficulty in expressing NFRs, because they are unsure of how to document them. Practitioners oftentimes forced them into a US template [23]. Through a literature study, we investigate the challenges in defining NFRs further in Sect. 4.1. In addition, we describe existing methods for defining NFRs in Sect. 4.2.

4.1   Challenges in Defining NFRs

Even though NFRs are deemed important for project success, they are notoriously difficult to define and validate. There are three main factors that make them more complex than functional requirements: (i) they have a strong impact on the architecture, (ii) they are hard to quantify, as they are of a qualitative nature rather than a quantitative one, and (iii) there is no one-size-fits-all approach. The challenges are described in the following paragraphs.

Architecture Level. As discussed in Sect. 2, NFRs should be considered at architecture level [4,31]. Ebert states that *"improving an architecture once it is not maintainable any more is impossible"* [7], but that delaying the implementation of technical requirements will not endanger the system in question.

However, he also explains that NFRs are often not measurable during the design phase [7]. So, while NFRs need to be considered during the design of the system and express requirements for the system as a whole, they can only be tested once the system has been built. The IREB guide follows this view and defines quality requirements as requirements that *"influence the system architecture more than functional requirements do"* and constraints as types of requirements that *"can constrain the system itself"* and impose limitations during development [28]. Also, this makes NFRs harder to trace than functional requirements [3,7].

Quantification. As stated previously, NFRs often cannot be measured during the design phase [7], but matters become more complicated if measurement of the NFRs becomes complex, or even impossible, in itself. Eckhardt *et al.* state that NFRs are often documented vaguely and without quantitative measures, making them difficult to test [8].

Glinz identifies three types of problems as a result of ambiguous and unverifiable quality requirements: (i) the quality of the system does not meet stakeholder expectations, (ii) the system outperforms the stakeholder expectations, potentially making the system more expensive than it needs to be, and (iii) developers and stakeholders cannot agree on whether quality requirements are met, as they cannot be measured objectively [11].

In their empirical study on NFR templates, Kopczyńska *et al.* [16] provide users with some guidance, by presenting quality characteristics for a single NFR. Two of those characteristics, individual completeness and verifiability, require the user to ensure that it is possible to verify the NFR.

Lack of a Single Approach. Previously we described that NFRs lack a common method [3,26] and that many definition methods exist, while for functional requirements the approach may seem more obvious given the context.

4.2   Available NFR Definition Methods

While NFRs may not have a best practice definition method like functional requirements in agile in the form of the Connextra template for USs [5], various approaches have been proposed over the years. Note that we consider NFR templates as a specific NFR definition methods. We therefore use the terms 'NFR definition method' and 'NFR template' interchangeably. We discuss a non-exhaustive selection of NFR definition methods in the following paragraphs.

Bowen *et al.* presented consumer-oriented software quality attributes, which link quality attributes to user concerns in the form of questions. For instance, when considering the performance of the software: *"How well does it utilize a resource?"* [2]. Mylopoulos *et al.* used these quality attributes in their goal graph modeling approach, which presents NFRs as related goals in a graph and shows whether and to what degree these goals are supported by the design of the system [24]. This evolved to a modeling formalism for representing how functional requirements affect soft goals (e.g., sharing of information), either positively or negatively, and these soft goals are then related to NFRs. This approach allows for modeling and reasoning about the impact of system attributes on NFRs; an NFR is satisfied when all its related soft goals are satisfied and it is not negatively impacted by any attributes [25].

Ebert specified NFRs using tables that contain quality goals, priority, measurable targets, related quality and release criteria, and applicable metrics. Using this approach, NFRs can be measured quantitatively [7]. The Quality-Aware Predesign Model (QAPM) also contains a table to represent quality requirements, which includes, among others: quality characteristic, threshold, applicability, and description [14]. Similarly, Cysneiros *et al.* presented the NFR description language that explains how an NFR should be described. The language includes a name, description, related design decisions, priority, and attributes [6].

The first four steps of the QUality PERformance (QUPER) approach also aim to define quality indicators for a system or product. A template was made to cover these first four steps and require information such as quality type, market expectations related to this quality (e.g. a five second response-time), quality indicators of competitor products and targets. This template focuses mainly on quantitative specifications [29].

Robertson & Robertson propose the use of "The system shall..." template, followed by some NFR the system should meet. However, this Volere Snow Card (VSC) template also includes a rationale, originator, fit criterion, dependencies and support materials among others. This template can also be used for functional requirements. For NFRs, they prescribe properties the NFRs should cover; for usability, they mention ease of remembering as example property [30].

Kopczyńska & Nawrocki presented a more specific template in 2014, called the Non-Functional Requirement Template (NoRT). This template differs for different types of NFRs, because it includes standard text and parameters the user needs to fill in. For instance, the performance requirement template is: *"[Average/maximum in <number>% cases] time between <request> and <response> should be longer than <time amount>* [15].

5   Treatment Design

We base the treatment design on requirements gathered from literature and the industry; we elicited the latter from practitioners through a focus group.

5.1   Meta-requirements from Literature

In our previous study on the definitions of NFRs and QRs, we identified four characteristics these definitions typically include [22]: (i) distinguished from functional requirements, (ii) describe a quality attribute the system or system component should exhibit, (iii) often include examples of NFR/QR types (e.g., availability), and (iv) may constrain functional requirements.

From these characteristics, we define three meta-requirements for the artifact (the first and fourth characteristics were combined into L-RQ1):

L-RQ1. The artifact must link an NFR to one or more functional requirement(s);

L-RQ2. The artifact must specify for which system or system component an NFR is relevant;

L-RQ3. The artifact must include examples of (quality) attributes.

5.2 Meta-Requirements from Industry

We invited three practitioners from Organization A to participate in a focus group to explain how they currently define NFRs and what the (dis)advantages are in available treatments, in autumn 2025. We selected two templates for the focus group: the VSC template [30] and NoRT [15].

We selected these two because they take different approaches regarding degree of freedom and granularity; the former is high-level and allows for a lot of freedom, while the second is more specific and restrictive. For the VSC template, we used the "*The system shall*" phrase and provided the participants with the additional guidance for NFRs presented in [30]. For NoRT, a few examples were made available (e.g., the performance format) and participants only needed to fill in the given parameters.

Current Way of Working. All three participants stated that they define NFRs based on functional requirements. In their opinion, the need of expressing an NFR depends on the functional requirement at hand. There is one exception, however, as Organization A has defined a set of *security* and *privacy* NFRs that are applicable to all projects and systems.

They do not use a specific format or template. One of the participants often uses a US template, another includes them as checklist items and the third often records NFRs as part of the acceptance criteria for a US. All participants reuse previously defined NFRs if possible.

Challenges in Defining NFRs. The main challenge the participants face in defining NFRs is making them quantifiable; if they are not, they are difficult to test (as stated in [8]). Adherence to some NFRs can only be assessed once the system is in place, according to the participants. One of them mentioned *availability* as an example, which needs the system to be up and running and it may evolve over time (see also [7]).

One participant explained that they would like to apply the same NFRs to all users or user groups, but this is sometimes not possible. This leads to having various levels of quality within an NFR, as the requirements are more strict for some user groups than others. This occurs when one type of NFR is considered more important (e.g., *accessibility* over *usability*). Moreover, this trade-off between NFRs should become apparent from their prioritization, but this is rarely the case as NFRs are defined in relation to functional requirements.

More generally, the participants stated that they lack guidelines or best practices (as described in [26]) for defining NFRs. It is also difficult to determine a level of quality across requirements, making it hard to determine a minimum threshold to meet and enforcing it (similar to [4,31]).

Evaluation of Available Treatments The participants defined NFRs using the VSC template and NoRT and were asked about the main benefits and limitations of the two treatments after using them. The most relevant feedback from the participants is presented in Table 2.

Table 2. Benefits and limitations of VSC and NoRT according to the focus group participants.

	VSC	NoRT
Benefits	The user has more freedom (it allows you to include motivations for example) The properties to consider are helpful It invites you to create a list	It helps you along, as part of the requirement is already included It is more specific
Limitations	Difficult to make it more specific/testable	If you include a template for every type of NFR, team members are less likely to read them Risk of filling it in for the sake of filling it in Not a one-size-fits-all-solution; users may need to deviate

The participants said that how much guidance you need, for instance via a template, depends on (i) your experience with writing NFRs, (ii) your experience with the system at hand, and (iii) the type of NFR you are working on.

The type of NFR matters, because 'user-oriented NFRs' (e.g., *usability*) are generally less clear and specific than 'technology-oriented NFRs' (e.g., *availability*). They explain that the second type is often easier to measure as they are objective, while the first type depends on the user and is therefore subjective. In addition, they consider the technology-oriented NFRs to be more stable, while the user-oriented NFRs can evolve over time. They think this distinction should be included in a template. A similar distinction is made in [7]; between user-oriented and development-oriented. Ebert, however, sees user-oriented as being of most interest to the customer, while the practitioners consider user-oriented as interaction with the user.

Ideally, they would prefer a combination of the two templates. The first should function as a starting point, which can then be refined to include more details. The participants appreciated the properties to consider in the first treatment and the template of the second treatment, because that makes the attributes you might want to describe explicit. They explained that this forces the users to consider everything, serves as a reminder, and prevents you from making assumptions (i.e., 'attribute x should be obvious for everyone').

We have summarized the feedback from the focus group participants into industry meta-requirements for the artifact:

I-RQ1. The artifact must include different (quality) attributes to consider;

I-RQ2. The artifact must allow for further refinement of an NFR;

I-RQ3. The artifact must distinguish between user-oriented and technology-oriented NFRs;

I-RQ4. The artifact must include a level of priority;

I-RQ5. The artifact must distinguish between NFRs that should be tested during run-time and can be tested offline;

I-RQ6. The artifact must distinguish between NFRs that should be tested periodically (or continuously) or once (prior to implementation);

I-RQ7. The artifact must specify whether the NFR is an exception and/or specification of a different NFR.

5.3   Artifact Development

First, we created a conceptual model to illustrate the relationships between the various concepts in the study; identified through literature and empirical research. This model can be seen as a high-level specification for the artifact. The conceptual model is shown in Fig. 2.

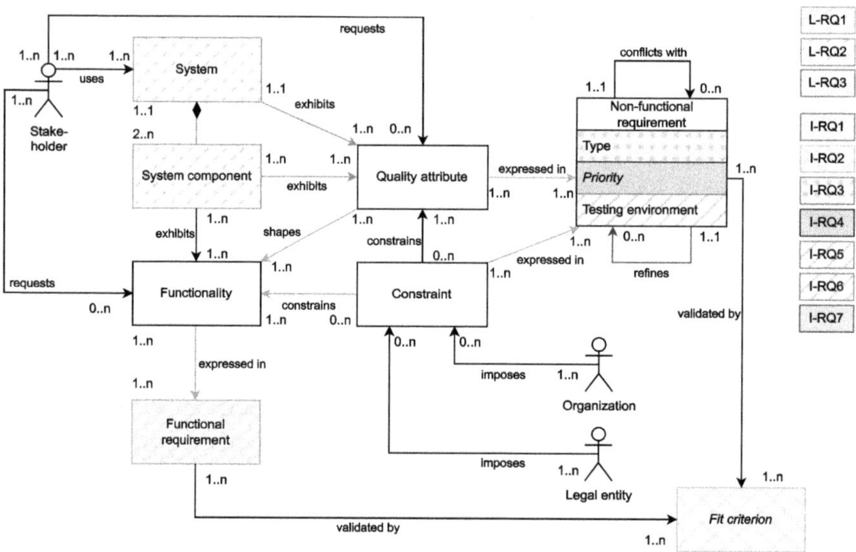

Fig. 2. Conceptual model of NFR and related concepts, highlighting elements that support the requirements for the artifact (included VSC elements are in italics).

In line with the literature [10], NFRs can express quality attributes or constraints. NFR have a type, hinting to the adoption of NFR taxonomies. This is partially covered in the quality characteristics for NFRs, which state that NFRs should be unambiguous [16]. NFRs constrain or shape functionality, so these functionality also need a common understanding. We assume, for example, that these functionalities are expressed in functional requirements (e.g., in USs).

We decided to relate quality attribute both to system components and to the system as a whole. While certain quality attributes can only be understood by looking at the system as a whole (e.g., performance), others need to be specified on individual components as part of a refinement process [27].

5.4 The iNFR Template

The developed artifact, the industry-NFR (iNFR) template, is shown in Fig. 3.

ID: NFR-0001			
Priority level: 1			
System (component): System Y			
Source *(choose one)*	X Stakeholder: End-user	O Own organization: …	O Legal entity: …
Type *(choose one per column)*	O Desire, user-oriented	O Usability O Other: …	
	X Desire, technology-oriented	O Efficiency O Maintainability O Portability X Reliability O Security O Other: …	
	O Constraint	O Cultural O Environmental O Implementation & design O Interface O Legal O Other: …	
Description *The system shall …* be available 99.8% of the time during office hours.			

Fit criteria
  1. Down time must not exceed 4.8 minutes per work week.
  2. Maintenance must be scheduled and performed on weekends.
  3. Users must be informed of scheduled maintenance 4 weeks in advance.			

Validation *(choose one)*	X Run-time online	O Run-time offline	O Compile-time
Testing *(choose one)*	X Continuous	O Periodical	O Single test
Conflicting NFR(s) *(mandatory in case of constraint)* n/a			
Impacted functional requirement(s) *(mandatory in case of constraint)* FR-0005			

Fig. 3. The developed iNFR template, showing a fictitious example.

The focus group stated that they would prefer a combination of the VSC and NoRT templates; start with a high-level description, which can be further refined. We met this request by using the *"The system shall"* phrase from the VSC template for the general description and including fit criteria, a term used by Robertson & Robertson to denote *"a quantification or measurement of the requirement such that you are able to determine whether the delivered product satisfies the requirement"* [30]. We also explicitly included NFRs types, as per the needs of the focus group (I-RQ3) and categorized them into three types: technology-oriented, user-oriented and constraints. In this categorization, we follow the practitioners' inputs rather than existing proposals like Ebert's [7].

For the NFR examples (L-RQ3/I-RQ1), we used the NFR classes listed by Eckhardt and colleagues: *efficiency, maintainability, portability, reliability, security,* and *usability,* because they were extracted from industry requirements specifications [8]. We assume that these are understood by other practitioners as well. In addition, for the constraints, we used Glinz's taxonomy for example types [10]. All types are included in alphabetical order in the template. For use in other contexts, we recommend using a taxonomy commonly used in that context. For instance, a company could select the taxonomy, so that all employees have a common understanding. We do not prescribe a specific taxonomy, because they can be domain-specific, but examples are presented in [2,7,8,10,30].

We also included fields that allow users to specify how and when the NFR should be validated and tested. The focus group also discussed NFRs that might conflict with other NFRs. We fulfilled this need by including "conflicting NFRs". Finally, we included a field for functional requirements that are impacted by the NFR in question. In a real-world setting, the template should be integrated into an issue tracking system.

6   Treatment Validation

As described in Sect. 3, we validated the template through expert opinion. All experts were given the NFR template, four fictitious example NFRs created using the template and a consent form. All interviews with the experts were conducted by the same researcher in autumn 2025. The experts were first asked to define a (fictitious) NFR for a self-chosen (fictitious) system using the empty template; the examples served as support material. The experts provided positive and negative feedback regarding fields in the template, which is summarized in Table 3.

The experts then evaluated whether the template could support practitioners in overcoming the challenges from the focus group. We identified four challenges, one of which, concerning quantifiability (*C3*), is confirmed by the literature, as discussed in Sect. 4. Finally, they were asked to rate the usefulness, ease of use and intention to use of the template. Both the challenges and the template were evaluated on a five-point Likert scale (from 1 – strongly disagree to 5 – strongly agree), the scores are shown in Table 4.

The consolidated scores per statement are visualized in Fig. 4. Note that 'strongly disagree' is not included, because this score was not observed.

The experts were generally positive, with some reservations, particularly for C4. They see potential, but would have to use the template from start to finish (refinement to implementation) in their development process to be able to assess the value of the template in overcoming this challenge (same for C1). Currently, there is no proof that these NFRs are testable (also related to C3) in this way and the testing field does not provide enough details for proper testing to be performed. All experts agreed that the template was useful and easy to use and that they intend to use the template again in the future to define an NFR.

Table 3. Feedback on template fields, where "responses" is the number of experts that provided the same feedback (out of the total of seven experts).

Template field	Feedback	Responses
ID	n/a	n/a
Priority	Default options (in line with organization) would be nice	1
System (component)	n/a	n/a
Source	Often apparent from description; can be considered redundant	3
	"Initiator" might be a better term	2
	Multiple sources should be possible	1
Type	Somewhat confusing; how to read and what is expected	3
	Easier to select a type than having to write one from scratch	4
Description	n/a	n/a
Fit criteria	Allow you to make the NFR more specific and quantifiable	6
Validation	Not immediately clear what the use of this field is	3
Testing	Nice that this is made explicit, as it forces you to consider this	3
	More fields to provide more details would be better	4
Conflicting NFRs	Nice that this is included, but still needs to be assessed manually	3
Impacted FRs	Dependencies are essential in the development process, important that this is included	2

Table 4. Validation results showing scores on the Likert scales for each expert (E), E6 and E7 are the consultants outside Organization A.

ID	Challenge statements	E1	E2	E3	E4	E5	E6	E7
C1	NFRs may conflict with others, which makes it more difficult to make the right decision in selecting which NFR(s) to implement.	4	4	3	4	4	4	4
C2	Some NFRs may be forgotten or overlooked.	4	4	4	4	4	4	5
C3	It is often difficult to make NFRs quantifiable and therefore testable.	4	5	3	5	2	5	3
C4	Some NFRs require specific circumstances for testing, but they are often not made explicit.	2	4	4	5	2	2	5
ID	**Template statements**	**E1**	**E2**	**E3**	**E4**	**E5**	**E6**	**E7**
T1	The template was useful for defining an NFR.	5	4	3	4	4	4	5
T2	The template was easy to use.	4	4	4	5	3	5	4
T3	I would use this template again to define an NFR.	4	5	4	4	4	4	4

7   Discussion

We use the design science research validity framework to discuss the threats to validity, categorized in criterion, causal, and context validity [17].

Criterion Validity. The meta-requirements for the artifact were determined by gathering input from a focus group containing participants from the target user group, namely practitioners. We triangulated these meta-requirements using literature; which often stated similar conclusions. We also gathered meta-requirements from literature, in addition to the industry meta-requirements.

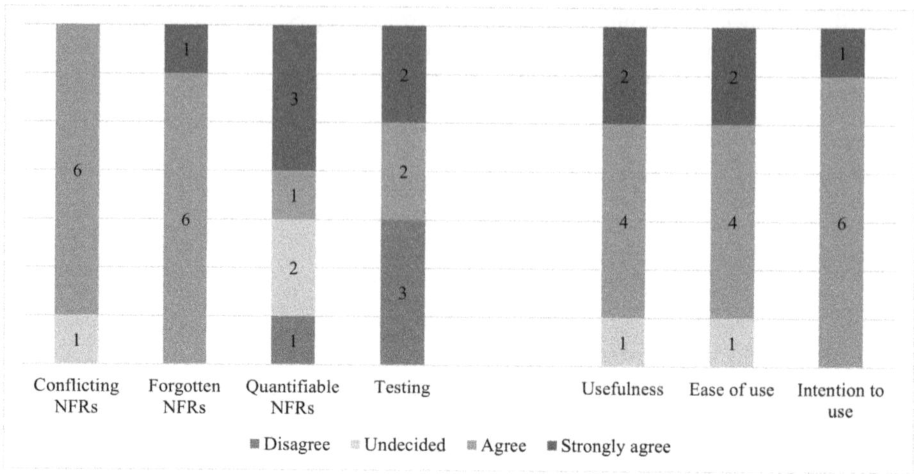

Fig. 4. Consolidated validation scores per statement.

Causal Validity. While validation of the artifact is limited and can only attest to the perceived mitigation of challenges, interviewees generally found the template useful for defining an NFR and would use the template again in the future. They did express doubts regarding some fields in the template, for instance, they are unsure how useful the template is in prioritizing conflicting NFRs. Similarly, they would need to use the template from refinement to implementation in the development process in order to estimate the usefulness of the validation and testing fields.

Context Validity. We elicited meta-requirements for the artifact from target end-users and performed validation through expert opinion. The focus group participants were involved in validation, as they are familiar with the described challenges, as well as two uninvolved experts to get a broader and more objective perspective. To gather more insight into the contextual validity, we also asked experts from different organizations to evaluate the template.

Future Work. While the interviewees stated an intention to use the artifact, it remains uncertain whether they will use it and, if so, to what extent. If the use of the NFR template results in higher quality NFRs was not considered in this study, but could provide valuable insight. Furthermore, the experts stated they would need to use the template in a full development process to be sure of the benefits regarding conflicts and testing. LLMs could potentially be used to help practitioners fill in and adhere to the template or even propose draft NFRs based on existing system documentation. Finally, we identify an opportunity to formalize the process described into a method.

8   Conclusion

We used a design cycle to address the design problem: *how to design an industry-specific template for defining NFRs?* We identified three meta-requirements from related literature, as well as seven meta-requirements from industry through a focus group session. We used these meta-requirements, as well as additional insights provided by the focus group participants, to create a conceptual model. The developed artifact, the iNFR template, is based on this model and industry needs. We then invited four practitioners to provide their expert opinion and validate the template. They expect that practitioners could be supported in overcoming the challenges described by the focus group, but would like to use the template in a full development process to test the full benefits. They valued the 'fit criteria' field most, as this helps make NFRs more specific and quantifiable. The experts generally found the template useful as well as easy to use and all experts expressed an intention to use the template to define an NFR again in the future. Through our iNFR-template, we propose a process for developing a situational NFR template that can be tailored to specific contexts and organizations, which can be used by others as well.

Data Availability Statement. Due to confidentiality agreements, no raw data could be shared. Instead, the focus group and interview protocols, as well as the iNFR template (including fictitious examples) are made available [21].

References

1. ISO/IEC/IEEE 29148:2018 systems and software engineering—Life cycle processes—Requirements engineering (2018), 2nd edn., December 2018
2. Bowen, T.P., Wigle, G.B., Tsai, J.T.: Specification of software quality attributes. Rome Air Development Center, Air Force Systems Command (1985)
3. Chung, L.: Representation and utilization of non-functional requirements for information system design. In: Andersen, R., Bubenko, J.A., Sølvberg, A. (eds.) Proceedings of the International Conference on Advanced Information Systems Engineering (CAiSE) 1991. LNCS, vol. 498, pp. 5–30. Springer, Heidelberg (1991). https://doi.org/10.1007/3-540-54059-8_78
4. Cleland-Huang, J., Settimi, R., Zou, X., Solc, P.: The detection and classification of non-functional requirements with application to early aspects. In: Proceedings of the International Requirements Engineering Conference, pp. 39–48. IEEE (2006)
5. Cohn, M.: User Stories Applied: For Agile Software Development. Addison-Wesley Professional (2004)
6. Cysneiros, L.M., do Prado Leite, J.C.S., de Melo Sabat Neto, J.: A framework for integrating non-functional requirements into conceptual models. Requirements Eng. **6**(2), 97–115 (2001)
7. Ebert, C.: Dealing with nonfunctional requirements in large software systems. Ann. Softw. Eng. **3**(1), 367–395 (1997)
8. Eckhardt, J., Vogelsang, A., Fernández, D.M.: Are "non-functional" requirements really non-functional? An investigation of non-functional requirements in practice. In: Proceedings of the International Conference on Software Engineering, pp. 832–842 (2016)

9. Giannakopoulou, D., Mavridou, A., Rhein, J., Pressburger, T., Schumann, J., Shi, N.: Formal requirements elicitation with FRET. In: Proceedings of the International Working Conference on Requirements Engineering: Foundation for Software Quality (2020)

10. Glinz, M.: On non-functional requirements. In: Proceedings of the IEEE International Requirements Engineering Conference, pp. 21–26. IEEE (2007)

11. Glinz, M.: A risk-based, value-oriented approach to quality requirements. IEEE Softw. **25**(2), 34–41 (2008)

12. Glinz, M.: A glossary of requirements engineering terminology: standard glossary of the Certified Professional for Requirements Engineering (CPRE) studies and exam, version 1.0. Tech. rep., IREB, Karlsruhe, Germany (2011)

13. Grimshaw, D.J., Draper, G.W.: Non-functional requirements analysis: deficiencies in structured methods. Inf. Softw. Technol. **43**(11), 629–634 (2001)

14. Kop, C., Mayr, H.C.: Conceptual predesign bridging the gap between requirements and conceptual design. In: Proceedings of the International Symposium on Requirements Engineering, pp. 90–98. IEEE (1998)

15. Kopczyńska, S., Nawrocki, J.: Using non-functional requirements templates for elicitation: a case study. In: Proceedings of the International Workshop on Requirements Patterns, pp. 47–54. IEEE (2014)

16. Kopczyńska, S., Nawrocki, J., Ochodek, M.: An empirical study on catalog of non-functional requirement templates: usefulness and maintenance issues. Inf. Softw. Technol. **103**, 75–91 (2018)

17. Larsen, K.R., Lukyanenko, R., Mueller, R.M., Storey, V.C., VanderMeer, D., Parsons, J., Hovorka, D.S.: Validity in design science research. In: Hofmann, S., Müller, O., Rossi, M. (eds.) Proceedings of the International Conference on Design Science Research in Information Systems and Technology, pp. 272–282. Springer, Cham (2020). https://doi.org/10.1007/978-3-030-64823-7_25

18. Lawrence, B., Wiegers, K., Ebert, C.: The top risk of requirements engineering. IEEE Softw. **18**(6), 62–63 (2001)

19. Lucassen, G., Dalpiaz, F., van der Werf, J.M.E., Brinkkemper, S.: Improving agile requirements: the quality user story framework and tool. Requirements Eng. **21**(3), 383–403 (2016)

20. Mavin, A., Wilkinson, P., Harwood, A., Novak, M.: Easy approach to requirements syntax (EARS). In: Proceedings of the IEEE International Requirements Engineering Conference, pp. 317–322. IEEE (2009)

21. Molenaar, S.: iNFR template online appendix (2026). https://doi.org/10.5281/zenodo.18267403

22. Molenaar, S., van den Berg, N., Dalpiaz, F., Brinkkemper, S.: Concept definition review: a method for studying terminology in software engineering. Inf. Softw. Technol. **180**, 107648 (2025)

23. Molenaar, S., Dalpiaz, F.: Improving the writing quality of user stories: a canonical action research study. In: Scanniello, G., Lenarduzzi, V., Romano, S., Vegas, S., Francese, R. (eds.) Proceedings of the International Product-Focused Software Process Improvement Conference, pp. 102–118. Springer, Cham (2025). https://doi.org/10.1007/978-3-032-12089-2_7

24. Mylopoulos, J., Chung, L., Nixon, B., et al.: Representing and using nonfunctional requirements: a process-oriented approach. IEEE Trans. Softw. Eng. **18**(6), 483–497 (1992)

25. Mylopoulos, J., Chung, L., Yu, E.: From object-oriented to goal-oriented requirements analysis. Commun. ACM **42**(1), 31–37 (1999)

26. Paech, B., Kerkow, D.: Non-functional requirements engineering-quality is essential. In: Proceedings of the International Working Conference on Requirements Engineering: Foundation for Software Quality Workshops, pp. 237–250 (2004)
27. Pohl, K.: Requirements Engineering: Fundamentals, Principles, and Techniques. Springer, Heidelberg, Germany (2010)
28. Pohl, K.: Requirements Engineering Fundamentals: A Study Guide for the Certified Professional for Requirements Engineering Exam-Foundation Level-IREB Compliant. Rocky Nook, Santa Barbara (2016)
29. Regnell, B., Svensson, R.B., Olsson, T.: Supporting roadmapping of quality requirements. IEEE Softw. **25**(2), 42–47 (2008)
30. Robertson, S., Robertson, J.: Mastering the Requirements Process: Getting Requirements Right, 3rd edn. Addison Wesley, Boston (2013)
31. Rozanski, N., Woods, E.: Software Systems Architecture: Working with Stakeholders Using Viewpoints and Perspectives, 2nd edn. Addison Wesley, Boston (2012)
32. Verhoeven, N.: Doing Research: The Hows and Whys of Applied Research, 5th edn. Boom uitgevers, Amsterdam (2019)
33. Wake, B.: INVEST in Good Stories, and SMART Tasks (2003). http://xp123.com/articles/invest-in-good-stories-and-smart-tasks/, Accessed 12 Mar 2025
34. Wieringa, R.: Design Science Methodology for Information Systems and Software Engineering. Springer, Heidelberg (2014). https://doi.org/10.1007/978-3-662-43839-8

Eliciting and Ingraining Cultural Elements in Digital Information Systems with CEFIS

Oscar A. Mondragon[1]([✉]) [iD], Josiah M. Heyman[1] [iD], Benito Mendoza[2] [iD],
Jeffrey Escamilla[1] [iD], Elizabeth D. Martin[1], Wellington Verduga[2], Melissa Ramirez[1],
Fatima Orpineda[1], Luis J. Franco[1] [iD], and Sugat Borthakur[1] [iD]

[1] The University of Texas at El Paso, El Paso, TX 79968, USA
{oamondragon,jmheyman}@utep.edu, {jescamilla2,edmartin,
mramirez57,forpineda,ljfranco,sborthakur}@miners.utep.edu
[2] New York City College of Technology, Brooklyn, NY 11201, USA
bmendoza@citytech.cuny.edu,
wellington.verduga@mail.citytech.cuny.edu

Abstract. This paper presents the Cultural Elements Framework for Information Systems (CEFIS) that supports the explicit representation and discussion of cultural considerations during Requirements Engineering (RE) for Digital Information Systems (DIS). This early-stage research framework is motivated by persistent challenges in designing trusted public-facing systems for culturally diverse populations. CEFIS structures cultural knowledge into inspectable Cultural Elements (CEs) that can be considered alongside traditional requirements artifacts. Rather than prescribing cultural requirements, the framework aims to make cultural assumptions visible, discussable, and traceable during early RE and design activities. A proof-of-concept (POC) application of CEFIS for a food assistance website serving a predominantly Hispanic population illustrates how selected CEs can be operationalized and reflected in prototype designs. This exploratory qualitative evaluation, conducted through focus groups, provides preliminary insights into how community members perceive culturally informed design choices when comparing new food-pantry website prototypes with the original site. The POC also highlighted methodological challenges associated with studying culture in RE contexts. Consistent with the goals of a Research Preview, this work does not evaluate effectiveness or generalizability; instead, it contributes structured conceptual framing, an initial operationalization, and a research agenda to stimulate discussion and future empirical work within the requirements engineering community.

Keywords: Cultural Elements · Requirements Engineering · Food Security · Trustworthy Information Systems

1 Introduction

Digital Information Systems (DIS) are essential for providing access to vital public and social services, including healthcare, education, and food assistance. In 2023, 36.8 million people in the United States lived in poverty, many qualifying for safety-net programs that rely on digital systems for information access and service delivery [1]. Despite widespread deployment, many such systems remain underutilized or mistrusted, particularly among culturally and linguistically diverse populations. Recent studies show that barriers to effective use often extend beyond usability or infrastructure limitations and are closely tied to cultural, linguistic, and contextual misalignments between systems and their intended users [2].

Within the broader literature on information access and equity, such misalignments have been shown to contribute to persistent disparities in how different populations engage with public-facing DIS [3]. These challenges are particularly evident in social services and food security contexts, where informational and procedural barriers limit access even when services are available [4].

In **requirements engineering (RE)**, prior work has highlighted the importance of ethics, values, and social context in system design [5–8]. While these approaches provide important conceptual foundations for considering human and societal concerns, they offer limited operational guidance for identifying, structuring, and tracing concrete cultural considerations during early RE activities. As a result, cultural assumptions are often addressed implicitly or deferred to later stages of design, rather than being treated as explicit artifacts within the RE process.

This paper introduces the **Cultural Elements Framework for Information Systems (CEFIS)** as an early-stage research framework to support the systematic integration of cultural considerations into RE. CEFIS structures cultural knowledge into explicit, inspectable **Cultural Elements (CEs)** grounded in anthropological and sociocultural theory [9, 10], and links them to system artifacts and design decisions. Rather than prescribing specific cultural requirements, CEFIS is intended to support reflection, discussion, and traceability of cultural considerations during RE and design activities.

CEFIS is informed by interdisciplinary foundations spanning cultural anthropology and sociocultural studies of trust and social organization [9, 10]. Prior work in culturally relevant interface design demonstrates the importance of making such cultural considerations explicit rather than implicit in system design decisions [11]. CEFIS is designed to complement existing RE practices and participatory approaches [12], making cultural assumptions and design choices more explicit, which can be validated by target user populations. This paper addresses the research question: **RQ1**: *How do users perceive UI components that ingrain cultural characteristics relevant to a population sector, including perceived motivation to use digital information systems in daily life?*

A proof-of-concept, addressing a food assistance pantry website serving a Hispanic community, examines the practical feasibility of applying CEFIS. Consistent with the goals of a Research Preview, this study does not aim to establish effectiveness or generalizability, but to demonstrate operationalization, surface methodological challenges, and open research questions.

2 Background and Related Work

Research on cultural considerations in information systems spans multiple disciplines, such as anthropology, human-computer interaction (HCI), information science, and RE. Foundational cultural theory emphasizes that culture comprises shared meanings, norms, and practices that shape how people interpret and interact with systems and institutions [9, 13]. In culturally diverse contexts, these shared meanings are closely linked to trust, social relationships, and perceptions of legitimacy [10].

Within HCI and information systems research, prior studies have shown that culturally relevant design features can influence user engagement and perceived appropriateness of digital interfaces, particularly for Hispanic and other minoritized populations [11]. However, much of this work focuses on interface-level adaptations and post-hoc evaluation, with limited attention to how cultural considerations are elicited, documented, and traced during early RE activities.

Several RE–adjacent approaches have sought to address ethical and social dimensions of system design. Value Sensitive Design (VSD) provides a framework for identifying and accounting for human values throughout the design process [5], while Value-Based Engineering (VBE) extends this perspective by offering process-level guidance aligned with IEEE 7000 for embedding ethical considerations into system development [6]. Norm Sensitive Design (NSD) further critiques value-centric approaches by emphasizing the role of social norms and contextual obligations in shaping acceptable system behavior [7]. While these approaches offer important conceptual insights, they do not provide concrete mechanisms for operationalizing culturally grounded requirements in a systematic and inspectable manner during RE.

Accessibility standards such as the Web Content Accessibility Guidelines (WCAG) demonstrate how principles of perceivable, operable, understandable, and robust design can be translated into concrete, testable criteria that guide system design and evaluation [8]. WCAG highlights the importance of structured frameworks that enable traceability and inspection; however, it does not consider broader cultural aspects like symbolism, community norms, or culturally rooted ideas of trust.

CEFIS builds on the above work by focusing on the elicitation and structuring of cultural considerations as first-class artifacts in RE. CEFIS complements value-oriented or norm-sensitive approaches by offering a lightweight, inspectable structure for reasoning about CEs and their implications during requirements prototyping. CEFIS may bridge the gap between high-level ethical frameworks and the practical realities of RE in culturally diverse, public-facing systems.

3 Cultural Elements Framework for Information Systems (CEFIS)

This paper introduces the Cultural Elements Framework for Information Systems (CEFIS) to guide human-centered design in identifying, documenting, and integrating culture into discrete elements mapped to user interface components within an information system. CEFIS is grounded in anthropological theories that categorize culture into three core Groups (i.e., Norms, Values, and Symbols), shaping how individuals interpret and engage with institutions and technologies [9, 13, 14]. Groups include CEs that map to user interface design choices.

Framework Structure: CEFIS organizes cultural knowledge into CEs, which represent culturally meaningful concepts that may influence system interpretation, interaction, or trust. Each CE is documented using a structured template that includes *Definition* (a concise description of the element), *Intent* (the rationale for why the element is relevant in a system context, *Generic Examples* (illustrative, cross-context examples), *In-Practice Examples* (domain- or population-specific manifestations), and *Design Implications* (potential influences on system artifacts such as content, workflows, or interface features). CEFIS is the result of an iterative process between anthropologists and CS professionals that delineates the basic elements of culture. Due to space limitations, only the basic work structure of CEFIS is presented here. CEFIS *Technical Report* provides a complete description. The report, user manual, and interactive framework are available in [15]. Figure 1 illustrates a static view of CEFIS as a Work Breakdown Structure organized from left to right.

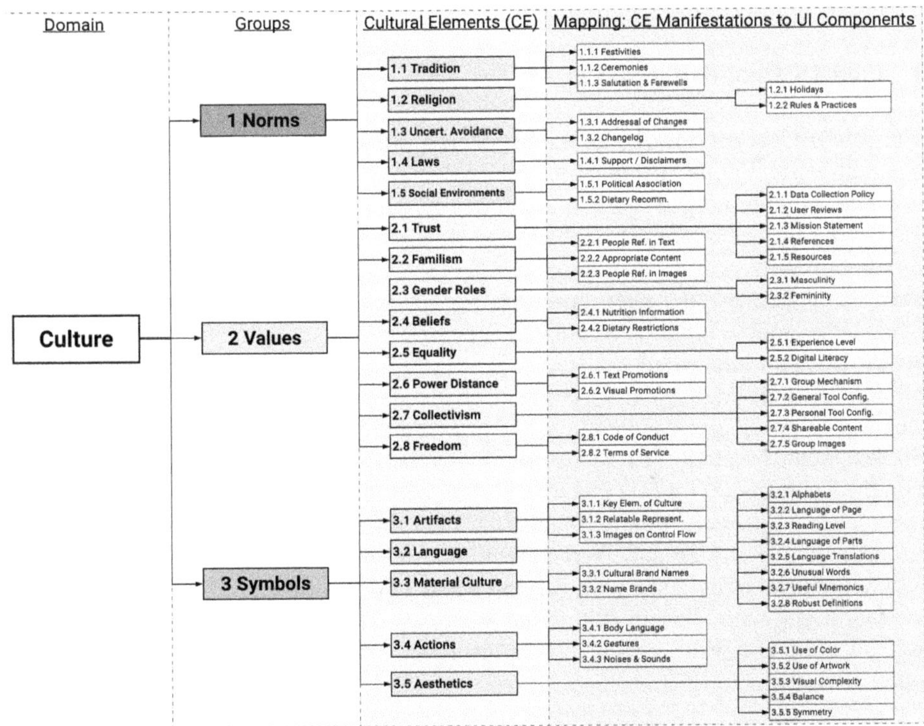

Fig. 1. Cultural Elements Framework for Information Systems (CEFIS) [15]

Limitations of CEFIS: The Groups and Cultural Elements included in CEFIS are not intended to be a holistic description of culture. For the sake of simplicity, this research team decided to assign CEs to a single Group and acknowledges that a) CEs may overlap between Groups, and b) relationships inside cultures among various CEs are not considered. Nevertheless, CEFIS is an initial step for proof of concept and provides a systematic approach for SWE to identify and implement culturally relevant aspects in the design of DIS for specific population sectors.

Tailoring CEFIS for Specific Populations or Domains: CEFIS provides CEs with associated definitions, intents, and generic examples intended to support reuse across domains. CEFIS allows culturally grounded tailoring when applied to specific population sectors, application domains, or both. Each CEs includes an *In-Practice* section that captures domain- or population-specific examples illustrating element manifestation in real-world systems. These examples should be authored by individuals who are members of the target culture or systematically elicited by domain experts from cultural insiders using established qualitative and ethnographic techniques. Prior work on Cultural Domain Analysis offers a methodological foundation for such elicitation, including free listing, pile sorting, and structured interviews to identify culturally salient concepts and relationships among them [16].

4   CEFIS Proof-of-Concept

A Proof-Of-Concept (POC) was conducted to explore the feasibility of applying CEFIS in a real-world setting. It illustrates how selected CEs can be identified, interpreted, and reflected in prototype designs, and how community members perceive these design choices during an exploratory qualitative evaluation. This POC does not aim to establish the effectiveness or generalizability of CEFIS but to surface methodological considerations, challenges, and open questions for future research. The POC was validated using focus groups, and its protocol was approved as exempt by the Institutional Review Board (IRB) for human subject studies. For the application context, this research team tailored CEFIS to address a) the needs and challenges of El Paso, Texas, a predominantly Mexican-origin Hispanic population, and b) the Food Security domain, by providing specific examples in all CE *In-Practice* sections. The POC was carried out in partnership with the Kelly Center for Food Hunger Relief, a local food pantry [17]. Food assistance systems are a vital part of public-facing DIS because they help people access essential resources who are often underserved by digital services. The target population for the system included individuals with varying levels of digital literacy, English proficiency, and familiarity with formal institutional processes. This context is relevant for examining how cultural considerations may influence the motivations of DIS users to engage with the system.

Applying CEFIS to Build Culturally Relevant Websites: Two Hispanic web developers used CEFIS as a guiding framework to create new website prototypes (bilingual and Spanish) intended to support access to food pantry services. Web developers, who have no prior knowledge of CEFIS or the Kelly Center website, were provided with the CEFIS technical report, user manual, and interactive framework [15] and were asked to use them as a reflective aid during the design process by identifying relevant Cultural Elements and their *In-Practice* section for examples related to Hispanics and food pantries. Web developers determined how to modify or add UI components, such as labels, buttons, text, images, sentiment-sensitive content, and panels, to reflect cultural traits. These instantiations informed decisions related primarily to content presentation, language use, symbolism, and interaction cues. The goal was not to enforce specific design outcomes, but to examine how CEs could inform design decisions when made explicit during early development activities. The new prototypes differed in how cultural considerations were expressed, enabling an exploratory comparison of design interpretations rather than a controlled experimental contrast measuring usability metrics. Web developers did not interact with food pantry users or customers.

Exploratory Evaluation Design: Two focus groups were designed and implemented: one bilingual and the other in Spanish. Each group included ten participants and met for about two hours. Participants received copies of the questionnaires, available at [15], which enabled them to compare images of the Kelly Center website with those of the new websites. Focus groups involved verbal group discussions of each question that were extensive, energetic, and rich. Participants could also write personal comments on the questionnaire. This process gathered insights into how target population users perceived the new prototypes. This evaluation was limited in scope. It was not designed to isolate the effects of individual CEs, measure the completeness of CEs, or assess how easy it was for developers to use CEFIS. Instead, the evaluation assessed whether culturally informed design choices were noticeable and meaningful to them.

Limitations and Scope: Because the study is on a single community-serving activity and in a culturally specific geographic setting, this initial validation is preliminary yet informative, as well as ethically important. The small sample size and qualitative nature of the evaluation limit the strength of claims regarding engagement or trust. These limitations are not treated as flaws but as boundary conditions appropriate to an early-stage research contribution that inform the research agenda outlined in Sect. 6.

5 Exploratory Findings and Observations

This section reports observations from the exploratory evaluation described in Sect. 4. These observations surface insights into how culturally informed design choices are perceived and identify methodological considerations for future research.

Coded Thematic Analysis of Participant Perceptions: Two initial codes were inductively derived and iteratively refined (i.e., one per focus group), comprising participant-written comments and session verbal transcripts. Two additional researchers reviewed, refined, and consolidated the codebooks. Themes were categorized into seven themes, 12 sub-themes, and 33 codes supported by participant quotations. A thematic map, available at [15], depicts relationships among themes and the cultural-linguistic complexities observed in this study. Participants reported that the prototypes were understandable, relevant to their needs, and the visual design drew their attention and fostered a strong sense of belonging. Bright red and green accents, images of chiles and fresh fruit, and scenes of neighbors sharing meals signaled that the pantry "was for us." One attendee added that the familiar food images "made me want to keep reading." These reactions reflect the intended effects of the CEFIS *Aesthetics* and *Artifacts* CE. Participants described the pantry as "an extension of my own family," reflecting alignment with community values and shared identity. Similarly, the themes of *Cultural Representation and Identity*, *Audience Connection and Emotion*, and *Motivation and Action Intent* created a unified sense of cultural response. These observations suggest that culturally informed design choices were noticeable to users; however, this POC does not permit attribution to specific CEs or the use of CEFIS itself.

Developer Reflections: Anecdotal developer reflections indicated that making cultural considerations explicit through structured CEs nurtured their inspection and reasoning during prototype design activities, and helped surface assumptions that might otherwise have remained implicit. Evaluation observations suggest that treating cultural considerations as explicit artifacts during early design is feasible and perceptible to users. Nonetheless, this work highlights the need for more rigorous evaluation designs and clearer differentiation between framework effects and design outcomes.

6 Research Agenda and Future Directions

Observations from the proof-of-concept surface several research questions. Moreover, it opens a broader future research agenda, including more evaluation designs, refined elicitation methods, and clearer role definitions in future studies.

Refining Elicitation and Framework Use. Future research concerns the systematic elicitation of CEs and their contextualized In-Practice examples. While the POC demonstrated the feasibility of populating CEFIS using expert interpretation and domain knowledge, future work should investigate structured elicitation approaches grounded in ethnographic and participatory methods, including techniques from Cultural Domain Analysis and participatory RE. Future studies should examine how intra-cultural diversity can be represented within the framework, avoiding overly homogeneous characterizations of culture. Evaluating CEFIS itself as a support artifact for RE is equally important. This includes studying its usability, perceived usefulness, and cognitive demands when used by requirements engineers, designers, and developers, as well as assessing how it influences requirement articulation and design rationale.

Designing Rigorous Evaluation Strategies. Future work should employ more rigorous evaluations to investigate the relationship between culturally informed requirements and system outcomes. This may include task-based usability studies, A/B testing of culturally differentiated designs, and mixed-method approaches that combine qualitative insights with quantitative measures. Such studies should distinguish between the effects of CEFIS as a framework for cultural considerations versus other approaches.

Generalization and Community Engagement. While this study focused on a food assistance context serving a Hispanic population, future research should explore the applicability of CEFIS across domains (e.g., healthcare, education) and the heterogeneity of user populations (e.g., age, language proficiency, education level, and income) to reveal which CEs are broadly reusable and which require substantial contextual tailoring. Moreover, CEFIS itself needs a thorough review by a team of cultural anthropologists. Other validations should examine multiple application stages: applying CEFIS prospectively (during requirements elicitation) or retrospectively as a diagnostic tool for identifying cultural blind spots in existing systems with limited utilization, as we did in this study. CEFIS may be especially valuable when SWE from a dominant culture (e.g., Anglo) design systems for unfamiliar cultures (e.g., Hispanics). For deployed systems,

CEFIS may enhance the cultural relevance of existing systems and websites. Another goal of this research agenda is to foster discussion within the RE community about the role of culture in RE practice. By positioning CEFIS as a reflective and inspectable framework rather than a prescriptive solution, this team invites feedback on CEFIS structure, assumptions, and integration with existing RE methods.

7 Conclusion

This paper presents CEFIS, an early-stage framework created to explicitly represent and discuss cultural considerations during RE for DIS. Driven by ongoing challenges in designing systems that are trusted and effectively adopted by culturally diverse populations, CEFIS organizes cultural knowledge into inspectable CEs that can be reasoned about alongside traditional requirements artifacts. Through a proof-of-concept application in a food assistance context for a Hispanic population, the results showed that CEFIS can identify relevant cultural characteristics rather than leaving them implicit. The exploratory findings from this study suggest that culturally informed design choices are noticeable and meaningful to users and that incorporating relevant cultural elements in the design of user interfaces is practical for designers, valuable for users, and may motivate the use and adoption of DIS. In line with the aims of a Research Preview, this work provides a structured framework for cultural elements, an initial implementation, and a research agenda to foster discussion within the RE community. This research group sees CEFIS as a foundation for further research into how cultural considerations can be systematically elicited, represented, and evaluated within requirements engineering processes.

Acknowledgments. This material is based upon work supported by the National Science Foundation under Grant No. 2131291. Any opinions, findings, conclusions, or recommendations expressed in this material are those of the author(s) and do not necessarily reflect the views of the National Science Foundation.

Disclosure of Interests. The authors declare that they have no competing interests.

Data Availability Statement. This study draws on IRB-approved qualitative focus group data. Questionnaires guided participant discussions, and recordings from two sessions informed development of the thematic codebook. Recordings were deleted after one month due to the sensitivity of the data and the risk of re-identification in a small, culturally specific community. The questionnaires, codebook, and CEFIS materials are available in [15].

References

1. U.S. Census Bureau: Poverty in the United States: 2023, https://www.census.gov/library/pub lications/2024/demo/p60-283.html, (2024).
2. Whitehead, L., Talevski, J., Fatehi, F., Beauchamp, A.: Barriers to and facilitators of digital health among culturally and linguistically diverse populations: qualitative systematic review. J. Med. Internet Res. **25**, e42719 (2023). https://doi.org/10.2196/42719

3. Lievrouw, L.A., Farb, S.E.: Information and equity. Annu. Rev. Inf. Sci. Technol. **37**, 499–540 (2003). https://doi.org/10.1002/aris.1440370112

4. Millerschultz, A., Nalley, L.L., McFadden, B., Nayga, R., Yang, W.: Required information as barriers to accessing groceries from food banks. Food Secur. **17**, 9–25 (2025). https://doi.org/10.1007/s12571-024-01516-2

5. Friedman, B., Kahn, P.H.Jr., Borning, A.: Value sensitive design and information systems. In: The Handbook of Information and Computer Ethics. pp. 69–101. John Wiley & Sons (2008). doi:https://doi.org/10.1002/9780470281819.ch4.

6. Spiekermann, S., Winkler, T.: Value-Based Engineering with IEEE 7000, https://papers.ssrn.com/abstract=4142396, (2022). doi:https://doi.org/10.2139/ssrn.4142396.

7. Martin, D.A., Clancy, R.F., Zhu, Q., Bombaerts, G.: Why do we need norm sensitive design? A weird critique of value sensitive approaches to design. Axiomathes. **33**, 1–19 (2023). https://doi.org/10.1007/s10516-023-09689-9

8. World Wide Web Consortium: Web Content Accessibility Guidelines (WCAG) 2.1, https://www.w3.org/TR/WCAG21/, (2025).

9. Kroeber, A.L., Kluckhohn, C.: Culture: a Critical Review of Concepts and Definitions. Harvard University, Peabody Museum of Archaeology and Ethnology (1952)

10. Vélez-Ibañez, C.G.: An Impossible Living in a Transborder World: Culture, Confianza, and Economy of Mexican-Origin Populations. University of Arizona Press, Tucson (2010)

11. Sachau, L.L., Hutchinson, S.R.: Trends in culturally relevant Interface design features for Latino web site users. Educ. Technol. Res. Dev. **60**, 1033–1050 (2012). https://doi.org/10.1007/s11423-012-9270-5

12. Ferreira, B., Conte, T., Diniz Junqueira Barbosa, S.: Eliciting requirements using personas and empathy map to enhance the user experience. In: Proceedings of the 29th Brazilian Symposium on Software Engineering (SBES), pp. 80–89 (2015). https://doi.org/10.1109/SBES.2015.14

13. Hofstede, G.: Culture's Consequences: Comparing Values, Behaviors, Institutions and Organizations Across Nations. SAGE (2001).

14. Hall, E.T.: Beyond culture. Knopf Doubleday Publishing Group (1976).

15. IS-CUCO Project: Repository-Cultural Elements Framework for Information Systems (CEFIS), https://ilink.cybershare.utep.edu/project-details-is-cuco.html.

16. Borgatti, S.P.: Elicitation techniques for cultural domain analysis. In: Schensul, J., LeCompte, E. (eds.) The Ethnographer's Toolkit, pp. 115–151. Sage Publications, Thousand Oaks, CA (1998)

17. Kelly Center for Hunger Relief – Helping El Pasoans in need address hunger and food insecurity.: https://kellyfresh.org/, Accessed 08 Jan 2026

Towards a Goal-Centric Assessment of Requirements Engineering Methods for Privacy by Design

Oleksandr Kosenkov[1,2]([✉]), Ehsan Zabardast[2], Jannik Fischbach[1],
Tony Gorschek[1,2], and Daniel Mendez[1,2]

[1] fortiss GmbH, Munich, Germany
{kosenkov,fischbach,gorschek,mendez}@fortiss.org
[2] Blekinge Institute of Technology, Karlskrona, Sweden
{oleksandr.kosenkov,ehsan.zabardast}@bth.se

Abstract. Implementing privacy by design (PbD) according to the General Data Protection Regulation (GDPR) is met with a growing number of requirements engineering (RE) approaches. However, the question of which RE method for PbD fits best the goals of organisations remains a challenge. We report our endeavor to close this gap by synthesizing a goal-centric approach for PbD methods assessment. We used literature review, interviews, and validation with practitioners to achieve the goal of our study. As practitioners do not approach PbD systematically, we suggest that RE methods for PbD should be assessed against organisational goals, rather than process characteristics only. We hope that, when further developed, the goal-centric approach could support the development, selection, and tailoring of RE practices for PbD.

Keywords: requirements engineering · empirical software engineering · privacy engineering · software compliance · privacy by design

1 Introduction

Achieving GDPR compliance during software engineering (SE), especially in the requirements engineering (RE) phase of the software development life cycle (SDLC). The number of RE methods trying to address GDPR compliance is constantly growing. In practice, the adoption of these methods and tools remains poorly supported [1,7], and ad-hoc approaches are widespread. One reason for this is the absence of concrete assessment criteria [1] for RE methods. The adoption of existing contributions in practice becomes cumbersome without any guidance on the selection and implementation of RE approaches. Existing SE process assessment approaches fail to address the specificity required for GDPR compliance. First, GDPR interpretation is complex and should address legal goals in a valid way in variable organizational conditions. Second, the GDPR mandates privacy by design (PbD), requiring regulatory requirements to be implemented throughout SDLC via RE and, in particular, integrated into requirements and system specification artefacts. Still, existing approaches consider

R. Guizzardi and J. Araújo (Eds.): REFSQ 2026, LNCS 16497, pp. 207–216, 2026.
https://doi.org/10.1007/978-3-032-21423-2_14

requirements and system specifications in isolation. Finally, regulatory compliance is an enterprise-level concern [9] requiring coordination and assessment of PbD methods across multiple development teams towards the achievement of enterprise goals. Yet, existing approaches do not sufficiently account for such goals. To facilitate the assessment of RE methods for PbD, we conducted a literature review, interviews, and synthesized and validated an initial version of a goal-centric assessment approach. Our approach is intended to guide organizations in choosing and tailoring or developing RE methods for PbD. We present our preliminary results to foster discussion and invite community feedback on the idea of goal-centric assessment of RE methods.

2   Background

Both "personal data protection by design" (Art. 25 GDPR) and the PbD principle, formulated in research, require controls to be considered from the beginning of the SDLC and implemented in the software design. We understand *privacy by design (PbD)* as the specification and implementation of requirements and system architecture in response to GDPR norms. We define *requirements engineering (RE) for PbD* as the requirements specification that captures requirements and early architecture (constraints) in response to GDPR norms, and effectively and correctly transmits specifications for implementation in the software design. We define *RE method characteristic* as a quality of an outcome and RE artifacts obtained by applying a method (e.g., specifications consistency). *RE method goal* is an ultimate purpose for which a method outcome is used and which drives the RE process (e.g., consistency supports the goal of managing risks).

3   Related Work

Existing studies suggest multiple RE methods for PbD or GDPR compliance (e.g., [8] identified 15 studies covering the RE-software design intersection for GDPR compliance), however, only some conduct an evaluation in practical settings or apply PbD-specific criteria. Studies in business process management and legal informatics suggest some systematic evaluation approaches for GDPR text processing (e.g., [2]), but do not consider such approaches in the context of SE. There are some general frameworks and approaches for SE and RE process assessment and improvement, such as CMMI, SPICE / ISO 33061, iFLAP, and Uni-REPM framework. However, these approaches do not address regulatory compliance, lack problem-orientation, explicit statement of method goals and improvements, and rather focus on process and/or product characteristics [13].

4   Methodology

Next, we report the methodology applied in this study to the extent necessary to explain the development of our goal-centric assessment approach and supports its subsequent discussion (for details see open data set and Fig. 1 for visual overview). This study was guided by the following research questions:

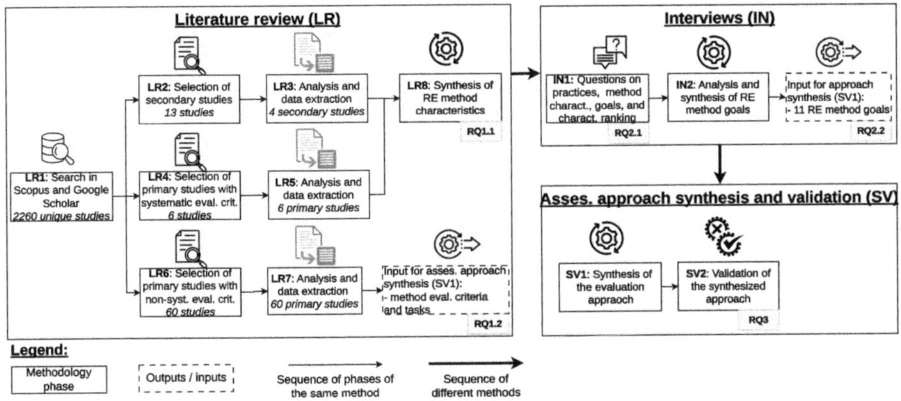

Fig. 1. Visual overview of the methodology

RQ1.1: What are the reported evaluation criteria for methods for PbD?

RQ1.2: What are the reported characteristics of methods for PbD?

RQ2.1: How do practitioners assess the method characteristics importance?

RQ2.2: What are the goals of practitioners in the process of RE for PbD?

RQ3: How useful and feasible is a goal-centric approach to the assessment of RE methods for PbD, according to practitioners?

To answer RQ1.1, RQ1.2 we executed a literature review and synthesized five RE method characteristics (MCs) essential for PbD. We conducted interviews with practitioners to answer RQ2.1, RQ2.2, and identified eleven method goals (MGs) to which method characteristics contribute. Finally, we answered RQ3 by validating the initial version of the assessment approach.

Literature Review (LR). After trial searches with different keywords, we excluded potentially limiting auxiliary terms (e.g., compliance) and executed the following query in Scopus and Google Scholar (without filters): *gdpr AND ("software engineering" OR "requirements engineering") AND (evaluation OR validation).* We retrieved **2260** unique primary studies (1777 from Scopus, the first 700 results from Google Scholar, and after removing 217 duplicates). We have not found any approach for systematically assessing RE methods for PbD, and, thus, we extracted the data for its synthesis from existing secondary studies (LR2-3), primary studies suggesting and evaluating new PbD methods systematically with tailored criteria (LR4-5), and primary studies suggesting new PbD methods, but assessing them with non-tailored criteria (LR6-7). We also extracted criteria from three publications on systematic evaluation of RE methods for system specification (e.g., [4]). We applied a thematic analysis [3] and meta synthesis [12] to synthesize (1) the RE method characteristics (LR8) using the data on systematic assessment of RE methods for PbD (LR2-5, and additional publications), and (2) our evaluation approach (SV1) using the data about non-systematic evaluation (LR6-7) in addition to the interviews results (IN1-2).

Interviews (IN). To answer RQ2.1, RQ2.2 we conducted semi-structured interviews [11]. We applied purposive sampling with snowballing to select participants involved in RE for PbD/GDPR compliance, with both technical insights and experience with GDPR, including both engineering roles (e.g., architects) and roles collaborating with them (e.g., lawyers). We adapted the Goal Question Metric (GQM) approach [14] to structure the interview process and further analysis. The GQM is an approach to defining and measuring software quality at three levels: (1) conceptual level, defining goals to be achieved, (2) operational level, defining questions for evaluating the achievement of goals, and (3) quantitative level, defining metrics or data required to answer the questions. For each method characteristic, we formulated open-ended questions about goals, questions, and metrics. At the end of the interviews, we asked to rank MCs (from 1—most important to 5—least important).

Synthesis and Validation of the Assessment Approach (SV). We synthesized the initial version of the assessment approach on the basis of the GQM approach, as briefly described above. The RE method goals identified in the interviews (IN2) served as a pivot for this. To iteratively develop our approach, we have used (1) questions, metrics, and additional comments identified in the interviews, (2) the relationship between method characteristics and goals, (3) the ranking of method characteristics assigned during the interviews, (4) evaluation criteria and tasks extracted from the literature. Where appropriate, we further decomposed method goals into subgoals. Lastly, the first author refined the approach on the basis of his knowledge of GDPR. We validated the usefulness and feasibility of our approach using screening and walkthrough of the assessment approach [6] (see Table 3 for an example of the approach provided to participants). Validation participants evaluated the *usefulness* (a quality of the components of our approach of being useful) and *feasibility* (a quality of being reasonable and likely to be applied for RE method assessment in practice) of each element of the approach (subgoals, questions, metrics) as positive or negative. See Table 1 for the number of positively evaluated components in relation to the total number of corresponding components (with the remaining evaluations being negative).

5   Results

Literature Review Results. The intersection between requirements and system specification for GDPR compliance is mentioned in multiple studies; however, there are no systematic approaches for the assessment of methods for PbD in practical settings. We found 6 primary studies suggesting new methods for PbD, which recognized and used a tailored evaluation of their contributions. The majority of the other primary studies have reused existing non-PbD-specific criteria for evaluation of their contributions. In the literature review, we extracted the following relevant data: (1) tasks, stakeholders, challenges to GDPR compliance from 4 relevant secondary studies (e.g., [8], (2) evaluation criteria applied for systematic evaluation of PbD methods in 6 primary studies (e.g., [2]), and (3) criteria and tasks (e.g., requirements conflict identification) for non-systematic evaluation of newly suggested PbD methods from 60 secondary studies.

RQ1.1: *The core reported systematic evaluation criteria for PbD methods are correctness, transparency, support of legal goals, activities, and documentation, support for both architectural and legal concepts.*

RQ1.2: *The five basic characteristics of RE methods (MCs) for PbD are as follows:*

MC1: Capturing legal domain knowledge is fundamental for represent legal concepts, identifying goals and architecturally significant requirements, and resolving the GDPR abstractness and engineering-legal perspectives gap. *MC2: Traceability & Consistency of Specifications* is mainly important to address challenges of certification and compliance provability. *MC3: Separation of Compliance & Non-Compliance Concerns* is important as regulated system components can require specific handling, and compliance can conflict with existing SE methods (e.g., outsourcing). *MC4: System Specification Transparency* enables involvement of stakeholders and supports their activities (e.g., risk management). *MC5: System Specification Flexibility* facilitates the architecture flexibility in response to changes in regulations or software, and maintenance of corresponding models.

Table 1. Overview of interviewee ID, company ID, role, general experience, experience with GDPR, ranking of method characteristics and evaluation of usefulness (U) and feasibility (F) of assessment approach components (subgoals, questions, metrics).

ID	Comp.	Role	Exp.	GDPR Exp.	MC1	MC2	MC3	MC4	MC5	Subg. (of 32) U	F	Quest. (of 148) U	F	Metric (of 172) U	F
I1	C1	Tech lead	4	3	5	4	2	3	1	-	-	-	-	-	-
I2	C1	Sales engineer	4	6	4	1	5	2	3	-	-	-	-	-	-
I3	C1	Stream lead	28	6	3	4	1	2	5	-	-	-	-	-	-
I4	C1	Data engineer	3,5	3,5	1	2	5	3	4	-	-	-	-	-	-
I5	C2	Web marketing spec.	8	5	1	2	5	4	3	32	32	146	137	167	158
I6	C3	Security manager	34	7	1	2	5	4	3	-	-	-	-	-	-
I7	C4	Data engineer	4	2	2	1	5	4	3	-	-	-	-	-	-
I8	C5	IT Compl.&Audit Head	30	7	2	3	1	5	4	-	-	-	-	-	-
I9	C6	Cloud Sec. Architect	14	5	1	3	5	2	4	-	-	-	-	-	-
I10	C7	Architect & Req-s Eng.	7	6	1	2	5	3	4	-	-	-	-	-	-
I11	C8	Project manager	20	7	1	2	3	4	5	-	-	-	-	-	-
I12	C8	Tech. project manager	3	3	1	3	4	2	5	-	-	-	-	-	-
I13	C9	Software developer	12	7	1	4	5	3	2	32	27	146	132	170	152
I14	C10	Software architect	15	7	1	4	5	3	2	-	-	-	-	-	-
I15	C11	Info. Security Expert	3	8	1	4	5	3	2	-	-	-	-	-	-
I16	C12	Data Protection Officer	7	7	-	-	-	-	-	32	32	147	141	152	142
I17	C13	Data Protection Advisor	4	4	-	-	-	-	-	31	16	137	98	158	75
I18	C14	Cloud Sec. Architect	2.5	5	-	-	-	-	-	31	30	140	131	150	141
I19	C15	Software Developer	7	2	-	-	-	-	-	29	28	141	135	159	152
Median					1	3	5	3	3						
Mode					1	2, 4	5	3	3, 4						
Sum					26	41	61	47	50						

Interview Results. Only 2 out of 15 interviewees used a specific RE method for PbD, I8 used a tool for compliance in different jurisdictions, and I14 used a data protection impact assessment tool for collaboration with lawyers. Other interviewees used ad hoc approaches (e.g., I1 interviewed lawyers). I1, I11, I14 reported having used some (≤ 4) of the questions and metrics in practice; the remainder were not previously used but potentially applicable. The highest number of the

190 goals was identified in connection with MC4 specification transparency (45 goals), and MC1 capturing legal knowledge (39 goals) (see Table 2).

RQ2.1: *The ranking of the RE method characteristics according to their importance is as follows: MC1: capturing legal knowledge, MC2: traceability and consistency, MC4: specification transparency, MC5: system specification flexibility, MC3: separation of compliance and non-compliance concerns (see Table 1).*

RQ2.2: *After a thematic analysis of the goals, we synthesized the following eleven core RE method goals for PbD (MGs):*

MG1: Facilitating GDPR compliance throughout SDLC includes subgoals for facilitating compliance in the design (e.g., controls modularity), implementation, and testing phases of SDLC, and integration into SDLC models.

MG2: achieving understandability of GDPR subgoals are related to understandability for the involved roles, common understanding, awareness about related aspects (e.g., risks), clarity of GDPR-to-system mapping, sustaining the understanding, best practices synthesis, and understandability of automation.

MG3: enabling decision-making includes subgoals for enabling decisions, compliance efficiency, balancing compliance, technical, business, and other needs, planning expenses, and effectively managing non-compliance (e.g., financial risk).

MG4: Documenting the required information includes subgoals addressing documentation availability, versioning, and history, documentation content, and characteristics, and documentation of GDPR-to-system mapping.

MG5: Facilitating compliance governance includes subgoals on using the processes supporting compliance (e.g., change management), identification of the required information, compliance gaps and the overall compliance status, execution of other governance types (e.g., IT governance), and compliance manageability.

MG6: Enabling response to changes subgoals focused on change identification (e.g., identifying what is likely to change), and facilitating the implementation of changes (e.g., implementation without impacting other components).

MG7: Verifiability&Validity of compliance has subgoals for clarity and availability of information for verification, capacity to trace the required information, addressing validity from stakeholders' perspectives, clarity of the information about the perspectives, sustaining validity, and knowing barriers to it.

MG8: Achieving effective communication on GDPR compliance implementation subgoals under MG consider the facilitation of cross-functional communication, achieving interaction between roles, translating between legal, technical, and business requirements, and communication in a common language.

MG9: facilitating GDPR compliance-related procedures focuses on facilitating procedures such as audits and compliance reviews.

MG10: addressing business concerns in PbD implementation is connected to facilitating business processes improvement, maximization of business outcomes.

MG11: Facilitating risk and security management focuses on intersections between GDPR compliance risks and security risks, controls, and their management.

Table 2. Overview of the number of method goals (MGs) mentioned in connection to method characteristics (MCs).

MC	MG1	MG2	MG3	MG4	MG5	MG6	MG7	MG8	MG9	MG10	MG11	Sum
MC1	3	14	6	4	2	1	2	4	-	-	3	**39**
MC2	7	3	3	6	4	4	5	-	1	-	-	**33**
MC3	4	2	6	2	2	1	3	2	1	1	-	**24**
MC4	4	8	7	10	-	1	1	5	4	1	4	**45**
MC5	9	1	3	1	4	10	-	1	1	-	-	**30**
MC6	3	2	1	1	7	-	-	1	1	3		**19**
Sum	**30**	**30**	**26**	**24**	**19**	**17**	**11**	**13**	**8**	**5**	**7**	**190**

Table 2 shows the number of goals grouped by MGs we synthesized and in relation to MCs with respect to which goals were mentioned. This data indicates that in the future it will be important to identify the contribution of MCs to MGs (e.g., MC1 capturing legal knowledge to MG2 achieving understandability).

Synhtesized Approach. The initial version of the approach was elaborated only to a limited degree, allowing for the validation of the core idea of building the RE method assessment around the method goals, rather than process characteristics, and starting a discussion with the community. The approach (see Table 3 for an excerpt), similarly to GQM, should allow the goal-centric assessment of RE methods for PbD (incl. ad hoc methods) on three levels of abstraction (1) a conceptual with 11 goals / 32 subgoals predefined (see 5) that should be achieved in the process of RE for PbD, (2) an operational (148 questions) focusing on the areas requiring assessment for the goals achievement, and (3) a quantitative with 172 metrics defining concrete criteria and metrics for addressing the corresponding questions. Unlike the GQM, our suggested assessment approach predefines the core approach components to embed the best practices for PbD. The approach can enable flexible assessment by allowing (1) selecting the relevant goals/subgoals requiring assessment and thereby scoping the corresponding questions and metrics, (2) extending existing components with the new ones (which will require development of the guidance for approach extension in the future; to date, we have not received any feedback about additional components required).

Table 3. An excerpt from the evaluation framework illustrating the structure of the framework

Goals	Subgoals	Questions	Criteria/Metrics
G1: Facilitating GDPR implementation throughout the SDLC	G1.1: facilitating software design and architecture	Q1.1.1: Does method support documenting GDPR compliance on software architecture level?	M1.1.1.1: documentation completeness
		Q1.1.2: Does method support architecture review engaging legal experts?	M1.1.2.1: reviews frequency
		Q1.1.3: Is it possible to discern GDPR compliance controls that need to be implemented?	M1.1.3.1: number of controls identified
		Q1.1.4: Is it clear what is the priority for controls implementation?	M1.1.4.1: prioritization available

The approach is applied in two phases (1) tailoring and (2) assessment. Following steps are required for tailoring (1.1) person conducting the assessment (assessor) reviews and selects the goals that organization is aiming to achieve in PbD and which require assessment, (1.2) subgoals belonging to selected goals are reviewed and selected, (1.3) questions belonging to selected subgoals are reviewed and selected, stakeholders required to answer these questions are identified, (1.4) the assessor independently or together with involved stakeholders selects the relevant metrics, and specifies the concrete steps for data collection (e.g., sources of data). This tailoring phase enables scoping of the assessment according to organizational needs. For the assessment execution, (2.1) data is collected, (2.2) answers to the questions are documented on the basis of the collected data, (2.3) subgoals achievement is documented, (2.4) the goals achievement and overall assessment results are documented. For the validation, only a general description and overview of the approach components (as in Table 3 and the open data set) were provided without the guidance for application.

Validation Results. During the validation, participants found the idea and structure of the approach to be clear, and mainly, questions related to concrete components emerged. Overall, the approach was evaluated positively (see next minimal and maximal number of components considered useful or feasible across validation participants or Table 1 for details). Reported non-feasibility of certain components was primarily related to participants' belief that specific concerns cannot be effectively addressed (e.g., communication in a common language).

RQ3: *Min 29 (90%)—max 32 (100%) of 32 subgoals were evaluated as useful, 16 (50%)—32 (100%) subgoals were considered feasible. 137 (92%)—147 (99%) of 148 questions evaluated useful and 98 (66%)—141 (95%) feasible. 150 (87%)—170 (99%) of 172 metrics were considered useful and 75 (44%)—158 (92%) feasible.*

6   Discussion

The conceptualization of PbD for GDPR compliance as a conjoint requirements and system specification was well received and aligned with the experience of practitioners. Our results point to the low maturity of RE methods for PbD in practice, for example, interviewees struggled to articulate their practices, some interviewees could not make an assessment, or changed it while answering. We suggest that such difficulties stemmed, at least in part, from the complex relations between method characteristics and goals. The positive validation of the initial version of our goal-centric approach provides the first indication that goals may be more suitable for assessment purposes. Our study shows that capturing legal knowledge (MC1) and specifications transparency (MC4) are critical for PbD, along with traceability (MC2). Also, practitioners need RE methods that not only support the subsequent SDLC phases and implementation of compliance controls but also account for internal organizational stakeholders (e.g., legal experts) and support their goals and activities (e.g., risk management). Our results support and concretize the idea that RE plays a fundamental role in supporting other phases of SDLC and is intertwined with them [10], and further suggest that RE contributes to the fulfillment of organizational goals and activities.

7   Limitations and Threats to Validity

To mitigate threats to the validity of the results, we followed guidelines for literature review [5], thematic analysis [3], interviews [11], and evaluation [6]. In the literature review, the authors used the selection criteria that did not require interpretation (e.g., defined evaluation criteria) and jointly discussed the intermediary results. We applied interview questions formulated and scoped using the structured GQM approach and asked about any additional considerations. Simplistic binary evaluation of the approach during the validation mainly served the purposes of the initial validation of the goal-centric assessment idea and identification of further improvement directions. To partially mitigate the threats to the results' generalizability, we involved participants in different professional roles, engaged in software requirements and system specification for GDPR compliance, and had expertise in both GDPR and software technologies.

8   Conclusion

Assessing RE methods for software compliance is essential due to their specificity, yet it is not systematic in practice. As RE for PbD demands the coordination of requirements with early architecture and subsequent SDLC phases, RE methods must capture legal knowledge and facilitate transparency of specification, along with providing traceability. Although practitioners often struggle to reason about practices in terms of method characteristics, they frequently pursue the same goals via different method characteristics, motivating a goal-centric assessment of RE methods. The validation of our vision of a GQM-inspired operationalization of such assessment points to its potential usefulness and feasibility in practice.

Before further developing the approach, we invite community feedback on the goal-centric RE method assessment and its synthesis process.

The open data is hosted on Zenodo (10.5281/zenodo.15760786) and website.

References

1. Alhirabi, N., Beaumont, S., Llanos, J.T., Meedeniya, D., et al.: Parrot: interactive privacy-aware internet of things application design tool. ACM IMWUT **7**(1), 1–37 (2023)
2. Bartolini, C., Lenzini, G., Santos, C.: An agile approach to validate a formal representation of the GDPR. In: Kojima, K., Sakamoto, M., Mineshima, K., Satoh, K. (eds.) JSAI International Symposium on AI. LNCS, vol. 11717. Springer, Cham (2018). https://doi.org/10.1007/978-3-030-31605-1_13
3. Braun, V., Clarke, V.: Using thematic analysis in psychology. Qual. Res. Psychol. **3**(2), 77–101 (2006)
4. Galster, M., Eberlein, A., Moussavi, M.: Comparing methodologies for the transition between software requirements and architectures. In: 2009 IEEE International Conference on Systems, Man and Cybernetics, pp. 2380–2385. IEEE (2009)
5. Kitchenham, B., et al.: Guidelines for performing systematic literature reviews in software engineering (2007)
6. Kitchenham, B., Linkman, S., Law, D.: DESMET: a method for evaluating software engineering methods and tools. Keele University (1996)
7. Klymenko, O., et al.: Understanding the implementation of technical measures in the process of data privacy compliance: a qualitative study. In: 16th Symposium ESEM, pp. 261–271 (2022)
8. Kosenkov, O., et al.: Systematic mapping study on requirements engineering for regulatory compliance of software systems. Inf. Softw. Technol. **178**, 107622 (2024)
9. Kosenkov, O., Unterkalmsteiner, M., Mendez, D., Fischbach, J.: Regulatory requirements engineering in large enterprises: an interview study on the European accessibility act. In: International Conference PROFES, pp. 204–220 (2024)
10. Nuseibeh, B., Easterbrook, S.: Requirements engineering: a roadmap. In: Proceedings of the Conference on the Future of Software Engineering, pp. 35–46 (2000)
11. Runeson, P., Höst, M.: Guidelines for conducting and reporting case study research in software engineering. EMSE **14**(2), 131–164 (2009)
12. Sandelowski, M., Barroso, J.: Handbook for Synthesizing Qualitative Research. Springer Publishing Company (2006)
13. Unterkalmsteiner, M., et al.: Evaluation and measurement of software process improvement—a systematic literature review. IEEE Trans. Software Eng. **38**(2), 398–424 (2011)
14. Van Solingen, R., Basili, V., Caldiera, G., Rombach, H.D.: Goal question metric (GGM) approach. Encyclopedia of Software Engineering (2002)

Trustworthiness in AI and Information Systems

Embedding Normative Requirements in Fuzzy Logic

Ziba Assadi[(✉)] and Paola Inverardi

Gran Sasso Science Institute, Viale Francesco Crispi, 7, 67100 L'Aquila, Italy
{ziba.assadi,paola.inverardi}@gssi.it

Abstract. Autonomous systems (AS) powered by AI components are increasingly integrated into the fabric of our daily lives and society, raising concerns about their ethical and social impact. To be considered trustworthy, AS must adhere to ethical principles and values. This has led to significant research on the identification and incorporation of ethical requirements in system design. A recent development is the introduction of SLEEC rules, which offer a comprehensive framework for representing ethical and normative considerations. This paper, based on a logical representation of SLEEC rules, presents a methodology to embed them into AS using fuzzy logic and test-score semantics. The use of fuzzy logic is motivated by the view of ethics as a domain of possibilities, which offers a way to deal with (soft) ethical dilemmas that AI systems may encounter. The approach is illustrated through a case study.

Keywords: AS · Ethics · SLEEC · Fuzzy Logic · Test-Score Semantics

1 Introduction

Autonomous Systems (AS) are increasingly integrated into many aspects of daily life and society, raising growing concerns about their ethical and social implications [11]. To be perceived as trustworthy, such systems must operate in accordance with well-defined ethical principles and human values. This requirement highlights the importance of embedding ethical considerations directly into their design and development processes. A recent contribution in this area is the introduction of the SLEEC (Social, Legal, Ethical, Empathetic, and Cultural) rules by Townsend et al. [25]. These rules represent high-level requirements that autonomous systems should not violate in their behaviour or decision-making.

In this paper, we propose an approach for translating SLEEC rules into a computational representation that can be embedded in AS, particularly robotic ones. We revisit the SLEEC rule for a healthcare robot introduced by Townsend et al. and present our own reformulation, which replaces the use of "unless" in the original model with explicit IF–THEN–ELSE structures. We argue that binary logic is insufficient to capture the nuances of human reasoning in ethically sensitive situations. To address this limitation, we extend boolean logic with fuzzy logic [30], which enables the modeling of graded ethical reasoning and the

R. Guizzardi and J. Araújo (Eds.): REFSQ 2026, LNCS 16497, pp. 219–228, 2026.
https://doi.org/10.1007/978-3-032-21423-2_15

representation of uncertainty in human decision-making. Our approach builds on test-score semantics [31], originally proposed by Zadeh (1982), to formalize vague or context-dependent concepts. By employing fuzzy logic, certain ethical requirements remain available at runtime as part of the system's decision-making engine [12]. This supports the system's ability to handle, and in some cases resolve, ethical dilemmas the system may face during interactions with humans.

Machine ethics has a long research history [23], including logical reasoning approaches such as deductive, non-monotonic, abductive, deontic, rule-based, event-calculus, knowledge-representation, and inductive logics [20]. This work explores fuzzy logic as a method for handling uncertainty and supporting graded ethical reasoning in autonomous systems. Fuzzy logic has been used to represent ethical vagueness in AI systems. Conceptual approaches use fuzzy logic to bridge subjective values and objective data or to represent degrees of ethical conformity without implementing complete fuzzy inference [6,13,27], while survey work discusses fuzzy logic at a high level as one of several machine ethics paradigms [17]. More computational studies apply fuzzy reasoning to model ethical risks and moral justification–particularly in AS without defuzzification or concrete decision outputs [7,15,16]. Partial implementations exist, including simulation-based ethical reasoning in UAVs, fuzzy expert systems, and neuro-fuzzy or argumentation-based hybrids, but these focus on ethical risk assessment or representation rather than full fuzzy ethical reasoning pipelines [10,21,22]. Overall, fully implemented and validated fuzzy ethical decision-making systems for machine ethics remain unexplored. The approach proposed in this paper contributes filling this gap.

The remainder of the paper is structured as follows. Section 2 reviews the existing formalization of SLEEC rules and their general structure. Section 3 discusses the nature of ethical rules and introduces fuzzy logic as a suitable reasoning framework. Section 4 outlines our methodology. Section 5 applies the approach to a case study showing how fuzzy logic can support ethical decision-making. Finally, Sect. 6 concludes the paper.

2   SLEEC Formalization and Refinement

Our approach builds on the methodology proposed by Townsend et al. [25] for eliciting SLEEC requirements for autonomous systems. Further studies have addressed the operationalization of these rules, including conflict resolution and redundancy analysis [9,24,26,28]. An example of a SLEEC rule, defined for a healthcare robot, is the following:

(1) *When the user tells the robot to open the curtains, then the robot should open the curtains, unless the user is 'undressed', in which case the robot does not open the curtains and tells the user 'the curtains cannot be opened while you, the user, are undressed.'*

An additional defeater rule was also introduced, utilized here and in [26].

(2) *unless the user is 'highly distressed', in which case the robot opens the curtains.*

The formalizations in [25,26] employ the Quinean interpretation of *unless* as an inclusive *or* [18]. However, using *unless* as a functional connective introduces logical inconsistencies, due to the lack of equivalence between $p \vee q \vee r$ and $(p \vee q) \wedge (p \vee r)$ [1]. In [2], two linguistic interpretations of *unless*–both functional and commutative–are presented. To avoid ambiguity, we follow the recommendation in [1] and replace *unless* with an explicit and more suitable for machine interpretation IF–THEN–ELSE structure. The reformulated rule is:

IF the user is dressed THEN open the curtains,

ELSE IF the user is not highly distressed THEN do not open the curtains,

ELSE open the curtains.

Then the general structure of a SLEEC rule – *When* c_0 *then* a_0 *unless* c_1 *in* which case a_1 *unless* c_2 *in* which case ... – according to the latter formalization for its conditions and actions (or defeaters) can be modeled as follows:

$$
\begin{array}{llll}
\texttt{if} & c_0 & \texttt{then} & a_0 \\
\texttt{else if} & c_1 & \texttt{then} & a_1 \\
\vdots & \vdots & \vdots & \vdots \\
\texttt{else if} & c_{n-1} & \texttt{then} & a_{n-1} \\
\texttt{else} & a_n & &
\end{array}
$$

This structure ensures logical consistency and supports direct translation into computational models, facilitating the embedding of ethical rules into AS.

3   The Need for Possibility and Fuzzy Logic

Ethical rules expressed in natural language are characterized by imprecision, gradability, and contextual dependency, introducing different levels of uncertainty in their evaluation and application. Their operationalization requires dealing with their inherent uncertainty, that favors possibility over probability: properties like moral consistency are feasible yet rare, and thus possible without being probable. Uncertainty can be handled using possibility theory [30]. A discussion of this modeling choice is provided in our previous work [3]. Based on this notion of possibility, we will use fuzzy logic to map linguistic terms like "highly distressed" into precise, machine-interpretable concepts, and to associate imprecise linguistic expressions with numerical values ranging between 0 and 1.

Fuzzy logic extends classical boolean logic to handle the concept of partial truth, where truth values are not absolute but vary between completely true and completely false. We will use possibility theory to assess the degree of compatibility of a moral property as an alternative to probability theory.

Possibility theory provides a mathematical framework for handling imprecision through graded representations of uncertainty (possibility distribution) without relying on statistical information, making it particularly suitable for reasoning about ethical rules expressed in natural language.

Test-score semantics [31] complements the framework by assigning partial applicability scores to linguistic concepts, which are then aggregated to compute the overall degree of satisfaction. Consider the example concerning our ethical rule that specifies that a user should not be undressed when the curtains are open. If the user sets a threshold for acceptable dressing, reasoning with possibility better reflects human perception than probability. For instance, wearing a sundress, with a degree of possibility above the threshold, may fully satisfy the notion of being dressed, whereas socks, below the threshold, contribute little and do not, and multiple pairs of socks do not increase the degree. We can observe that reasoning with possibility aligns more closely with human perception than with probability. Moreover, the possibility of dressing is best represented by the maximum value among the garment categories of choice.

4   Methodology

Our semi-formal representation of SLEEC rules in natural language provides a foundation for their full logical formalization and subsequent embedding within AS. Achieving this transformation, however, requires the elimination of all forms of semantic ambiguity. Most natural language expressions inherently convey nuances of possibility and degree. For instance, in our example, the phrase "highly distressed" involves both the possibility of a user being "distressed" and the degree or intensity associated with the quantifier "highly". Our semantic framework is based on the possibility theory and the test-score semantics [30,31], both introduced by Zadeh, which form the theoretical foundation of our method. Test-score semantics computes partial scores of linguistic concepts under possibility-based reasoning. Partial scores are then aggregated to produce final degrees representing the satisfaction of each ethical rule.

Our workflow is structured into three main stages. First, we identify an explanatory database (Descriptive data) composed of explicit and implicit necessities (Designation)–where the denotative and connotative aspects of natural language, as discussed in [19], provide useful insights into the notions of explicitness and implicitness. Second, we perform possibility distribution and degree assignment to these necessities, followed by their combination and compatibility checking through fuzzification (Compilation). Finally, we quantify the resulting outcomes through defuzzification (Fig. 1).

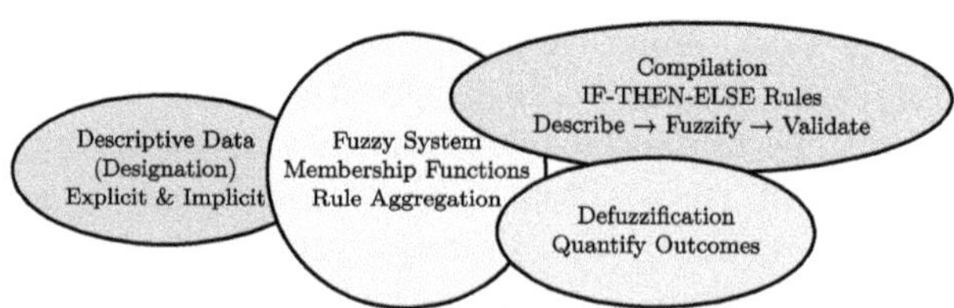

Fig. 1. The 3-stage method

This process embodies the foundation of test-score semantics, which associates every natural language concept with a degree of applicability. In our approach, concepts are partially evaluated through membership functions, their partial test-score degrees are aggregated to obtain overall scores, and compatibility among them is assessed using fuzzy rules.

4.1 Preliminaries for Fuzziness

Consider all components of SLEEC rules as a universe U or domain of discourse. The possibility function POSSIBILITY $\triangleq \mu : U \to [0,1]$ is a fuzzy membership function that maps a variable in U to a value in $[0,1]$. The possibility distribution (membership degrees) of the distress variable $x \in$ {Quite calm, ..., Quite distressed} is given by μ(Quite calm) $= 0, \ldots, \mu$(Normal) $= 0.5, \ldots, \mu$(Quite distressed) $= 1$.
$F = \{(x_1, 0), \cdots, (x_j, \mu_F(x_j)), \cdots, (x_n, 1)\}$ is a representation of fuzzy sets as a collection of ordered pairs, each consisting of an element of the universe and its corresponding membership value.

Designation. We use Carnap's method to assign formal notation to entities according to their extension and intension nature [5]. The term "designator" was introduced by Carnap for all expressions to which a semantic analysis is applied. By definition, the extension of a term or predicate is the corresponding class, and its intension is the corresponding property.

For instance, USER and CURTAINS are terms that are extensively designated according to their explicit meanings. In contrast, OPEN, DRESSED, and DISTRESSED are predicates that are intensively designated to capture their implicit senses–namely, OPEN referring to the action of grabbing and pulling the cord, DRESSED to the user having clothes on, and DISTRESSED to physiological or behavioral symptoms such as variations in blood pressure, body temperature, or heart rate, depending on age. The modifier HIGHLY functions as a quantification term, intensively designated to represent specific degrees of distress.

Descriptive Data. Descriptive data are derived for each SLEEC rule according to their extensional and intensional designations. In our conditional propositions, only the IF part requires a specific designation, as the THEN part corresponds to a boolean action. In the example under consideration, all designations are intensional and therefore implicit, and their descriptive data can be defined as
$DD \triangleq DRESSED[Clothes; \mu_{DC}]+ DISTRESSED[Age; \mu_A$, Blood Pressure; μ_{BP}, Body Temperature; μ_{BT}, Heart Rate; $\mu_{HR}]+ HIGHLY[Distressed; \mu_{HD}]$.

Compilation. The formalized SLEEC rules, structured as nested IF-THEN-ELSE statements, exhibit the logical completeness required for system-level compilation and embedding. The process involves (i) describing the relevant data, (ii) fuzzifying non-absolute or graded concepts, and (iii) validating the resulting representation through compilation and compatibility testing.

4.2   Fuzzification

Fuzzification represents a controlled balance between crisp values and linguistic variables. It involves abstracting precise numerical data into vague or imprecise linguistic categories, thereby enabling the classification of large numeric ranges into a limited and interpretable set of linguistic labels.

Dressed or Undressed. Depending on personal preferences or cultural factors, users may define the concept of being dressed according to the number or combination of garments worn. In such cases, we propose the use of a discrete membership function to represent this variability. By applying discrete membership functions to upper- and lower-body garments and defining an appropriate threshold, the overall membership function for the concept of dressing can be constructed: $\mu_{DC}(x) = 1$ if $\sum_i \mu_C(x_i) \geq T$, else 0, where $\mu_C(x_i) = \text{Poss}\left(\bigcup_j x_{i_j}\right) = \max_j \text{Poss}(x_{i_j})$. For example, imagine a user having just one sock and a hat on and having established a threshold T. Assuming that one sock $\triangleq x_{i_s}$, hat $\triangleq x_{i_h}$ and $\mu_C(x_{i_{s_j}}) = 0.12$, $\mu_C(x_{i_{h_j}}) = 0.11$, $T = 0.8$, first step of fuzzification results in $\Sigma_i \mu_C(x_i) = 0.12 + 0.11 = 0.23 < 0.8 = T$. Since the sum is less than T, we proceed to the second phase. Here, we find that the user's membership function is defined as $\mu_{DC}(x) = 0$. As a result, the system diagnoses the user as undressed due to the insufficient level of dressing indicated by the membership values.

Distress Indicators. Distress in individuals can stem from several physiological factors, including fluctuations in blood pressure, body temperature, and heart rate. These vital signs are classified based on age and we can divide them into three categories as Low, Medium, or High, depending on age group: Young, Middle, or Old. For instance, let's consider a 40-year-old individual. According to scientific medical information provided by Harvard Health Publishing, the ranges for these indicators would typically be outlined in terms of what is considered normal, elevated, or concerning for that age group. Assuming that the patient is monitored and the healthcare professionals can access these data this categorization helps assess an individual's health status and determine if they are experiencing distress due to abnormal readings in these vital signs. For a 40-year-old, the heart rate membership function can be defined as $\text{HR}_{40}(x)$: Low for $x < 60$, Low-to-Medium for $60 \leq x < 90$, Medium for $90 \leq x \leq 153$, Medium-to-High for $153 < x \leq 180$, and High for $x > 180$.

The speed of decision-making depends on different types of membership functions [14], such as Triangular, Trapezoidal, Piecewise linear, Gaussian and Singleton. We use membership functions proposed by Zadeh [29] for the possible distribution of age as Young, Middle-aged, and Old (see [4] for details). And the trapezoidal membership function to convert the crisp values of the rest of the indicators to fuzzy sets [1]: $\mu(x; x_1, x_2, x_3, x_4) = \max(\min(\frac{x - x_1}{x_2 - x_1}, 1, \frac{x_4 - x}{x_4 - x_3}), 0)$.

Compatibility Test by Fuzzy Rules. On the strength of the membership functions, the system recognizes a number in the interval $[0, 1]$ as a degree for dressing and indicators of distress. Our fuzzy system requires a set of rules for aggregating the partially tested results into an overall assessment that reflects the compatibility of the SLEEC rule with the descriptive data. Essentially, these rules are needed to infer the user's state regarding dressing and distress before making a decision about opening the curtains. Fuzzy rules enable the system to make decisions based on imprecision, as they convert fuzzy sets into linguistic values. In the context of the formalized SLEEC rule applied in nursing homes:

$$\texttt{if } c_0 \texttt{ then } a_0, \quad \texttt{else if } c_1 \texttt{ then } a_1 \equiv \neg a_0, \quad \texttt{else } a_2 \equiv a_0.$$

Proposition c_0, which refers to a dressed user, can be categorized as boolean due to its boolean membership function. Similarly, proposition a_0 is also boolean, as it relates to the action of opening or not opening the curtains. Proposition c_1, which concerns a user being not highly distressed, remains somewhat ambiguous at this stage. The linguistic variables combined with logical connective symbols are essential for constructing if-then rules. These fuzzy if-then rules are pivotal in controlling the output variables. The inference engine selects the optimal variables, emulating boolean logic with basic operators. This variable indicates the user's level of distress, taking into account measurements such as age, blood pressure, body temperature, and heart rate. The fuzzy rule base for the nursing home SLEEC system consists of up to $3^5 = 243$ rules; the complete rule set is provided in Table 2 of [4]. The i-th rule combines age (A_i), blood pressure (BP_i), heart rate (HR_i), and body temperature (BT_i) to infer a distress level (D_i) using the linguistic terms shown in the table. As an example: **IF** A is *Old* $\wedge$ BP is *High* $\wedge$ HR is *High* $\wedge$ BT is *High*, **THEN** D is *High*.

4.3   Defuzzification

Fuzzy outputs are converted to numeric, crisp values via defuzzification. We use the center of gravity (COG) method:

$$D^*(\mathbf{x}) = \frac{\sum_i D_i \cdot \min(\mu_{A_i}(x_1), \mu_{BP_i}(x_2), \mu_{HR_i}(x_3), \mu_{BT_i}(x_4))}{\sum_i \min(\mu_{A_i}(x_1), \mu_{BP_i}(x_2), \mu_{HR_i}(x_3), \mu_{BT_i}(x_4))} \tag{3}$$

where $\mathbf{x} = (x_1, x_2, x_3, x_4)$ are the crisp input values for Age, Blood Pressure, Heart Rate, and Body Temperature [4].

5   Excerpt of Applying the Method

In the following, we present an excerpt illustrating how our method evaluates distress using formula (2), and discuss how this formulation supports the management of ethical dilemmas in humanrobot interaction. Due to the complexity of the defuzzification process, only the final outcome is reported. Figure 2 illustrates the defuzzification of the aggregated fuzzy outputs for distress based on $D^*(x)$, $x = (a, bp, hr, bt)$, computed by formula (3). Each colored region represents one of the distress levels–Low, Medium, or High. The height of each region is adjusted based on how well the input data (age, blood pressure, body temperature, and heart rate) satisfy the conditions of that rule, which is calculated as the minimum of their membership values $\left(\min\left(\mu_{A_i}(x_A), \mu_{BP_i}(x_{BP}), \mu_{BT_i}(x_{BT}), \mu_{HR_i}(x_{HR})\right)\right.$. D_i is the centroid (center) of the trapezoidal distress output for rule i, representing the typical numeric value of that distress level (in Fig. 2: Low ~ 0.2, Medium ~ 0.5, and High ~ 0.8 distress).

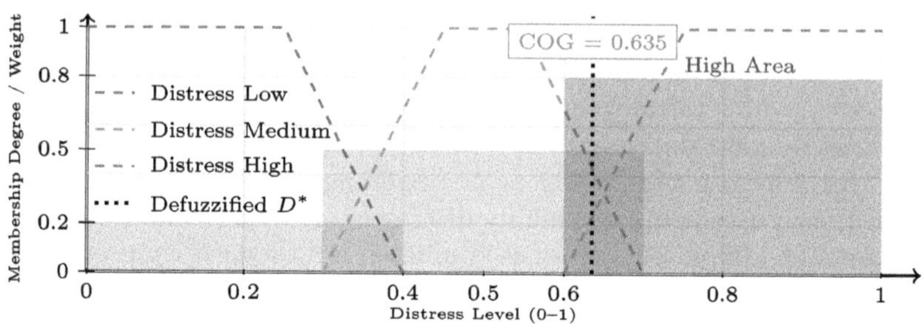

Fig. 2. Defuzzification of the aggregated fuzzy distress output.

When two fuzzy sets overlap (e.g., Medium and High Distress), the region with the larger aggregated area pulls the centroid (defuzzified value, D^*) toward itself. As a result, D^* tends to be located within the region contributing more to the overall fuzzy area. In this example, a defuzzified value of $D^* = 0.635$ lies within the overlap between the Medium and High regions but is pulled toward the High side, indicating a high distress state. In this fuzzy configuration, when the defuzzified value lies in the overlap between Medium and High Distress, the dominant distress level is determined by the larger aggregated area; values above 0.6 are dominated by the High distress region and are therefore interpreted as High Distress. Therefore, the threshold of distress for triggering the curtain-opening action should be set to 0.6.

Our method provides a means for addressing ethical dilemmas in humanrobot interaction scenarios. The scenario obtained by combining formulas (1) and (2) poses a clear ethical dilemma: opening the curtains may violate the user's privacy, whereas refraining from action may conflict with the user's expressed preferences and potentially compromise their health in the presence of high distress. To address this dilemma, we estimate the user's level of distress through fuzzy inference and dynamically balance competing ethical considerations, allowing the robot to decide whether to preserve privacy or act in support of the user's autonomy and health. In contrast, prior work addresses such dilemmas by resolving inconsistencies among SLEEC rules at a static analysis stage, typically by discarding one option [8,9].

6   Conclusion

In our work, we embed SLEEC rules into the AI system by defining a dataset that appropriately represents each rule's conceptual dimensions and by generating corresponding distributions using relevant membership functions. As expected, some rules require the introduction of new concepts–such as our definition of "highly distressed". This process results in a preliminary dataset but does not yet yield executable commands. Starting from a semi-formalized IF–THEN SLEEC rules we use fuzzy rules to perform aggregation and compatibility testing. At this stage, the presence of non-boolean linguistic values requires their defuzzification into single numeric values, making them interpretable and actionable within the system. The process we introduced allows and steers fine grain operationalization of the SLEEC rules that permit their management at run time in the decision engine of the AS. This is key to manage ethical dilemma that may require actual pieces of information that can only be available at execution time. Future work concerns the full specification of the method and its implementation in a real case health care scenario currently under development in our robotic lab.

Data Availability Statement. not applicable as no new data was created or analyzed in this paper.

References

1. Assadi, Z.: Logical formalisms for ethics. In: Proc. Int. Conf. Inf. Tech. Soc. Good (GoodIT'24), pp. 416–419 (2024)
2. Assadi, Z.: Non-quineian unless. In: XXI Brazilian Logic Conf. p. 263 (2025)
3. Assadi, Z., Inverardi, P.: Fuzzy logic in ethical AI. In: The 9th Women in Logic Work, pp. 27–29 (2025)
4. Assadi, Z., Inverardi, P.: Fuzzy representation of norms (2026). arXiv:2601.04249
5. Carnap, R.: Meaning and Necessity: A Study in Semantics and Modal Logic. Univ. Chicago, 30th ed. (1988)
6. Cervantes, J.-A., Rodríguez, L.F., López, S., Ramos, F., Robles, F.: Autonomous agents and ethical decision-making. Cogn. Comput. **8**(2), 278–296 (2016)
7. Dyoub, A., Lisi, F.A.: Towards ethical risk assessment of symbiotic AI systems with fuzzy rules. In CEUR Workshop Proceedings **3881**, 36–49 (2024)
8. Feng, N., et al.: Analyzing and debugging normative requirements via satisfiability checking. In: Proceedings of the IEEE/ACM 46th International Conference on Software Engineering ICSE '24, Article No. 214, pp. 1–12
9. Feng, N., et al.: Supplementary Material for [8]. https://github.com/NickF0211/LEGOS-SLEEC
10. Griffin, H., Ghahremani, M., Gegov, A.: Fuzzy expert system based extension of SWI-prolog for evaluating AI ethics. In: IEEE 12 Int. Conf. Intel. Sys, pp. 1–6 (2024)
11. Inverardi, P.: The challenge of human dignity in autonomous systems. In: Werthner, H., et al. (eds.) Perspectives on Digital Humanism, pp. 25–29. Springer (2022)
12. Inverardi, P., Mori, M.: Requirements models at run-time to support consistent system evolutions. In: 2 Int. Requirements@Run.Time, pp. 1–8 (2011)
13. Kaufmann, M., Meier, A.: Fuzzy ethizität: Radar für ethische künstliche intelligenz. HMD Praxis der Wirtschaftsinformatik **59**(2), 538–555 (2022)
14. Kim, S., Lee, M., Lee, J.: A study of fuzzy membership functions for dependence decision-making in security robot system. Neural Comput. Appl. **28**(1), 155–164 (2017)

15. Narayanan, A.: Ethical judgement in intelligent control systems for autonomous vehicles. In: 2019 Australian and New Zealand Control Conference (ANZCC), pp. 231–236 (2019)
16. Narayanan, A.: When is it right and good for an intelligent autonomous vehicle to take over control (and hand it back)? (2019) arXiv:1901.08221
17. Narayanan, A.: Machine ethics and cognitive robotics. Curr. Robot. Rep. 4(2), 33–41 (2023)
18. Quine, W.V.O.: Methods of Logic. New York, revised ed. edition (1959)
19. Rieger, B.B.: Feasible fuzzy semantics: on some problems of how to handle word meaning empirically. Words, Worlds, Contexts 6, 193–209 (1981)
20. Russell, S.J., Norvig, P.: Artificial Intelligence: A Modern Approach. Pearson (2016)
21. Sholla, S., Mir, R.N., Chishti, M.A.: A fuzzy logic-based method for incorporating ethics in the internet of things. Int. J. Ambient Comput. Intell. 12(3), 98–122 (2021)
22. Smith, G.G.: Design of ethical autonomous agents for unmanned aerial vehicles using fuzzy logic. Master's thesis, Florida Institute of Technology (2022)
23. Tolmeijer, S., Kneer, M., Sarasua, C., et al.: Implementations in machine ethics: a survey. ACM Comput. Surv. 53(6), 1–38 (2021)
24. Townsend, B., Parnell, K.J., Yaman, S.G., Nemirovsky, G., Calinescu, R.: Normative conflict resolution through human–autonomous agent interaction. J. Resp. Tech. 21, 100114 (2025)
25. Townsend, B., Paterson, C., Arvind, T.T., et al.: From pluralistic normative principles to autonomous-agent rules. Mind. Mach. 32(4), 683–715 (2022)
26. Troquard, N., Sanctis, M.D., Inverardi, P., Pelliccione, P., Scoccia, G.L.: Social, legal, ethical, empathetic, and cultural rules: Compilation and reasoning. Procee. AAAI Conf. Arti. Intell. 38(20), pp. 22385–22392 (2024)
27. Xu, J.: Semantic representation of fuzzy ethical boundaries in AI (2025)
28. Yaman, S.G., Ribeiro, P., Cavalcanti, A.: Specification, validation and verification of social, legal, ethical, empathetic and cultural requirements for autonomous agents. J. Syst. Softw. 220, 112229 (2025)
29. Zadeh, L.A.: Quantitative fuzzy semantics. Inf. Sci. 3(2), 159–176 (1971)
30. Zadeh, L.A.: Fuzzy sets as a basis for a theory of possibility. Fuzzy Sets Sys. 1(1), 3–28 (1978)
31. Zadeh, L.A.: Test-score semantics for natural languages and meaning-representation via pruf. Fuzzy Sets, Fuzzy Logic, and Fuzzy Systems, pp. 542–586 (1996)

Fairness as a First-Class Requirement: A Fairness Hazard Analysis Approach to Socio-Technical Processes

Giovanna Broccia[1]([✉])(iD), Lucio Lelii[1], Roberto Cirillo[1], Dario Di Nucci[3], Samuel Fricker[4], Fabio Palomba[3], Giorgio O. Spagnolo[1], and Alessio Ferrari[1,2](iD)

[1] ISTI-CNR, Pisa, Italy
{giovanna.broccia,lucio.lelii,roberto.cirillo,spagnolo}@isti.cnr.it,
alessio.ferrari@ucd.ie
[2] University College Dublin, Dublin, Ireland
[3] University of Salerno, Salerno, Italy
{ddinucci,fpalomba}@unisa.it
[4] University of Applied Sciences and Arts Northwestern Switzerland,
Windisch, Switzerland
samuel.fricker@fhnw.ch

Abstract. *Context and Motivation.* Fairness in socio-technical systems is increasingly recognised as a critical requirement, especially in processes involving human-AI interaction. Fairness hazards are situations or factors that threaten the fair treatment of individuals or groups. If left unaddressed, they can accumulate into systemic bias. Therefore, ensuring fairness must be treated as a first-class requirement during system design, rather than a post-hoc fix. *Question/Problem.* Systematic methods for identifying fairness hazards in socio-technical workflows and translating them into requirements-level mitigations are still missing. *Principal Ideas/Results.* We propose Fairness Hazard Analysis (FHA), an adaptation of hazard analysis methods from the safety-critical domain to analyse fairness in socio-technical processes. FHA is demonstrated through an AI-assisted hiring case and supported by *HumAInFlow*, a modelling and simulation platform. The approach is preliminarily evaluated through two focus groups. The feedback from participants highlights FHA's usefulness for structured fairness analysis, the importance of diverse expertise, and the potential for deeper integration within HumAInFlow. *Contribution.* This work offers a novel method for integrating fairness into requirements analysis of socio-technical workflows, and provides an LLM-based tool to automate the analysis, marking a shift from bias detection to bias prevention with *fairness-by-design*.

1 Introduction

As artificial intelligence (AI) technologies are increasingly deployed in everyday activities and mediate decisions that affect people's lives, the risks of biased or

R. Guizzardi and J. Araújo (Eds.): REFSQ 2026, LNCS 16497, pp. 229–244, 2026.
https://doi.org/10.1007/978-3-032-21423-2_16

inequitable outcomes have become more visible and urgent. In socio-technical systems, where humans and AI agents interact, these risks can be amplified: biases may propagate across actors and processes, leading to compounding fairness issues over time [16].

Despite its relevance, fairness is often treated as a post-hoc evaluation concern rather than a requirement to be engineered from the outset [13]. Ensuring fairness, however, requires systematic attention comparable to safety and security, calling for requirements engineering (RE) methods that can identify and mitigate fairness risks early in the design process.

Recent work has introduced the notion of *fairness debt*, conceptualising fairness issues as liabilities that accumulate when unaddressed and become increasingly difficult and costly to resolve [27]. While research on algorithmic fairness has produced a wide range of metrics and mitigation techniques, most are typically applied at the AI model or dataset level. Consequently, there remains a lack of operational methods that requirements engineers can apply to analyse and address fairness in socio-technical workflows [26].

To address this gap, we propose Fairness Hazard Analysis (FHA), an adaptation of hazard analysis methods from safety engineering [11]. FHA treats fairness issues as hazard-like states that may emerge and propagate through human-AI workflows, enabling their systematic identification, analysis, and mitigation. This analogy is motivated by the conceptual parallel between safety and fairness: just as safety engineering aims to identify and control conditions that could lead to harm, fairness engineering can systematically anticipate and mitigate conditions that may cause inequitable outcomes. By treating fairness issues as hazard-like states that can propagate through human-AI workflows, FHA provides a structured way to trace and control the accumulation of fairness debt [27] before it leads to systemic bias.

To illustrate the approach, we applied FHA to an AI-assisted hiring process. We also introduce a tool named HumAInFlow for modelling, simulating and analysing socio-technical workflows and support FHA. The approach and tool have been qualitatively evaluated through two focus groups involving diverse experts, aimed at gathering feedback on its clarity and usefulness, and on the suitability of HumAInFlow as a supporting tool for conducting FHA. Major points of improvements are the need to frame fairness concepts within specific contexts, the enhancement of analytical rigour and simulation capabilities, and the strengthening of usability and interoperability of the tool.

It should be noted that the primary focus of this study is the FHA method, while the supporting tool is used as an initial instantiation to explore and operationalise it; both are currently at the proof-of-concept level, i.e., Technology Readiness Level (TRL) 3. This study is part of a larger design science [32] endeavour, where we have currently performed the phases of problem investigation, treatment design, and preliminary validation in a controlled environment (through the focus groups). These will be later followed by implementation, i.e., application in a real-world problem context, and evaluation, i.e., systematic assessment in practice, where HumAInFlow will be used more extensively to support the application and empirical validation of FHA..

Related Work. Fairness in algorithmic and socio-technical systems has traditionally been addressed through metrics and mitigation techniques applied to data or models. While effective for local parity, these approaches often abstract away the organisational and human contexts in which decisions occur. Foundational critiques emphasise that fairness must be reasoned about at the system level: abstraction from social context can conceal structural inequities and reproduce systemic harms [10,25,27]. Recent studies have begun to explore how fairness and broader human values can be operationalised throughout the system lifecycle. *Values@Runtime* proposes mechanisms to capture and adapt to stakeholder values during operation [3], while *ReFair* focuses on fairness-requirement elicitation in machine learning systems through a context-aware recommender system [14]. Empirical analyses further show that fairness is still treated as a secondary quality attribute: developers lack systematic, lifecycle-oriented methods to specify, trace, and maintain fairness requirements [23,31]. In parallel, safety and security engineering provide well-established hazard-analysis frameworks for early identification and mitigation of risks [19]. Recent work demonstrates that system-safety methods can also uncover social and ethical risks in machine-learning systems [24]. However, explicit translations of fairness risks into actionable, requirements-level controls across human-AI workflows remain scarce.

Goal-oriented requirements engineering approaches such as i* [33] and KAOS [9] provide powerful abstractions for modelling stakeholder goals, dependencies, and obstacles, and have been successfully used to reason about non-functional concerns through softgoals and constraints. However, these approaches primarily focus on goal satisfaction and conflict resolution, and provide limited support for analysing how risks such as fairness issues, may emerge, propagate, and accumulate across socio-technical workflows over time. FHA is therefore positioned as complementary: while goal-oriented models capture what the system should achieve, FHA focuses on identifying and controlling fairness-related hazard conditions arising from interactions between human and AI actors.

FHA systematically identifies fairness hazards using empirically established sources of fairness debt, analyses how these hazards may propagate across socio-technical workflows, and derives requirements-level mitigations with explicit traceability to the unfair outcomes they are intended to prevent. While FHA is structurally inspired by safety hazard analysis, it goes beyond a direct substitution of "safety" with "fairness" by grounding hazard identification in normative fairness-debt sources rather than system failure modes, explicitly distinguishing undesirable bias from contextually justified differentiation, and treating mitigation as a reconfiguration of socio-technical workflows rather than purely technical controls.

2   Background

2.1   Bias, Fairness, and Hazards

Bias, the systematic deviation from objective accuracy in judgment, often arises when data or decisions reflect unequal representation or pre-existing human prejudices [30]. In AI systems, bias frequently originates from the human-generated datasets used for training [15]. Fairness, in this context, involves mitigating such systematic errors to ensure that AI-supported outcomes do not perpetuate or amplify inequities across demographic or social groups [22].

However, recent evidence shows that fairness cannot be considered a static property of algorithms alone, as human-AI interactions can create feedback loops that dynamically shape and intensify biases in human cognition and behaviour [16]. These feedback effects represent significant hazards: risks that extend beyond technical malfunction to encompass psychological, social, and ethical consequences [7]. When biased AI systems influence human perception and judgment, they may not only distort individual decision-making but also reinforce societal disparities, making the identification and correction of these feedback-driven hazards a critical challenge for responsible design of AI systems [1].

2.2   Fairness Debt

Fairness debt was introduced to explain how fairness issues in software systems accumulate when they are not explicitly managed throughout the software lifecycle [27]. Aligned with the definitions of technical debt [2] and social debt [28], fairness debt represents the latent socio-technical liabilities that result from fairness oversights, omissions, or trade-offs made during development and operation.

De Souza Santos et al. [27] identify several root causes of fairness debt across the software lifecycle: **(i) cognitive bias**, arising from developers' subjective assumptions; **(ii) requirements bias**, from incomplete or non-inclusive elicitation; **(iii) design bias**, introduced through architectural or interface choices; **(iv) historical bias**, stemming from legacy data that reproduces inequities; **(v) training bias**, due to unrepresentative datasets; **(vi) model bias**, produced by algorithmic simplifications or parameter settings; **(vii) testing bias**, when validation overlooks fairness metrics; and **(viii) societal bias**, reflecting broader structural inequalities in the system's context.

These causes are not isolated but interdependent, meaning that fairness issues can propagate across lifecycle stages: for example, an unaddressed requirements bias may evolve into design or testing bias downstream. Over time, the accumulation of such debts increases the risk of systemic inequities, reputational damage, and regulatory non-compliance. Although defined in the context of software development, several of these root causes—particularly cognitive, societal, and requirements bias—can also emerge within the human components of socio-technical systems. Human decision-makers interacting with software systems may, for instance, over-rely on algorithmic recommendations, apply subjective evaluation criteria, or reproduce social stereotypes. This socio-technical interpretation reinforces that fairness debt is not purely a software engineering concern but a property of the entire human-software ecosystem. Hence, it should be treated as a managed and traceable property of socio-technical systems, requiring continuous attention rather than post-hoc correction.

This work builds on this idea by using the identified root causes of fairness debt to structure the identification of fairness hazards in socio-technical workflows through the proposed FHA approach.

2.3 Hazard Analysis

Hazard analysis is a foundational concept in system safety engineering, aimed at identifying and mitigating conditions that could lead to undesired or unsafe system states [11]. A hazard is typically defined as a state or set of conditions that, together with certain triggers, can result in harm or loss [18]. The purpose of hazard analysis is to anticipate such conditions as early as possible, evaluate their causes and potential consequences, and design appropriate preventive or corrective controls [20].

Among the most commonly used hazard analysis techniques, the Preliminary Hazard Analysis (PHA) is a qualitative, top-down approach that provides an initial overview of potential hazards, even before detailed system design information is available [11]. Its objective is to capture early insights concerning potential risk sources, their likely causes and effects, and to propose preliminary mitigation strategies, which are documented in a hazard table. A PHA generally follows a structured sequence of activities. The process begins with system definition, followed by the identification of potential hazardous conditions, failures, and actions. Each identified hazard is then examined to determine its possible causes and the severity and likelihood of its potential consequences. The combination of severity and likelihood provides a preliminary basis for assessing risk and prioritising hazards that require further attention. Finally, preventive or control measures are proposed to eliminate each hazard or reduce its associated risk to an acceptable level. The process is iterative: as the system design matures, new information can refine both the identified hazards and the proposed mitigations.

This work takes inspiration from PHA to conceptualise FHA—a socio-technical adaptation that treats fairness deficiencies as hazard-like conditions. FHA retains the PHA structure to identify, trace, and mitigate fairness hazards across socio-technical workflows.

3 Fairness Hazard Analysis

We adapt PHA to identify and mitigate fairness issues in FHA systematically. FHA treats fairness issues—e.g., biased decisions, unbalanced access to information, or unequal treatment of agents—as hazard-like conditions that can arise during socio-technical processes, enabling their structured analysis and mitigation at the requirements level.

Consistent with the structure of PHA, FHA follows the sequential process described below (cfr. Figure 1). Each step is carried out by a team of analysts with diverse expertise in RE, data science, ethics, software engineering, and the specific system domain. These experts are trained to recognise fairness issues and reason about their propagation across socio-technical processes, ensuring consistency in hazard identification, classification, and mitigation planning.

Step A. System Definition. As in PHA, the first step defines and models the socio-technical process, its actors, and their interactions.

Step B. Fairness Hazard Identification. Each actor within the process is examined by the analysts in terms of the fairness-debt root causes [27], systematically assessing whether and how any of these causes may give rise to fairness hazards

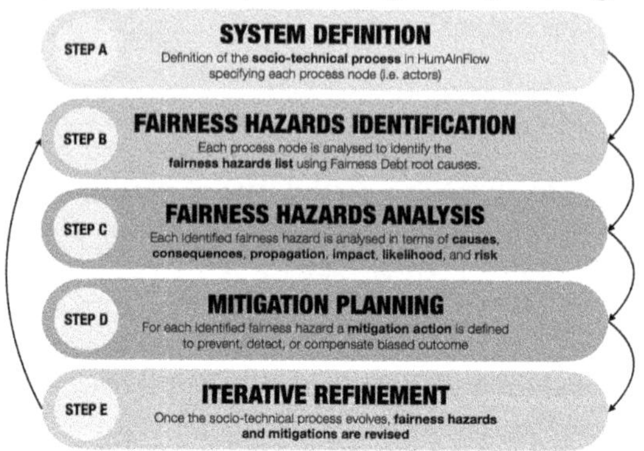

Fig. 1. FHA process

within that part of the process. Analysts draw on multiple sources when identifying fairness hazards, including prior empirical studies on fairness debt, organisational policies, regulatory guidelines, and domain-specific scenarios. FHA supports collaborative sense-making among analysts with complementary backgrounds, allowing hazards to be iteratively refined rather than exhaustively predefined. This step results in a fairness-hazard list documenting the potential fairness issues and where they could emerge.

Step C. Fairness Hazard Analysis. Each identified fairness hazard is analysed in terms of its consequences, propagation, impact (degree of unfair treatment), and likelihood (probability of occurrence) through a collaborative review process where analysts discuss and resolve differing judgments to reach consensus. Impact ranges from none (intentional or justified differentiation) to critical (structural unfairness breaching ethical, legal, or organisational norms), while likelihood expresses how often a fairness issue may occur—from rare to systemic. Combining impact and likelihood allows analysts to prioritise fairness risks. FHA distinguishes between undesirable bias, which causes harm and requires mitigation, and justified or goal-aligned differentiation, which may be acceptable in context. The latter is recorded for transparency and traceability. While such cases are assigned no risk and require no mitigation, their explicit documentation supports accountability and prevents unexamined assumptions from becoming implicit sources of fairness debt.

This step produces a table reporting each hazard, its consequences, propagation, and qualitative risk classification.

Step D. Mitigation Planning. For each fairness hazard, FHA defines control actions at the requirements level that modify the socio-technical workflow to prevent, detect, or compensate for unfair outcomes. Mitigation is achieved by introducing or adjusting workflow nodes and by implementing specific controls at critical decision points. These controls may include procedural additions–such as inserting human review or consensus nodes for high-impact decisions–as well as technical interventions, for instance, refining or constraining AI behaviour through targeted prompt engineering, introducing fairness-aware scoring functions, or enforcing transparency and auditability checkpoints.

Step E. Iterative Refinement. As in traditional PHA, FHA is an iterative process. Once the socio-technical process evolves or new empirical evidence emerges, fairness hazards and mitigations are revisited.

4   Sample Case

AI-assisted hiring systems can enhance recruitment quality by improving efficiency and reducing the transactional workload of human personnel. Nevertheless, insufficiently investigated biases may lead to unfair practices and discriminatory outcomes based on factors such as gender, race, ethnicity, or personality traits [8]. We select the AI-assisted hiring process as a representative case because it involves complex and continuous human-AI interactions and decision-making steps that are particularly sensitive to fairness concerns, as largely demonstrated by previous literature on fairness engineering [12]. These characteristics make it an ideal context for illustrating how FHA can uncover and mitigate fairness hazards in socio-technical workflows. To conduct the analysis, a team of three analysts, who are authors of this paper, applied the FHA to the selected case.

Step A. System Definition. The AI-assisted hiring process comprises four operational nodes (cf. Figure 2). The *Data Ingestor* receives the job description and candidates' curricula, and extracts structured features and job requirements.

These are provided to the *AI Prescreener*, which produces a ranked shortlist of candidates based on feature–requirement matching. The *Human Recruiter* receives both the ranked shortlist and the original curricula, reviews them, and possibly overrides the AI's ranking to select interview candidates. All intermediate artefacts—the extracted features, AI shortlist, and recruiter decisions—are finally transmitted to the *Audit Node*, which consolidates the records into a persistent log for traceability.

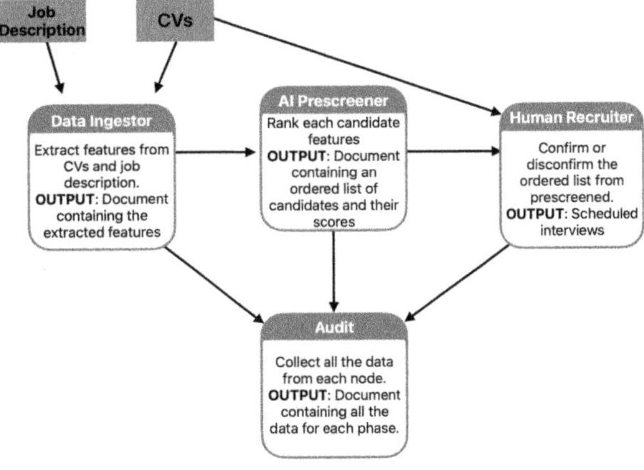

Fig. 2. AI-assisted hiring workflow

Table 1. Identified Fairness Hazards (FH$_i$) across workflow nodes, with examples and detailed root causes.

ID	Node	Hazard Description	Example(s)	Root Cause(s)
FH$_1$	Data Ingestor	**Historical Bias.** CVs and job ads reflect past inequities (e.g., gender imbalance, unequal access to roles). The Ingestor encodes these disparities into structured data.	Career breaks due to maternity leave are interpreted as lower experience.	**Historical bias; Requirements bias**
FH$_2$	Data Ingestor	**Data Representativeness Deficit.** Parsing or extraction fails to capture diverse CV formats, languages, or trajectories, leading to incomplete representation.	Foreign degrees not recognised; Nonstandard CVs partially parsed.	**Training bias; Requirements bias**
FH$_3$	Data Ingestor	**Requirements Bias in Job Descriptions.** Subjective or exclusionary job terms are ingested without inclusivity checks.	"Young and dynamic" or "native English speaker" disadvantage certain groups.	**Requirements bias; Societal bias**
FH$_4$	AI Prescreener	**Training Data Imbalance.** The ranking model is trained on demographically skewed datasets, reinforcing dominant patterns.	Historical hires (mostly men) bias the model toward male-typical CVs.	**Training bias; Historical bias**
FH$_5$	AI Prescreener	**Proxy Feature Bias.** Certain features act as proxies for ranking.	Higher-ranked universities or institutions lead to higher candidate scores.	**Model bias; Training bias**
FH$_6$	AI Prescreener	**Transparency Deficit.** Lack of interpretability prevents auditors from identifying bias.	Recruiters receive rankings without explanations for scores.	**Design bias; Testing bias**
FH$_7$	Human Recruiter	**Confirmation Bias.** Recruiters overly rely on AI rankings, disregarding contradictory evidence.	Human recruiters interview only top-ranked candidates or highlight candidate weaknesses to justify a low score.	**Cognitive bias; Design bias**
FH$_8$	Human Recruiter	**Cognitive Bias.** Recruiters apply subjective heuristics or stereotypes during evaluation.	Foreign-sounding names rated as less suitable.	**Cognitive bias; Societal bias**

Step B. Fairness Hazard Identification. Each of the nodes defined in Step A is examined by the analysts for hazard identification. The identified fairness hazards (FH$_i$) are then jointly discussed and refined, resulting in the list provided in Table 1 and used in Step C.

Step C. Fairness Hazard Analysis. The fairness hazards are analysed in terms of its consequences, propagation, impact, likelihood, and risk, as shown in Table 2. Some identified biases represent undesirable conditions that may lead to high-risk fairness issues and therefore require prompt mitigation (e.g., FH$_1$ or FH$_4$ can systematically disadvantage underrepresented candidates and propagate through multiple workflow nodes). Others, however, correspond to intended or contextually acceptable behaviours (e.g., preferential weighting of candidates from prestigious universities) and are consequently assigned no risk and not subject to mitigation.

Step D. Mitigation Planning. Table 3 summarises all the mitigation strategies defined to prevent, detect, or compensate for unfair outcomes, while Fig. 3 shows the updated workflow. Some of the mitigations have a direct impact on the workflow by modifying or extending its execution (e.g., adding the *Feature-Validation* node to mitigate FH$_2$ or refining the prompt used in the *AI Prescreener* node to mitigate FH$_1$). Others act as informative or procedural controls, supporting awareness and organisational learning for the future (e.g., the

Table 2. Fairness risk assessment for identified hazards.

ID	Potential consequences	Impact *(i)*	Likelihood *(l)*	Risk *(i*l)*	Propagation
FH_1	Systemic exclusion of minority candidates; reputational damage.	High	Likely	High	Data Ingestor $\rightarrow$ AI Prescreener; Human Recruiter
FH_2	Misclassification/omission of nonstandard CVs; missed talent.	High	Likely	High	Data Ingestor $\rightarrow$ AI Prescreener; Human Recruiter
FH_3	Disadvantage for certain demographic/social groups.	Moderate	Possible	Medium – High	Data Ingestor $\rightarrow$ AI Prescreener; Human Recruiter; Audit
FH_4	Ranking bias; systematically lower scores for minorities.	High	Likely	High	AI Prescreener $\rightarrow$ Human Recruiter; Audit
FH_5	Higher-ranked institutions or companies receive higher scores, intentionally reflecting desired selection criteria.	None	Likely	None	AI Prescreener $\rightarrow$ Human Recruiter; Audit
FH_6	Inability to detect/contest biased rankings.	High	Possible	Medium – High	AI Prescreener $\rightarrow$ Human Recruiter; Audit
FH_7	Amplification of prescreening bias; reduced accountability.	High	Likely	High	Human Recruiter $\rightarrow$ Audit
FH_8	Inconsistent/unfair human assessments.	High	Likely	High	Human Recruiter $\rightarrow$ Audit

detailed report on historical bias produced to mitigate FH_1, or the report on biased terms used in the job description issued by the *Requirements-Check* node to mitigate FH_3). As previously mentioned, some of the identified fairness hazards are not mitigated, as they represent expected behaviour (e.g., FH_5 is not mitigated because candidates from high-ranked universities are intentionally prioritised according to the desired selection criteria).

Step E. Iterative Refinement. Once all the mitigation actions have been performed, the new workflow is analysed from Step B.

5 HumAInFlow

HumAInFlow is a no-code, agentic platform, that we designed to model, simulate, and analyse socio-technical workflows where humans and software, including AI agents, co-exist and collaborate [6]. The platform is planned for open-source release following completion of validation and testing phases. Unlike existing agentic AI frameworks (e.g., Langflow, Flowise AI, AutoGen Studio), HumAInFlow explicitly represents human roles as first-class nodes and allows their simulation through large language models (LLMs)—by instantiating personas through embedded prompts—making it suitable for studying processes that combine automated reasoning with human judgment.

We used HumAInFlow as a supporting tool for the AI-assisted hiring analysis, modelling and simulating all workflow nodes and mitigation strategies through LLMs (Fig. 4 shows the original, non-mitigated, workflow).

This setup enables end-to-end analysis of socio-technical interactions under controlled and reproducible conditions. Within FHA, HumAInFlow supports both the identification and assessment of fairness hazards by allowing analysts to model workflow components—human and technical—as autonomous agents whose behaviour can be systematically varied. For instance, intentionally biased

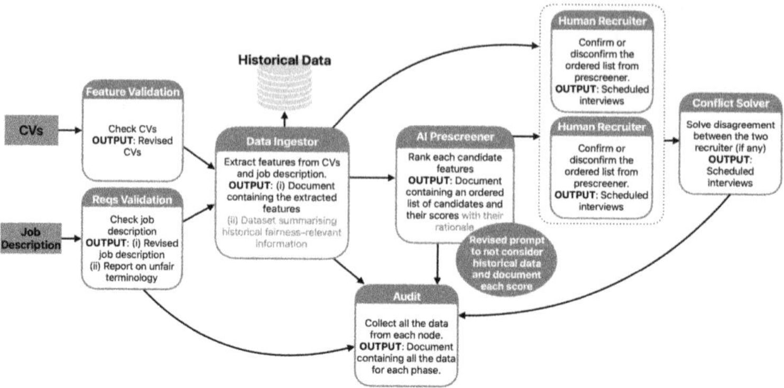

Fig. 3. AI-assisted hiring workflow with mitigation strategies

Table 3. Summary of mitigation actions for identified fairness hazards.

ID	Workflow modification/control	Expected effect
FH$_1$	Extend the *Data Ingestor Node* to produce an additional output dataset summarising historical fairness-relevant information.	Document historical bias for future hiring processes.
	Refine the prompt in the *AI Prescreener Node* to explicitly disregard historical imbalances during ranking.	Prevent replication of historical inequities in candidate scoring.
FH$_2$	Add a *Feature-Validation Node* between the user interface and the *Data Ingestor* to enforce a structured CV submission format.	Ensure completeness and comparability of candidate data; reduce representational bias due to unstructured or nonstandard CVs.
FH$_3$	Add a *Requirements-Check Node* at the input stage to automatically scan job descriptions for potentially biased or exclusionary terminology.	Detect and neutralise linguistic or cultural bias in job descriptions.
	The *Requirements-Check Node* generates a *Fairness Report* passed as input to the *Audit* Node to inform HR personnel about flagged terminology.	Support organisational awareness and long-term bias reduction in job descriptions.
FH$_4$	Retrain the *AI Prescreener* model using synthetic, demographically balanced data to counteract skewed patterns in the original training set.	Reduce model bias during candidate ranking by ensuring that historical or demographic imbalances do not influence learned representations.
FH$_6$	Implement prompt engineering rules that explicitly instruct the *AI Prescreener* to document the rationale behind each candidate ranking.	Improve transparency, interpretability, and contestability of AI decisions.
FH$_7$ and FH$_8$	Introduce a second *Human Recruiter Node* operating in parallel with the first, to independently review the AI-generated shortlist.	Mitigate overreliance on AI outputs and subjective judgments.
	Add a *Disagreement Discussion Node* to consolidate and compare the evaluations of the two recruiters, simulating a consensus phase when discrepancies occur.	Resolve divergences between human reviewers.

or imperfect nodes (e.g., a human recruiter affected by confirmation bias or an AI prescreener overvaluing specific features) can be introduced to observe how their behaviour influences downstream decisions. This allows analysts to system-

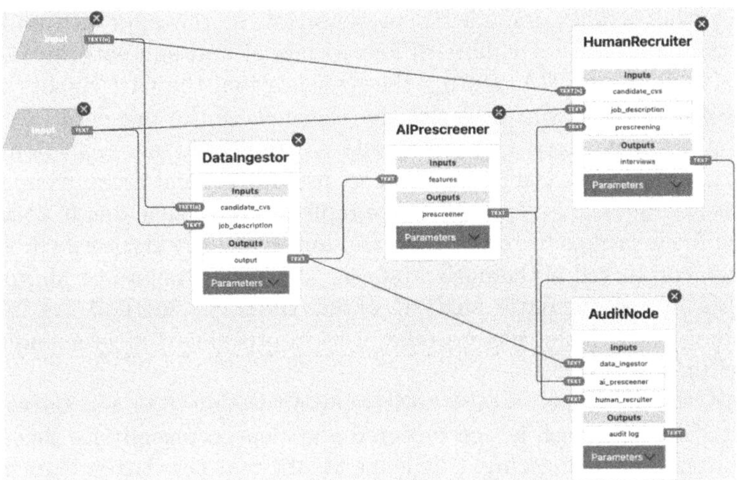

Fig. 4. AI-assisted hiring workflow modelled in HumAInFlow

atically examine how fairness hazard can emerge and propagate. Furthermore, mitigation strategies can be modelled and simulated within the same environment to evaluate their effectiveness in reducing or eliminating bias.

For simulation purposes, the model provides a simplified abstraction of reality. For instance, human discussions or model retraining are represented by additional simulation nodes or prompt engineering mechanisms. To ensure a realistic representation of each actor in the AI-assisted hiring process, a careful prompt engineering phase was conducted to design prompts that could reproduce the expected behaviour of both human and technical entities. Standard prompting techniques—such as chain-of-thought reasoning and persona-based design—were applied in accordance with the OpenAI guidelines [21]. Since fairness hazards may also emerge from the wording or framing of prompts, three authors of this paper independently reviewed and iteratively refined all node prompts, selecting the formulations that best balanced realism and neutrality.

6 Preliminary Evaluation

At this stage, the FHA method and HumAInFlow are at the proof of concept level. Given their preliminary nature, we did not evaluate them across different scenarios, but we performed a first *treatment validation* with users in a controlled environment—following design science terminology and concepts—to identify relevant points of improvements before actual *implementation*, i.e., introduction of the artifact in practice. We validated the approach in two two-hour focus groups with 6 people each, involving twelve academics (33.4% Female, 66.7% Male) with different degrees of expertise in fairness (58% Basic or None, 42% Intermediate to Advanced). The focus groups were moderated by the first and last authors. They included a presentation of the approach and a video showing the capability of HumAInFlow to model and simulate socio-technical workflows to support FHA. During the presentation, the participants could ask questions and provide observations. At the end of the presentation, a set of eight questions was posed to participants to trigger further reflection on FHA and HumAInFlow, concerning ease of use, usefulness, and recommendations for improvement—questions reported in the replication package due to space limitations. The focus groups were recorded and automatically transcribed. Then, the last author conducted a thematic analysis to identify points of improvements. The results of the thematic analysis about the FHA method are in Table 4, while Table 5 reports the themes related to improvement recommendations for the HumAInFlow tool.

Overall, the participants were positive about the method and the tool, specifying that: "The approach feels structured and clear, especially for those familiar with requirements engineering."; "It helps identify fairness issues throughout the process...not only in the AI component."; and that "The tool nicely complements the method...it translates the analysis steps into something operational."

They also provided several recommendations for improvements. Concerning the method (Table 4), participants emphasised the need to clarify and contextualise the concept of fairness by explicitly defining it within each analysis context and incorporating ethical frameworks that distinguish between acceptable and unacceptable biases. They suggested improving bias detection and representation through better tool support, clearer distinctions between human and algorithmic sources, and support for exploring hidden biases. They also highlighted the need to enhance FHA's analytical rigour and usability via clearer risk-evaluation guidance, domain-specific templates, and practical examples, and recommended integrating automated mitigation suggestions, human-AI collaboration mechanisms, and transparent documentation of mitigation rationales. They also encouraged positioning fairness as an ongoing, reflective practice by embedding feedback loops into the method and reframing bias identification as a constructive opportunity for learning and ethical growth.

Concerning the tool (Table 5), participants highlighted the importance of improving its overall usability to better manage complex socio-technical workflows. They recommended introducing automated layout, hierarchical representations, and semi-automatic abstractions to enhance clarity and reduce visual clutter. Strengthening model validation and knowledge reuse was also considered essential, suggesting pre-execution checks, debugging breakpoints, and mechanisms to warn about known fairness hazards or mitigation patterns when reusing components. The group particularly valued the tool's simulation and analytical potential, encouraging the ability to model biased human or AI agents, as well as feedback loops, to explore how bias propagates and evolves over time. In terms of extensibility and interoperability, participants proposed a modular plugin architecture and textual export options to facilitate integration with external models and analytical tools.

Table 4. Recommendations for improving the Fairness Hazard Analysis method

Improvement Area	Recommendation	Rationale / Description	Exemplary Quote (Participant)
1. Clarify and Contextualize Fairness Concepts	Define fairness explicitly for each analysis context	The concept of fairness is inherently subjective; the method should require explicit ethical framing and domain-specific definitions.	"For me, the word 'fairness' itself is tricky. What's fair depends on perspective—fairness is inherently biased."
	Distinguish between acceptable and unacceptable bias	The tool could allow users to tag certain biases as "intended" or "undesired" to reflect context-dependent ethics.	"There are desired and undesired biases—for instance, preferring candidates from high-ranking universities might be intentional."
	Include ethical principle templates	Offer pre-defined ethical or fairness frameworks (e.g., distributive justice, equal opportunity) to guide consistent analysis.	"Every system should state openly which ethical principles it follows, so users know what definition of fairness applies."
2. Strengthen Bias Detection and Representation	Enhance bias-identification support in the tool	Add structured prompts, examples, and checklists for detecting common human and algorithmic biases.	"AI systems often perpetuate existing inequalities, like paying men more than women."
	Model both human and algorithmic biases distinctly	The method should clearly separate bias types and provide visualization of how they interact.	"You should distinguish between human and machine biases—and possibly even combine their strengths to reduce weaknesses."
	Support exploration of hidden biases	Include sensitivity analysis or simulation tools to uncover biases not explicitly known by analysts.	"But how do we detect biases we don't know about?"
3. Improve Analytical Rigor and Usability of FHA	Provide clearer guidance on risk evaluation	Develop scales or calibration aids for judging likelihood and impact to reduce subjectivity.	"Judging likelihood and impact is subjective—calibration is needed."
	Offer domain-specific templates or libraries	Create FHA templates for common socio-technical domains (e.g., hiring, healthcare) to ease application.	"It's important to start with frequent, well-known recruitment cases—that's where this model can bring the most value."
	Provide interactive tutorials or example analyses	Tutorials can make the structured steps of FHA easier to apply and interpret.	"The approach feels structured and clear, especially for those familiar with requirements engineering."
4. Enhance Fairness Mitigation and Iteration Support	Integrate mitigation strategy suggestions	When a hazard is identified, the tool could suggest potential mitigation actions (e.g., retraining models, adding review nodes).	"If we know a bias exists—for example, gender bias in historical data—we can retrain models or balance datasets to mitigate it."
	Promote human-AI collaboration mechanisms	Explicitly model roles for human oversight, such as review checkpoints or multi-human consensus steps.	"Use two human recruiters and a discussion node to reduce over-reliance on AI."
	Support documentation of mitigation rationale	Encourage users to record why certain actions were chosen, increasing transparency and accountability.	"The tool allows process simulation to uncover unexpected biases through analysis of outputs."
6. Support Reflective and Ongoing Fairness Practice	Encourage iterative, dialogic reflection	Build feedback mechanisms for revisiting fairness assumptions as systems evolve.	"Fairness itself must be contextually defined."
	Frame bias as a learning opportunity	Treat the discovery of bias as a positive step toward ethical improvement, not merely a flaw.	"We're all biased about what counts as bias! Some biases might align with ethical values or goals."

Finally, they recommended broadening the analytical scope of the tool to assess the side effects of fairness interventions on other system qualities and to consider differentiated impacts across multiple stakeholder groups.

As a preliminary validation, the evaluation is subject to limitations in terms of reliability, validity, and generalisability, following established criteria for qualitative research [17]. Regarding reliability, given the proof-of-concept maturity of the method (TRL 3), we adopted a formative qualitative evaluation aimed at identifying improvement opportunities. Exploratory focus groups are commonly used at this stage to support early artifact evaluation and refinement [29], with thematic analysis ensuring consistency in data interpretation [4]. Concerning validity, although the analysis followed a systematic procedure, the results may be affected by the Hawthorne effect, as participants were aware of being observed. Finally, generalisability is limited by the exclusive involvement of academic participants and a single illustrative case; broader validation with industry

Table 5. Recommendations for HumAInFlow

Improvement Area	Recommendation	Rationale / Description	Exemplary Quote (Participant)
1. Usability & Visualization	Provide auto-layout and clearer node arrangement	Reduce visual clutter in complex workflows; support automatic layouting so links and dependencies remain readable as models grow.	"The interactions between nodes are tangled; we need a clearer layout."
	Add hierarchical views / macro-nodes	Allow grouping nodes into higher-level "macro-nodes" and switching between levels of granularity to manage complexity.	"It would help to group single nodes into a macro-node and get a higher-level view."
	Semi-automatic high-level abstractions	Offer semi-automated clustering/abstraction of related nodes to generate higher-level visualizations without extra modeling burden.	"High-level views could be auto-generated to avoid modeling every abstraction level by hand."
2. Model Validation & Knowledge Reuse	Pre-execution validation & breakpoints	Add preflight checks (missing links, invalid connections) and debugging breakpoints to pinpoint execution failures early.	"Does the tool signal when something does not make sense?"
	Warnings on risky patterns / loops	Detect problematic loops or ill-formed connections and guide users to resolve non-termination or structural errors.	"We discussed adding breakpoints to understand where the problem arises."
	Memory of known hazards & reuse guidance	When importing nodes/models, surface past analyses (known fairness risks, typical mitigations) and suggest checks by node type.	"When importing something, the tool could run an analysis and warn: you should add a mitigation here."
3. Simulation & Analytical Capabilities	Simulate biased agents and propagation	Let users simulate biased humans/LLMs to observe how bias propagates through the socio-technical workflow and where mitigations help.	"I want to simulate a biased human or AI and see how the bias propagates and whether mitigation works."
	Temporal/feedback-loop simulation	Support time-evolving scenarios and feedback loops to evaluate whether mitigations hold over repeated interactions.	"Consider simulating feedback loops to verify if mitigations survive in the long term."
4. Extensibility & Interoperability	Plugin architecture for models/nodes	Enable adding local/remote models and custom nodes via plugins so organizations can integrate proprietary or fine-tuned components.	"It would be nice to add plugins or new nodes not initially foreseen by the system."
	Textual export/import (JSON/XML)	Provide an editable textual representation for complex models to support versioning, reviews, and interoperability with other tools.	"Having a textual representation of the diagram helps manage complex models."
5. Broader Analytical Scope	Assess side-effects on other NFRs	When planning fairness mitigations, analyze collateral impacts on other qualities (e.g., performance, usability, security).	"Mitigating fairness may affect other non-functional requirements; we should reason about side effects too."
	Multi-stakeholder impact weighting	Allow per-actor impact/risk weighting and trade-offs, since hazards may affect stakeholders differently.	"Risks can differ for recruiters vs. candidates; we should weight impacts and tailor mitigations."

practitioners, multiple application contexts, and longitudinal studies is left as future work.

7   Conclusion

This paper introduced Fairness Hazard Analysis (FHA), a structured approach for identifying, analysing, and mitigating fairness risks in socio-technical workflows. By adapting hazard analysis principles from safety engineering, FHA enables fairness-by-design through early, requirements-level reasoning rather than post-hoc evaluation. The AI-assisted hiring case and preliminary focus group evaluation demonstrated the method's feasibility and its value in promoting interdisciplinary reflection on fairness. Future work will extend FHA to larger, practitioner-led case studies and integrate automated support for bias detection and mitigation within the HumAInFlow platform, advancing fairness as a first-class non-functional requirement in socio-technical system design.

Acknowledgments. Research supported by the EU Project CODECS GA 101060179. The authors acknowledge the use of ChatGPT to refine the text.

Data Availability Statement. We made our supplementary material available in [5].

References

1. Afreen, J., Mohaghegh, M., Doborjeh, M.: Systematic literature review on bias mitigation in generative ai. AI and Ethics pp. 1–53 (2025)
2. Alves, N.S., et al.: Identification and management of technical debt: a systematic mapping study. Inf. Softw. Technol. **70**, 100–121 (2016)
3. a Bennaceur, A., Hassett, D., et al.: Values@runtime: an adaptive framework for operationalising values. In: ICSE – SEIS pp. 175–179. IEEE (2023)
4. Braun, V., Clarke, V.: Using thematic analysis in psychology. Qual. Res. Psychol. **3**(2), 77–101 (2006)
5. Broccia, G., et al.: Fairness as a first-class requirement: A fairness hazard analysis approach to socio-technical processes - supplementary material (2025). https://doi.org/10.5281/zenodo.17472752
6. Broccia, G., et al.: Humainflow : a no-code platform for modelling and simulating human-ai workflows. Tech. Rep. 011, ISTI-CNR (2025)
7. Chen, C., et al.: Ethical perspective on ai hazards to humans: a review. Medicine **102**(48), e36163 (2023)
8. Chen, Z.: Ethics and discrimination in artificial intelligence-enabled recruitment practices. Human. Social Sci. Commun. **10**(1), 1–12 (2023)
9. Dardenne, A., Van Lamsweerde, A., Fickas, S.: Goal-directed requirements acquisition. Sci. Comput. Program. **20**(1–2), 3–50 (1993)
10. Dolata, M., Schwabe, G., Schwabe, D.: Fairness as a sociotechnical concept in information systems. Inf. Syst. J. **33**(4), 970–995 (2023)
11. Ericson, C.A., et al.: Hazard Analysis Techniques for System Safety. John Wiley & Sons (2015)
12. Fabris, A., Messina, S., Silvello, G., Susto, G.A.: Algorithmic fairness datasets: the story so far. Data Min. Knowl. Disc. **36**(6), 2074–2152 (2022)
13. Farahani, A., et al.: On adaptive fairness in software systems. In: Proceedings of SEAMS, pp. 97–103. IEEE (2021)
14. Ferrara, C., et al.: Refair: toward a context-aware recommender for fairness requirements engineering. In: Proceedings of ICSE. IEEE (2024)
15. Gichoya, J.W., et al.: AI pitfalls and what not to do: mitigating bias in AI. Br. J. Radiol. **96**(1150), 20230023 (2023)
16. Glickman, M., Sharot, T.: How human-ai feedback loops alter human perceptual, emotional and social judgements. Nat. Hum. Behav. **9**(2), 345–359 (2025)

17. Leung, L.: Validity, reliability, and generalizability in qualitative research. J. Family Med. Primary Care **4**(3), 324–327 (2015)
18. Leveson, N.G.: Safeware: system safety and computers. ACM (1995)
19. Leveson, N.G.: Engineering a Safer World: Systems Thinking Applied to Safety. MIT Press, Cambridge, MA (2011)
20. Lutz, R.R.: Analyzing software requirements errors in safety-critical, embedded systems. In: Proceedings of RE, pp. 126–133. IEEE (1993)
21. OpenAI: Openai cookbook: Examples and guides for using the openai api. https://github.com/openai/openai-cookbook (2025). Accessed 15 Oct 2025
22. Pagano, T.P., et al.: Bias and unfairness in machine learning models: a systematic review on datasets, tools, fairness metrics, and identification and mitigation methods. Big Data Cogn. Comput. **7**(1), 15 (2023)
23. Palomba, F., Ferrara, C., Sellitto, G., De Lucia, A., Ferrucci, F.: Fairness-aware machine learning engineering: how far are we? ESE **29**(1), 9 (2024)
24. Rismani, S., et al.: Applying system-theoretic process analysis (stpa) to identify ethical and social risks in machine learning systems. In: Proceedings of FAccT, pp. 2540–2553. ACM (2023)
25. Selbst, A.D., Boyd, D., et al.: Fairness and abstraction in sociotechnical systems. In: Proceedings of FAT*, pp. 59–68. ACM (2019)
26. Soremekun, E., Papadakis, M., Cordy, M., Le Traon, Y.: Software fairness: an analysis and survey. ACM Comput. Surv. (2022)
27. de Souza Santos, R., et al.: Software fairness debt: Building a research agenda for addressing bias in ai systems. ACM TOSEM **34**(5), 1–21 (2025)
28. Tamburri, D.A., et al.: Social debt in software engineering: insights from industry. J. Internet Serv. Appl. **6**(1), 10 (2015)
29. Tremblay, M.C., et al.: Focus groups for artifact refinement and evaluation in design research. Commun. Assoc. Inf. Syst. **26**(1), 27 (2010)
30. Varona, D., Suárez, J.L.: Discrimination, bias, fairness, and trustworthy AI. Appl. Sci. **12**(12), 5826 (2022)
31. Voria, G., et al.: Fairness-aware practices from developers' perspective: a survey. Inf. Softw. Technol. **182**, 107710 (2025)
32. Wieringa, R.: Design Science Methodology for Information Systems and Software Engineering. Springer (2014)
33. Yu, E.S.: Modelling Strategic Relationships for Process Reengineering. Ph.D. thesis, University of Toronto (1995)

Specifying Fairness and Transparency Requirements for Public Benefit Allocation

Amanda Aline F.C. Vicenzi[1] , José Siqueira de Cerqueira[2(✉)] ,
Pekka Abrahamsson[2] , and Edna Dias Canedo[1]

[1] Department of Computer Science, University of Brasília (UnB), Brasília, DF, Brazil
amandaaline3@gmail.com, ednacanedo@unb.br
[2] Faculty of Information Technology and Communication Sciences,
Tampere University, Tampere, Finland
{jose.siqueiradecerqueira,pekka.abrahamsson}@tuni.fi

Abstract. Context and motivation: The increasing adoption of AI in public administration requires translating ethical and legal expectations into verifiable requirements. In Brazil, AI is increasingly explored to support eligibility assessment and allocation in social programs, yet there is limited guidance on how to specify and validate fairness and transparency in such high-stakes settings. **Question/problem:** This research preview investigates how fairness and transparency can be operationalized as measurable non-functional requirements (NFRs) for AI-supported social benefit allocation. **Principal ideas/results:** As a proof-of-concept, we simulate scholarship allocation using ProUni data and assess the model through predictive performance, group fairness metrics, and SHAP-based explainability evidence. Results indicate satisfactory accuracy while revealing measurable racial disparities, motivating bias mitigation. **Contribution:** We propose an initial RE-oriented framework that integrates fairness indicators, explainability artifacts, and accountability mechanisms into specification and validation checkpoints, supporting early-stage discussion and feedback on responsible AI in digital government.

Keywords: Responsible AI · Non-Functional Requirements · Fairness · Transparency · Digital Government

1 Introduction

The digitalization of public services has accelerated the adoption of Artificial Intelligence (AI) to improve efficiency, scalability, and resource allocation in public administration [12,17]. In Brazil, AI-based approaches are increasingly considered to support decision-making in social programs, including eligibility assessment and benefit allocation. However, in high-stakes public contexts, algorithmic decisions may affect citizens' rights and reproduce or amplify historical inequalities embedded in data and institutional practices [1,4,9,15]. From a software engineering perspective, these risks translate into ethical non-functional requirements (NFRs) such as fairness, transparency, and accountability, which are often weakly specified, validated, and monitored. In practice, AI systems are frequently assessed primarily through predictive performance, while ethical properties are addressed later or informally [13], a particularly critical issue in public-sector settings subject to constitutional principles and data protection obligations.

Operationalizing ethical requirements requires measurable criteria and auditable evidence. Explainability plays a central role, as stakeholders must be able to understand and scrutinize the drivers of automated recommendations. Techniques such as SHapley Additive exPlanations (SHAP) provide global and local insights into feature influence, supporting transparency and bias diagnosis [18]. From a requirements engineering (RE) perspective, such explainability artifacts can serve as validation evidence, strengthening traceability between ethical principles, requirements, and system behaviour.

This research preview investigates how fairness and transparency can be specified as verifiable NFRs for AI-based social benefit allocation, using the University for All Program (ProUni) as an illustrative context. ProUni is a Brazilian federal scholarship initiative launched in 2004 to expand access to higher education based on socioeconomic and educational criteria. We conduct a proof-of-concept audit using a simulated predictive model inspired by ProUni data, assessing fairness through quantitative metrics and transparency through SHAP-based analyses. Based on these insights, we propose an initial RE-oriented framework that integrates ethical principles, legal constraints, and measurable fit criteria into specification and validation checkpoints, aiming to stimulate discussion on systematic approaches to ethical requirements in digital government.

2 Background and Related Work

The adoption of AI in public-sector decision-making has expanded rapidly in recent years, particularly in domains such as education, health, and social assistance [1]. While data-driven systems promise efficiency and scalability, their use in high-stakes public contexts raises persistent concerns regarding fairness, transparency, accountability, and compliance with fundamental rights [3]. When algorithmic outputs influence access to social benefits, these concerns must be addressed not only as ethical issues but also as explicit system-level requirements.

A substantial body of research has documented algorithmic bias as a central risk in AI-supported decision systems, especially when historical data encode structural inequalities [8]. In public-sector applications, biased outcomes may directly undermine principles of equality, impersonality, and legality. To address these risks, prior work on fairness aware AI proposes quantitative metrics such as Statistical Parity Difference, Equal Opportunity Difference, and Disparate Impact to assess group-level disparities [10]. Toolkits such as IBM AIF360 [2] operationalize these metrics; however, their use is typically detached from RE artifacts, such as fit criteria, validation checkpoints, or traceability mechanisms.

Complementary to fairness assessment, explainable AI (XAI) techniques have been proposed to enhance transparency and trust in algorithmic decisions. Methods such as SHapley Additive exPlanations (SHAP) provide global and local interpretability, enabling stakeholders to inspect feature influence and diagnose potential bias [18]. Although XAI is often treated as a post hoc analysis mechanism, recent studies highlight its relevance for accountability and regulatory compliance. Nevertheless, the systematic use of explainability artifacts as validation evidence for ethical NFRs remains under-explored in RE research.

At the governance level, international initiatives such as the OECD AI Principles [14], the UNESCO Recommendation on AI Ethics [11], and the European Union AI Act [19] emphasize transparency, non-discrimination, accountability, and human oversight, particularly for high-risk AI systems. Despite their normative importance, these frameworks provide limited guidance on how ethical principles can be translated into verifiable system requirements or embedded into software development practices. In Brazil, this gap is reflected in the coexistence of constitutional principles, LGPD obligations, and national AI strategies that still lack concrete engineering level operationalization [16].

From a methodological perspective, many AI projects follow established data mining and machine learning lifecycles, such as CRISP-DM [5]. While such lifecycles offer structured guidance for technical activities, ethical concerns such as fairness and transparency are typically addressed implicitly within phases like business understanding or evaluation, rather than specified through measurable fit criteria or systematically validated across the lifecycle. RE research has therefore emphasized the need to operationalize ethical principles as NFRs, enabling their specification, validation, and monitoring alongside traditional quality attributes [15]. However, existing approaches often remain conceptual or focus on isolated techniques, without demonstrating integrated workflows that combine fairness metrics, explainability artifacts, and accountability mechanisms.

Our research addresses a gap at the intersection of AI lifecycles and RE. Rather than proposing a new end-to-end development process, we extend established lifecycles such as CRISP-DM with an explicit RE layer that treats fairness and transparency as verifiable NFRs. This layer is operationalized through measurable fit criteria, explainability-based validation evidence, and traceability links between ethical principles, legal norms, and system-level requirements. Grounded in a preliminary case study from Brazilian digital government, this work contributes an early-stage, RE-oriented perspective on translating ethical AI principles into actionable and auditable engineering practices.

3 Study Setting

This research preview examines whether AI-based decision-support models in public administration may reproduce or amplify social inequalities, and how ethical requirements can be operationalized and assessed within the AI lifecycle. We focus on fairness and transparency as verifiable NFRs in a digital government context, guided by the following research questions:

RQ1. To what extent can AI-based predictive models for public benefit allocation exhibit measurable disparities across social groups?

RQ2. How can fairness and transparency be specified and assessed as NFRs within a context-sensitive framework for AI development in the Brazilian public sector?

To address **RQ1**, we conducted a preliminary audit of a predictive model simulating scholarship allocation in the University for All Program (ProUni), evaluating predictive performance, explainability, and fairness indicators. To address **RQ2**, we derived an initial framework that embeds fairness and transparency as measurable NFRs within the RE process. The study follows the CRISP-DM methodology [5], extended with two RE-oriented checkpoints: **RE-1 (Specification)**, which defines explicit fairness and transparency criteria, and **RE-2 (Validation)**, which verifies compliance using quantitative fairness metrics and explainability evidence.

The dataset was obtained from the Brazilian Federal Government Open Data Portal (MEC) and contains records of ProUni scholarships awarded between 2005 and 2020. Available attributes include region, institution, field of study, modality, study shift, scholarship type, and sociodemographic variables (sex, race/colour, age, disability). As the public dataset includes only successful applicants, a synthetic set of non-beneficiaries was generated to enable supervised learning and exploratory fairness auditing. This synthetic data was used solely for proof-of-concept purposes and does not aim to reproduce real allocation outcomes. Categorical variables were one-hot encoded, and a target variable (`PROBABILIDADE _BOLSA`) was introduced to simulate approval likelihood. Data were split into training (80%) and testing (20%) sets, with numerical features standardized using `StandardScaler`. We employed `XGBRegressor` [6], selected for its robustness with tabular data.

Model performance was evaluated using MAE, MSE, RMSE, R^2, and MAPE [20]. The model achieved satisfactory predictive performance (MAE = 0.125). Explainability was assessed using SHAP, providing global and local insights into feature influence and supporting transparency oriented validation [18]. The most influential attributes included region, race/colour, scholarship type, and year of award. Group fairness was evaluated using Statistical Parity Difference (SPD), Equal Opportunity Difference (EOD), and Average Odds Difference (AOD) [10]. The unmitigated model exhibited measurable disparities across racial groups (odds ratio = 1.04, $p < 0.001$). Applying the Reweighing technique from AIF360 reduced disparities across all metrics (SPD: −0.09 to −0.02; EOD: −0.06 to −0.01; AOD: −0.07 to −0.01). The results indicate that predictive accuracy alone is insufficient to assess AI systems in sensitive public-sector contexts. Fairness auditing revealed group-level disparities prior to mitigation, while explainability analyses supported transparency and traceable validation of ethical NFRs. These findings provide initial evidence addressing **RQ1** and inform the proposed RE-oriented framework addressing **RQ2**.

4   An Ethical Framework for AI in Government

Grounded in Article 37 of Brazil's 1988 Constitution legality, impersonality, morality, publicity, and efficiency, this framework treats fairness and transparency as first-class NFRs for AI systems in government. Rather than proposing a new AI lifecycle, it introduces an explicit RE layer that complements existing lifecycles by enabling the specification, validation, and monitoring of ethical requirements. Insights from the ProUni case illustrate that models evaluated solely through predictive performance may produce indirect discrimination, reinforcing the need to embed equity criteria from the outset and to audit them continuously. Figure 1 summarizes the framework around two RE checkpoints: **RE-1 (Specification)** and **RE-2 (Validation)**.

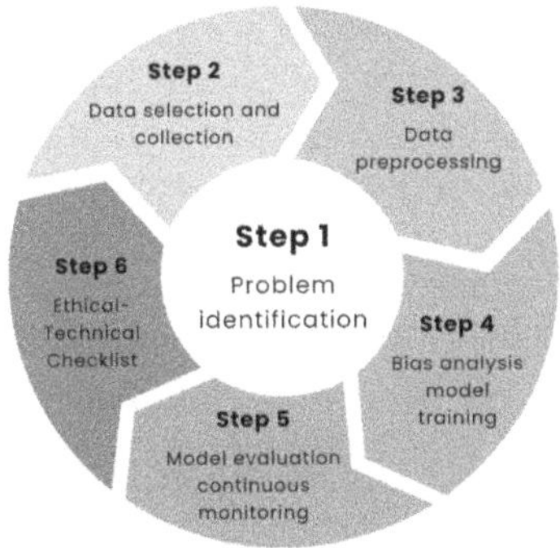

Fig. 1. Ethical framework for AI in Brazilian digital government with RE checkpoints for fairness and transparency.

Problem Identification and Data Selection. AI initiatives in public administration should begin with a contextualized problem definition, identifying affected social groups and intended policy outcomes. Ethical data selection must be guided by relevance, representativeness, and non-discrimination [7]. Sensitive attributes should be retained not removed to enable bias detection and mitigation. In the ProUni case, the availability of data only for awarded scholarships limited impartiality assessment, motivating the use of complementary public sources or controlled synthetic data strictly for exploratory fairness auditing.

Data Preprocessing. Preprocessing decisions directly affect fairness and must therefore be auditable. Public-sector datasets often contain missing or "Not Informed" values for sensitive attributes. Ethical preprocessing requires diagnosing missingness patterns, applying statistically sound treatments, and documenting all transformations. Removing sensitive attributes to "avoid bias" is counterproductive, as it prevents bias detection. Transparent documentation of cleaning and encoding decisions supports traceability and accountability.

Model Evaluation and Monitoring. Evaluation extends beyond technical performance to include verification of ethical NFRs. In the ProUni proof-of-concept, fairness auditing revealed measurable disparities across racial groups, motivating mitigation actions. Explainability techniques such as SHAP provide local and global insights into influential features, supporting transparency and managerial oversight [18]. Human oversight remains essential, as quantitative indicators must be interpreted in light of public policies and social context. Continuous monitoring and documented mitigation cycles are required to sustain legality and public trust over time.

RE Checkpoints and Fit Criteria. At **RE-1 (Specification)**, ethical requirements are defined with explicit fit criteria, such as: (i) **Fairness**: $|SPD|$, $|EOD|$, $|AOD| \leq 0.02$ for protected attributes; (ii) **Disparate Impact**: DI within $[0.8, 1.25]$; (iii) **Transparency**: provision of local SHAP-based explanations within predefined latency and fidelity thresholds; and (iv) **Auditability**: complete decision trails stored for all inferences over a defined retention period. At **RE-2 (Validation)**, compliance is verified through fairness reports, explainability artifacts, and records of mitigation and re-evaluation.

Reflective Dimensions. To avoid a purely procedural checklist, the framework incorporates five reflective dimensions guiding documentation and justification across the lifecycle: (i) algorithmic sensitivity and informational justice; (ii) epistemic transparency and cognitive accessibility; (iii) technical responsibility and accountability; (iv) social sustainability and institutional reflexivity; and (v) regulatory compliance and data governance. These dimensions promote evidence based reflection rather than binary compliance judgments. The framework broadens fairness assessment beyond statistical metrics by integrating legal, ethical, and institutional considerations into RE artifacts. In the Brazilian context where a consolidated AI law is still under discussion (Bill No. 2338/2023), it provides a structured and auditable path for aligning AI-supported public decisions with constitutional principles and fundamental rights.

5   Discussion

Performance, Fairness, and Validation. The results confirm that predictive performance alone is insufficient for evaluating AI systems in sensitive public-sector contexts. Although the proof-of-concept model achieved satisfactory accuracy, fairness auditing revealed measurable racial disparities, indicating the risk of reproducing historical inequalities through automated decisions. The reduction of these disparities after bias mitigation reinforces the need to treat fairness verification as a formal validation activity (RE-2 checkpoint), rather than as a post hoc concern. These findings highlight that accuracy and fairness must be jointly assessed throughout the AI lifecycle.

Legal, Institutional, and Managerial Implications. The observed disparities are directly related to constitutional principles of equality and non-discrimination, as well as to obligations established by the LGPD. AI-based decision-support systems that produce group-level disparities without systematic monitoring or mitigation may conflict with the public sector's duty to prevent indirect discrimination. By enabling traceable auditing and validation of ethical requirements, the proposed framework helps translate legal and constitutional principles into operational system-level criteria, supporting both regulatory compliance and managerial oversight.

Implications for Requirements Engineering Practice. From a RE perspective, the framework operationalizes fairness, explainability, and auditability as NFRs that must be specified, validated, and monitored alongside traditional quality attributes. Fairness metrics such as SPD and EOD serve as quantitative proxies for ethical compliance, while explainability artifacts support transparency, interpretability, and debugging. Auditability, in turn, enhances accountability and maintainability by enabling traceability of model decisions and periodic review. Integrating these attributes into AI development and validation workflows strengthens trustworthiness and societal legitimacy, particularly in digital government contexts.

Positioning with Respect to Existing Frameworks. Unlike existing AI governance initiatives that primarily articulate high-level ethical principles, the proposed framework focuses on their operationalization within software engineering practice. Rather than replacing established AI lifecycles, it complements them with an explicit RE layer that provides concrete fit criteria, validation evidence, and traceability mechanisms. This positioning bridges the gap between normative ethical guidance and day-to-day engineering activities in public-sector AI development.

> **RQ1. Preliminary Insight.** AI-based models for social benefit allocation may exhibit measurable group-level disparities when trained on historically constrained or unbalanced data, underscoring the need for explicit fairness requirements and validation checkpoints.
>
> **RQ2. Preliminary Insight.** Fairness and transparency can be specified and assessed as measurable NFRs through an RE-oriented approach that combines fairness metrics, explainability artifacts, and traceability mechanisms.

6   Conclusion

This research preview examined how fairness and transparency can be operationalized as verifiable NFRs for AI-based decision-support systems in digital government. Using a proof-of-concept predictive model inspired by the CRISP-DM methodology, the study illustrated that predictive performance alone is insufficient in high-stakes public-sector contexts. The ProUni case highlighted measurable fairness disparities and showed how explainability and bias mitigation techniques can support ethical auditing of AI models.

Beyond the case illustration, the paper proposed an initial requirements oriented framework that integrates fairness and transparency into the AI lifecycle through explicit RE checkpoints for specification and validation. Grounded in Brazilian constitutional principles and data protection regulations, the framework translates abstract ethical and legal obligations into measurable criteria, validation evidence, and audit trails, complementing existing AI lifecycles rather than replacing them. As an early-stage investigation, this work does not claim definitive validation of the proposed framework. Instead, it aims to stimulate discussion within the RE community on how ethical requirements for AI systems can be systematically specified, validated, and monitored in public-sector applications. Future work will empirically evaluate the framework in real governmental settings and refine its criteria and validation mechanisms across different policy domains.

Acknowledgments. This work was supported by CONVERGENCE of Humans and Machines (220025) and the EVIL-AI "The identification and the mitigation of the negative effects of Artificial Intelligence Agents" (JAES/2024/EVIL-AI) projects by Jane and Aatos Erkko Foundation and the "Multifaceted ripple effects and limitations of human-AI interplay at work, business and society (SYNTHETICA)" project (358714) by Research Council of Finland. We thank the Conselho Nacional de Desenvolvimento Científico e TecnolÃşgico (CNPq), Grant Nº 300883/2025-0.

Data Availability Statement. The data that support the findings of this study are openly available in Zenodo at https://zenodo.org/records/17410424.

References

1. de Almeida, P.G.R., dos Santos Júnior, C.D.: Artificial intelligence governance: understanding how public organizations implement it. Gov. Inf. Q. **42**(1), 102003 (2025). https://doi.org/10.1016/J.GIQ.2024.102003
2. Blow, C.H., Qian, L., Gibson, C., Obiomon, P., Dong, X.: Comprehensive validation on reweighting samples for bias mitigation via aif360 (2023). https://arxiv.org/abs/2312.12560
3. Casillas, J.: Bias and discrimination in machine decision-making systems. Ethics Artif. Intell. **41**, 13–38 (2024)
4. de Cerqueira, J.A.S., Azevedo, A.P.D., Leão, H.A.T., Canedo, E.D.: Guide for artificial intelligence ethical requirements elicitation - RE4AI ethical guide. In: 55th Hawaii International Conference on System Sciences, HICSS, pp. 1–10. ScholarSpace, http://hdl.handle.net/10125/80015 (2022)
5. Chapman, P., et al.: The crisp-dm user guide. In: 4th CRISP-DM SIG Workshop in Brussels in March, vol. 1999, pp. 1–14. sn, NCR Systems Engineering Copenhagen, https://s2.smu.edu/~mhd/8331f03/crisp.pdf (1999)
6. Chen, T., Guestrin, C.: Xgboost: A scalable tree boosting system. In: Proceedings of the 22nd ACM sigkdd international conference on knowledge discovery and data mining, vol. 1, pp. 785–794. arXiv, https://arxiv.org/abs/1603.02754 (2016)
7. Gebru, T., Morgenstern, J., Vecchione, B., Vaughan, J.W., Wallach, H., Iii, H.D., Crawford, K.: Datasheets for datasets. Commun. ACM **64**(12), 86–92 (2021)
8. Gentelet, K., Mizrahi, S.K.: A human-centered approach to ai governance: Operationalizing human rights through citizen participation. In: Human-Centered AI, pp. 215–230. Chapman and Hall/CRC, https://www.taylorfrancis.com/chapters/oa-edit/10.1201/9781003320791-24/human-centered-approach-ai-governance-karine-gentelet-sarit-mizrahi (2024)

9. Gonçalves, C.D., de Paoli Menescal, E., de Mendonça, F.L.L., Canedo, E.D.: Trust in AI: perspectives of c-level executives in brazilian organizations. In: Proceedings of the XXIII Brazilian Symposium on Software Quality, SBQS 2024, Salvador, Bahia, Brazil, November 5-8, 2024, pp. 147–157. ACM, https://doi.org/10.1145/3701625.3701654 (2024)

10. González-Sendino, R., Serrano, E., Bajo, J., Novais, P.: A review of bias and fairness in artificial intelligence. Int. J. Interact. Multimed. Artif. Intell. **9**, 1–13 (2023)

11. Kettemann, D.M.C.: UNESCO recommendation on the ethics of artificial intelligence. Conditions Implement. Germany **1**, 1–43 (2022)

12. Lin, K., Shen, C., Cheng, S.: Applications of AI in digital governance services for local taxes- a case of the local tax bureau of taichung city government. In: Proceedings of the 25th Annual International Conference on Digital Government Research, DGO 2024, Taipei, Taiwan, June 11-14, 2024, pp. 6–18. ACM, https://doi.org/10.1145/3657054.3657056 (2024)

13. Mellouli, S., Janssen, M., Ojo, A.: Introduction to the issue on artificial intelligence in the public sector: Risks and benefits of AI for governments. Digit. Gov. Res. Pract. **5**(1), 1:1–1:6 (2024). https://doi.org/10.1145/3636550

14. OECD: Recommendation of the council on artificial intelligence. OECD: Paris, France pp. 1–12 (2024). https://legalinstruments.oecd.org/en/instruments/OECD-LEGAL-0449, originally adopted on 22 May 2019; amended on 3 May 2024

15. de Paula Porto, D., et al.: Ethical requirements in the age of artificial intelligence: a systematic literature review. In: Proceedings of the 21st Brazilian Symposium on Information Systems, SBSI 2025, Recife, Brazil, May 19-23, 2025, pp. 663–672. SBC, https://doi.org/10.5753/sbsi.2025.246613 (2025)

16. Presidência da República do Brasil: Lei n° 13.709, de 14 de agosto de 2018. https://www.planalto.gov.br/ccivil_03/_ato2015-2018/2018/lei/l13709.htm (2018)

17. Reis, A.R., Lopes, J.M., da Costa, J.M., de Jesus, T.F., Torres, T.P.d.R.: Artificial intelligence as a tool applicable to public administration: a look at the human resources area. ARACÊ **6**(4), 18213–18238 (Dec 2024). https://doi.org/10.56238/arev6n4-422

18. Salih, A.M., et al.: A perspective on explainable artificial intelligence methods: shap and lime. Adv. Intell. Syst. **7**(1), 2400304 (2025)

19. Sonsini, W., Parliament, T.E.: The EU artificial intelligence act. European Union pp. 1–10 (2024). https://www.wsgr.com/a/web/qrkz1SnNzWw6nk7B3oAyDa/10-things-you-should-know-about-the-eu-artificial-intelligence-act_v2.pdf

20. Tatachar, A.V.: Comparative assessment of regression models based on model evaluation metrics. Int. Res. J. Eng. Technol. (IRJET) **8**(09), 0056–2395 (2021)

Formal Methods

Provably Relevant HAL Interface Requirements for Embedded Systems

Manuel Bentele[1,3]([✉])(iD), Andreas Podelski[1](iD), Axel Sikora[2,3](iD),
and Bernd Westphal[4](iD)

[1] University of Freiburg, Freiburg, Germany
bentele@informatik.uni-freiburg.de
[2] Offenburg University of Applied Sciences, Offenburg, Germany
[3] Hahn-Schickard Institute, Villingen-Schwenningen, Germany
[4] German Aerospace Center, Oldenburg, Germany

Abstract. **[Context and Motivation]** Embedded applications often use a Hardware Abstraction Layer (HAL) to access hardware. Improper use of the HAL can lead to incorrect hardware operations, resulting in system failure and potentially serious damage to the hardware. **[Question and Problem]** The question is how one can single out, among a possibly large set of HAL interface requirements, those that are indisputably relevant for preventing this kind of system failure. **[Ideas and Results]** In this paper, we introduce a formal notion of relevance. This allows us to leverage a formal method, i.e., software model checking, to produce a mathematical proof that a requirement is indisputably relevant. We propose an approach to extract provably relevant requirements from issue reports on system failures. We present a preliminary case study to demonstrate that the approach is feasible in principle. The case study uses three examples of issue reports on embedded applications that use the SPI bus via the *spidev* HAL. **[Contribution]** The overall contribution of this paper is to pave the way for the study of approaches that support the systematic identification of requirements essential for preventing a specific kind of system failure.

Keywords: Requirements Engineering · Embedded Systems · Hardware Abstraction Layer (HAL) · HAL Interface Requirements · Serial Peripheral Interface (SPI) · Formal Methods · Software Model Checking

1   Introduction

Developing application code that uses a HAL to access hardware of an embedded system poses specific requirements engineering challenges. Besides the usual system and software requirements, which are typically defined at the start of a project, HAL interface requirements are often ignored until later, perhaps too late: The improper use of the HAL can lead to incorrect hardware operations resulting in system failure and potentially serious hardware damage.

Unlike system requirements, which vary depending on the specific application, interface requirements are determined by the HAL and can be reused across multiple system designs. Example 1 illustrates a typical HAL interface requirement that defines the correct use of HAL functions through a dependency.

> **Example 1**: HAL interface requirement
>
> A call of the function `write` shall be preceded by a call of the function `init`.

This HAL interface requirement ensures that the application code only calls the HAL function `write` to send data via a communication device after it has initialized the device through a call of the HAL function `init`. If this requirement is violated, the communication device will not be operational and no data can be sent via the device. Such a violation can lead to serious system failures.

HAL interface requirements specify the needs that hardware manufacturers (who provide the HAL) impose on software developers of embedded systems (who write the application code). Software developers must adhere to the HAL interface requirements to ensure the correct use of HAL functions when writing application code. In general, however, the set of HAL interface requirements for a given hardware can be overwhelming large, which may be one reason why they are often ignored until later in the software development process or, in the worst case, when their violation has indeed caused a system failure. This raises naturally the question how one can single out, among a possibly large set of HAL interface requirements, those that are indisputably relevant for preventing this kind of system failure that can lead to potentially serious hardware damage.

In this paper, we address exactly this problem and introduce a novel criterion which can be defined precisely and unambiguously. The idea of the criterion is to help identify requirements that are *provably relevant* for preventing system failures. We call this criterion *relevant*, for short. The criterion allows us to leverage a formal method, i.e., software model checking [11], to produce a mathematical proof that a requirement is relevant (and, in this sense, provably relevant).

We propose an approach to extract provably relevant requirements from issue reports on system failures. The approach comes in two versions. In the first version, one infers a candidate requirement from the issue report and then applies software model checking to check whether the candidate requirement is a relevant requirement, or not. In the second version, one assumes that one is given a (possibly large) set of HAL interface requirements for, say, a specific HAL. The approach is then to take the whole set as a set of candidate requirements and apply software model checking to each of them. In the second version, the approach relies on the fact that the application of software model checking as a formal method is fully automatic.

We present a preliminary case study to demonstrate that the approach may be feasible in principle (we leave a full-fledged case study to future work). We use three examples of issue reports on embedded applications that use the SPI bus via the *spidev* HAL. To carry out the approach in its second version, we use a set of 26 HAL interface requirements for the *spidev* HAL (the set of all HAL interface requirements for the *spidev* HAL that are of a specific form); we check each of those on the two versions of each of the three application programs.

The contribution of this paper is to define a precise and unambiguous criterion that can be used to single out requirements, to propose an approach to use that criterion, and to present a preliminary case study to demonstrate that the approach is feasible in principle. The overall contribution is to pave the way for the study of approaches that support the systematic identification of requirements essential for preventing a specific kind of system failure.

The remainder of the paper is structured as follows: Sect. 2 introduces our approach. Section 3 presents a preliminary case study. Section 4 discusses related work. Section 5 concludes the paper.

2   An Approach Based on Relevance

In this section, we introduce a formal notion of relevance and an approach. Given an issue report on a system failure, we present two variants of the approach: one that extracts a single interface requirement from the issue and checks its relevance, and the other checks a given set of candidate requirements for relevance.

2.1   Notion of Relevance

Intuitively, we consider a requirement to be relevant if its validity is essential to prevent a system failure. Definition 1 captures this intuition precisely.

Definition 1 (Relevance). *A requirement R is* relevant *if there exists a system that comes in two versions: a faulty version, i.e., a system that exhibits a system failure, and a repaired version, i.e., a system that no longer exhibits the system failure, such that the original application program in the faulty system violates R and the new application program in the repaired system satisfies R.*

For Definition 1, we note two remarks: (1) The definition is based on an existential condition. That is, we have a criterion that allows us to confirm relevance. It does not allow us to conclude that an interface requirement will never become relevant. (2) To make the definition practically useful, we need to apply it to existing system failures. In theory, it may always be possible to build an artificial system that witnesses the relevance of a given interface requirement.

2.2   Extract and Check a Single Candidate Requirement
for Relevance

The approach involves several stakeholders. Hardware manufacturers are only partly involved. They provide the HAL, particularly its documentation and occasionally the source code. However, the extent and quality of the HAL documentation are often moderate. Development companies are the primary users of the approach. Their embedded software developers are especially interested in ensuring that the application code interacts correctly with the HAL. The goal here

260   M. Bentele et al.

is to single out the provably relevant HAL interface requirements. Developers can then concentrate on the provably relevant HAL interface requirements to write more reliable application code for embedded systems. Figure 1 illustrates the approach embodied as a process chart. The approach comprises two parts. Initially, we extract a candidate requirement from a given issue report and subsequently, we formally prove the relevance of the candidate requirement. A detailed description of each part is provided below to explain the steps involved.

Extract Candidate Requirement from Issue Report. In the first part of the process, a developer extracts a requirement from a given issue report on a system failure observed in a faulty embedded system using a HAL (see the blue

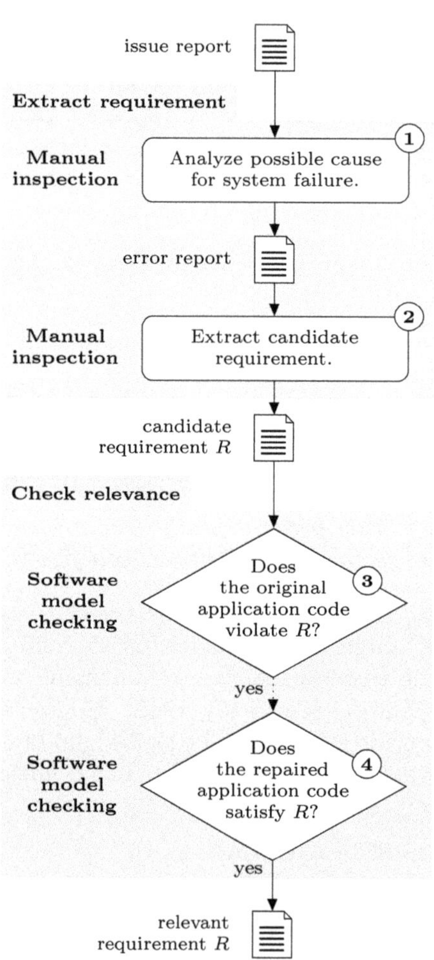

Fig. 1. Overall approach. The application code comes in two versions: the original version exhibits the system failure, the repaired version does not.

The extracted requirement serves as a candidate that may be responsible for the system failure, i.e., the violation of the requirement captures the failure and the satisfaction of the requirement witnesses the absence of the failure.

Inspect Issue Report. In Activity 1 (Manual inspection), the developer carefully analyzes the cause of the system failure from the issue report in the faulty system to create an error report. Such a report should identify and describe the error, its underlying cause, and include details about the current configuration and state at failure.

For example, an application program in an embedded system, that uses the HAL functions `init` and `write` of Example 1 from Sect. 1 to operate a communication device, sends messages to an actuator to open and close a train door. Suppose an issue report describes the observable system failure: the train door does not close. During inspection, the developer investigates the underlying cause of this failure. The developer analyzes the embedded system and finds that the actuator is not moving. Using analysis and debugging techniques, the developer identifies that the communication device is not in an operational state, preventing messages from being sent to the actuator by calling the HAL function `write`. Further inspection reveals that the communication device is never initialized. A call of the HAL function `init` in the application code is missing. The developer documents this cause in the error report, including details about the system, specifically the missing HAL function call, and notes that the communication device is not initialized. If the issue report already contains these details, the developer can skip the activity and continue with Activity 2. Finally, the activity produces a comprehensive error report.

Extract Candidate Requirement. In Activity 2 (Manual inspection), the developer extracts a candidate requirement based on the insights provided in the error report, especially focusing on the underlying cause that may indicate improper HAL usage. In our example from Activity 1, the developer suspects that the functions from the HAL are not being used correctly. To prevent improper HAL usage, the HAL functions must follow specific sequences to operate the hardware correctly. These sequences can be prescribed by dependencies between HAL functions where certain functions depend on the successful execution of others. To model this relationship, we use a binary relation representing a dependency between two HAL functions. For a pair of HAL functions f_1 and f_2, the dependency $f_1() \lhd f_2()$ ("f_2 depends on f_1") expresses that a call of f_1 must precede a call of f_2 in the application code of an embedded system. We call such a pair of HAL functions a *temporal dependency*. The developer carefully investigates the cause from the report to identify a dependency between HAL functions that may be related to the error. Hereby, the developer consults the HAL documentation and if possible the HAL implementation to determine if a dependency exists. Based on such a dependency, the developer extracts a temporal dependency as a candidate requirement.

In our example from Activity 1, the developer consults the HAL documentation, focusing on the HAL function `init` mentioned in the error report. The HAL documentation contains a textual description of the HAL interface requirement shown in Example 1 from Sect. 1. This requirement defines a dependency between the HAL functions `init` and `write`. Using this information, the developer extracts a candidate requirement by formalizing the dependency as the temporal dependency $\texttt{init}() \lhd \texttt{write}()$. The developer suggest that this temporal dependency could be responsible for the system failure. Finally, the activity produces the candidate requirement R for the relevance check.

Check Relevance of Extracted Candidate Requirement. The relevance check is the second part of the process (see the green box in Fig. 1) and requires as input the candidate requirement R. The check involves two decisions (depicted in diamond shape in Fig. 1) to witness the relevance of R according to Definition 1. For the two decisions, we leverage a formal method, specifically software model checking (see, e.g., [11]), to formally prove the relevance of R. For clarity, we explain below the two decisions of the relevance check.

First Decision of Relevance Check. In the first step of the relevance check, we apply software model checking to the original application code of the faulty system, where we expect to detect a violation of R. If the decision returns the result 'yes', a violation is found. The violation indicates that R remains a candidate for relevance. Contrarily, if no violation is detected, it implies that R is not responsible for the system failure from the issue report. In this case, the developer may return to Activity 2 to extract another candidate requirement and repeat the relevance check.

Second decision of relevance check. In the second step of the relevance check, we again apply software model checking, this time to the application code of the system in the repaired version. Hereby, we aim to confirm that R is no longer violated. Consequently, we expect that the application code in the repaired version satisfies R. If the decision returns the result 'yes', the relevance check witnesses that R is indeed a relevant requirement. Otherwise, if the decision returns the result 'no', R is still violated. In this case, R could not be proven relevant and the developer may return to Activity 2 to extract another candidate requirement and repeat the relevance check.

2.3 Check a Set of Candidate Requirements for Relevance

We introduce an alternative approach for obtaining relevant interface requirements, embodied as a process chart in Fig. 2. This alternative approach of the relevance check is well-suited for use in industrial settings where companies collect issues in internal issue trackers. Most of these issues have already been resolved, i.e., the corresponding faulty systems have been repaired and the reported system failures no longer occur. But it remains unclear which requirements are relevant to prevent the system failures.

Here, the alternative approach can be applied retrospectively to single out relevant requirements. Unlike the overall approach, this alternative does not require the manual extraction of a candidate requirement from a given issue report. Instead, the alternative lifts the relevance check for a single candidate requirement (as shown in Fig. 1) to a finite set of candidate requirements $\mathcal{R}$. The set $\mathcal{R}$ is fixed for a given HAL interface and can be inferred from the HAL documentation and, if possible, from the HAL implementation.

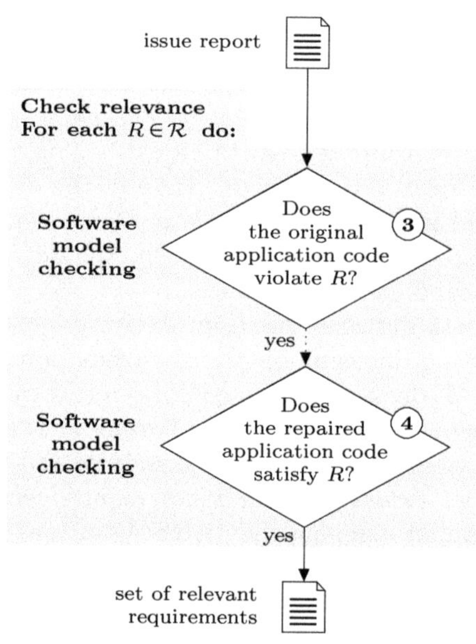

Fig. 2. Alternative approach. The finite set of candidate requirements $\mathcal{R}$ is fixed for a given HAL interface. The application code comes again in two versions: the original version exhibits the system failure, the repaired version does not.

Our formal notion of relevance allows us to leverage software model checking in order to simultaneously prove the relevance of each requirement $R \in \mathcal{R}$, as explained in Sect. 2.2. If R is proven relevant (i.e., both decisions return 'yes') we add it to a finite set of relevant requirements. Ideally, this set contains exactly one relevant requirement to emphasize the significance of relevance. Multiple relevant requirements indicate that a system failure is masked by other failures.

3   Preliminary Case Study

In this section, we present a preliminary case study where we apply the approach from Sect. 2 to three issue reports on system failures. Our goal is to evaluate the approach. Specifically, we aim to address the following research questions:

RQ1: Is the approach to extract a relevant HAL interface requirement from an issue report on a system failure feasible in principle?

RQ2: For each system failure, is there only one single requirement that is relevant for the system failure?

The motivation behind RQ2 is our impression that the significance of relevance as a means to single out requirements is weakened in the case where two requirements are relevant for the same system failure. To be able to give at least a preliminary answer to RQ2 we narrow down the question by restricting the set of requirements to the set of temporal dependencies that can be inferred for a given HAL. This gives us a finite number of requirements and allows us to check each of them on the two versions of each system.

3.1   System Failures in Embedded Systems

The system failures stem from issues that have recently received some attention in newsgroups, as discussed among several places including [15–17]. The issue reports concern embedded systems and provide structural system descriptions but they do not explicitly state interface requirements at all.

Overview of Systems. The embedded systems share a common structure, as illustrated in Fig. 3, which specifically depicts the embedded system in [16]. While this schematic representation focuses on that particular example, it is important to note that the other two systems are similarly structured.

SPI bus and spidev HAL. The embedded systems use the Serial Peripheral Interface (SPI) [13] as a communication bus to connect the system's hardware, in particular a computer or microcontroller, to a peripheral device. The peripheral device is specifically an actuator like a display controller in [15], a sensor in [16], or an unspecified device in [17]. The SPI bus is operated in a master/slave configuration where the integrated SPI controller of the computer or microcontroller serves as master to control the bus communication. Conversely, the SPI controller of the peripheral device serves as slave. The computer or microcontroller runs an application program that uses the *spidev* HAL[1] to operate the SPI bus via the master SPI controller (see Fig. 3). The *spidev* HAL comprises several software layers to support SPI controllers from various manufacturers and uses POSIX system calls to provide a HAL interface. Proper operation of the SPI controller by the embedded application requires the use of HAL functions such as `open` to initialize the SPI controller. Configuration and data transfers are then performed through HAL functions like `ioctl`, `read`, and `write`. The `ioctl` function uses specific SPI constants[2] to set parameters such as mode, speed, and bit order for SPI data transfers.

HAL interface requirements. Interface requirements between the application program and the *spidev* HAL (see dashed purple box in Fig. 3) solely depend on the HAL. These requirements have to be satisfied during the runtime of the system. Otherwise runtime errors can occur that may lead to serious system failures.

Currently, such HAL interface requirements do not exist for the *spidev* HAL. To address RQ1, we extract a candidate requirement for each of the three system failures according to our overall approach from Sect. 2.2. To address RQ2, we systematically infer a set of requirements for the *spidev* HAL to apply our alternative approach from Sect. 2.3 retrospectively on the three systems.

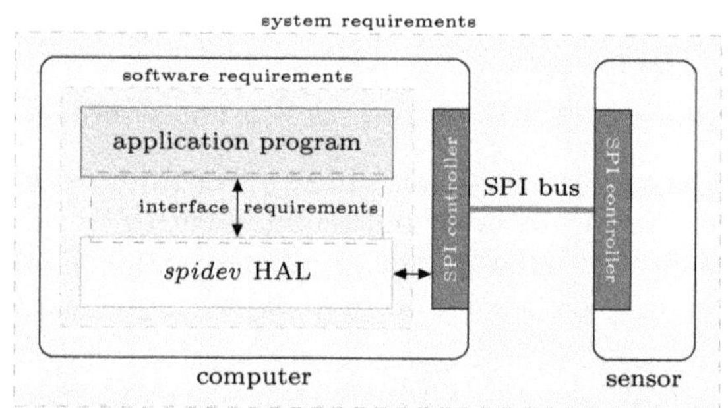

Fig. 3. Architecture of the embedded system from the issue report in [16].

Replicated Systems and Corresponding Failures. While the reports offer some insights into the issues and the used embedded systems, they do not provide the complete application code or sufficient details of the hardware setup to clone each system. We rebuild the embedded systems with the hardware to replicate system failures corresponding to those reported in the issue reports. With the rebuild, we make sure that an error in each system lead to a system failure from the issue reports, i.e., that it is a real error (as opposed to a *theoretical* error which cannot appear in a practical environment). We create three applications that correspond to the applications from the issue reports: control an actuator (cf. [15]), read sensor measurements (cf. [16]), and test communication (cf. [17]).

---

[1] The *spidev* HAL with its userspace API is part of the Linux kernel repository and available at https://git.kernel.org/pub/scm/linux/kernel/git/torvalds/linux.git/tree/Documentation/spi/spidev?h=v5.3.

[2] For reasons of readability, we have omitted the prefix `SPI_IOC_` for all SPI constants from the *spidev* HAL and we have abbreviated the SPI constant `MESSAGE` with `MSG` (also see Table 1).

In the following, we describe the three embedded systems and their observations that align with the ones from the issue reports.

> **Embedded system 1: I/O Expander**
>
> **System description**: The system 'I/O Expander' is designed to control a Microchip MCP23S17 input/output expander, which offers 16 configurable input/output pins. This system setup involves a master SPI controller on the computer and a slave SPI controller in the MCP23S17. The application program uses the *spidev* HAL to communicate with the MCP23S17, operating through a specified sequence of initialization and control commands.
>
> **Failure observation**: Upon executing the program, a system failure is observed in which pin A0 of the MCP23S17 does not activate as expected. This failure corresponds to the issue reported in [15], where the actuator (a display controller) fails to be controlled reliably.

> **Embedded system 2: Accelerometer**
>
> **System description**: The application 'Accelerometer' sends control commands to an Analog Devices ADXL345 accelerometer, which measures acceleration along three axes. This system employs a similar master/slave configuration, where the computer acts as the SPI master and the ADXL345 acts as the SPI slave. The application program retrieves sensor data by transmitting commands through the *spidev* HAL, similar to how it might be executed in the original system.
>
> **Failure observation**: When running this application, we could observe a failure where no acceleration data can be received from the ADXL345. This observation aligns with the system failure described in the issue report from [16], where a sensor fails to provide measurements.

> **Embedded system 3: *spidev*-Test**
>
> **System description**: The application program '*spidev*-Test' is generally used by developers to test the functionality of newly developed SPI components. In this case, we utilize this application to test the communication with the ADXL345 accelerometer. The system uses the same SPI master/slave configuration, with the computer configured to check the connectivity and data flow through the ADXL345.
>
> **Failure observation**: In executing this application, a failure occurs where the communication test fails to return a valid device ID. This observes the issue reported in [17], where the sanity check for communication with a peripheral device does not succeed.

3.2 Extract and Check Candidate Requirements from System Failures

We apply our overall approach from Sect. 2.2 to the three issue reports in order to address RQ1. We obtain the original application code from our replicated systems, where each system exhibits a failure.

Inspect Issue Reports. The three issue reports describe system failures observed during operation and related to the SPI bus. While the application code is syntactically correct and can be compiled and run, the issue reports indicate that the errors are not trivial. Manual inspection of the system failures reveals that each application code properly initializes the SPI controller using the HAL function `open`, but omits essential configuration calls, causing the controller to operate with default settings. This misconfiguration leads to communication failures, as there is no universal agreement on a default configuration for SPI controllers. In the 'I/O Expander' code, the missing `ioctl(WR_MAX_SPEED_HZ)` call causes clock speed mismatches. In the 'Accelerometer' code, the absent `ioctl(WR_MODE32)` call results in polarity and phase mismatches. In the '*spidev*-Test' code, the missing `ioctl(WR_BITS_PER_WORD)` call causes word size mismatches in data transfers between the master and slave SPI controller.

Extract Candidate and Check Relevance. Following our overall approach, we extract a candidate requirement for each issue from the insights of the inspection. Specifically, we extracted the temporal dependencies δ_{26} (for 'I/O Expander'), δ_{17} (for 'Accelerometer'), and δ_{23} (for '*spidev*-Test') as candidates (shown in detail in Table 1). We conduct the relevance check on the three candidates where we apply software model checking carried out by the verification tool ULTIMATE AUTOMIZER [10] in version 0.3.0.[3]

Validity of Temporal Dependencies. Software model checking of the relevance check verifies the validity of extracted requirements within a C program that uses *spidev* functions from the HAL. We encode this validity through assertions in an annotated version of the program.

The annotation, shown schematically in Listing 1, adds auxiliary statements of two kinds: update statements that only modify auxiliary variables, and assert statements. For each temporal dependency of the form $\delta : f_1() \triangleleft f_2()$, we insert an update statement in the code for the implementation of function f_1 and an assert statement in the function f_2, in addition to the declaration of an auxiliary variable for the temporal dependency δ. In each execution, the value of the auxiliary variable (the *ghost state*) flags whether the call of the function f_1 has (or has not yet) taken place. We use the ANSI/ISO C Specification Language (ACSL) [5], an annotation language for C supported by a variety of verification tools. The encoding of the validity is independent of the particular application code and solely depends on the HAL.

---

[3] ULTIMATE AUTOMIZER is part of the open-source program analysis framework ULTIMATE and available at https://www.ultimate-pa.org.

```
 1    /*@ ghost int state_d1 = 0; */
 2
 3    int open(const char *path, int oflag, ...)
 4    {
 5        int ret = ...;
 6
 7        /*@ ghost state_d1 = 1; */
 8        return ret;
 9    }
10
11    ssize_t read(int fd, void *buf, size_t nbyte)
12    {
13        /*@ assert (state_d1 == 1); */
14
15        return ...;
16    }
```

Listing 1. Encoding the validity of a temporal dependency in an application program through the validity of an assertion in an annotation of the application program. Given the temporal dependency δ_1 : **open**() ◁ **read**() from Table 1, the annotation consists in adding ghost code (in green) to the *spidev* functions **open** and **read**. The code snippets here refer to the original implementation of the *spidev* functions from the HAL. The annotation does not modify the application program in other than the shown places.

Experimental Results. In the first step of the relevance check, we apply ULTI-MATE AUTOMIZER on each of the three application programs to verify the validity of the corresponding candidate temporal dependency. The verification results reveal that one assert statement is violated in each faulty application program. We inspect each violation (using the failure path from the verification result) to witness that the violated assert statements are indeed part of the program annotation. Based on the program annotation, we do a reverse-lookup to locate the temporal dependencies, to which these violated assert statements belong. The verification results witness that each application program violates one of the three candidate temporal dependencies.

In the second step of the relevance check, we again apply ULTIMATE AUTOMIZER, this time to each of the application programs in the repaired version. We obtain the repaired version by manual repair of the error in each faulty application program. The failure path from each verification result can guide us to localize the errors, so that the repaired application programs no longer cause the observed system failures. From the check, we obtain the verification results, which witness that all assertions in each of the three application programs are satisfied. Thus, all three candidate temporal dependencies are satisfied and indeed relevant. Our overall approach to obtain a relevant interface requirement succeeds in all three cases of our case study and is feasible in principle (**RQ1**).

3.3   Check a Set of *spidev* HAL Interface Requirements for Relevance

We apply our alternative approach from Sect. 2.3 retrospectively to the three issue reports in order to address RQ2. We obtain the application code in the original, faulty version from the replicated systems, and in the repaired, correct version from our experiments addressing RQ1.

Infer a Set of Candidate Requirements. The approach requires a set of interface requirements, for which we infer temporal dependencies from the *spidev* HAL. We use a systematic method to infer the temporal dependencies where we investigate all pairs of HAL functions. For each pair, we consult the documentation of the HAL and, if possible, the HAL implementation to determine if a dependency exists. Confirmed dependencies are added as temporal dependencies to the set. Finally, we obtain the set of temporal dependencies shown in Table 1.

Check Relevance of Candidates. For each of the three issue reports, we apply the relevance check to the set of temporal dependencies from Table 1. We again utilize ULTIMATE AUTOMIZER, this time to simultaneously verify the validity of all temporal dependencies from the set. This requires that we encode the validity of all temporal dependencies as annotation in both versions of each application program.

Experimental Results. Table 2 shows the experimental results of the relevance check. Three out of the total 26 candidate temporal dependencies (namely δ_{17}, δ_{23}, and δ_{26}) are formally proven relevant. These three requirements are responsible for the system failures from the three issue reports. For each system failure, we obtain exactly one provably relevant HAL interface requirement (**RQ2**). This finding emphasizes the significance of relevance in our preliminary case study.

Table 1. Candidate temporal dependencies inferred from the *spidev* HAL.

δ_1	: open()	◁ read()
δ_2	: open()	◁ write()
δ_3	: open()	◁ ioctl(MSG)
δ_4	: open()	◁ close()
δ_5	: open()	◁ ioctl(RD_MODE)
δ_6	: open()	◁ ioctl(WR_MODE)
δ_7	: open()	◁ ioctl(RD_MODE32)
δ_8	: open()	◁ ioctl(WR_MODE32)
δ_9	: open()	◁ ioctl(RD_LSB_FIRST)
δ_{10}	: open()	◁ ioctl(WR_LSB_FIRST)
δ_{11}	: open()	◁ ioctl(RD_BITS_PER_WORD)
δ_{12}	: open()	◁ ioctl(WR_BITS_PER_WORD)
δ_{13}	: open()	◁ ioctl(RD_MAX_SPEED_HZ)
δ_{14}	: open()	◁ ioctl(WR_MAX_SPEED_HZ)
δ_{15}	: ioctl(WR_MODE32)	◁ read()
δ_{16}	: ioctl(WR_MODE32)	◁ write()
δ_{17}	: ioctl(WR_MODE32)	◁ ioctl(MSG)
δ_{18}	: ioctl(WR_LSB_FIRST)	◁ read()
δ_{19}	: ioctl(WR_LSB_FIRST)	◁ write()
δ_{20}	: ioctl(WR_LSB_FIRST)	◁ ioctl(MSG)
δ_{21}	: ioctl(WR_BITS_PER_WORD)	◁ read()
δ_{22}	: ioctl(WR_BITS_PER_WORD)	◁ write()
δ_{23}	: ioctl(WR_BITS_PER_WORD)	◁ ioctl(MSG)
δ_{24}	: ioctl(WR_MAX_SPEED_HZ)	◁ read()
δ_{25}	: ioctl(WR_MAX_SPEED_HZ)	◁ write()
δ_{26}	: ioctl(WR_MAX_SPEED_HZ)	◁ ioctl(MSG)

Table 2. Experimental results of the applied relevance check to the inferred temporal dependencies for the *spidev* HAL from Table 1. The set listed in under 'Result' is exactly the set of interface requirements that the check determines to be violated. That is, the complement contains those that the check determines to be correct.

| Application program | | | Result | Verification | |
| name | version | size | incorrect | time | mem. |
		[LOC]		[s]	[MB]
I/O Expander	faulty	172	$\{\delta_{26}\}$	5.37	343
	repaired	180	$\emptyset$	5.91	379
Accelerometer	faulty	284	$\{\delta_{17}\}$	7.70	468
	repaired	292	$\emptyset$	9.18	526
spidev-Test	faulty	764	$\{\delta_{23}\}$	971.13	1359
	repaired	768	$\emptyset$	914.20	1820

3.4   Discussion

The results from our preliminary case study demonstrate that we obtain the same relevant HAL interface requirements using the overall approach as well as the alternative relevance check. This consistency indicates convergence and robustness of our approach. In our preliminary case study, we did not encounter the scenario where one system failure masks other ones, which indicates that several requirements might be relevant. Masking failures could occur if a developer forgets to insert not only the HAL function calls for the configuration of the master SPI controller but also the call to initialize the SPI controller, leading to several observable system failures that may mask one another. While this case could potentially arise, our alternative relevance check from Sect. 2.3 can obtain several relevant requirements even in the presence of masking failures.

The experimental results from Table 2 also indicate that the verification of the validity of temporal dependencies itself is not a challenge in this case study (cf. last two columns of Table 2). Even the more complex application program '*spidev*-Test' with 764 lines of code (including the annotation) in its faulty version can be verified within 17 min where the memory consumption never exceeds 1.9 GB.[4] For this reason, it does not seem useful to evaluate the efficiency of other software model checking tools or formal verification methods.

3.5   Threats to Validity

The primary threat concerns the limited generalizability of our findings, as our approach was only applied to specific example cases. Further research is needed to confirm the applicability of the approach across diverse industrial embedded systems. Additionally, the evaluation involved the same team of developers who created the approach, which could introduce bias. More research and independent assessment is needed to confirm the generalizability of our findings.

---

[4] All verification runs with Ultimate Automizer were carried out and measured on a regular desktop computer with quad-core CPU at 3.4 GHz, 8 GB of memory, running Arch Linux with Linux kernel 6.12.45.

The scalability of our approach is theoretically possible but limited by software model checking, particularly due to state explosion in complex or concurrent systems. One potential solution is to manually reduce the corresponding application programs to smaller, simplified versions that still exhibit the observed system failures. The approach is also unable to handle complex temporal dependencies, but this is not an inherent limitation. The primary challenge resides in the capabilities of the software model checker, with scalability issues arising from system complexity rather than the requirements themselves.

Our approach is not fully sound and may produce false negatives, potentially missing relevant HAL interface requirements. Additionally, the correctness of the results depends on properly added program annotations. Errors in the annotations could lead to incorrect results. However, automation of annotation generation can mitigate this risk. In our context, incorrect annotations are likely to be detected since they are written only once for a HAL (the same one used across all application programs in the preliminary case study).

The relevance of HAL interface requirements relies heavily on the representativeness of observed system failures. The lack of case studies and the often imprecise failure descriptions limit our understanding of potential issues. Due to the unavailability of original systems, we replicated comparable embedded systems to reproduce the failures. However, results from these replicas cannot be directly generalized to the original systems. In industrial practice, access to actual systems would reduce the need for replication to obtain application code.

4   Related Work

In this section, we cover work related to the topics in this paper. We focus on areas such as formal requirements engineering, interface requirements, and methods for deriving requirements.

Requirements Engineering. There is a rich body of work on formal requirements engineering; see, e.g., [1,8,14]. While this work is closely related to ours in both spirit and underlying techniques, such as SAT/SMT solving and model checking, it does not employ software model checking to evaluate a criterion for identifying a specific subset of requirements. In contrast, our relevance criterion explicitly determines whether a requirement is provably relevant, allowing us to single out a subset of requirements (the provably relevant ones). Its formal nature ensures unambiguity and clarity, which helps to identify the provably relevant HAL interface requirements that are essential for preventing system failures.

Temporal Dependencies. The class of temporal dependencies which we used to define the set of 26 candidate requirements are temporal requirements. These requirements correspond to the precedence requirement pattern in the hierarchy outlined in [9]. The class of temporal dependencies is restrictive enough to enable a systematic selection of candidate requirements; yet, it is expressive enough to include relevant interface requirements, as shown in our preliminary case study.

Deriving Requirements. Previous work [7], building upon the work in [2] and [12], proposes different algorithms to automatically derive interface requirements from an existing library implementation for its safe and permissive use. These approaches require the presence of explicit safety requirements (e.g., invariants) within the library implementation, which serve as a basis for the automatic inference of a possibly comprehensive set of interface requirements. In contrast, our approach does not depend on safety requirements defined a priori. Instead, the primary objective of our approach is to derive a concise set of HAL interface requirements by single out the relevant ones that are essential for preventing system failures. A similar line of research is the specification mining based on statistical or stochastic methods where interface requirements are automatically derived from a set of error-free application programs that properly interact with the interface, e.g., see [3,4]. The mined specifications are utilized to detect so-called API (mis)uses. The existing approaches to automatically mine interface requirements may be contrasted with our approach to derive relevant HAL interface requirements: the former relies on programs that properly use a given interface, whereas the latter relies in the existence of programs that do not. Exploring how one can exploit this apparent complementariness remains an open area for future research.

5 Conclusion

In this work, we introduced a formal relevance criterion for requirements engineering, based on system failures. The criterion allows us to single out those requirements that are essential for preventing system failures. Its formal nature ensures unambiguity and clarity, which helps to identify relevant requirements.

We presented an approach to extract provably relevant requirements, specifically HAL interface requirements, by formally proving their relevance within a defined process. HAL interface requirements define the correct use of a HAL interface in application programs for embedded systems. Our approach to single out relevant HAL interface requirements starts by analyzing issue reports that mention observable system failures. From these reports, we infer candidate requirements for the correct use of the HAL interface. We then formally prove the relevance of each candidate requirement by leveraging software model checking. This relevance check is an essential process step, as it witnesses that an interface requirement is indisputably responsible for an observed system failure.

We evaluated our approach in a preliminary case study on three examples of issue reports related to embedded application programs that use the SPI bus via the *spidev* HAL. The experimental results demonstrate the practical feasibility of our approach. We were able to obtain a relevant interface requirement for each mentioned system failure from the three issue reports. Each relevant interface requirement is essential in preventing an observable system failure. Embedded software developers should concentrate on such relevant requirements to prevent specific kinds of system failures, such as those mentioned in the issue reports.

Acknowledgments. Part of this study was funded by the Deutsche Forschungsgemeinschaft (DFG, German Research Foundation) – 503812980.

Data Availability Statement. The dataset for the findings of the preliminary case study is available on Zenodo [6] and enables reproduction and validation of the results.

Disclosure of Interests. The authors declare that they have no competing interests that could have appeared to influence the work reported in this paper.

References

1. Alrajeh, D., Kramer, J., Russo, A., Uchitel, S.: Elaborating requirements using model checking and inductive learning. Trans. Softw. Eng. **39**(3), 361–383 (2013). https://doi.org/10.1109/tse.2012.41
2. Alur, R., Černý, P., Madhusudan, P., Nam, W.: Synthesis of interface specifications for Java classes. SIGPLAN Notices **40**(1), 98–109 (2005). https://doi.org/10.1145/1047659.1040314
3. Amann, S., Nadi, S., Nguyen, H.A., Nguyen, T.N., Mezini, M.: MUBench: a benchmark for API-misuse detectors. In: Proceedings of MSR, pp. 464–467. ACM (2016). https://doi.org/10.1145/2901739.2903506
4. Amann, S., Nguyen, H.A., Nadi, S., Nguyen, T.N., Mezini, M.: A systematic evaluation of static API-misuse detectors. Trans. Softw. Eng. **45**(12), 1170–1188 (2019). https://doi.org/10.1109/tse.2018.2827384
5. Baudin, P., et al.: ACSL: ANSI/ISO C Specification Language. Frama-C (2024). https://frama-c.com/download/acsl-1.20.pdf, version 1.20
6. Bentele, M., Podelski, A., Sikora, A., Westphal, B.: Replication dataset for provably relevant HAL interface requirements for embedded systems. Replication package (2026). https://doi.org/10.5281/zenodo.17441552
7. Beyer, D., Henzinger, T.A., Singh, V.: Algorithms for interface synthesis. In: Proceedings of CAV, pp. 4–19. Springer (2007). https://doi.org/10.1007/978-3-540-73368-3_4
8. Degiovanni, R., Alrajeh, D., Aguirre, N., Uchitel, S.: Automated goal operationalisation based on interpolation and SAT solving. In: Proceedings of ICSE, pp. 129–139. ACM (2014). https://doi.org/10.1145/2568225.2568323
9. Dwyer, M.B., Avrunin, G.S., Corbett, J.C.: Patterns in property specifications for finite-state verification. In: Proceedings of ICSE, pp. 411–420. ACM (1999). https://doi.org/10.1145/302405.302672
10. Heizmann, M., et al.: ULTIMATE AUTOMIZER and the search for perfect interpolants (competition contribution). In: Proceedings of TACAS, pp. 447–451. Springer (2018). https://doi.org/10.1007/978-3-319-89963-3_30
11. Heizmann, M., Hoenicke, J., Podelski, A.: Software model checking for people who love automata. In: Proceedings of CAV, pp. 36–52. Springer (2013). https://doi.org/10.1007/978-3-642-39799-8_2
12. Henzinger, T.A., Jhala, R., Majumdar, R.: Permissive interfaces. Softw. Eng. Notes **30**(5), 31–40 (2005). https://doi.org/10.1145/1095430.1081713
13. Hill, S.C., Jelemensky, J., Heene, M.R., Groves, S.E., DeBrito, D.N.: Queued serial peripheral interface for use in a data processing system. Patent US-4958277 (1990). https://image-ppubs.uspto.gov/dirsearch-public/print/downloadPdf/4958277
14. Palma, F., Susi, A., Tonella, P.: Using an SMT solver for interactive requirements prioritization. In: Proceedings of ESEC/FSE, pp. 48–58. ACM (2011). https://doi.org/10.1145/2025113.2025124

15. SPI connection between RPi and ATmega32. Raspberry Pi Forum (2016). https:// forums.raspberrypi.com/viewtopic.php?p=881605
16. Reading values from MCP3002 not working [...]. Raspberry Pi Forum (2019). https://forums.raspberrypi.com/viewtopic.php?t=230569
17. *spidev* sanity check not working. Stack Exchange (2019). https://raspberrypi. stackexchange.com/questions/102286/spidev-sanity-check-not-working

A Practical and Complete Method for Detecting rt-Inconsistencies in Real-Time Requirements

Nico Hauff[(✉)] [iD], Elisabeth Henkel[iD], Elisabeth Fünfgeld,
Vincent Langenfeld[iD], and Andreas Podelski[iD]

University of Freiburg, Freiburg, Germany
`hauffn@informatik.uni-freiburg.de`

Abstract. **[Context and motivation]** Methods to automatically detect an rt-inconsistency, a notorious defect in real-time requirements, have proven to be practically useful. Existing methods scale to industrial examples. They are, however, not complete, meaning that they cannot detect every rt-inconsistency. **[Question/problem]** The question is whether one can achieve both scalability and completeness. **[Principal ideas/results]** We adapt an existing (incomplete) method so that it takes, as a configurable parameter, a set of candidate subsets of requirements. We develop an algorithm that selects such a set, guaranteed to be large enough to ensure completeness, yet potentially small enough to ensure scalability. Our experimental evaluation demonstrates that the resulting complete method indeed scales to industrial examples. It can detect previously unknown defects and, rather than incurring an overhead, can even be more efficient. **[Contribution]** We present—to the best of our knowledge—the first method for detecting rt-inconsistencies that is both practical and complete. We prove its completeness and present an experimental evaluation.

Keywords: formal methods · requirements analysis · real-time requirements · rt-consistency (real-time consistency)

1 Introduction

Methods for automatically detecting defects in formalized requirements have been shown to be useful in various industrial settings [9]. For real-time requirements, rt-inconsistency is an example of a defect that is notoriously hard to detect without an automatic method. Roughly, an rt-inconsistency can arise from the interplay of time constraints [11,12]. To give some intuition, we illustrate rt-inconsistency informally through an example. Consider the two informal real-time requirements below.

r_1: *If the high-precision sensor is requested, it must be active within 3 seconds.*
r_2: *If system diagnostic is active, the high-precision sensor must be inactive for at least 2 seconds.*

Although these requirements are jointly consistent – meaning that there exist systems that can satisfy both, circumstances may still arise in which they conflict. Consider the trace shown in Fig. 1. At time point $t = 1$, the sensor request

R. Guizzardi and J. Araújo (Eds.): REFSQ 2026, LNCS 16497, pp. 274–289, 2026.
https://doi.org/10.1007/978-3-032-21423-2_19

sensReq is set. Due to requirement r_1, the sensor must be active (*sensOn*) within the next 3 seconds. At time point $t = 3$, system diagnostic is activated (*diagOn*). By requirement r_2, the sensor must be inactive for at least 2 seconds. If the sensor is not turned on during the time interval $[1, 4]$, any continuation of the trace after time point $t = 4$ will result in the violation of either requirement r_1 or r_2, since the first requires the sensor to be activated while the second requires it to remain inactive. The set of the two requirements is thus rt-inconsistent.

It has been shown that existing automatic methods to detect rt-inconsistencies can be practical, i.e., scale to industrial examples of real-time requirements [6,7]. The existing methods are, however, not complete; i.e., they do not detect all rt-inconsistencies. Detecting some, though not all rt-inconsistencies may be useful, but it is unsatisfactory from a conceptual and from a pragmatic point of view. Before starting the repair of these defects, the user wants to know about all rt-inconsistencies, and after finishing the repair, the user wants to make sure that all rt-inconsistencies have indeed been eliminated and no new ones have been introduced.

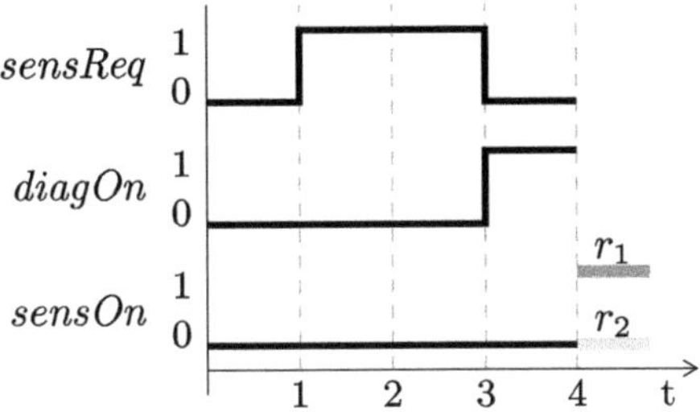

Fig. 1. Witness for the rt-inconsistency of requirements r_1 and r_2.

This raises the question whether can one design a method that is both practical and complete. In this paper, we provide a positive answer. We introduce a new method, prove its completeness, and present an experimental evaluation demonstrating that it scales to industrial-scale examples.

We can adapt an existing (incomplete) method so that it takes, as a configurable parameter, a set $\mathcal{C}$ of candidates, where each candidate is a subset of the given set $\mathcal{R}$ of requirements.[1]

As our main technical contribution, we develop an algorithm to configure the parameter as a function of $\mathcal{R}$. The algorithm can select the set $\mathcal{C}$ in such a way that it is guaranteed to be large enough to ensure completeness, yet potentially small enough to ensure scalability. The algorithm takes the set $\mathcal{R}$ of requirements and returns a set $\mathcal{C}$ of candidates. Each candidate in $\mathcal{C}$ is not necessarily rt-inconsistent in the context of the whole set $\mathcal{R}$ of requirements, and perhaps not even rt-inconsistent if taken by itself. This over-approximation results in a loss of precision, which is acceptable as long as it is outweighed by the gain in efficiency.

Given a set $\mathcal{R}$ of requirements, the new method first applies the algorithm to compute $\mathcal{C}$ and then applies the existing, adapted method with the parameter $\mathcal{C}$. We formally prove that the new method is complete. Our experimental

---

[1] In the case where $\mathcal{C}$ consists of all subsets of $\mathcal{R}$ of size 2, we obtain the practical, but incomplete method from [6,7]. In the case where $\mathcal{C}$ is the set of all subsets of $\mathcal{R}$, we obtain a method that is complete but practically unrealistic; it is of theoretical interest only (idem for the case where $\mathcal{C}$ is the singleton set $\{\mathcal{R}\}$).

evaluation demonstrates that it is also practical; i.e., the new method scales to the same industrial examples of real-time requirements that have been used to demonstrate the scalability of the existing (incomplete) method by Langenfeld et al. [6,7].

The experimental evaluation shows that the new method is more effective in finding defects. On the examples, the new method has unearthed rt-inconsistencies that were previously unknown in these industrial examples, and that could not be detected by the existing method for intrinsic reasons. The fact that these rt-inconsistencies were previously unknown may serve as an indication that completeness is not just a conceptual issue.

Furthermore, the experimental evaluation shows that, rather than incurring an overhead as the price to pay for the detection of new defects, the new method is comparable in efficiency with the existing automated method both in terms of time and memory consumption (and sometimes even more efficient).

In summary, the contribution of this paper is to present a method for detecting rt-inconsistencies that is both practical and complete (Sect. 2), to prove the completeness (Sect. 3), and to present an experimental evaluation (Sect. 4).

Outline Section 2 introduces the new method. Section 3 presents the formal foundation of the method and proves completeness. Section 4 presents the experimental evaluation. Section 5 discusses related work. Section 6 concludes.

2   Overview

In this section, we give an informal presentation of the new method. We postpone formal definitions until Sect. 3.

The method takes as input a set $\mathcal{R}$ of formalized requirements. From now on, we consider $\mathcal{R}$ to be fixed. The method checks whether $\mathcal{R}$ is rt-inconsistent, that is, whether there exists a system behaviour that satisfies all requirements in $\mathcal{R}$ up to some point in time t, but necessarily violates at least one of them as time progresses.

The method is based on two new properties, *weak* rt-inconsistency and *contextual* rt-inconsistency. Their definition refers to the syntax of the representation of a requirement as a logical formula, i.e., a *countertrace*; see Sect. 3.1.

If a subset R of $\mathcal{R}$ is minimal rt-inconsistent, then R is also weakly rt-inconsistent.[2] The converse is not true in general. That is, if R is minimal weakly rt-inconsistent, then R is not necessarily rt-inconsistent. Equivalently, if R is not weakly rt-inconsistent, then R is either not rt-inconsistent or (it is rt-inconsistent but then) it is not *minimal* rt-inconsistent.

The rt-inconsistency of $\mathcal{R}$ is equivalent to the existence of a contextual rt-inconsistent subset R of $\mathcal{R}$. Furthermore, if a subset R of the set of requirements $\mathcal{R}$ is minimal contextually rt-inconsistent, then R is also weakly rt-inconsistent, and it is even minimal weakly rt-inconsistent.

---

[2] A subset R of $\mathcal{R}$ is *minimal* [weakly, contextually] rt-inconsistent if it is [weakly, contextually] rt-inconsistent and no proper subset of R has this property.

The property of contextual rt-inconsistency of subsets R of $\mathcal{R}$ is upward closed, i.e., the property extends from R to any superset R' of R in $\mathcal{R}$. An upward closed set can be represented by the (in general, exponentially smaller) set of its minimal elements.

We adapt an existing (incomplete) method to check the rt-inconsistency of a set $\mathcal{R}$ of requirements so that it takes a set $\mathcal{C}$ of *candidate* subsets of $\mathcal{R}$ as a configurable parameter. Given $\mathcal{C}$, the adapted method computes the set of all candidate subsets in $\mathcal{C}$ that are contextually rt-inconsistent.

The new method consists of two steps. The first step computes the set of all minimal *weakly* rt-inconsistent subsets of $\mathcal{R}$. The second step uses this set for the parameter $\mathcal{C}$ in the adapted method and computes the set of all minimal *weakly* rt-inconsistent subsets (i.e., the candidate subsets in $\mathcal{C}$) that are contextually rt-inconsistent.

In Sect. 3, we prove that the set computed in the second step is exactly the set of minimal contextually rt-inconsistent subsets of $\mathcal{R}$.

To summarize, the new method computes the set of all minimal contextually rt-inconsistent subsets of $\mathcal{R}$ and returns the answer yes ("$\mathcal{R}$ is rt-inconsistent") if and only if the computed set is non-empty.

3   Completeness

This section presents the formal foundation for the method presented in Sect. 2.

3.1   Preliminaries (rt-Inconsistency)

We present formal requirements in the logic of countertrace formulas [4], a subset of formulas in the temporal logic of Duration Calculus [10].

A *countertrace* (CT) formula is a formula of the form $\pi_0 \,;\, \pi_1 \,;\, \dots \,;\, \pi_{n-1} \,;\, true$, where π_i denotes a phase and the chop operator ; separates two phases. A *phase* refers to a non-zero time interval, which can either be unconstrained (i.e., the *true*-phase) or constrained by a state expression P, denoted as $\lceil P \rceil$, referring to a time interval in which P is satisfied. The duration of a phase may be constrained by $\ell \sim t$, where $\sim \in \{<, \leq, >, \geq\}$ and t is a non-zero duration. A phase is hence formally defined by $\pi := true \mid \lceil P \rceil \mid \pi \wedge \ell \sim t$. The semantics of a state expression P is defined via interpretations. An *interpretation* $\mathcal{I}[\![P]\!]$: $\mathbb{R}_{\geq 0} \to \{0, 1\}$ maps each point in time $t \in \mathbb{R}_{\geq 0}$ to 1 if P holds at t, and to 0 otherwise. We write $\mathcal{I}_P(t)$ to denote the valuation of P at time t. By $\mathcal{I}, [b, e]$ and $\mathcal{I}, [b, e)$, we denote the segment of interpretation $\mathcal{I}$ in the inclusive and exclusive time interval between time points b and e, respectively. The satisfaction of a CT formula by an interpretation segment is defined as follows:

$$\mathcal{I}, [b, e] \models \lceil P \rceil \qquad \text{if } \mathcal{I}_P(t) = 1 \text{ for almost all } t \in [b, e] \text{ and } b \neq e,$$

$$\mathcal{I}, [b, e] \models \ell \sim t \qquad \text{if } e - b \sim t,$$

$$\mathcal{I}, [b, e] \models \pi_1; \pi_2 \qquad \text{if } \mathcal{I}, [b, m] \models \pi_1 \text{ and } \mathcal{I}, [m, e] \models \pi_2 \text{ for some } m \in [b, e].$$

A CT formula φ is satisfied by an interpretation ($\mathcal{I} \models \varphi$) if every prefix of it satisfies φ (($\mathcal{I}, [0, t]) \models \varphi$ for all t). We can use a CT formula φ to present a requirement r by negation, i.e., to define behaviour that is not allowed. That is, if an interpretation satisfies the CT formula φ then it violates the requirement r.

We say a requirement is *active* in phase π_i (under interpretation $\mathcal{I}$ at time point t) if there is an interpretation segment such that $(\mathcal{I}, [0, t]) \models \pi_0 ; \dots ; \pi_i$. By the term *seeping* through phases, we refer to the fact that by extending an interpretation segment with a specific duration and variable valuation, more than one subsequent phase becomes active.

For notational convenience, we write $inv(\pi)$ to refer to the state expression of phase π. We use $op(\pi)$ to denote the function that returns the operator of phase π if it has one and None otherwise, i.e., $op(\pi) \in \{<, \leq, >, \geq, \text{None}\}$. By the Boolean predicate $Sat(F)$ we denote the predicate that is true if and only if the Boolean formula F is satisfiable.

In the remainder of this section, the term requirement refers to its representation as a CT formula. An interpretation $\mathcal{I}$ satisfies a set $\mathcal{R}$ of requirements if it satisfies all requirements in $\mathcal{R}$, formally: $\mathcal{I} \models \mathcal{R}$ if $\mathcal{I} \models r$ for all $r \in \mathcal{R}$.

Following the terminology from [11], we call a set of the requirements $\mathcal{R}$ *rt-inconsistent* if there exists an interpretation $\mathcal{I}$ and a time point t such that the interpretation segment until time point t satisfies all requirements in $\mathcal{R}$ but cannot be extended to a full interpretation satisfying all requirements in $\mathcal{R}$. Formally, $(\mathcal{I}, [0, t]) \models \mathcal{R}$ but $\mathcal{I} \not\models \mathcal{R}$. By convention, we write $\mathcal{I} \not\models \mathcal{R}$ to stand short for: $\mathcal{I}' \not\models \mathcal{R}$ for any interpretation $\mathcal{I}'$ where $(\mathcal{I}, [0, t]) = (\mathcal{I}', [0, t])$. We note the subtle fact that the interpretation might be infinitely extendable towards a time point $t_0 > t$ such that the requirements are still satisfied, but no interpretation reaching t_0 would do so. Formally (using the similar convention as above), $(\mathcal{I}, [0, t_0)) \models \mathcal{R}$ and $(\mathcal{I}, [0, t_0]) \not\models \mathcal{R}$.

3.2   Weak rt-Inconsistency

We define the property weak rt-inconsistency of a subset $R \subseteq \mathcal{R}$ as the conjunction of the properties $\Phi(R)$, $\Psi(R)$, and $\chi(R)$ which we will introduce next.

$\Phi(R)$: *The conjunction of the invariants of the critical phases of all requirements in R is satisfiable.* The fact that this condition is necessary for the rt-inconsistency of $\mathcal{R}$ follows from the fact that there must exist a satisfying prefix of an interpretation. In particular, the interpretation must satisfy the *critical phases* in time points right before a violation may become unavoidable.

$\Psi(R)$: *The conjunction of the non-violation conditions of all requirements in R is unsatisfiable.* The fact that this condition is necessary for the rt-inconsistency of $\mathcal{R}$ follows from the fact that the unavoidability of the violation of a requirement is due to the fact that the requirements impose conditions (i.e., the *non-violation conditions*) that cannot be satisfied simultaneously.

$\chi(R)$: *At least one requirement in R specifies a time bound.* The fact that this condition is necessary for the rt-inconsistency of $\mathcal{R}$ follows from the fact that only the specification of a time bound can enforce the change of a variable valuation over time.

We now define critical phases and non-violation conditions. Intuitively, the critical phases of a requirement r are defined as the phase indices i such that, when phase π_i in r is active in the current interpretation segment, the violation of requirement r can become unavoidable by any extension of this segment. Requirements, for which seeping is possible may have more than one critical phase. A requirement whose phases do not correspond to a critical phase is assigned index -1.

Definition 1 (Critical phases). *For a requirement r of the form $\pi_0 ; \pi_1 ; \cdots ; \pi_n ; true$, the phase index i of a phase π_i with $i \in \{0, \cdots, n\}$ is an element of the set of critical phases $Crit(r)$ if the following four conditions are satisfied:*

1. *phase π_i is not the last phase:*
$$i < n$$

2. *the invariants of all its subsequent phases π_{i+1} to π_n are simultaneously satisfiable:*
$$Sat\Big(\bigwedge_{k=i+1}^{n} inv(\pi_k) \Big)$$

3. *no subsequent phase π_{i+1} to π_n has a lower time bound:*
$$\forall i < j \leq n.\ op(\pi_j) \notin \{>, \geq\}$$

4. *phase π_i has a lower time bound or it does not imply the invariants of subsequent phases π_{i+1} to π_n:*
$$op(\pi_i) \in \{>, \geq\}\ or\ \neg\Big(inv(\pi_i) \Rightarrow \bigwedge_{k=i+1}^{n} inv(\pi_k) \Big)$$

If none of the phase indices 0 to n is contained in $Crit(r)$ then $Crit(r) := \{-1\}$.

If a violation can occur from a phase of a requirement, then this phase is a critical phase. This can be seen as follows: The first condition excludes the last phase to be critical, as the last phase of a requirement is always a *true*-phase, and reaching this phase corresponds to the violation of the requirement. Intuitively, the second condition ensures that all subsequent phases of a critical phase can be seeped through in a single step (i.e., with a specific variable valuation), while the third establishes that no time bound enforces to stay in a subsequent phase. The fourth condition guarantees that being in a critical phase does not necessarily result in seeping to the last phase but either requires a specific variable valuation or to exceed a time bound.

In general, a requirement can have multiple critical phases. We can, however, replace such a requirement by multiple copies of the requirement such that in each copy exactly one critical phase is singled out. Thus, without loss of generality, we can assume that each requirement comes with exactly one critical phase.

This means that $Crit(r)$ is always a singleton. We write $Crit(r) = i$ instead of $Crit(r) = \{i\}$.

We next define the critical invariant of a requirement.

Definition 2 (Critical invariant). *For a requirement r of the form $(\pi_0 \,; \pi_1 \,; \cdots \,; \pi_n \,; true)$, the critical invariant is given as*

$$
critInv(r) := \begin{cases} \neg inv(\pi_0) & \text{if } Crit(r) = -1, \\ inv(\pi_i) & \text{if } Crit(r) = i \text{ and } 0 \le i \le n. \end{cases}
$$

For each critical phase of a requirement the non-violation condition defines constraints on observables to prevent an immediate violation of the requirement when being active in the critical phase. Intuitively, the non-violation condition specifies a valuation on observables such that the last phase of the requirement cannot be reached.

Definition 3 (Non-violation condition). *For a requirement r of the form $(\pi_0 \,; \pi_1 \,; \cdots \,; \pi_n \,; true)$, the non-violation condition is given as*

$$
Nvc(r) := \begin{cases} \neg inv(\pi_0) & \text{if } Crit(r) = -1, \\ \neg inv(\pi_i) & \text{if } Crit(r) = i \text{ and } op(\pi_i) \in \{>, \ge\} \\ & \quad \text{and } \bigvee_{j=i+1}^{n-1} inv(\pi_j), \\ \bigvee_{j=i+1}^{n-1} \neg inv(\pi_j) & \text{otherwise.} \end{cases}
$$

A requirement is not violated if we choose a variable valuation that satisfies the non-violation condition of a requirement.

We can now formally define the three properties and the property of weak rt-inconsistency.

Definition 4 (Weak rt-inconsistency). *The property Φ holds for a requirements set R if the conjunction of the critical invariants of all requirements in R is satisfiable, formally,*

$$
\Phi(R) \Leftrightarrow Sat\Big(\bigwedge_{r \in R} critInv(r) \Big).
$$

The property Ψ holds for a requirements set R if the conjunction of the non-violation conditions of all requirements in R is not satisfiable, formally,

$$
\Psi(R) \Leftrightarrow not\ Sat\Big(\bigwedge_{r \in R} Nvc(r) \Big).
$$

The property χ holds for a requirements set R if one of the requirements $r \in R$ contains a time bound, formally,

$$
\chi(R) \Leftrightarrow op(\pi_i) \neq \textbf{None} \text{ for some } r \in R \text{ where } r = (\pi_0 \,; \ldots \,; \pi_n) \text{ and } i < n.
$$

The property weak rt-inconsistency holds for a requirements set R if the conjunction of the properties $\Phi(R)$, $\Psi(R)$ and $\chi(R)$ holds:

$$
R \text{ weakly rt-inconsistent } \Leftrightarrow \Phi(R) \text{ and } \Psi(R) \text{ and } \chi(R).
$$

Before we prove that each of the properties is a necessary condition for rt-inconsistency, we introduce the following terminology. A requirement $r \in R$ is said to be *involved* in the rt-inconsistency of a set R if and only if r is contained in at least one minimal rt-inconsistent subset of R.

Lemma 1. *If the requirements set R is rt-inconsistent and R is minimal, then $\Phi(R)$ holds.*

Proof. Let R be a set of requirements such that R is intrinsically rt-inconsistent and R is minimal. By the definition of (intrinsic) rt-inconsistency, there exists a satisfying finite prefix of an interpretation such that any extension of this prefix leads to a violation of some requirement $r \in R$. Therefore the last phase of the requirement r must become active under this extension. This necessitates that the critical phase of r is active directly before the violation occurs (by definition of critical phases). As R is minimal, all other requirements in R are involved in the rt-inconsistency. To make the violation unavoidable, all other requirements in R must enforce a specific variable valuation to prevent their own violation. However, this situation can arise only if all other requirements in R are also in their critical phase. The conjunction of critical invariants of all requirements in R must hence be satisfiable and thus $\Phi(R)$ must hold. $\qquad\square$

Lemma 2. *If the requirements set R is rt-inconsistent, then $\Psi(R)$ holds.*

Proof. Proof by contradiction. Let R be a set of requirements such that R is intrinsically rt-inconsistent, and let $\Psi(R)$ evaluate to *false*, i.e., the conjunction of non-violation conditions of all requirements in R is satisfiable. From the definition of (intrinsic) rt-inconsistency, there must exist a finite prefix of an interpretation that is not extendable to a full interpretation. By the definition of critical phases, every requirement $r \in R$ involved in the rt-inconsistency must be in its critical phase immediately before the violation happens. By definition, the non-violation condition of a critical phase specifies a valuation on observables that extends the finite prefix to a full interpretation without violating the requirement. Since the conjunction of the non-violation conditions of all requirements in R is satisfiable, there is a valuation that extends the prefix without violating any requirement in R. That contradicts the assumption that R is rt-inconsistent. $\qquad\square$

Lemma 3. *If the requirements set R is rt-inconsistent, then $\chi(R)$ holds.*

Proof. Proof by contradiction. Let R be a requirements set such that R is intrinsically rt-inconsistent and $\chi(R)$ does not hold, i.e., no requirement in R specifies a time bound.
The critical invariants of all requirements in R must be simultaneously satisfiable prior to the valuation leading to the rt-inconsistency (Lemma 1). As no requirement in R specifies a time bound, none of it can enforce a variable valuation that

must hold at a specific point in time. Each interpretation segment satisfying all critical invariants can thus be extended to a satisfying full interpretation. The given set must hence be rt-consistent, which contradicts our assumption.   □

The following theorem is a direct consequence of Lemmas 1 to 3.

Theorem 1. *If the requirements set R is rt-inconsistent and minimal, then R is weakly rt-inconsistent.*

3.3 Contextual rt-Inconsistency

We now define the notion of contextual rt-inconsistency (in the context of $\mathcal{R}$).

Definition 5 (Contextual rt-inconsistency). *The requirements set $R \subseteq \mathcal{R}$ is rt-inconsistent in the context $\mathcal{R}$ if there exists an interpretation $\mathcal{I}$ such that the interpretation segment until some time point t satisfies all requirements in $\mathcal{R}$ but cannot be extended to a full interpretation satisfying all requirements in R, formally, $(\mathcal{I}, [0, t]) \models \mathcal{R}$ and $\mathcal{I} \not\models R$.*

We observe that the rt-inconsistency of $\mathcal{R}$ is equivalent to the existence of a set $R \subseteq \mathcal{R}$ that is contextually rt-inconsistent, formally, if

$$X(\mathcal{R}) = \{R \subseteq \mathcal{R} \mid R \text{ contextually rt-inconsistent}\}$$

then

$$\mathcal{R} \text{ rt-inconsistent} \Leftrightarrow X(\mathcal{R}) \neq \emptyset.$$

We are interested in minimal contextually rt-inconsistent subsets R of $\mathcal{R}$, i.e., $R \subseteq \mathcal{R}$ such that R is contextually rt-inconsistent and any proper subset of R is not.

Theorem 2. *If the subset of requirements $R \subseteq \mathcal{R}$ is minimal contextually rt-inconsistent, then R is minimally weakly rt-inconsistent.*

Proof. Let $R \subseteq \mathcal{R}$ be minimal contextually rt-inconsistent. One can show, using the same line of reasoning as in the proofs of Lemmas 1 to 3, that a minimal contextual rt-inconsistent subset R of $\mathcal{R}$ is weakly rt-inconsistent.

Now, let $R' \subseteq R$ such that R' is weakly rt-inconsistent, i.e., $\Phi(R')$, $\Psi(R')$ and $\chi(R')$ hold. We show that such an R' must be equal to R. Since R is contextually rt-inconsistent, $(\mathcal{I}, [0, t]) \models \mathcal{R}$ holds. Since $\Psi(R')$ holds, the conjunction of the non-violation conditions of all $r \in R'$ is unsatisfiable. As the finite prefix $(\mathcal{I}, [0, t])$ is reachable, and the conjunction of the non-violation conditions is unsatisfiable, $\mathcal{I} \not\models R'$ holds. Therefore R' is contextually rt-inconsistent with respect to $\mathcal{R}$. The minimality of R with respect to contextual rt-inconsistency then implies $R' = R$. This concludes the proof that R is minimal weakly rt-inconsistent.   □

We next show the converse direction under an extra assumption.

Lemma 4. *If the subset of requirements $R \subseteq \mathcal{R}$ is minimal weakly rt-inconsistent and contextually rt-inconsistent with respect to $\mathcal{R}$, then R is also minimal with respect to the contextual rt-inconsistency.*

Proof. Let $R \subseteq \mathcal{R}$ be minimal weakly rt-inconsistent and contextually rt-inconsistent, and let $R' \subset R$. Since R is minimal with respect to weak rt-inconsistency, R' is not weakly rt-inconsistent. The conjunction of the properties $\Phi(R')$, $\Psi(R')$ and $\chi(R')$ does not hold. Since $\Phi(R) \Leftrightarrow Sat(\bigwedge_{r \in R} critInv(r))$ and $R' \subset R$, it follows that $\Phi(R')$ must hold. If $\Psi(R')$ or $\chi(R')$ does not hold, Lemma 2 and Lemma 3, respectively, imply that R' is not rt-inconsistent. Hence, by definition, $(\mathcal{I}, [0, t]) \not\models \mathcal{R}$ or $\mathcal{I} \models R'$ must hold. In the first case, since $R' \subset R \subseteq \mathcal{R}$, we have $(\mathcal{I}, [0, t]) \not\models \mathcal{R}$. In either case, R' is not contextually rt-inconsistent. Since R' is not contextually rt-inconsistent while R is, and $R' \subset R$, R is minimal with respect to contextual rt-inconsistency. $\qquad\square$

We also observe that the property of contextual rt-inconsistency for subsets $R \subseteq \mathcal{R}$ is upward closed. This means that, if we have two subsets R and R' of $\mathcal{R}$ such that R is contextually rt-inconsistent and $R \subseteq R'$, then also R' is contextually rt-inconsistent. This means that we can represent the set of all contextually rt-inconsistent subsets of $\mathcal{R}$ by the upward closure of the set of the minimal contextually rt-inconsistent subsets of $\mathcal{R}$, formally, if

$$MinX(\mathcal{R}) = \{R \in X(\mathcal{R}) \mid R \text{ minimal}\}$$

then

$$X(\mathcal{R}) = \uparrow MinX(\mathcal{R})$$

where we define upward closure as usual, i.e., $\uparrow M = \{S \mid \exists S' \in M.\, S' \subseteq S\}$ for a set M of sets. As a consequence of the fact that $\uparrow M$ is empty if and only if M is empty, for any set M of stes, we have that $\mathcal{R}$ is rt-inconsistent if and only if $MinX(\mathcal{R}) \neq \emptyset$, formally:

$$\mathcal{R} \text{ rt-inconsistent} \Leftrightarrow MinX(\mathcal{R}) \neq \emptyset.$$

We remind the reader that the property of rt-inconsistency is not upward closed for the reason that possibly $(\mathcal{I}, [0, t]) \not\models \mathcal{R} \cup \{r\}$ for some $r \notin \mathcal{R}$.

3.4 Putting Things Together

In Sect. 2 we give an informal presentation of the new method. Formally, the first step of the new method computes the set $\mathcal{C}$ of all minimal weakly rt-inconsistent subsets $R \subseteq \mathcal{R}$, i.e.,

$$\mathcal{C} = \{R \subseteq \mathcal{R} \mid R \text{ weakly rt-inconsistent and minimal}\}.$$

The second step of the new method is to compute the set $\mathcal{M}$ of all subsets $R \subseteq \mathcal{R}$ such that R is an element of the set $\mathcal{C}$ of candidates and R is contextually rt-inconsistent, i.e.,

$$\mathcal{M} = \{R \subseteq \mathcal{R} \mid R \in \mathcal{C} \text{ and } R \text{ contextually rt-inconsistent}\}.$$

We can now formally relate the set $MinX(\mathcal{R})$ of minimal contextual rt-inconsistent subsets of $\mathcal{R}$, to the set $\mathcal{M}$, i.e., the set computed by the new method presented.

Theorem 3. *The set $\mathcal{M}$ is equal to the set of minimal contextual rt-inconsistent subsets of $\mathcal{R}$, formally:*

$$\mathcal{M} = MinX(\mathcal{R}).$$

Proof. We first show $\mathcal{M} \subseteq MinX(\mathcal{R})$: Let $R \in \mathcal{M}$. By definition, R is a candidate, i.e., $R \in \mathcal{C}$, and R is contextually rt-inconsistent with respect to $\mathcal{R}$. Since $R \in \mathcal{C}$, R is minimal weakly rt-inconsistent. Since R is minimal weakly rt-inconsistent, it is also minimal contextually rt-inconsistent (Lemma 4). Therefore, $R \in MinX(\mathcal{R})$.

Now we show $MinX(\mathcal{R}) \subseteq \mathcal{M}$: Let $R \in MinX(\mathcal{R})$. By definition, R is minimal contextually rt-inconsistent. By Theorem 2, R is also minimal weakly rt-inconsistent. Hence, R is a candidate, i.e., $R \in \mathcal{C}$. Since the new method collects exactly those candidates that are contextually rt-inconsistent, it follows that $R \in \mathcal{M}$. $\qquad\square$

We obtain the equivalence $\mathcal{R}$ rt-inconsistent $\Leftrightarrow \mathcal{M} \neq \emptyset$. This concludes the proof of the completeness of the new method. The completeness corresponds to the $\Rightarrow$ direction in the above equivalence: If $\mathcal{R}$ is rt-inconsistent then the method returns yes. The $\Leftarrow$ direction corresponds to the soundness of the method: If the method returns yes, then $\mathcal{R}$ is rt-inconsistent.

4   Evaluation

We have implemented the method described in Sect. 2 in the program analysis framework ULTIMATE as part of the requirements analysis tool ULTIMATE REQCHECK. The implementation builds on an existing tool chain used for the analysis of rt-inconsistency [7]. For the evaluation of our method, we considered the following questions.

RQ1 Is the new (complete) method to detect rt-inconsistencies practical? Does it scale to the same industrial examples that have been used to demonstrate the scalability of the (incomplete) method from [7]?

RQ2 How effective is the candidate extraction as a filter? How large is the proportion of the discarded candidates among all possible candidates?

RQ3 Is the additional effort for achieving completeness worth it?
  (a) Can the complete check detect previously unknown rt-inconsistencies?
  (b) What is the cost of completeness in terms of additional time and memory consumption?

We evaluated our implementation of the complete rt-inconsistency check by analyzing eleven sets of industrial requirements. Sets *dev01* to *dev10* are taken from publicly available benchmarks based on BOSCH requirements, which have been formalized and obfuscated. These are the same industrial examples of real-time requirements that have been used to demonstrate the scalability of the existing (incomplete) methods from [6,7]. The set *abz* is a set of automotive requirements published by Houdek et al. [5]. The formalizations of all requirements result from applying the process described in [1]. The resulting formalized requirements in the pattern language HANFORPL [3] are mapped into countertrace formulas within ULTIMATE REQCHECK. The benchmarks were executed using Linux 6.8.12-13-pve with Java OpenJDK 21.0.2 and Python 3.11 on an AMD EPYC 9354P 32-Core CPU with 3.25 GHz and 377 GiB RAM and they were performed using the benchmarking tool benchexec 3.30. ULTIMATE REQCHECK was run in version 0.3.0-wip.mf.rtiPreCheck-cacdf88. Each analysis was assigned 80 GB of RAM, 8 cores and an 8h timeout per benchmark.

Findings. The benchmark results are shown in Tables 1, 2, and 3[4]. Table 1 shows the results of applying the complete rt-inconsistency check on the industrial requirements sets. It shows an identifier for the requirements set (ID), the number of requirements (r), as well as the size of the subset of real-time requirements (rt). Result columns show the number of rt-inconsistencies that were found broken down to the size of their minimal representative (rti_2, rti_3, rti_5, and rti_7), as well as the total analysis time (T) and peak memory consumption (M). No analysis exceeded the eight hour timeout or the memory limitation. Although, most rt-inconsistencies found involve

Table 1. Results of the complete rt-inconsistency check. Columns show an identifier (ID), requirements count (r), real-time requirements count (rt), inconsistencies of set size i (rti_i), total analysis time (T), and peak memory consumption (M).

ID	r	rt	rti_2	rti_3	rti_5	rti_7	T (h:m:s)	M (GB)
dev01	26	21	6	0	0	0	54	1.7
dev02	50	47	13	0	0	0	18:20	4.6
dev03	52	11	0	0	1	0	12	0.5
dev04	58	53	13	0	0	0	17:28	4.2
dev05[3]	68	64	4	0	0	0	1:02:11	4.4
abz	83	52	23	4	0	0	20:16	7.0
dev06	100	95	109	0	0	0	4:22	5.2
dev07	107	80	38	0	0	0	3:11	4.8
dev08	263	234	73	4	0	0	3:29:24	9.8
dev09	407	358	46	0	0	4	4:18:54	10.6
dev10	699	543	0	0	0	0	4:39:19	12.3

[3] The rt-inconsistency check for one candidate was cancelled due to an internal time out of the trace abstraction plugin.

two requirements, the analysis also found eight rt-inconsistencies that each involved three requirements (i.e., in *dev08* and *abz*), one that involves five requirements (i.e., in *dev03*), and four that each involve seven requirements (i.e., in *dev09*). These rt-inconsistencies were not detected by the incomplete method checking only pairs of requirements. No minimal rt-inconsistencies with more than seven requirements involved were found.

Table 2 shows the results of applying the first step of the method, which extracts the set $\mathcal{C}$ of candidates, *candidate extraction* for short. It shows the number of subsets to be considered in the pairwise check without candidate extraction (n_2), the number of candidates of cardinality two if the extraction

[4] A replication package for the benchmarks can be found at doi.org/10.5281/zenodo.18305869.

would have been used (c_2), and the number of candidates for the complete check (c).

For both cases, it also shows the number of false positives among the candidates (fp_2, fp), i.e., the number of candidates that were not confirmed as rt-inconsistent by the check. The number of required sets without candidate extraction (i.e., the power set cardinality 2^r) is omitted. For the pairwise check, the candidate extraction reduces the number of considered sets by between 98% (*dev02*) and 100% (*dev03*). For the complete check, this effect is even higher.

The candidate extraction by itself is complete but in general it is not sound, i.e., if no candidate is extracted ($\mathcal{C} = \emptyset$) then $\mathcal{R}$ is not rt-inconsistent but extracting a candidate ($\mathcal{C} \neq \emptyset$) does not in general mean that $\mathcal{R}$ is rt-inconsistent. The cases where $\mathcal{C} = \emptyset$ will be rare in general.

Table 3 shows the resources consumed across different configurations of the rt-inconsistency check. Result columns show total analysis time and peak memory consumption for the check using subsets of size two to five (Incomp$_2$ to Incomp$_5$), the complete check (Comp) and the candidate extraction (Cand). Compared to Incomp$_2$, the complete check requires at most 2.6 GB more memory (*abz*) and, in the best case, 1.2 GB less (*dev10*).

Table 2. Results of the candidate extraction. Columns show the identifier (ID), number of requirements (r) and the number subsets to be considered for the pairwise check without candidate extraction (n_2); the number of extracted candidates in case of pairwise check and full check (c_2, c) and for each the number of false positives among them (fp_2, fp).

ID	r	n_2	c_2	fp_2	c	fp
dev01	26	650	8	2	8	2
dev02	50	2,450	47	34	47	34
dev03	52	2,652	0	0	1	0
dev04	58	3,306	47	34	47	34
dev05	68	4,556	6	2	6	2
abz	83	6,806	47	24	101	74
dev06	100	9,900	112	3	112	3
dev07	107	11,342	41	3	41	3
dev08	263	68,906	124	51	131	54
dev09	407	165,242	81	35	102	52
dev10	699	487,902	31	31	36	36

In terms of runtime, the complete check ranges from taking 1 hour and 40 minutes longer (*dev09*) to being 43 minutes faster (*dev10*). While the difference in resource consumption between the complete check and the pairwise check (Incomp$_2$) is rather subtle, it becomes pronounced in contrast to the checks considering subsets of size three to five (Incomp$_3$ to Incomp$_5$). For subsets of size three, two requirements sets exceeded the memory limit and five the time limit, whereas only three sets ran successfully(*dev01*, *dev03*, and *dev07*). For set *dev07*, the complete check finished in less than 4 minutes, whereas Incomp$_3$ required 90 minutes. Similarly, sets *dev06* and *dev10* reached the memory limit after almost 4 hours and more than 7 hours, respectively, whereas the complete check successfully finished the analyses in less than 5 minutes and less than 5 hours, respectively. Analyses for subset sizes four and five were continued only for requirements sets that that completed the prior check within the given time and memory limit. For all requirements sets, candidate extraction takes only few seconds to minutes and is thus negligible in relation to the runtime of the rt-inconsistency analysis.

Based on the benchmark results, we conclude that the complete rt-inconsistency check scales well on the same industrial sets that were previously used to demonstrate the scalability of the incomplete method in [7]. The fact that the new, complete method can detect previously unknown defects shows that completeness is not merely a theoretical issue. We hence conclude that a complete method to detect rt-inconsistencies can be practical (**RQ1**). The candidate extraction reduces the number of sets to be considered during the complete check substantially. The proportion of the discarded candidates among all possible candidates is 98% and higher. The filter is hence effective (**RQ2**). The complete check detects rt-inconsistencies that are not detected by the incomplete method. While achieving completeness incurs almost no additional cost (sometimes even reduces it) compared to $Incomp_2$, the complete check is substantially less costly, in both memory usage and runtime, than $Incomp_3$. In this sense, achieving completeness not only increases the effectiveness of the check but also its efficiency (**RQ3**).

Table 3. Resource consumption across different configurations of the rt-inconsistency check. Columns show an identifier (ID), number of requirements (r), total analysis time (T in h:m:s), and peak memory consumption (M in GB) for each setup: check using subsets of size 2 to 5 ($Incomp_2$ to $Incomp_5$), complete check (Comp), and candidate extraction only (Cand). Exceeding the time or memory limit is indicated by TO and OOM, respectively. Checks for subset sizes 4 and 5 were run only if the preceding check completed without exceeding time or memory limits.

ID	r	$Incomp_2$ T	M	$Incomp_3$ T	M	$Incomp_4$ T	M	$Incomp_5$ T	M	Comp T	M	Cand T	M
dev01	26	53	1.5	1:28	2.1	45:47	18.1	4:57:07	OOM	54	1.7	5	0.3
dev02	50	20:25	4.4	TO	18.6	-	-	-	-	18:20	4.6	10	0.3
dev03	52	27	1.1	1:25	2.1	23:06	7.3	TO	65.2	12	0.5	6	0.3
dev04	58	19:59	5.2	TO	23.9	-	-	-	-	17:28	4.2	10	0.3
dev05	68	1:02:27	4.1	TO	19.3	-	-	-	-	1:02:11	4.4	13	0.3
abz	83	9:57	4.4	TO	30.1	-	-	-	-	20:16	7.0	8	0.3
dev06	100	4:26	4.9	3:52:06	OOM	-	-	-	-	4:22	5.2	16	0.3
dev07	107	4:13	4.7	1:30:04	54.9	TO	38.4	-	-	3:11	4.8	19	0.3
dev08[5]	263	3:58:36	-	-	-	-	-	2:43	OOM	3:29:24	9.8	28	0.4
dev09	407	2:39:01	9.7	TO	35.9	-	-	-	-	4:18:54	10.6	11:24	0.5
dev10	699	5:22:16	13.5	7:19:37	OOM	-	-	-	-	4:39:19	12.3	48	0.5

[5] The analyses of *dev08* with $Incomp_2$ to $Incomp_4$ were cancelled due to an exception unrelated to our implementation. For comparison, we included the runtime of $Incomp_2$ as reported in [7].

Threats to validity.   For **RQ1–3**: The benchmarks that we use in our experiments stem from the automotive context. We do not know to what extent the experimental results can be extrapolated to a set of real-time requirements in a different context. For **RQ3**: Our comparison of the performance of an incomplete and a complete check applies to the specific example where the complete check has been obtained from the incomplete one by a transformation. We do not know to what extent the results of the comparison extend to another pair formed by an incomplete and a complete check in the case where the two checks are not related. Thus, to be perfectly precise, the research question here refers to the effort of turning an incomplete into a complete check.

5   Related Work

Here, we discuss only work that is most directly related. The approach in [11] is to translate each single real-time requirement into a timed automaton and then take the product, which becomes exponentially large. Compared to [11], the method in [6,7] does not construct the parallel product of timed automata explicitly, which can make the method scalable. However, the method is not complete as it only checks subsets of fixed size (namely, size two) for rt-inconsistency within the context of the full set of requirements.

The existing method from [6,7] reduces the task of checking rt-inconsistencies to a *program analysis* task; i.e., it transforms a given set of real-time requirements into a program in a specific programming language (Boogie [8]) and then applies software model checking [2] to the resulting program. The executions of the program account for all system behaviors that are possible according to the real-time requirements; importantly, the executions also account for the continuous passing of time. Roughly, a system behavior can run into an rt-inconsistency if and only if an execution of the program can end in a *deadlock* state. In such a state, the passing of time is blocked. This models the fact that, if time continues to pass, the corresponding system behavior will violate at least one of the real-time requirements.

The absence of an execution with a deadlock is a safety property for the program. The safety property is specified through an assertion (on a syntactic level, we insert an `assert()` statement in the program). The assertion is constructed from a set of conjunctions where each conjunct corresponds to one requirement (technically, the conjunct depends on a *phase* of the requirement). The size of the assertion grows exponentially in the number of requirements. The check of the assertion becomes prohibitively costly. The new method presented in this paper can be seen as a way to address exactly this problem: The task of the first step in the new method is to judiciously select a set of subsets of requirements. The second step then constructs a new assertion that contains one conjunction for each subset in this set. The conjuncts within each conjunction correspond one-to-one to the requirements of that subset.

In comparison with the representation used by the method of [6,7], the more abstract representation of real-time requirements as CT formulas leads to the efficient check of weak rt-inconsistency in the first step of the new method.

6 Conclusion

We have obtained a new sound and complete method for detecting rt-inconsistencies by integrating a new, unsound but complete method into an existing, sound but incomplete method. We have adapted the existing method to detect a specific kind of request so that it takes a configurable parameter, i.e., a set of candidates. We have developed an algorithm that selects a suitable value for the parameter, i.e., a set that is large enough to ensure completeness but small enough to ensure scalability to industrial examples. For future work, we may explore to what extent one can apply this principle to other methods to detect defects in requirements.

Acknowledgements. Authors N. Hauff, E. Henkel, V. Langenfeld, and A. Podelski were supported by the Bundesministerium für Bildung und Forschung (BMBF, Federal Ministry of Education and Research, Germany), reference no. 03VP11880 *System Valid.*

Data Availability Statement. Experimental Data from Sect. 4 is available at doi.org/10.5281/zenodo.18305869. The tool ULTIMATE REQCHECK is available as open source github.com/ultimate-pa.

References

1. Dietsch, D., Langenfeld, V., Westphal, B.: Formal requirements in an informal world. In: 2020 IEEE Workshop On Formal Requirements (FORMREQ), pp. 14–20. IEEE (2020)
2. Heizmann, M., Hoenicke, J., Podelski, A.: Software model checking for people who love automata. In: CAV. Lecture Notes in Computer Science, vol. 8044, pp. 36–52. Springer (2013)
3. Henkel, E., Hauff, N., Langenfeld, V., Eber, L., Podelski, A.: Systematic adaptation and investigation of the understandability of a formal pattern language. Requir. Eng. **29**(1), 3–23 (2024)
4. Hoenicke, J.: Combination of processes, data, and time. Ph.D. thesis, Carl von Ossietzky University of Oldenburg (2006)
5. Houdek, F., Raschke, A.: Adaptive exterior light and speed control system. In: ABZ. Lecture Notes in Computer Science, vol. 12071, pp. 281–301. Springer (2020)
6. Langenfeld, V.: Formalisation and analysis of system requirements. Ph.D. thesis, University of Freiburg, Freiburg im Breisgau, Germany (2023)
7. Langenfeld, V., Dietsch, D., Westphal, B., Hoenicke, J., Post, A.: Scalable analysis of real-time requirements. In: RE, pp. 234–244. IEEE (2019)
8. Leino, K.R.M.: This is Boogie 2. Manuscript KRML **178**(131) (2008)
9. Lorch, R., et al.: Formal methods in requirements engineering: survey and future directions. In: FormaliSE@ICSE, pp. 88–99. ACM (2024)
10. Olderog, E., Dierks, H.: Real-time systems - formal specification and automatic verification. Cambridge University Press (2008)
11. Post, A., Hoenicke, J., Podelski, A.: rt-inconsistency: a new property for real-time requirements. In: FASE. LNCS, vol. 6603, pp. 34–49. Springer (2011)
12. Post, A.C.: Effective correctness criteria for real-time requirements. Ph.D. thesis, University of Freiburg (2012)

Automata-Represented Requirements in HANFORPL
A Visual Approach for Requirements Engineering Practice and Formal Reasoning

Tobias Kolzer[iD], Vincent Langenfeld[(✉)][iD], Nico Hauff[iD], Elisabeth Henkel[iD], and Andreas Podelski[iD]

University of Freiburg, Freiburg im Breisgau, Germany
`langenfv@informatik.uni-freiburg.de`

Abstract. **[Context]** Visual notations play an important role in requirements engineering by supporting communication and validation, while formal methods provide a foundation for rigorous analysis. **[Problem]** Automata with a formal semantics are typically not intended for direct use by requirements engineering practitioners, while visual approaches commonly used in requirements engineering do not support formal reasoning. **[Principal Ideas]** We introduce *Automata-Represented Requirements*, a visual approach that combines visual requirements modelling with a pattern-based language for formalizing real-time requirements and its underlying formal semantics. The approach aims to enable intuitive specification of behavioural requirements together with formal reasoning. **[Contribution]** We outline the design of Automata-Represented Requirements and describe its formal foundations. The approach is implemented as part of HANFORPL, a pattern-based language and system for formalizing real-time requirements. Using illustrative examples from requirements engineering practice, we demonstrate how visual modeling and formal reasoning can be effectively integrated.

Keywords: requirements engineering · visual modelling · formal semantics · automata · HanforPL

1 Introduction

Requirements engineering (RE) plays a central role in the development of complex software systems by providing a foundation for communication, validation, and early analysis.

Visual notations are widely used in RE practice because they can ease shared understanding among stakeholders. They are suitable in particular for documenting system behaviour in terms of transitions between operation modes [10]. At the same time, formal methods offer well-established techniques for rigorous reasoning about system behaviour, enabling the detection of inconsistencies,

© The Author(s), under exclusive license to Springer Nature Switzerland AG 2026
R. Guizzardi and J. Araújo (Eds.): REFSQ 2026, LNCS 16497, pp. 290–299, 2026.
https://doi.org/10.1007/978-3-032-21423-2_20

incompleteness, vacuity, redundancy, unrealizability or unintended consequences at an early stage [2,5–9].

Despite their complementary strengths, visual requirements modelling and formal reasoning are often addressed separately. Automata and related formal models provide a precise semantics and a solid basis for verification and analysis. However, these models are typically developed with formal method experts in mind and are rarely tailored to the needs and working practices of RE practitioners. On the other hand, existing visual approaches to requirements focus primarily on usability, communication, and documentation, but are generally not designed to support formal reasoning or automated analysis. This separation leads to a persistent gap between visual practitioner-oriented requirements representations and formally well-founded models. As a consequence, formal analysis is often postponed to later development phases or requires a manual and error-prone translation of requirements into formal artifacts. This situation limits the practical applicability of formal methods in RE and weakens the traceability between informal requirements discussions and formal analyses.

In this paper, we address this gap by proposing Automata-Represented Requirements, a visual approach that combines practitioner-friendly requirements modelling with precise formal semantics. The central idea is to represent behavioural requirements using an automata-based notation that, while grounded in a formal model suitable for analysis, remains accessible to practitioners; in fact, it is reminiscent of visual notations already used in industrial requirements documents, albeit informally. Practitioners interact with visual representations that align with their usual modelling activities, while the underlying semantics enables formal reasoning without requiring explicit exposure to formal notation.

We realize our visual approach in the existing HANFORPL infrastructure [5]. HANFORPL offers a pattern-based (restricted-grammar) natural language tailored to requirements engineering practice. HANFORPL assigns a formal semantics by translating requirements to countertraces (CTs), a fragment of Duration Calculus, a logic for reasoning about real-time behaviour. This translation enables formal reasoning about properties such as rt-inconsistency analysis of real-time requirements [8]. We integrate the visual approach seamlessly into HANFORPL by introducing new patterns that accommodate an isomorphic textual representation of the visual models. By construction, we tightly couple practitioner-oriented visual models with the formal representations (for analysis), eliminating the need for separate representations or manual translations. Finally, new and existing patterns coexist and can be freely combined, allowing visual models to enrich textual requirements and vice versa.

As a research preview, this paper focuses on presenting the core ideas, design decisions, and intended use of Automata-Represented Requirements in HANFORPL, and illustrate the approach using representative examples from RE practice. The paper aims to demonstrate the feasibility of combining visual requirements modelling and formal reasoning within a single coherent framework and to outline directions for future empirical evaluation and tool support.

Our contributions is threefold. First, we identify and articulate the gap between formal automata-based models and practitioner-oriented visual requirements approaches. Second, we introduce Automata-Represented Requirements as a means to bridge this gap by unifying visual modelling and formal semantics. Third, we present the realization of this approach in the infrastructure of HANFORPL and discuss its potential to support both RE practice and formal reasoning.

2   HANFORPL and CTs

In this section, we give a glimpse of HANFORPL; for a full exposition, see [8,9].

Requirements in HANFORPL are obtained by instantiating patterns, i.e., natural language sentences with placeholders. In the example requirement below, the variables C and L refer to the observables `CarAhead` and `LightOff` and range over the (here, boolean) values of these observables.

```
Globally it is always the case that if  C  holds then  L  holds
after at most 0.25 seconds
```

For its formal semantics, the above requirement is given as the CT formula.

$$true; \lceil C \wedge \neg L \rceil \wedge \ell \geq 0.25; true$$

Intuitively, a CT formula expresses what must *not* happen so that the requirement becomes satisfied. That is, a behaviour of a system satisfies the requirement if it is not possible to divide the time axis into intervals such that the behaviour satisfies the constraint of each interval. Or, equivalently, a behaviour of a system *violates* the requirement if it possible to divide the time axis into intervals such that the behaviour satisfies the constraint of each interval. In the example, a behaviour violates the requirement if it is possible to divide the time axis into three intervals such that the behaviour satisfies C (the signal `CarAhead` is on) but does not satisfy L (the signal `LightOff` is not on) during the whole duration of the second interval, and the length ℓ of the second interval exceeds 0.25. The expression *true* in the first and third interval expresses that no constraint is imposed on the violating behaviour on the time points in these intervals.

Formally, a behaviour of a system is modelled as a function that assigns to each time point t (a positive real number) a valuation v, where a valuation gives a value to each variable.

As for the syntax, a CT formula is a concatenation (via the *chop* operator ";") of *phases*. Each phase is described by a boolean expression over (type bool, int or real) variables such as C and L that stand for the value of an observable. A phase may come with a conjunct of the form $\ell \sim c$ to express a time bound such as $\ell \geq 0.25$. Here, ℓ is a duration variable, $\sim$ is an arithmetic comparison operator, and c is a constant of type real.

3   ARRs and CTs

In this section, we use examples to illustrate the structure of Automata-Represented Requirements. We define the formal semantics of each ARR by translating it into a set of counter traces (CTs). We present a sequence of example ARRs $A_1, \ldots, A_4$, that loosely correspond to successive refinement steps and illustrate the different constructs for building up an ARR.

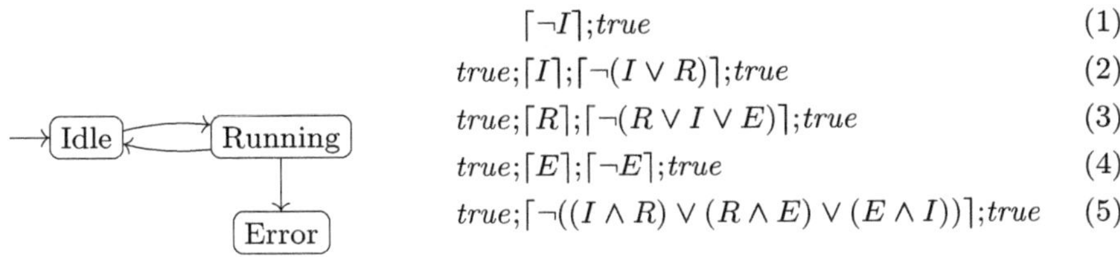

$$\lceil \neg I \rceil; true \tag{1}$$
$$true; \lceil I \rceil; \lceil \neg(I \vee R) \rceil; true \tag{2}$$
$$true; \lceil R \rceil; \lceil \neg(R \vee I \vee E) \rceil; true \tag{3}$$
$$true; \lceil E \rceil; \lceil \neg E \rceil; true \tag{4}$$
$$true; \lceil \neg((I \wedge R) \vee (R \wedge E) \vee (E \wedge I)) \rceil; true \tag{5}$$

Fig. 1. ARR A_1 **Fig. 2.** CTs for ARR A_1.

Basic Transitions. The ARR A_1 in Fig. 1 is given by its locations $Idle$, $Running$ and $Error$, and directed edges between them. Intuitively, the locations represent system modes and the edges represent transitions between them.

The ARR A_1 is translated into the set of the five CTs shown in Fig. 2. The CTs use a boolean variable for each location, here I, R and E. Intuitively, the value of the boolean variable encodes whether the system is in the corresponding mode or not. As described in Sect. 2, a CT defines *violating* behaviours. A behaviour satisfies the ARR A_1 if it is not violating any CTs in the set.

Initially, a behaviour that satisfies the ARR must be in the mode $Idle$, which is singled out as the initial mode. Accordingly, CT (1) expresses that a behaviour violates the ARR A_1 if the time axis can be divided into two intervals such that the behaviour does not satisfy the constraint I during the duration of the first interval; i.e., the behaviour assigns the value *false* to the boolean variable I at each time point t in the interval. The boolean constant *true* expresses that no constraint is imposed on the violating behaviour during the second interval.

The CTs 2 to 4 represent the outgoing transitions of a location, for each of the three locations $Idle$, $Running$ and $Error$ which have, respectively, one outgoing transition, two or none.

The CT (2) expresses that a behaviour violates the ARR A_1 if the time axis can be divided into four intervals such that the behaviour satisfies the constraint I in the second interval but, in the third interval, the behaviour satisfies neither I nor R. Intuitively, the violating behaviour has left the mode $Idle$ without going into the mode $Running$, the only possible successor mode of $Idle$.

The CT (3) expresses the outgoing transitions of mode $Running$ in exactly the same way as CT (2). The CT (4) expresses that a behaviour violates the ARR

A_1 if it leaves the location *Error*, which does not have any possible transition into another location.

Finally, the CT (5) expresses that a behaviour violates the ARR A_1 if it satisfies the conjunction of two variables of different locations. Intuitively, the violating behaviour is being in two locations of the ARR A_1 at the same time.

Transitions with Conditions and Events. The ARR A_2 in Fig. 3 has transitions labelled with conjunctions of guards over the variables such as *rpm* (of type int) and *failure* (of type bool) and with events such as *reset* and *ebrake*.

In general, transitions may be labelled by conjunctions of guards and events. Intuitively, if a guard is satisfied, the transition is enabled and the behaviour *may* take the transition. If an event happens, the transition is enforced and the behaviour *must* take the transition. The ARR A_2 is translated into the set of CTs which contains the CTs (1) and (5) and the five CTs shown below.

$$true; \lceil I \rceil; \lceil \neg (I \vee (R \wedge rpm \geq 120)) \rceil; true \tag{6}$$

$$true; \lceil R \wedge r \rceil; \lceil \neg (R \vee (E \wedge (f \vee e))) \rceil; true \tag{7}$$

$$true; \lceil R \wedge \neg r \rceil; \lceil \neg ((R \wedge \neg r) \vee (E \wedge (f \vee e)) \vee (I \wedge (rpm \leq 130 \wedge r))) \rceil; true \tag{8}$$

$$true; \lceil R \wedge e \rceil; \lceil \neg (R \vee (E \wedge f) \vee (I \wedge (rpm \leq 130 \wedge r))) \rceil; true \tag{9}$$

$$true; \lceil R \wedge \neg e \rceil; \lceil \neg ((R \wedge \neg e) \vee (E \wedge (f \vee e)) \vee (I \wedge (rpm \leq 130 \wedge r))) \rceil; true \tag{10}$$

The CT (6) is equal to the CT (2) up to the addition of the guard $rpm \geq 120$. The CT (6) expresses that a behaviour violates the ARR A_2 if the time axis can be divided into four intervals such that the behaviour satisfies the constraint I in the second interval but, in the third interval, the behaviour does not longer satisfy I, and, moreover, it does not satisfy R or it does not satisfy the guard

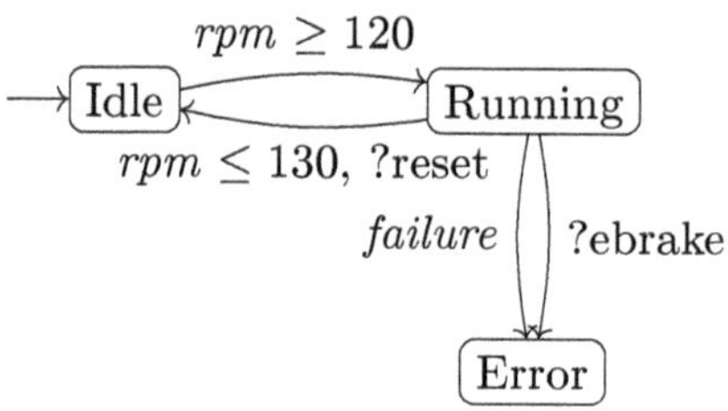

Fig. 3. ARR A_2

$rpm \geq 120$. Intuitively, the violating behaviour has left the mode *Idle* without going into the mode *Running*, or it has perhaps taken the transition but the transition is not enabled (because the guard is not satisfied).

The transition from the mode *Running* to the mode *Idle* is labelled by the event *reset* (in conjunction with the guard $rpm \leq 130$). The transition gives rise to two CTs, (7) and (8), which account for the two ways in which a behaviour can violate the ARR A_2: the event *reset* does not take place or it does.

The fact that the event *reset* takes place between two intervals is encoded by the fact that the value of the corresponding variable, here r, changes from *false* to *true* between two intervals. Thus, if the value of the variable r is already *true* in the first interval, then its value can obviously not go from *false* to *true* between the two intervals, which means that the event *reset* did not take place.

Now, CT (7) expresses that a behaviour violates the ARR A_2 if, even though the event *reset* did not take place, the behaviour left the mode *Running* without taking the transition that could possibly be enabled, namely the transition from the mode *Running* to the mode *Error*; i.e., the behaviour was in the mode *Running* in the second time interval but not in the third, and the value of the variable r is already *true* in the second time interval.

The CT (8) expresses that a behaviour violates the ARR A_2 if, even though the event *reset* takes place, the behaviour left the mode *Running* without taking the transition that is enforced by the event *reset* (if the guard $rpm \leq 130$ is satisfied). This is the transition from the mode *Running* to the mode *Idle*; i.e., the behaviour was in the mode *Running* in the second time interval but in the third interval it is not in the mode *Idle* (where it should be, by the fact that the transition to the mode *Idle* must be taken).

Location Invariants. The ARR A_3 in Fig. 4 has locations that are annotated with invariants: the location *Idle* with the negation of the boolean variable *failure* and the location *Running* with the expression $rpm \geq 120$ over the variable rpm of type int.

The ARR A_3 is translated into the set of CTs containing CTs (1) and (5) from the translation of A_1, the five CTs (6) – (10) added for the translation of A_2, and the CTs in Fig. 5.

The CT 11 expresses that a behavior violates the ARR A_3 if there is an interval where it is in location *Idle* and *failure* is *true*. The CTs in Fig. 5 can already be formulated in the existing fragment of HANFORPL (by instantiating the *Invariance* pattern).

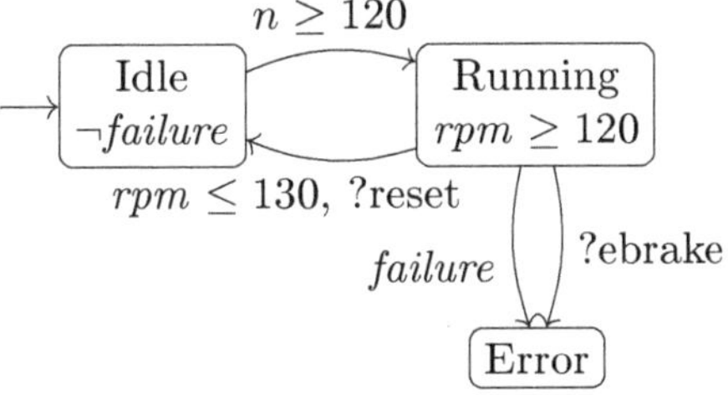

Fig. 4. ARR A_3.

$$true; \lceil I \wedge f \rceil; true \qquad (11)$$
$$true; \lceil R \wedge \neg (rpm \geq 120) \rceil; true \qquad (12)$$

Fig. 5. CTs for A_3.

Time Bounds. The ARR A_4 in Fig. 6 has transitions and locations with time bounds such as ≥ 20.0 and $\ell < 200.0$. The ARR A_4 is translated into the set of CTs containing all CTs from ARR A_3, namely CTs (1), (5) and (6) – (10), as well as the CTs in Fig. 7. The CT (14) expresses that a behavior violates the ARR A_4 if it stays in the location *Running* during an interval whose length exceeds 5.0 (encoded by the constraint $\ell \geq 5$) and, moreover, the transition into the location *Error* was enforced (encoded by e) and all other transitions to the same target are not enabled (encoded by $\neg f$). The CT (15) expresses that a behavior violates the ARR A_4 if it stays in the location *Running* during an interval that is strictly smaller than the time bound 200.0 which is attached to the location *Running*. It can already be formulated in the existing fragment of HANFORPL, namely by instantiating the *DurationBound* pattern.

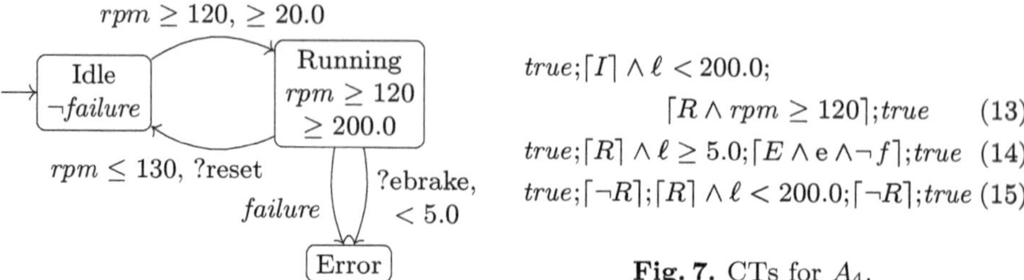

Fig. 6. ARR A_4.

$$true; \lceil I \rceil \wedge \ell < 200.0;$$
$$\lceil R \wedge rpm \geq 120 \rceil; true \qquad (13)$$
$$true; \lceil R \rceil \wedge \ell \geq 5.0; \lceil E \wedge e \wedge \neg f \rceil; true \quad (14)$$
$$true; \lceil \neg R \rceil; \lceil R \rceil \wedge \ell < 200.0; \lceil \neg R \rceil; true \quad (15)$$

Fig. 7. CTs for A_4.

4   Implementation

The implementation of our extension of HANFORPL comprises two parts. First, we provide a graphical editor to support specification input in the most accessible form for practitioners. Second, we extend HANFORPL [8] with a set of patterns that allow ARRs to be expressed in a textual form. This enables working with ARRs in settings without a graphical editor, such as requirements management tools, and supports inter-tool communication using HANFORPL as an interchange format. The implementation is available as part of the HANFOR open-source software at github.com/ultimate-pa.

Graphical Editor. We have implemented a graphical editor that enables the creation and modification of ARRs using their native graphical representation; see the snapshot in Fig. 8. The graphical editor is fully integrated into the HANFOR infrastructure and can be used in parallel with the editor for textual requirements. This allows users to enhance ARRs with textual requirements. Existing analysis toolchains, such as REQCHECK [5], can be applied without modification.

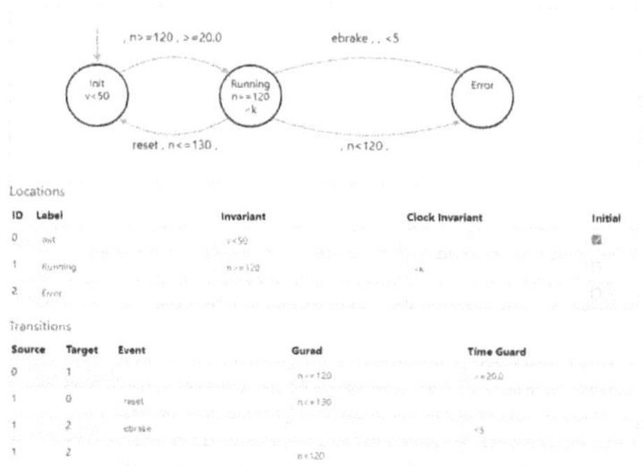

Fig. 8. Editing the ARR A_4.

New HANFORPL patterns. We have added a new set of patterns to the existing HANFORPL patterns. This enables the representation of an ARR by a set of textual requirements. These requirements are primarily used to represent the edges of an ARR. The two requirements shown in Fig. 9 translate the two transitions between the locations *Idle* and *Running* of the ARR A_4. Internally, the graphical representation of an ARR is translated into a set of textual requirements. This translation permits the seamless integration of ARRs into the HANFOR infrastructure.

- Globally, if in location `Idle` for at least `20.0` time units, transition to `Running` is enabled if guard $rpm \geq 120$ holds.
- Globally, if in location `Running` then transition to `Idle` if event `reset` fires and guard $rpm \leq 130$ holds.

Fig. 9. Requirements translating two transitions of the ARR A_4.

5   Evaluation Preview

The development of the formal framework builds on our experience from several industrial formal analysis projects and aims to provide a precise yet practical means for specifying ARRs in real-world settings.

The evaluation of our approach will be guided by the following two hypotheses:

R_1 ARRs are sufficiently expressive to formally capture industrial requirements.
R_2 The semantics of ARRs is sufficiently intuitive to be used by requirements engineering practitioners without prior training.

To evaluate R_1, we plan to deploy the proposed patterns and graphical extensions in industrial projects conducted using HANFOR. We will observe whether ARRs are used to formalise state-machine-like requirements, or whether classical patterns are instead employed to approximate the intended behaviour. For each instance, a post-hoc expert assessment will construct the alternative representation and analyse the respective limitations of both approaches.

To evaluate R_2, we plan to conduct a controlled experiment with practitioners who have little to no prior experience with HANFORPL. Participants will be presented with examples of ARRs represented either graphically or using patterns and will be asked to judge whether given example behaviours satisfy or violate the specified requirements, following an evaluation setup comparable to [6].

6   Related Work

We distinguish the related work along three dimensions: formal semantics, graphical representation, and orientation toward requirements engineering practitioners.

A first class of related work comprises formal approaches that do not provide a graphical, automaton-like input representation. Examples include the tool RAT [2], assuming requirements in LTL, as well as FRET [3] and related pattern languages such as EARS-CTL, which offer temporal-logic formalization through restricted natural language. While it is possible to encode automaton-like behaviour in these approaches, practitioners must manually infer how individual constructs can be combined to form an automaton. As a consequence, edge cases and under-specification are not immediately apparent, even to experienced users.

A second class consists of graphical approaches without a fixed formal semantics, such as UML state machines and Statecharts [4]. These notations provide rich graphical modelling capabilities but do not aim to define a precise, semantics.

A third class includes graphical approaches that do provide a formal foundation but are not intended for use by RE practitioners, as they impose a high formal barrier of entry. For example, RATSY [2] supports graphical specification in the form of Büchi automata, but requires users to understand and manipulate formal concepts such as location invariants and events, which are not naturally aligned with requirements-level modelling. Similarly, Timed Automata [1], although graphically represented, demand substantial familiarity with the underlying formalism.

In contrast to these approaches, our work combines a graphical, automaton-based representation with a precise formal semantics while explicitly targeting the needs and practices of requirements engineering practitioners.

7   Conclusion

In this research preview, we introduced *Automata-Represented Requirements*, a visual approach that integrates visual requirements modelling with formal semantics. The approach is designed to support requirements engineering practitioners by providing an intuitive, practitioner-oriented representation of behavioural, mode-based requirements, while at the same time offering a precise formal foundation suitable for automated reasoning and analysis.

By grounding visual models in a formally defined semantics and embedding them seamlessly into the HANFORPL infrastructure, ARRs bridge the gap between practitioner-oriented visual representations and formally well-founded models used for verification. This integration eliminates the need for manual translations and enables formal analysis to be applied directly to visually specified requirements.

As outlined in Sect. 5, future work will focus on empirically evaluating the approach in practical settings, assessing its usefulness for requirements engineering practice, and further investigating how visual modelling and formal reasoning can be effectively combined within a single coherent framework.

Data Availability. The tools ULTIMATE REQCHECK and HANFOR are available as open source at github.com/ultimate-pa.

References

1. Alur, R., Dill, D.L.: A theory of timed automata. Theor. Comput. Sci. **126**(2), 183–235 (1994)
2. Bloem, R., et al.: RATSY - a new requirements analysis tool with synthesis. In: Touili, T., Cook, B., Jackson, P. (eds.) CAV 2010. LNCS, vol. 6174, pp. 425–429. Springer, Heidelberg(2010). https://doi.org/10.1007/978-3-642-14295-6_37
3. Giannakopoulou, D., Pressburger, T., Mavridou, A., Rhein, J., Schumann, J., Shi, N.: Formal requirements elicitation with FRET. In: REFSQ Workshops. CEUR Workshop Proceedings, vol. 2584. CEUR-WS.org (2020)
4. Harel, D.: Statecharts: a visual formalism for complex systems. Sci. Comput. Program. **8**(3), 231–274 (1987)
5. Hauff, N., Henkel, E., Kolzer, T., Langenfeld, V., Podelski, A.: Hanfor: Requirements formalisation and beyond. In: REFSQ Workshops. CEUR Workshop Proceedings, vol. 3959. CEUR-WS.org (2025)
6. Henkel, E., Hauff, N., Langenfeld, V., Eber, L., Podelski, A.: Systematic adaptation and investigation of the understandability of a formal pattern language. Requir. Eng. **29**(1), 3–23 (2024)
7. Katis, A., Mavridou, A., Giannakopoulou, D., Pressburger, T., Schumann, J.: Capture, analyze, diagnose: Realizability checking of requirements in FRET. In: Shoham, S., Vizel, Y. (eds,) CAV 2022. LNCS, vol. 13372, pp. 490–504. Springer, Cham (2022). https://doi.org/10.1007/978-3-031-13188-2_24
8. Langenfeld, V.: Formalisation and analysis of system requirements. Ph.D. thesis, University of Freiburg, Freiburg IM Breisgau, Germany (2023)
9. Post, A., Menzel, I., Podelski, A.: Applying restricted English grammar on automotive requirements — does it work? In: REFSQ, pp. 166—-180 (2011)
10. Vogelsang, A., Femmer, H., Winkler, C.: Take care of your modes! an investigation of defects in automotive requirements. In: Daneva, M., Pastor, O. (eds.) REFSQ 2016. LNCS, vol. 9619, pp. 161–167. Springer, Cham (2016). https://doi.org/10.1007/978-3-319-30282-9_11

LLMs use in RE

Supporting Stakeholder Requirements Expression with LLM Revisions: An Empirical Evaluation

Michael Mircea$^{(\boxtimes)}$, Emre Gevrek, Elisa Schmid , and Kurt Schneider

Leibniz Universität, Welfengarten 1, 30167 Hanover, Germany
`{michael.mircea,elisa.schmid,kurt.schneider}@inf.uni-hannover.de`

Abstract. [**Context and Motivation**] Stakeholders often struggle to accurately express their requirements due to articulation barriers arising from limited domain knowledge or from cognitive constraints. This can cause misalignment between expressed and intended requirements, complicating elicitation and validation. [**Question/Problem**] Traditional elicitation techniques, such as interviews and follow-up sessions, are time-consuming and risk distorting stakeholders' original intent across iterations. Large Language Models (LLMs) can infer user intentions from context, suggesting potential for assisting stakeholders in expressing their needs. This raises the questions of (i) how effectively LLMs can support requirement expression and (ii) whether such support benefits stakeholders with limited domain expertise. [**Principal Ideas/Results**] We conducted a study with 26 participants who produced 130 requirement statements. Each participant first expressed requirements unaided, then evaluated LLM-generated revisions tailored to their context. Participants rated LLM revisions significantly higher than their original statements across all dimensions—*alignment with intent, readability, reasoning*, and *unambiguity*. Qualitative feedback further showed that LLM revisions often surfaced tacit details stakeholders considered important and helped them better understand their own requirements. [**Contribution**] We present and evaluate a stakeholder-centered approach that leverages LLMs as articulation aids in requirements elicitation and validation. Our results show that LLM-assisted reformulation improves perceived completeness, clarity, and alignment of requirements. By keeping stakeholders in the validation loop, this approach promotes responsible and trustworthy use of AI in Requirements Engineering.

Keywords: LLMs · Requirements Engineering · Requirements Elicitation · Scientific Evaluation · Human-In-The-Loop · Human-AI-Collaboration

1 Introduction

Eliciting and validating stakeholder needs is a central challenge in Requirements Engineering (RE). These tasks are inherently complex because cognitive and

R. Guizzardi and J. Araújo (Eds.): REFSQ 2026, LNCS 16497, pp. 303–319, 2026.
https://doi.org/10.1007/978-3-032-21423-2_21

social factors hinder stakeholders from accurately expressing their intentions, including memory limitations, societal pressures, and articulation barriers [12]. While retrieval and reporting barriers arise from limited recall and context dependence, articulation barriers often stem from tacit knowledge or vocabulary mismatches between stakeholders and engineers [12]. This challenge may be particularly pronounced among stakeholders with limited technical or domain knowledge. Consequently, requirements must be elicited through interactive dialogue rather than simply gathered from stakeholder statements [16], to enable clarification and shared understanding. Current approaches such as interviews rely on communication-intensive exchanges in which RE experts uncover stakeholders' underlying needs [16]. Effective elicitation, however, requires substantial domain understanding; without it, resulting artifacts may be low in quality, misaligned with stakeholder intent, or lacking clarity and reasoning [5]. To mitigate this, elicitation is often conducted iteratively across multiple sessions [16], allowing practitioners to contextualize and refine stakeholder input into artifacts such as user stories [6]. These artifacts form the basis for validation and development but make multi-session formats time-intensive and prone to misalignment, as delays can cause stakeholders to forget or reinterpret their original intentions.

Large Language Models (LLMs) may be able to bridge this gap due to their strong natural language capabilities and domain understanding. Beyond the current evidence of LLM ability to simulate empathetic behavior [11], existing work explicitly shows that the in-context learning capabilities of LLMs can be effective at identifying user intent [8]. Given sufficient stakeholder context, they may accurately express needs from the stakeholder's perspective, reducing articulation barriers. Their efficiency also enables immediate validation by the stakeholder, supporting low-latency iteration within a single elicitation session.

User Stories are a popular requirements artifact [6], which provide an effective medium for this collaboration, as their structured yet accessible format bridges the gap between stakeholders and developers. Each user story captures stakeholder, functionality, and rationale, in a form understandable to both parties. This dual interpretability allows LLM-generated user stories to be validated directly by stakeholders and subsequently used in development without reformulation, minimizing the risk of misinterpretation between elicitation and implementation [6].

In this paper, we investigate if the capabilities of LLMs to infer user intent and tacit knowledge can assist stakeholders in expressing software requirements more effectively, more specifically to create pre-validated, high-quality user stories aligned with stakeholder intent. We propose a collaborative elicitation approach in which LLMs help stakeholders refine and understand their needs in real time. We aimed at answering the following research questions through an empirical study:

- **RQ1:** How effective are LLMs in assisting stakeholders in expressing their requirements?
- **RQ2:** Is this expression support particularly beneficial for stakeholders with limited domain expertise?

The results of our study show that LLM-assisted revisions were consistently perceived as clearer, better reasoned, and more aligned with stakeholder intent than original statements, with large effects across all evaluated dimensions.

The remainder of this paper is structured as follows: Sect. 2 discusses related work on LLMs in RE. Section 3 describes the study design and methodology. Section 4 presents quantitative and qualitative results. Section 5 discusses implications and limitations. Section 6 outlines threats to validity, and Sect. 7 concludes with future research directions.

2   Related Work

There is a rapidly growing body of research exploring the use of Large Language Models in Requirements Engineering (LLM4RE) [3,15]. While LLMs are tested for various tasks, the nature of the evaluation is most commonly focused around automation, rather than collaborative systems [15]. Given the well-documented risks of hallucination and misalignment [3], recent works emphasize the need for Human-in-the-Loop (HITL) approaches in both the design and evaluation of LLM-based systems [13,15]. Our work aligns with this direction through an AI-in-the-Loop perspective [7], where the human drives the elicitation process and the AI assists through contextual reformulation and clarification. This approach aims to counteract hallucination concerns by maintaining stakeholder agency while reducing cognitive and articulation barriers.

Several studies have examined the potential of LLMs for elicitation and specification tasks. Ronanki et al. [9] compared requirements for trustworthy AI generated by ChatGPT with those written by RE experts. Other expert reviewers rated the LLM-generated requirements as acceptable to high across criteria such as atomicity, consistency, and correctness, but the authors stressed that true requirements must originate from or be validated by the customer, not RE experts. Similarly, Santos et al. [10] and Akin et al. [1] assessed ChatGPT's ability to generate user stories using frameworks such as QUS and INVEST. Both found that ChatGPT could produce user stories of comparable formal quality to those written by humans, though their evaluations were conducted by RE experts rather than stakeholders. Consequently, these studies primarily assessed adherence to structural quality metrics rather than alignment with stakeholder intent or validity of content. Hymel and Johnson [4] extended this line of work by comparing LLM- and human-generated requirements for fifty participant-submitted project ideas. Each idea was transformed into requirements by both a human expert and GPT-4, and the originating participants rated both versions for alignment and completeness. LLM-generated requirements received higher alignment scores and comparable completeness, demonstrating that LLMs can efficiently produce coherent first drafts of requirements.

Collectively, existing studies treat LLMs as independent producers of requirements whose outputs are later validated by others (often not stakeholders). In contrast, our work examines LLMs as stakeholder-centered articulation aids that assist in reformulating and clarifying requirements while keeping the stakeholder as the final validator. Rather than assessing LLM performance from an expert standpoint, we focus on how LLM-assisted reformulations improve stakeholders' ability to express, understand, and ultimately validate their own requirements. This perspective positions LLMs not as autonomous requirement generators, but as supportive systems that help bridge articulation gaps and foster more inclusive, human-centered elicitation practices.

3   Study Design

This study examines how LLMs can support stakeholders in articulating software requirements by inferring intent and improving clarity and completeness. Unlike approaches focused on automating requirement generation [1,10], we explore LLMs as collaborative aids that refine and reformulate stakeholder statements. To enhance external validity, we selected a specific software family, integrated development environments (IDEs), and involved real users as stakeholders. Since only stakeholders themselves can judge whether a generated requirement accurately represents their needs, they directly validated the LLM revisions. To analyze effects across domain familiarity, both novice and experienced users were included. Participation was voluntary and uncompensated.

3.1   Methodology

The study was conducted as a guided survey with a moderator who ensured participant understanding while minimizing influence. Figure 1 illustrates the overall process. Participants first provided informed consent and were briefed on the study's purpose (including the use of AI) and data protection measures. The LLM used was a GDPR-compliant, data-isolated instance of GPT-4o (*OpenAI*). The survey consisted of three phases:

1. **Pre-survey:** Participants provided contextual data and initial requirements.
2. **LLM intervention:** Moderator inserted stakeholder attributes and requirements into a structured prompt template, generating revised requirements.
3. **Post-survey:** Participants evaluated the LLM revisions and compared them against their original statements.

Pre-survey. The pre-survey consisted of two parts:

1. **Gathering stakeholder attributes:** Participants reported demographic and contextual information to enable personalized prompt conditioning. Collected variables included age (binned in five-year intervals), gender, education, work experience, and IDE experience (described in natural language).

2. **Task instruction and initial requirements:** Participants formulated five requirements for a new IDE using the user story format ("As a [user], I want [goal] so that [benefit]"). This was to allow for fair comparison with LLM-revisions. The moderator ensured consistent format adherence.

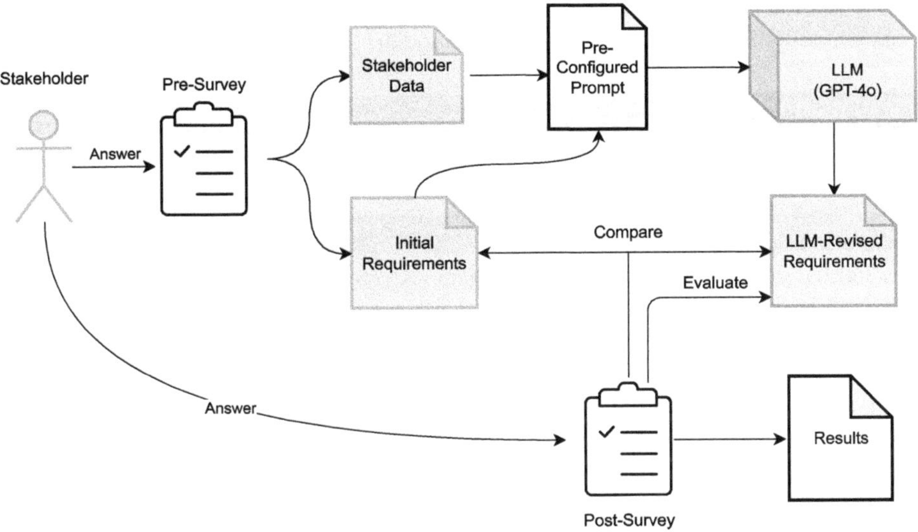

Fig. 1. Methodology of our study design. Stakeholder and their produced artifacts are colored green, LLM and generated artifacts are colored blue. (Color figure online)

LLM Intervention. Prompt design followed Google's Prompt Engineering Whitepaper [2]. Iterative pilot testing led to a modular template parameterized with stakeholder data from the pre-survey. This ensured transparency, reusability, and reproducibility. We employed a modular one-shot prompt engineering strategy combining role prompting, contextual prompting, task instruction, and output constraints. The conceptual components of the final prompt are summarized below (the full prompt is included in our supplementary material[1]).

Definition of Variables

Defines variables from the pre-survey for use as contextual placeholders (e.g., **age**, **work experience**), ensuring consistent and efficient prompt contextualization.

Role Prompting

Specifies the LLM's assumed role to shape tone and reasoning style. The model acted as a *Product Owner* responsible for articulating and refining user stories.

---

[1] https://figshare.com/s/ba3cd02a6b69a49846f7.

> **Contextual Prompting**
>
> Provides the LLM with stakeholder background and project context, enabling phrasing from the stakeholder's perspective with the clarity of a *Product Owner*.

> **Task Instruction**
>
> Instructs the LLM to revise stakeholder requirements for clarity, completeness, and understandability, adapting detail and vocabulary to the given persona.

> **Specified Output**
>
> Constrains output format ("As a [user], I want [goal] so that [benefit]").

> **One-Shot Example**
>
> Includes a sample input–output pair to demonstrate the expected reasoning process and guide the model's response style.

Post-survey. The post-survey captured both quantitative and qualitative feedback. We determined "effectiveness" as used in **RQ1** ("How effective are LLMs in assisting stakeholders in expressing their requirements?") based on a systematic literature review [5] of user stories and their most common defects, as well as further aspects regarding perceived improvements. To measure effectiveness, participants compared each LLM-revised requirement with its original version on a five-point semantic differential scale (much worse $\rightarrow$ much better) across the following dimension:

Set 1: Comparison of original statements and revisions

- **Alignment**: Representation of stakeholder intent.
- **Readability**: Ease of understanding.
- **Reasoning**: Clarity of rationale behind the requirement.
- **Unambiguity**: Degree to which the requirement avoids ambiguity.

Additionally, participants answered binary questions assessing deeper cognitive and reflective effects:

Set 2: Evaluation of each revision

- **Surfacing tacit knowledge (completeness)**: Did the revision introduce aspects they had not explicitly stated, but considered important?
- **Comprehension**: Did the revision help them understand their own needs?
- **Correctness**: Did the revision introduce factual or logical errors?

Finally, participants provided overall impressions of the revisions:

- **Perceived strengths**: Aspects the stakeholders liked in particular.
- **Perceived weaknesses**: Unfitting or disruptive aspects.
- **Particular omissions**: Any cases, where a revision omitted or obfuscated previously mentioned, important details of a requirement.

3.2 Data Analysis

The analysis combined quantitative ratings and qualitative free-text responses. For **RQ1**, we tested whether LLM-assisted revisions were perceived as differing in quality from the original stakeholder statements. Participants rated each LLM-revised requirement relative to their original statement on four dimensions using a five-point semantic differential scale (1 = much worse, 3 = equal, 5 = much better). To avoid dependence between repeated measures, each participant's five ratings per dimension were aggregated using the median. Wilcoxon signed-rank tests were used to assess whether participants' median ratings differed from the neutral (equal) midpoint of the scale. The neutral values were retained in the calculation. Effect sizes were computed as $r = Z/\sqrt{N}$. For each evaluation dimension, we formulated the following hypotheses:

- H_0: The median perceived effect of LLM revisions is equal to the neutral midpoint of the scale.
- H_1: The median perceived effect of LLM revisions differs from the neutral midpoint of the scale.

For **RQ2**, we examined whether perceived effectiveness differed between low- and high-experience stakeholders. To enable between-group correlation analysis with this relatively small sample size, the first two authors independently classified participants' experience levels into two groups based on parameters captured in the pre-survey: self-reported IDE usage and work experience. Disagreements were resolved through discussion. The analysis was conducted using Mann–Whitney U and Chi-square tests:

- H_0: There is no difference between groups in perceived effectiveness.
- H_1: There is a difference between groups in perceived effectiveness.

Corrections for multiple testing were applied using Bonferroni (RQ1) and Holm procedures (RQ2), respectively.

4 Results

4.1 Participant Overview

A total of 26 participants took part in the study, resulting in 130 paired comparisons. The final participant population was comprised of software engineering students and professionals from Germany with varying levels of technical and professional expertise, resulting in a classification of 16 low-experience and 10 high-experience participants.

4.2   Quantitative Results: All Participants

Comparison of Original and LLM-Revised Requirements. Figure 2 illustrates the individual participant ratings ($N = 130$ requirement pairs) comparing the LLM-revised requirements to their original statements across four dimensions: *Alignment, Readability, Reasoning,* and *Unambiguity.*

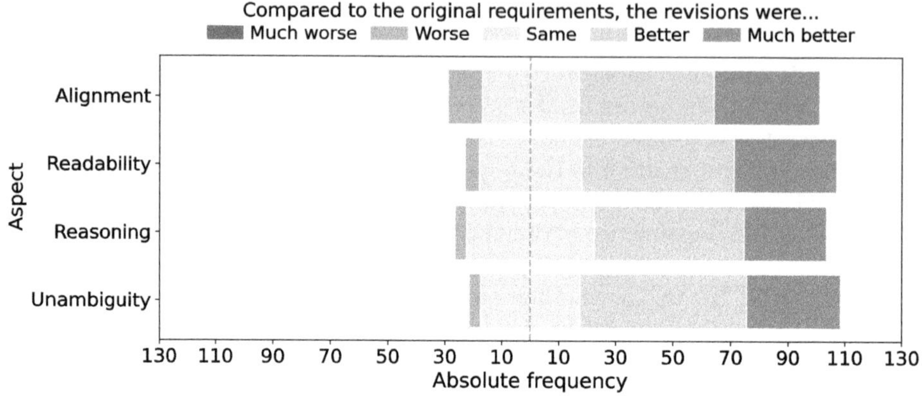

Fig. 2. Participant ratings comparing LLM-revised to original requirements in four dimensions. Bars show the proportion of ratings on a five-point scale from LLM-revisions being "much worse" to "much better."

Across all dimensions, LLM-revised requirements were rated higher than their original counterparts. The statistical analysis was performed on aggregated data per participant ($N = 26$), with the results presented in Table 1. Wilcoxon signed-rank tests against the neutral value confirmed that these improvements were statistically significant across all dimensions ($p < 10^{-5}$), with large effect sizes ($r = .876$–$.878$). To account for multiple testing across the four evaluated dimensions, a Bonferroni correction was applied ($\alpha_{\text{adj}} = 0.0125$). All effects remained well below this threshold, indicating robust and consistent improvements.

Table 1. Wilcoxon signed-rank test results comparing original and LLM-revised requirements (aggregated per participant, $N = 26$). Reported are median ratings, test statistic (W), p-values, and effect sizes (r).

Dimension	Median	W	p	r
Alignment	Better	0.0	$< .001$	.878
Readability	Better	0.0	$< .001$	.878
Reasoning	Better	0.0	$< .001$	.878
Unambiguity	Better	0.0	$< .001$	.876

The results of the statistical analysis are notably similar across dimensions due to the data aggregation by median smoothing out within-subject variance. Therefore, we repeated the analysis treating all 130 samples as independent observations. While this approach underestimates p-values due to non-independence, it revealed subtle nuances in effect sizes: *Readability*, *Reasoning*, and *Unambiguity* showed similarly strong effects ($r \approx .85$), whereas *Alignment* was slightly lower ($r = .76$), more accurately reflecting the slight differences between the dimensions visible in Fig. 2.

Supplementary Yes/No Responses. Figure 3 summarizes participants' binary responses on whether the LLM revisions: (1) surfaced tacit details they forgot mentioning, (2) improved their understanding of the requirement, or (3) introduced any factual or logical errors. The results are visually divided between low- and high-experience participant responses.

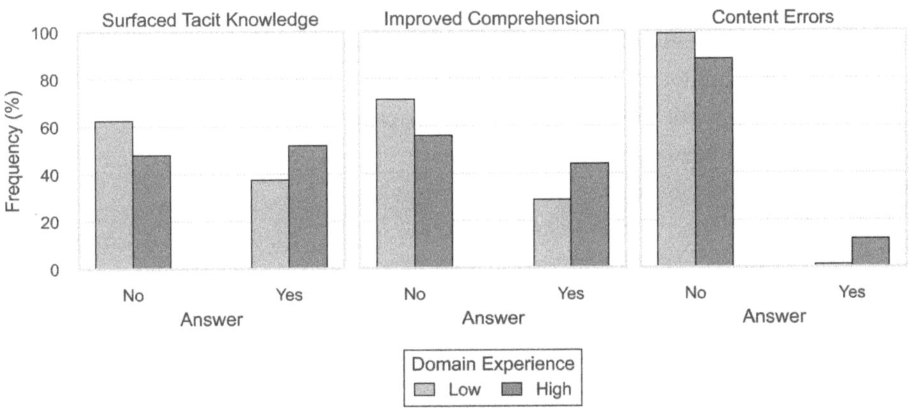

Fig. 3. Proportion of perceived improvements or issues in LLM-revised requirements ($N = 130$). Each bar shows the percentage of participants in the low- and high-experience groups answering "Yes" or "No."

In 43% of all evaluations, participants indicated that the LLM revisions correctly surfaced additional aspects they had not originally mentioned, while 35% stated that the revisions improved their understanding of the underlying requirement. Only 5% of revisions (7 out of 130) were perceived to introduce factual or logical inaccuracies. A closer look at the responses suggests that high-experience participants more frequently recognized added details and improved comprehension, but also identified a greater number of content-related errors (six cases compared to one among low-experience participants).

4.3 Qualitative Analysis

To complement the quantitative data, responses to the concluding questions were analyzed thematically through manual open coding of the free-text answers without the use of dedicated qualitative analysis software.

Perceived Strengths. Participants commented on strengths of the revised requirements. Table 2 summarizes the resulting themes and their frequency of mention. Most comments emphasized improvements in clarity, readability, and linguistic quality, with several participants also noting that the revisions added useful details or supported their understanding of the requirements.

Table 2. Perceived strengths of LLM-revised requirements.

Theme	Mentions
Clearer and more precise formulations	13
Improved readability, sentence structure, and word choice	13
Additional details and elaborations	7
Support in understanding and expressing requirements	5
Reduced misunderstandings and clarified meaning	4
More professional and polished writing style	4
Preserved the original idea and intent	2

Perceived Weaknesses. Participants were also invited to comment on any aspects of the LLM-generated revisions they found distracting or unhelpful. Thematic analysis of these free-text responses revealed that, while many explicitly stated that they perceived no issues, a minority of participants reported issues related to loss of meaning, complexity, or over-elaboration. Table 3 summarizes the main themes and their frequency of mention.

Table 3. Perceived weaknesses of LLM-revised requirements.

Theme	Mentions
Loss of meaning, focus, or thematic deviation	9
Overly elaborate or unnecessarily complex phrasing	3
Ambiguous or unclear wording	2
Minimal change or redundant adjustment	1

Lost or Omitted Details. Finally, participants were asked whether any important details or meanings were lost in the LLM-generated revisions. Most participants (20 out of 26) reported no loss of information in any of their five evaluated revisions. Among the few who did, two distinct types of meaning loss were described: one participant noted that certain words meant to be preserved were replaced or rephrased, resulting in a subtle linguistic loss of meaning, while another indicated that the revision missed the core content of their requirement.

4.4   Comparison by Experience Level

Figure 4 visualizes the distribution of ratings across low- and high-experience participants for each evaluated dimension, while the corresponding statistical results are summarized in Table 4. Overall, the boxplots show largely similar response patterns between experience groups, with median ratings consistently favoring the LLM-revised requirements across all dimensions. A Mann–Whitney U test revealed a small raw difference for readability (raw $p_{raw} = .045$), suggesting that more experienced stakeholders may have perceived stronger linguistic improvements. However, this difference did not remain significant after applying Holm's correction for multiple comparisons ($p_{adj} = .18$). All other dimensions showed no statistically significant differences between groups. Complementary Chi-square tests on the full scale distributions confirmed this pattern, indicating no meaningful distributional shifts.

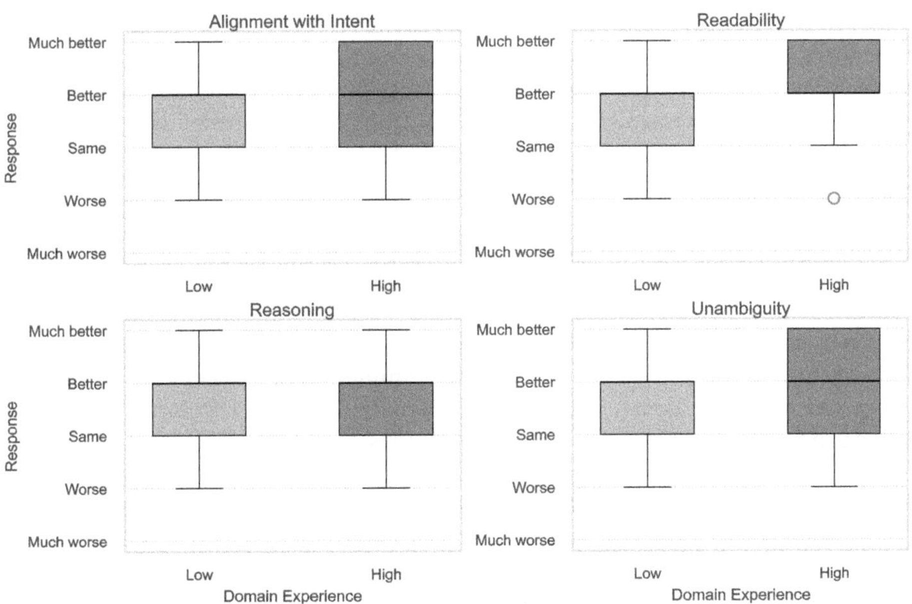

Fig. 4. Comparison of responses from low- and high-experience stakeholders. *Note.* Comparison of low- and high-experience participants across four evaluation dimensions.

Table 4. Mann-Whitney U and Chi-square test results comparing experience groups across the four evaluation dimensions. Holm-adjusted p-values (p_{adj}) for $k = 4$.

Dimension	U	p_{MWU}	$p_{MWU,adj}$	χ^2	p_{Chi}	$p_{Chi,adj}$
Alignment with Intent	1903.5	.630	.630	4.10	.251	.502
Readability	1604.5	**.045**	.180	5.01	.171	.684
Reasoning	1984.5	.939	.939	0.42	.936	.936
Unambiguity	1813.0	.340	.680	3.98	.264	.528

5   Discussion

5.1   Interpretation of Findings

The results demonstrate that LLM-assisted revisions substantially improved the overall quality of stakeholder requirements. Participants rated the revised statements significantly higher across all four evaluated dimensions, with large and consistent effect sizes at the participant level. The apparent uniformity of responses is partly attributable to median aggregation and partly reflects consistent, if minor, perceived improvements across participants, particularly for linguistic dimensions. Further cognitive biases possibly contributing to the uniform responses are discussed in 6. Notably, none of the revisions were rated as 'much worse' by any participant. While we anticipated linguistic improvements, it was surprising that *Alignment* also increased significantly and that many revisions were reported to improve completeness and enhance understanding. When viewed at the requirement level, the relative pattern across dimensions provides more nuance: the strongest improvements appeared in *Readability*, *Reasoning*, and *Unambiguity* ($r \approx .85$), suggesting that current LLMs excel primarily in linguistic refinement, structural clarity, and logical articulation. Nevertheless, *Alignment* ($r = .76$) also showed a strong improvement, indicating that LLM assistance can help stakeholders express their underlying needs more faithfully.

The qualitative results corroborate these findings: participants emphasized clearer phrasing, smoother sentence structure, and helpful elaborations as major strengths, while only a few noted over-elaboration or semantic drift. Most did not perceive any information loss, and when meaning deviations occurred, they were either lexical (word choice) or conceptual (focus shift). These isolated instances of altered meaning highlight the importance of keeping LLM4RE systems within a collaborative validation loop to ensure that humans remain the ultimate authority on requirements correctness and intent.

Differences between low- and high-experience participants were small and statistically non-significant after adjustment for multiple testing, suggesting that the benefits of LLM support are similar across different levels of stakeholder expertise. Interestingly, experienced participants tended to rate the revisions slightly higher and more often reported improved understanding and additional beneficial details. This trend, while contrary to our initial expectation that novices would benefit most from expression support, may suggest that experienced users are better able to recognize nuanced improvements and critically evaluate precision of requirements. This interpretation is reinforced by the fact that the same group also identified many more inaccuracies or errors, indicating heightened sensitivity rather than diminished benefit.

5.2   Interpretive Limitations

Although the observed effect sizes were very strong, several interpretive limitations must be considered before deriving implications for RE practice. Further, methodological limitations will be discussed in Sect. 6.

Domain Specificity and Stakeholder Type. The study focused on requirements related to IDEs. While this choice ensured that the authors could verify the plausibility of participant statements and LLM revisions, it also represents a highly technical and structured context. All participants were active IDE users, implying familiarity with abstract reasoning and formalized expression. Consequently, the linguistic and cognitive demands in this domain may differ substantially from those in less technical contexts. In stakeholder groups with limited articulation ability (e.g., patients, educators, or elderly users), the effects of LLM support might vary. Further, IDEs are an established software category. The performance of LLMs to infer stakeholder needs may be lower when applying them to novel or innovative projects. Future studies should therefore examine whether similar improvements occur in non-technical or multidisciplinary RE settings.

Evaluation Design and Perceived Quality. Our evaluation compared pairs of user stories. While this ensured fair and controlled comparisons, it may not fully reflect real-world elicitation dynamics, which are often more unstructured and conversational. Moreover, the quality judgments were based on stakeholder perception rather than external expert evaluation. While this focus was intentional and already justified in the earlier sections, we recognize our results capture only perceived improvements in requirement quality. Therefore, our approach does not replace technical analyses. Subsequent RE processes must still ensure factual accuracy, feasibility, and consistency with system goals.

5.3   Implications for RE Practice

The findings suggest several implications for how LLMs can be responsibly integrated into RE practice. First, LLMs can serve as effective articulation support during early elicitation activities. Participants consistently rated LLM revisions as clearer, more reasoned, and less ambiguous than their original statements. Combined with the expert-based evaluation from related works [1,10], this indicates that LLMs can help stakeholders formulate high-quality requirements in real time. This capability could be leveraged in interviews, workshops, or novel digital elicitation tools to help stakeholders express their needs more precisely before analyst inspection. Second, the observed improvements in comprehension and completeness highlight LLMs' potential to act as reflective partners in elicitation. Stakeholders frequently reported that model-generated revisions surfaced tacit details they had not articulated and helped them better understand their own requirements. Embedding such LLM assistance in interactive elicitation processes may therefore promote early validation and richer stakeholder reflection, leading to more accurate and aligned requirements from the start.

However, the occasional semantic drift observed underscores that such support must remain collaborative. LLMs should not replace stakeholders or practitioners in RE processes but rather complement them as a liaison. Keeping both parties in the loop ensures that improved formal quality does not come at the cost of alignment with stakeholder needs or traceability, promoting responsible, human-centered application of AI in Requirements Engineering.

Finally, the findings suggest practical design directions for future RE tools. Since perceived benefits were similar across experience levels, LLM-based assistance could be broadly applicable when tailoring phrasing and feedback depth to stakeholder attributes and expertise. Further, integrating such tools into distributed or asynchronous elicitation formats (i.e. online questionnaires, chat-based interviews or app reviews) could substantially improve requirement clarity and mutual understanding without increasing process overhead.

6   Threats to Validity

This section discusses potential threats to validity following Wohlin et al. [14].

Construct Validity. Our operationalization of "effective" expression support was based on the stakeholders' own perception of quality and alignment. This intentionally emphasizes subjective assessment over objective correctness, as only stakeholders can judge whether a requirement accurately represents their intent or enhances their understanding. Perceived improvement does not necessarily imply factual correctness or feasibility, however these qualities of LLM-generated user stories were already investigated by related works [1,4,10].

Internal Validity. To guarantee informed consent, participants were informed that the study involved an AI-based technology, which may have influenced their evaluations. There is a pronounced similarity across the evaluated dimensions, suggesting potential biases in the ratings. Some participants might have rated LLM outputs more favorably due to an *appeal-to-authority* or *social desirability* bias, while others may have rated them more critically due to skepticism toward AI. Since participants evaluated revisions of their own requirements, self-evaluation factors could also have influenced effects. Furthermore, the LLM's role of *Product Owner* may have shaped stylistic outcomes associated with professional quality. We counteracted this by keeping the same user story structure for both original and revised statements. Finally, our prompts included different context information, including stakeholder attributes, to tailor the model's phrasing to an adequate level of complexity. While this aligns with guidelines [2], we did not empirically verify the effect of these attributes against a zero-shot baseline. Therefore, the impact of individual prompt components remains an unverified assumption that may have influenced performance.

Conclusion Validity. The modest participant sample ($N = 26$, 16 low, 10 high) limits statistical power for subgroup analyses. To address dependence among repeated measures, we aggregated ratings per participant before hypothesis testing, which reduced within-subject variation. However, while this leads to more accurate statistical measures, aggregating by median smooths out some nuances in the data. We therefore additionally performed an exploratory reanalysis using all individual ratings which produced comparable patterns with more nuanced insights on effect sizes, suggesting robustness.

External Validity. The study was conducted in a realistic application context but limited to users of IDEs. This represents a technically literate population that may be more articulate and comfortable with structured reasoning than typical end users. Consequently, the observed effects may not generalize to less technical domains such as healthcare or education, where articulation barriers and domain-specific language differ substantially. Moreover, the study was conducted with a single, GDPR-compliant instance of GPT-4o. Different model versions or prompts could yield different results.

7 Conclusion and Future Work

This work investigated how LLMs can support stakeholders in expressing their software requirements more effectively. Using a stakeholder-centered design, we found that LLM-assisted revisions were consistently rated higher than original stakeholder statements across all evaluated dimensions (*Alignment, Readability, Reasoning,* and *Unambiguity*). These results indicate that LLMs can help bridge articulation barriers, leading to clearer and more complete requirements, while preserving stakeholder intent. Qualitative findings further suggest that such assistance can help stakeholders better understand and thus validate their own requirements. Our results highlight the potential of integrating LLMs as articulation and validation aids in early requirements elicitation, particularly in interviews, workshops, or digital elicitation tools. However, occasional meaning drift emphasizes that LLMs should complement, not replace, humans. Keeping stakeholders at the center of the validation loop remains essential for trustworthy and responsible use of LLM4RE systems and practices.

Future work should examine the generalizability of these results in less technical or multidisciplinary domains, explore the impact of contextual attributes in prompting, and evaluate integration of LLM expression support in interactive RE practices or tools. Further research is also needed to determine how well such systems can adapt their phrasing complexity, detail level, and clarification strategies to different stakeholder profiles and contexts.

Data Availability Statement. Our supplementary material is available at https://figshare.com/s/ba3cd02a6b69a49846f7.

Disclosure of Interests. The authors have no competing interests to declare that are relevant to the content of this article.

References

1. Akin, E., Meattle, H.: How well can ChatGPT create user stories compared to humans? Tech. rep., University of Gothenburg, Department of Informatics (2024). https://gupea.ub.gu.se/handle/2077/80161, technical report / pre-print
2. Boonstra, L., et al.: Prompt engineering. https://www.kaggle.com/whitepaper-prompt-engineering (2025), whitepaper. Accessed 14 Oct 2025
3. Cheng, H., et al.: Generative ai for requirements engineering: A systematic literature review. arXiv preprint arXiv:2409.06741 (2024). https://arxiv.org/abs/2409.06741, preprint
4. Hymel, C., Johnson, H.: Analysis of LLMs vs human experts in requirements engineering. arXiv preprint arXiv:2501.19297 (2025)
5. Kustiawan, Y.A., Lim, T.Y.: User stories in requirements elicitation: a systematic literature review. In: 2023 IEEE 8th International Conference On Software Engineering and Computer Systems (ICSECS), pp. 211–216. IEEE (2023)
6. Lucassen, G., Dalpiaz, F., Werf, J.M.E.v.d., Brinkkemper, S.: The use and effectiveness of user stories in practice. In: International working conference on requirements engineering: Foundation for software quality, pp. 205–222. Springer (2016)
7. Natarajan, S., Mathur, S., Sidheekh, S., Stammer, W., Kersting, K.: Human-in-the-loop or ai-in-the-loop? automate or collaborate? In: Proceedings of the AAAI Conference on Artificial Intelligence. vol. 39, pp. 28594–28600. AAAI Press (2025)
8. Rodriguez, J.A., Botzer, N., Vazquez, D., Pal, C., Pedersoli, M., Laradji, I.: Intentgpt: few-shot intent discovery with large language models. arXiv preprint arXiv:2411.10670 (2024). https://arxiv.org/abs/2411.10670, preprint
9. Ronanki, K., Berger, C., Horkoff, J.: Investigating chatgpt's potential to assist in requirements elicitation processes. In: 2023 49th Euromicro conference on software engineering and advanced applications (SEAA), pp. 354–361. IEEE (2023)
10. Santos, R., Freitas, G., Steinmacher, I., Conte, T., Oran, A.C., Gadelha, B.: User stories: Does ChatGPT do it better? In: Proceedings of the 27th International Conference on Enterprise Information Systems (ICEIS 2025) – Volume 2, pp. 47–58. SciTePress (2025)
11. Sorin, V., et al.: Large language models and empathy: systematic review. J. Med. Internet Res. **26**, e52597 (2024)
12. Tourangeau, R., Rips, L.J., Rasinski, K.: The Psychology of Survey Response. Cambridge University Press, Cambridge, UK (2000)
13. Vogelsang, A.: From specifications to prompts: on the future of generative large language models in requirements engineering. IEEE Softw. **41**(5), 9–13 (2024)
14. Wohlin, C., Runeson, P., Höst, M., Ohlsson, M.C., Regnell, B., Wesslén, A.: Experimentation in software engineering, vol. 236. Springer (2012)

15. Zadenoori, M.A., Dąbrowski, J., Alhoshan, W., Zhao, L., Ferrari, A.: Large language models (LLMs) for requirements engineering (re): A systematic literature review. arXiv preprint arXiv:2509.11446 (2025). https://arxiv.org/abs/2509.11446, preprint
16. Zowghi, D., Coulin, C.: Requirements elicitation: a survey of techniques, approaches, and tools. In: Engineering and Managing Software Requirements, pp. 19–46. Springer (2005)

Opportunities and Limitations of GenAI in RE: Viewpoints from Practice

Anne Hess[1]([✉]) [iD], Andreas Vogelsang[2] [iD], Xavier Franch[3] [iD],
Andrea Herrmann[4] [iD], Sylwia Kopczyńska[5] [iD], and Alexander Rachmann[6] [iD]

[1] University of Applied Sciences Würzburg-Schweinfurt, Würzburg, Germany
`Anne.Hess@thws.de`
[2] University of Duisburg-Essen, Essen, Germany
`andreas.vogelsang@uni-due.de`
[3] Universitat Politècnica de Catalunya, Barcelona, Spain
`xavier.franch@upc.edu`
[4] Herrmann & Ehrlich, Stuttgart, Germany
`herrmann-ehrlich@gmx.de`
[5] Poznan University of Technology, Poznań, Poland
`sylwia.kopczynska@cs.put.poznan.pl`
[6] Hochschule Niederrhein, Krefeld, Germany
`Alexander.Rachmann@hs-niederrhein.de`

Abstract. Context and motivation: With the rapid advancement of AI technologies, there is an increasing need to understand how AI can be effectively integrated into RE processes. In recent years, several studies have explored the potential and challenges of applying GenAI to support or even automate RE-related activities.

Question/problem: Despite the existing body of knowledge on AI's potential for supporting RE activities, there is limited evidence on its practical applicability and limitations from an industry perspective.

Principal ideas/results: To address this gap, we conducted a survey with RE practitioners in collaboration with the IREB Special Interest Group on AI & RE. In addition to describing our research methodology and survey design, we present insights from our quantitative and qualitative data analyzes. These insights include practitioners' perspectives on current usage scenarios, concerns, experiences—both positive and negative—as well as training needs related to using GenAI in requirements elicitation, analysis, specification, validation, and management.

Contribution: This study provides empirical evidence on the practical use of GenAI in RE, offering insights into its benefits, challenges, and training needs. The findings inform future research and industry strategies, guiding effective AI integration and skill development for improved RE processes and results.

Keywords: GenAI · Requirements Engineering · Opportunities · Limitations · Experience · Industry · Survey

© The Author(s), under exclusive license to Springer Nature Switzerland AG 2026
R. Guizzardi and J. Araújo (Eds.): REFSQ 2026, LNCS 16497, pp. 320–335, 2026.
https://doi.org/10.1007/978-3-032-21423-2_22

1   Introduction

Requirements Engineering (RE) is a crucial discipline in software development, which provides the foundation for successful project results by ensuring that stakeholder needs are precisely elicited, analyzed, specified, validated, and managed [1,14]. In recent years, the integration of Artificial Intelligence (AI) into RE processes has emerged as a promising approach to improve both the efficiency and effectiveness of performing the aforementioned RE-related activities [6,7,9,13,17]. Research in this area spans a wide range of AI-based approaches, supporting requirements elicitation and classification [2,18], requirements specification [11], or requirements prioritization [3,15].

Beyond these contributions, a growing number of empirical studies, particularly literature reviews, have examined how AI is being applied within RE, reflecting the increasing interest in leveraging AI techniques to support and even automate various RE-related activities [4,5,8,12,16,20]. These studies highlight both the potential benefits and challenges of integrating AI into RE processes, contributing to a growing and diverse body of work that evolves with advancements in AI technologies. Notably, the research suggests that although AI can accelerate RE activities and improve result quality, it also raises concerns regarding the reliability and semantic accuracy of AI-generated artifacts, reinforcing the necessity of continued human oversight.

While knowledge on AI's potential and limitations in RE exists, there is limited evidence concerning its practical applicability from an industry perspective. To address this gap, we conducted an online survey among RE practitioners to investigate their use and perceptions of Generative AI (GenAI) in professional contexts. Our analysis of the elicited quantitative and qualitative data offers insights into typical usage scenarios, concerns, and threats impeding GenAI adoption in RE. It also highlights both positive and negative experiences associated with GenAI in RE-related activities and identifies training needs.

This study was carried out as part of our collaboration within the Special Interest Group on Artificial Intelligence & Requirements Engineering of the International Requirements Engineering Board (SIG #AIREB[1]). The group is dedicated to exploring how AI technologies can enhance and transform RE, aiming to establish standards, identify best practices, and offer guidance and training to responsibly integrate AI into RE processes.

The remainder of this paper is structured as follows: Sect. 2 describes the methodology and design of the study. Section 3 presents the results obtained from both quantitative and qualitative data analysis. In Sect. 4 we discuss our findings in relation to existing research and potential threats to validity. Finally, Sect. 5 concludes the paper with a summary of the key insights and outlines directions for future work.

---

[1] https://ireb.org/en/community/special-interest-group/sig-aireb, last access October 23rd, 2025.

2   Study Design and Methodology

Research Objective and Research Questions. As motivated in the introduction section, our study aimed to explore how RE practitioners use and perceive GenAI in their professional activities. To achieve this goal, we derived the following research questions.

- RQ1: How frequently do RE practitioners use GenAI in their work and for which RE activities?
- RQ2: What factors prevent RE practitioners from using GenAI, and what concerns do they have about its use in RE?
- RQ3: What positive and negative experiences have RE practitioners encountered when using GenAI in RE and how do they assess its usefulness and harmfulness?
- RQ4: In which areas do RE practitioners see a need for additional training on GenAI?

To address these research questions, we conducted an online questionnaire-based survey among practitioners. This cost-effective method allowed us to collect and analyze data from a large sample, providing an overview of GenAI usage in RE. The study was designed according to the guidelines proposed by Wohlin et al. [19] and Molléri et al. [10].

Survey Instrument. Our questionnaire comprised a total of 37 questions (both open and closed questions), organized into several sections:

- **Introduction** outlined the survey's objectives, relevant policies, estimated completion time, and provided contact information of the research team;
- **Demographics and Experience** gathered data on participants' professional experience both overall and in RE, their organization's size, current role, industry sector, country, experience with specific RE activities, and previous exposure to GenAI tools like ChatGPT;
- **Use of GenAI in RE** investigated its application across various RE activities, including elicitation, analysis, specification and modeling, validation and quality assurance, and management. In addition to gathering insights on positive and negative experiences, we identified reasons and barriers that prevented participants from using GenAI in RE. We also collected data on the perceived usefulness, as well as the limitations and risks associated with GenAI in each RE activity and related tasks/usage scenarios;
- **Training Needs** questioned respondents whether they would like to receive additional training, preferred training formats, and the skills perceived as most essential for effectively adopting AI in RE;
- **Closing section** asked for final remarks and optional comments.

The survey questions were developed and validated through an iterative process. The core objectives, along with the initial topics, ideas, and concepts, were introduced and discussed during one of our regular meetings within the SIG #AIREB. Building on these discussions, the first two authors drafted an initial structure and a set of questions, which were presented at a subsequent follow-up meeting. Additionally, the initial questionnaire was distributed by email to all 35 members of the SIG, as not all members could attend the meetings. Feedback gathered during the meeting and via email from members (including input from the other four authors) was incorporated into the set of questions, which was then implemented on the LimeSurvey platform[2], chosen for its accessibility, usability, and security features. The survey was set up to collect anonymous responses. Before its public distribution, the survey underwent a final validation round and was pilot-tested again within the SIG #AIREB to ensure quality and clarity. This final validation led to minor adjustments in wording, spelling, and question order. No major changes were necessary following the pilot study, and the finalized questionnaire (see link below) was used in the data collection phase. All responses collected during the final validation were deleted and not included in the analysis phase.

Target Population and Sample. We defined the target population as participants in software development projects and product teams who have experience in RE. We aimed to obtain a diverse sample including practitioners from various countries, domains, and organizational contexts, thereby reflecting the diversity of RE practice in industry.

Distribution Strategy. Since no single distribution channel provides direct access to a representative sample of the target population, we employ multiple online dissemination strategies. The survey was distributed through: 1) direct contacts of the authors and an author's newsletter, 2) LinkedIn social media accounts of both the SIG #AIREB and authors, 3) IREB newsletter, and 4) the mailing list of the RE Specialist Group of the German Informatics Society (mid-February 2025).

Data collection occurred between November 1, 2024, and March 31, 2025. Due to public invitations, the exact response rate can't be calculated, but with about 130 participants starting the survey and 57 completing it, the response rate is considered low (which is typical for online surveys).

Analysis Strategy. In this analysis activity, all authors were involved. We conducted both quantitative and qualitative analysis. For closed-ended questions, such as multiple-choice and Likert-scale items, we applied descriptive statistics and frequency analysis. For open-ended questions, we performed a manual thematic analysis, systematically reviewing textual responses to identify recurring codes, themes, and patterns related to our research questions, particularly positive and negative experiences (RQ3). Two authors developed the initial coding schema after several consolidation meetings and pilots. This schema was reviewed by two other authors, which led to a revised iteration. The final coding schema, detailed in our codebook, includes 14 themes and 52 codes (see the shared material linked below for more information).

Before starting data analysis, we screened all responses to the survey. Although only 57 participants completed the survey, we decided to include all data in the analysis, as we believe the presence of unanswered questions does

---

[2] https://www.limesurvey.org/, last access on January 18, 2026.

not compromise the validity of the data. Unfortunately, we were unable to reliably interpret the reasons for these omissions, as they could stem from various factors, such as participants' lack of confidence due to limited experience with GenAI or fatigue from the lengthy survey questions. We also retained responses from participants with lower RE expertise, as they represent potential target groups for future RE training. For traceability, during our thematic analysis, we explicitly marked the responses of the participants who did not complete the survey.

3   Results

3.1   Participants and Demographics

According to our records in the Limesurvey tool, 130 people started the survey via the link that we shared via various channels and shared demographics and other data, but only 57 completed the survey (see also previous Sect. 2). The majority of our participants are employed in industry, particularly in large enterprises (74), medium enterprises (16), small enterprises (8), and micro-entreprises (6). The other respondents characterized their organization as research-technology transfer (8), and as university/research (6). There was a diversity of application domains in which the participants worked over the past 5 years, but more than half of the participants worked in the IT / Software domain (84). Moreover, most of the participants indicated a professional experience of more than 10 years in the RE discipline (63), followed by 6–10 years (26), and 3–5 years (21). A total of 17 people indicated an experience level of less than 2 years or being new to the topic of RE. Although we aimed for geographic diversity, most of the respondents were from European countries (116). Few participants were from Asia (9), North America (4), South America (3), Africa (2), and Australia or New Zealand (1).

3.2   RQ1: Utilization of GenAI in RE

Figure 1 shows the percentage of respondents who have already applied GenAI in RE in general and for specific RE activities. The figure illustrates that over half of the respondents have utilized GenAI in RE, mainly for specification and elicitation. GenAI was applied the least frequently in requirements management.

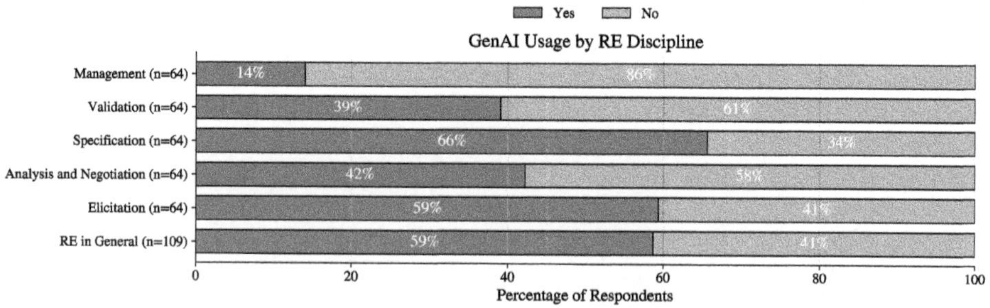

Fig. 1. Have you used GenAI for RE?

3.3   RQ2: Barriers, Limitations and Threats

For participants who had not yet used GenAI in RE or encountered circumstances preventing its use, we further explored the underlying reasons. As Fig. 2a shows, ethical and legal concerns were the most frequently reported barriers, followed by lack of awareness or knowledge, insufficient organizational support, and low-quality results. Additionally, Fig. 2b summarizes the threats and limitations perceived by all respondents when using GenAI in RE. Among these, hallucinations and over-reliance on AI were identified as the most frequent issues.

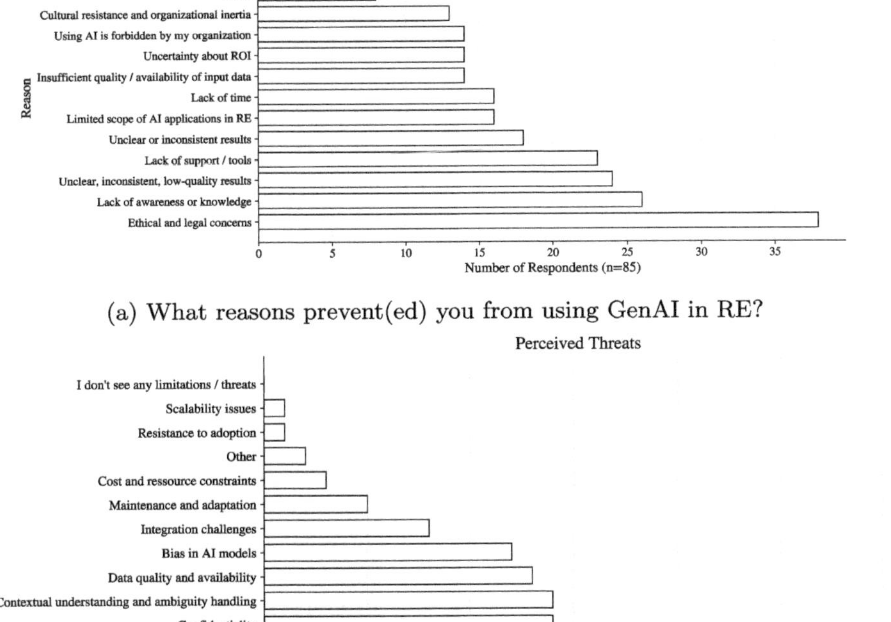

(a) What reasons prevent(ed) you from using GenAI in RE?

(b) Select up to three limitations/threats that you see in GenAI in RE.

Fig. 2. Bar charts showing (a) reasons that prevented respondents from using GenAI in RE and (b) perceived threats and limitations.

3.4 RQ3: Applying GenAI in RE Experience, Usefulness and Harmfulness

Requirements Elicitation. As shown in Fig. 1, elicitation is one of the two activities where more than half of the respondents have already used GenAI. We asked these respondents about their positive and negative experiences using GenAI in the context of elicitation. Thematic analysis of their comments revealed that GenAI is most beneficial for "generation" tasks or "NLP" tasks like generating requirements (e.g., based on interview results), formulating questions (e.g., for interview preparation), and summarizing content in large documents. Some respondents compared GenAI to "roles" like a sparring partner or assistant, particularly valuable during brainstorming sessions or when serving as a domain expert. Respondents generally found GenAI to be the most advantageous when supporting easy activities, with time savings being the most cited benefit, followed by output quality and output completeness. However, output quality was also highlighted as a significant drawback, particularly due to hallucinations and overly simplistic results. These issues lead to human-experienced challenges, such as the need for human reviews, lack of trust, and potential time waste.

These findings are consistent with the observations derived from the quantitative data analysis. Figure 3a shows how practitioners assess the usefulness and harmfulness of GenAI for specific tasks within requirements elicitation. The results show that most of the respondents had positive experiences with GenAI, particularly in preparation tasks such as preparing surveys, workshops, or field studies. For these tasks, respondents assessed GenAI to be rather useful and cause little to no harm. Using GenAI for data analysis was evaluated as useful, but it also seems to have some risks.

Requirements Analysis and Negotiation. As shown in Fig. 1, analysis and negotiation exhibit relatively low GenAI, with around 58% of the respondents not having used it. Those who did apply GenAI in this area found it useful for "requirements analysis", in particular for identifying conflicts between requirements and enhancing or reformulating them. However, respondents emphasized that such benefits require users' knowledge of GenAI and effective prompting. As with elicitation, time consumption was noted as a major drawback, largely due to the need for human reviews stemming from issues such as hallucinations and unusable outputs.

Figure 3b presents how practitioners assess the usefulness and harmfulness of GenAI for specific analysis and negotiation tasks. The results show that respondents generally find GenAI helpful for tasks such as requirements categorization and grouping, gap analysis, where usefulness ratings are high and harmfulness is perceived as low. However, tasks that involve trade-off analysis or stakeholder alignment and consensus building are seen as more challenging: while some usefulness is recognized, respondents also report a higher potential for harm, indicating that these tasks may require more caution and human oversight.

Requirements Specification and Modeling. Specification is the activity where GenAI has been adopted by 66% of the respondents (Fig. 1), which is

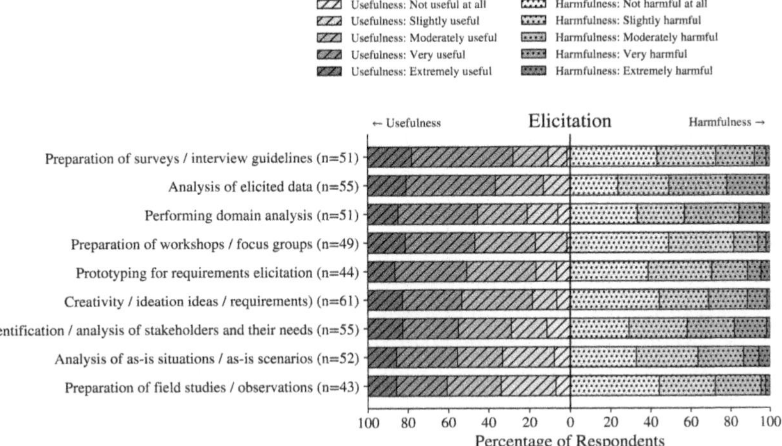

(a) Elicitation

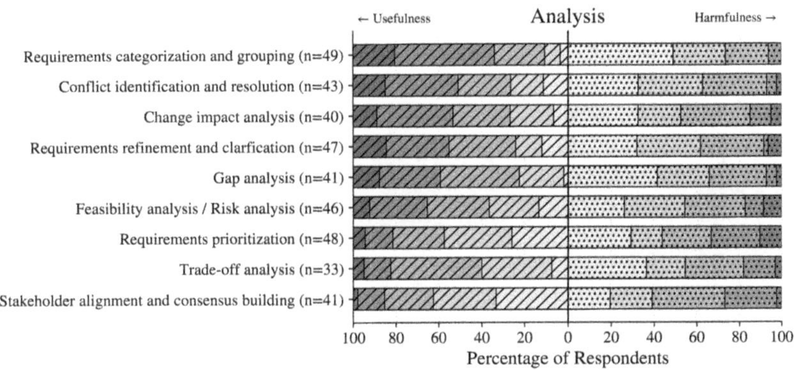

(b) Analysis and Negotiation

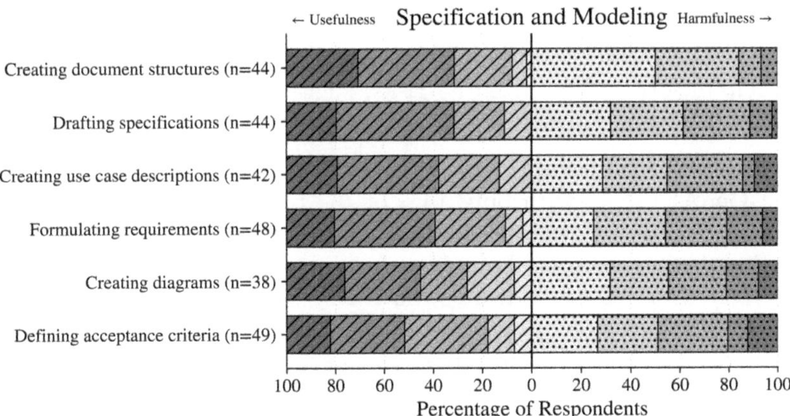

(c) Specification and Modeling

Fig. 3. How useful/harmful is GenAI for certain RE tasks?

the largest share among all activities. The thematic analysis of comments on positive and negative experiences highlighted GenAI's benefits in "model management" tasks, such as model creation and translation, and "modeling process" tasks like suggesting missing aspects. Its support for "generation" tasks, particularly in generating acceptance criteria, was also noted. Respondents frequently mentioned time savings and improved output quality as key advantages. However, drawbacks included output quality issues such as hallucinations, incorrect solutions, dubious acceptance criteria, and inappropriate modeling suggestions, all of which require thorough proofreading.

As shown in Fig. 3c, respondents perceive GenAI to be particularly useful for creating document structures and drafting specifications, with low levels of perceived harmfulness. Tasks such as formulating requirements, creating diagrams, and defining acceptance criteria are also overall positively evaluated, though with slightly more mixed experiences. The results suggest that practitioners see value in GenAI as a support tool for producing and structuring specification content, but that its application still requires careful review to avoid quality issues.

Requirements Validation and Quality Assurance. Figure 1 shows that validation is an RE activity with relatively little reported usage of GenAI: 39% of respondents have already applied it in this context. Compared to the previously discussed RE activities, we received fewer comments on positive and negative experiences. The analysis revealed that GenAI was especially beneficial for "validation planning" tasks, such as identifying quality criteria, and for "property/concept validation" tasks, like ensuring requirements' consistency and adherence to standards or norms. Although drawbacks such as hallucinations and the need for human reviews were noted, they were mentioned less frequently than in other activities.

The analysis of the quantitative data illustrated in Fig. 4a shows that GenAI is considered especially useful for tasks such as identifying inconsistencies, detecting incomplete or unclear requirements, and creating test cases, which receive high usefulness ratings and low perceived harmfulness. More complex validation activities, such as validation against stakeholder needs or planning and conducting reviews, receive more mixed evaluations. While some practitioners find GenAI helpful, others see potential risks, suggesting that these activities still rely heavily on human expertise and judgment.

Requirements Management. Management is the activity with the lowest reported GenAI usage, with only 14% of the respondents indicating previous use (Fig. 1). Thematic analysis of their comments did not provide significant information due to the limited number of responses. The quantitative data analysis, illustrated in Fig. 4b, indicates that while GenAI is seen to be moderately useful for tasks such as requirement tracking, maintaining traceability and configuration management, its perceived usefulness is less pronounced compared to other activities, although the harmfulness ratings are low. More strategic or process-related tasks, such as change management or assessment of requirements processes, are considered less suitable for GenAI support. In general, the results suggest that the role of GenAI in the management of requirements is currently limited, likely due to the complexity and organizational nature of these tasks.

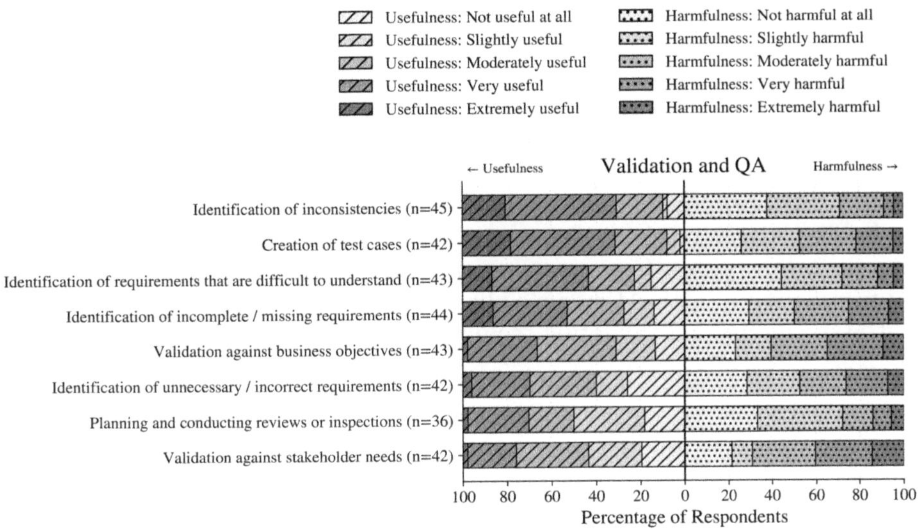

(a) Validation and QA

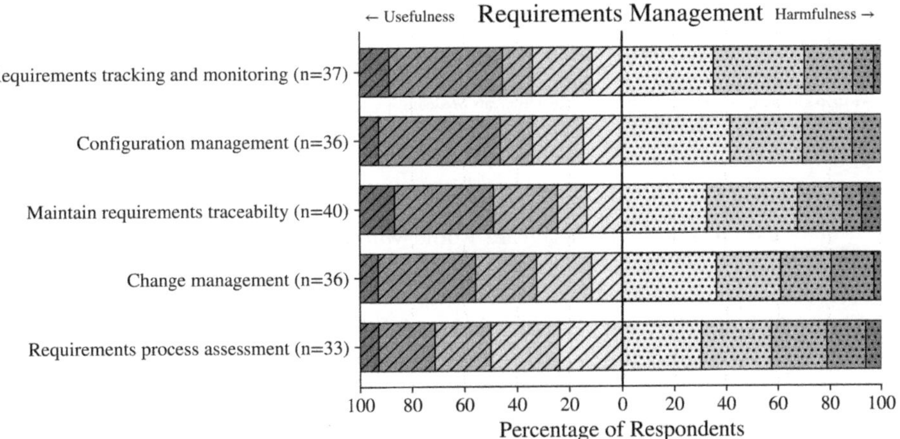

(b) Requirements Management

Fig. 4. How useful/harmful is GenAI for certain RE tasks?

3.5 RQ4: Training and Skills

A large part of our respondents (90%) agreed that the set of skills of requirements engineers will need to change as AI becomes more prevalent in RE.

The survey responses highlight that requirements engineers will increasingly need skills in AI literacy, prompt engineering, and critical evaluation. Many emphasized the importance of understanding how AI works, its limitations, and how to effectively use AI tools to support, but not replace, their work. Prompting skills were repeatedly mentioned, along with the ability to validate and critically assess AI-generated outputs, given risks of errors, biases, or hallucinations. Respondents also noted a shift in focus from detailed documentation to higher-level skills such as stakeholder management, communication, risk awareness, and ethical considerations. In general, requirement engineers must adapt by learning to collaborate with AI responsibly, ensuring that human expertise remains central in guiding and validating requirements.

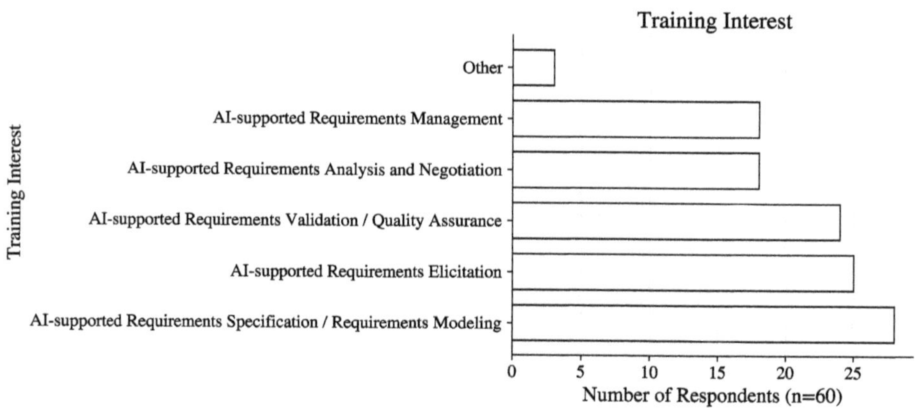

Fig. 5. For which activities would you like to receive training?

Figure 5 shows that our respondents were interested in receiving training in all areas of RE. AI-supported requirements specification and modeling was selected most often. Elicitation, validation, and QA were of similar interest. Negotiation and management were less frequently mentioned, but still selected by 30% of the respondents. Respondents expressed a strong interest in training that helps them practically apply AI across all RE activities:

Elicitation: using AI for prompting, analyzing documents and legacy data, and preparing interviews or questionnaires; in analysis and negotiation, supporting gap identification and structured discussions; **Specification and Modeling**: transforming unstructured inputs into well-structured requirements, diagrams, and models; **Validation and Quality Assurance**: using NLP, test generation, semantic checks, and conflict detection; **Management**: AI-supported impact analysis, prioritization, and tool integration.

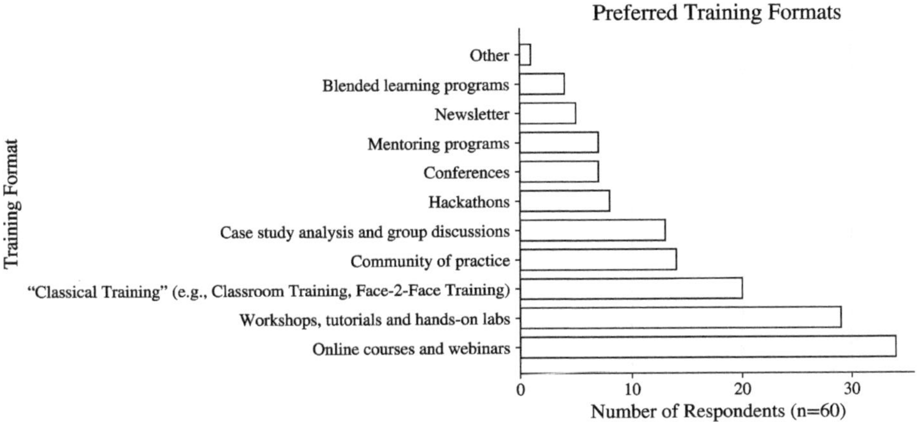

Fig. 6. Which training format do you prefer? You can select up to three training formats.

Across all phases, respondents also emphasized the importance of training on limitations, risks, and ethical considerations, as well as the practical integration of these concepts into existing processes and domain-specific contexts. Figure 6 shows that our respondents prefer online courses and webinars in addition to workshops, tutorials, and hands-on labs. Blended learning, newsletters, mentoring programs, conferences, and hackathons were less popular among the participants.

4 Discussion

4.1 Comparison with Related Work

According to our study, the RE activities most supported by AI in practice are primarily specification and modeling, as well as elicitation, followed by analysis and negotiation, validation and, lastly, requirements management. However, the literature reviews analyzed during our research indicate different emphases in academic publications. Table 1 compares the relative importance of these supported RE activities. In our survey, participants could select multiple RE activities, resulting in a cumulative response rate of 220 percent for "yes" answers. These responses are normalized to sum up to 100 in the table.

The six meta-studies [4,5,8,12,16,20] analyzed conclude that the application of AI can accelerate RE activities and improve the quality of the results, while also bringing some challenges. Especially, humans are still needed to validate the semantic correctness of the results. This is consistent with our findings. However, these studies summarize mainly primary studies from science.

One study [12] considers all activities in software engineering, while another [10] even all activities in engineering, including RE. These studies investigate research trends, highlighting which RE phases utilize LLMs/GenAI, alongside the models used, challenges faced, and future prospects. There have been

Table 1. GenAI usage per RE activity in percent: comparison with related work

RE activity	Our study	Vasudevan and Reddi-vari [16]	Zadenoori et al. [20]*	Cheng et al. [4]
Elicitation	26.8	12.5	22	26.8
Analysis and negotiation	19.1	47.5	19	28.0
Specification	30.0	27.5	12	22.0
Validation	17.7	10.0	22	17.9
Management	6.4	2.5	12	5.4

*not counting category "other"

two comparable surveys examining the adoption of generative AI in practical software engineering. However, these surveys also focused on GenAI usage at the broader level of software engineering phases, with RE being only one component [7,8]. In contrast, our survey not only explores which RE activities incorporate AI but also delves into specific RE usage scenarios within those activities, providing a more detailed perspective.

In our survey, we investigate the factors that hinder GenAI usage and the threats associated with its usage. Through the analysis of the six meta-studies [4, 5,8,12,16,20], we found that these studies identified a similar mix of challenges, encompassing both preventing factors and threats, as our findings did. Key issues include concerns about confidential information data privacy [4,5,8] and a lack of interpretability that affects stakeholder trust and limits control over the results generated [4,5,8,16]. Further challenges include the need for extensive high-quality datasets for AI training [5,8,16], ensuring the accuracy and reliability of the output [5,8,12], and the integration of domain knowledge to refine AI [5,8, 12]. Limitations also involve the absence of advanced logical reasoning essential for complex problem-solving [8,12], technical challenges such as computational power needs, and ethical concerns, including bias, fairness, and privacy [4,5]. Additional issues relate to legal and regulatory compliance [4,5], integrating text and graphical data in various formats [8], computation costs [4], reproducibility of results [4], hallucinations [4], and the ambiguity and complexity of natural language [5]. Other challenges include integrating AI into existing toolchains [5], the risk of over-reliance on AI leading to de-skilling of experts [5], ensuring security and robustness against malicious manipulations [5], the need for new user skills in AI utilization and interpretation [8], and the ongoing requirement to update and retrain models with the latest data [8].

4.2   Threats to Validity

Construct Validity. There is a risk that respondents may have interpreted certain terms or questions differently. To mitigate this threat, we used commonly used terminology, explained key concepts, and conducted a pilot study in which participants reviewed the questionnaire for clarity and understandability. To further reduce evaluation apprehension, the survey was conducted anonymously, without requiring any personal data.

Content Validity. To mitigate the risk that the questions are not representative of what they aim to measure, participants in the pilot study were asked whether changes were needed to better capture the research questions. Nevertheless, we acknowledge that including additional questions could have allowed for a more comprehensive exploration of the phenomenon under investigation.

Internal Validity. A potential threat to the study is the trustworthiness of responses. However, we did not find evidence to suggest that participants intentionally provided false answers. Another potential threat concerns the ability of the respondents' to accurately complete the questionnaire. We assumed that participants would have no difficulty using the LimeSurvey platform, which employs standard question formats, and that they would have sufficient English proficiency to understand the questions. To ensure clarity, we conducted a pilot study to verify the ease of comprehension of the questionnaire.

Since the study relies on self-reported data, responses can be influenced by self-serving and social desirability biases. Participants might overstate their adherence to recommended or modern practices or understate challenges. To mitigate these threats, the survey was anonymous and focused on concrete behaviors rather than evaluative judgments. The results should be interpreted as practitioners' perceptions rather than objective measurements.

This study is exploratory and descriptive. Given the non-random sampling and ordinal nature of the variables, the analysis was limited to descriptive statistics to avoid overinterpretation. More advanced statistical and demographic analysis are deferred to future studies.

External Validity. The main threat pertains to the number and the representativeness of respondents and the projects or products they had experience with. Based on our study design and analysis of demographic data, the respondents represented a diverse set of software project participants (holding various roles, working in different organizations and industry sectors, etc.). This diversity helps mitigate the risk of bias toward a particular context. Although the sample appears appropriate for the objectives of the survey, we acknowledge that it may not be representative of all possible contexts, especially considering geographical diversity. Sampling and self-selection bias were mitigated by distributing the survey through various professional channels, though voluntary participation may still limit generalizability.

Conclusion Validity. We tried to ensure that our qualitative analysis accurately reflected the data. Two researchers independently conducted qualitative coding, and two additional authors subsequently verified the correctness of the assigned codes. Discrepancies were discussed until consensus was reached, after which the final conclusions were drawn collaboratively.

5   Conclusions

This paper presents the design and findings of an online survey with RE practitioners on their use and perception of GenAI. Most respondents primarily use GenAI for specification, modeling, and elicitation, with less frequent use in requirements management. Key barriers include ethical concerns, lack of awareness, insufficient support, and low-quality output. Time savings are a major benefit, but issues like hallucinations and over-reliance on AI necessitate careful review to ensure quality. Most respondents agreed that requirements engineers' skills must evolve as AI becomes more integrated into RE.

Our study contributes to the literature by focusing on GenAI use in RE activities and related usage scenarios from practitioners' perspectives. Positive experiences may inspire other practitioners to adopt GenAI in their work context. Researchers could replicate this study to track the evolution of AI usage or to address current limitations by exploring regional differences with larger sample sizes. Finally, the results of the survey are intended to motivate the development of methods, tools and training programs to improve AI-supported RE activities by advancing skills in AI literacy, prompt engineering, and critical evaluation.

Acknowledgments. We thank the respondents for sharing their valuable experience and the members of the SIG #AIREB for their participation in the pilot study. This work was partially supported by Grant PID2024-156019OB-I00 funded by MICIU/AEI/10.13039/501100011033 and by ERDF, EU.

Data Availability Statement. The survey instrument (questionnaire), codebook, anonymized raw responses, and analysis materials supporting the findings of this study are publicly available via Zenodo at https://doi.org/10.5281/zenodo.17429345. All shared data were de-identified prior to publication to protect participant privacy.

Declaration of interest. The authors have no competing interests to declare.

References

1. Alsanoosy, T., Spichkova, M., Harland, J.: Cultural influence on requirements engineering activities: a systematic literature review and analysis. Requirements Eng. **25**(3), 339–362 (2020)
2. Anders, M., Paech, B.: Ferere: Feedback requirements relation using large language models. In: Hess, A., Susi, A. (eds.) Requirements Engineering: Foundation for Software Quality (REFSQ), pp. 89–105. Springer (2025)
3. Anwar, R., Bashir, M.B.: A systematic literature review of ai-based software requirements prioritization techniques. IEEE Access **11**, 143815–143860 (2023)
4. Cheng, H., et al.: Generative AI for Requirements Engineering: A Systematic Literature Review. arXiv preprint (2025). https://arxiv.org/abs/2409.06741
5. Rosado da Cruz, A.M., Cruz, E.F.: Machine learning techniques for requirements engineering: a comprehensive literature review. Software **4**(3), 14 (2025)
6. Dalpiaz, F., Niu, N.: Requirements engineering in the days of artificial intelligence. IEEE Softw. **37**(4), 7–10 (2020)

7. Hess, A., Immich, T., Tamanini, J., Biedenbach, M., Koch, M.: Opportunities and limitations of ai in human-centered design a research preview. In: Mendez, D., Moreira, A. (eds.) Requirements Engineering: Foundation for Software Quality, pp. 149–158. Springer Nature Switzerland, Cham (2024)

8. Kretzschmar, M., Dammann, M.P., Schwoch, S., Braun, F., Saske, B., Paetzold-Byhain, K.: Evaluating the current role of generative ai in engineering development and design-a systematic review. In: Proceedings of the Norddesign Conference (2024)

9. Liu, K., Reddivari, S., Reddivari, K.: Artificial Intelligence in Software Requirements Engineering: State-of-the-Art. In: 2022 IEEE 23rd International Conference on Information Reuse and Integration for Data Science (IRI), pp. 106–111 (2022)

10. Molléri, J.S., Petersen, K., Mendes, E.: An empirically evaluated checklist for surveys in software engineering. Inform. Softw. Technol. **119** (2020)

11. Navrotskyi, M., Gordieiev, O., Gordieieva, D.: An approach to developing a software requirements specification template for greenfield projects using artificial intelligence. In: 2024 14th International Conference on Dependable Systems, Services and Technologies (DESSERT), pp. 1–7 (2024)

12. Nguyen-Duc, A., et al.: Generative artificial intelligence for software engineering-a research agenda. J. Softw.: Pract. Exper. **55**(11), 1806–1843 (2025)

13. Oriol, M., Motger, Q., Marco, J., Franch, X.: Multi-agent debate strategies to enhance requirements engineering with large language models. In: 2025 IEEE 33rd International Requirements Engineering Conference (RE), pp. 527–534 (2025)

14. Pohl, K.: Requirements engineering fundamentals: a study guide for the certified professional for requirements engineering exam-foundation level-IREB compliant. Inc, Rocky Nook (2016)

15. Radwan, A.M., Abdel-Fattah, M.A., Mohamed, W.: Smart agile prioritization and clustering: an ai-driven approach for requirements prioritization. IEEE Access **13**, 127335–127350 (2025)

16. Vasudevan, P., Reddivari, S.: The role of generative ai models in requirements engineering: a systematic literature review. In: Proceedings of the 2025 ACM Southeast Conference (ACMSE 2025), pp. 188–194. ACM (2025)

17. Vogelsang, A.: From specifications to prompts: On the future of generative large language models in requirements engineering. IEEE Softw. **41**(5), 9–13 (2024)

18. White, J., Hays, S., Fu, Q., Spencer-Smith, J., Schmidt, D.C.: ChatGPT prompt patterns for improving code quality, refactoring, requirements elicitation, and software design, pp. 71–108. Springer Nature Switzerland (2024)

19. Wohlin, C., Runeson, P., Höst, M., Ohlsson, M.C., Regnell, B., Wesslén, A.: Experimentation in software engineering. Springer Science & Business Media (2012)

20. Zadenoori, M.A., Dąbrowski, J., Alhoshan, W., Zhao, L., Ferrari, A.: Large Language Models (LLMs) for Requirements Engineering (RE): A Systematic Literature Review. arXiv preprint (2025). https://arxiv.org/html/2509.11446v1

A Comparative Study of Large and Small Language Models for Domain Model Extraction

Cheng Yi Chou[ID], Fatma Başak Aydemir[✉][ID], and Fabiano Dalpiaz[ID]

Utrecht University, Utrecht, The Netherlands
`c.y.chou@students.uu.nl`, `{f.b.aydemir,f.dalpiaz}@uu.nl`

Abstract. Large language models can derive conceptual models from textual requirements, offering an off-the-shelf alternative to traditional rule-based and machine-learning-based methods. [*Question/Problem*] Comparative evidence on the validity and completeness of different large and smaller language models for the domain model derivation task remains limited. [*Principal ideas/Results*] We compare GPT-o1, Llama3-8B, and Qwen-14B with the rule-based Visual Narrator using nine datasets containing user stories and corresponding domain models. Each language model was prompted with structured templates and evaluated on class and association extraction through precision, recall, and F-scores. GPT-o1 outperformed the smaller language models and matched or exceeded Visual Narrator in most tasks. Small language models produced competitive but less consistent results, revealing efficiency–accuracy trade-offs. [*Contribution*] We provide a systematic comparison of large language models, small language models, and rule-based modeling approaches and offer an updated evaluation framework to guide future research on the balance between scale, performance, and interpretability of the automated techniques for domain model extraction.

Keywords: user stories · domain modeling · large language models · small language models · Visual Narrator

1 Introduction

Model extraction and derivation from natural language requirements have long received attention from the requirements engineering (RE) community. Analysts and researchers have sought methods to transform natural language descriptions into various types of dynamic and static conceptual models. Early work relied on rule-based techniques and linguistic heuristics [1, 17], which achieved precision through explicit patterns but often failed to generalize beyond predefined contexts. Machine and deep learning pipelines [20] improved automation but required data annotation for training, limiting their applicability in practical settings.

The emergence of large language models (LLMs) offers a new opportunity to revisit this challenge. Trained on extensive corpora and capable of contextual reasoning, LLMs can interpret natural language text with greater semantic depth than earlier approaches [16]. They promise adaptability across domains, flexibility in representing diverse modeling tasks, and the potential to generate structured models directly from

R. Guizzardi and J. Araújo (Eds.): REFSQ 2026, LNCS 16497, pp. 336–351, 2026.
https://doi.org/10.1007/978-3-032-21423-2_23

plain language. However, questions remain about their consistency, completeness, and alignment with human modeling practices; issues that require systematic investigation.

Recent studies have begun to examine the capabilities and limitations of LLMs in software modeling. Ferrari et al. [12] demonstrated that ChatGPT can generate sequence diagrams from textual descriptions but struggles with completeness and contextual precision. Chen et al. [7] compared prompt strategies for domain model generation, showing that examples improve accuracy, whereas chain-of-thought reasoning adds little benefit. Bragilovski et al. [6] found that GPT-4 can approach human recall in class identification but still exhibits distinct error profiles. While these studies highlight the potential of LLMs, few have compared them directly with small language models (SLMs) or rule-based systems using a shared evaluation framework.

Emerging work suggests that small language models (SLMs) may offer complementary advantages in software modeling tasks. Owing to their reduced parameter count and narrower training scope, SLMs can exhibit more predictable behavior and lower hallucination rates in constrained domains. Their lighter computational footprint enables cost-efficient fine-tuning and on-premise deployment, which is particularly attractive for industrial settings with privacy or resource constraints. Moreover, SLMs are often open, less bound to contractual limitations and specific deployment platforms, making them more easily integrable with rule-based or symbolic techniques, facilitating hybrid approaches that combine statistical learning with explicit domain knowledge. These characteristics position SLMs as a promising alternative for scenarios where transparency, controllability, and efficiency are critical [21,23,24].

This work addresses the lack of SLM evaluations in domain model derivation by conducting a systematic comparison of three language models—GPT-o1 as an LLM, Llama3-8B and and Qwen-14B as SLMs—against the established rule-based system Visual Narrator (VN) [17] for domain model extraction from usere stories. Our goal is to assess whether LLMs and SLMs can derive domain models that are not only syntactically valid but also semantically correct and as complete as possible. We focus on two essential elements of domain modeling (classes and associations) and evaluate model quality using established information-retrieval metrics and qualitative error analysis.

Our results reveal that GPT-o1 consistently produces models that outperform those of the SLMs and often match or exceed the rule-based baseline. The SLMs deliver competitive but less stable outcomes, revealing trade-offs between computational efficiency and modeling accuracy. These findings open new directions for research on the balance between model scale, performance, and interpretability in automated domain modeling.

The contributions of this paper are threefold. First, we introduce Visual Narrator 2.0, an LLM-capable version of the state-of-the-art rule-based domain model extraction tool Virtual Narrator. Second, we develop and integrate an additional evaluation component that refines existing model quality dimensions and supports replication and benchmarking in future studies. Third, we provide a detailed empirical evaluation across nine benchmark datasets, combining statistical and qualitative analyses. Together, these contributions advance the understanding of how LLMs can support RE tasks and lay the foundation for scalable and context-aware model extraction.

This paper is structured as follows. Section 2 presents the related work. Sec. 3 details our research method. Section 4 describes the evaluation. Section 5 discusses the results and Sect. 6 concludes the paper.

2   Related Work

The derivation of conceptual models from textual requirements is a long-standing strand of research [27]. Prior work has explored the automated generation of diverse artifacts such as class diagrams [8], sequence diagrams [12], and goal models [13,22] from natural language specifications. In this study, we focus specifically on domain models, which capture the key concepts and relationships within a problem space.

Arora et al. [1] implement a pipeline using Stanford Core NLP and GATE NLP tool kits to extract domain models from shall statements with heuristics. The pipeline extracts domain concepts, associations, generalizations, cardinalities, and attributes and is evaluated on private industrial datasets. Later, Arora et al. [2] use active learning to reduce superfluous entities and relations identified automated techniques. Lucassen et al. [17,19] introduce Visual Narrator (VN), which applies NLP and heuristic-based rules to user stories to automatically extract conceptual models, aiming to minimize human intervention while improving the interpretability of user requirements. Saini et al. propose DoMoBOT [20], an interactive domain model extraction tool combining rules and neural networks powered by spaCy [14] and GloVe [18] word embeddings.

Arulmohan et al. [3] explore how LLMs support domain model derivation from natural language text in agile product backlogs. They use GPT-3.5 in their experiments, which is outperformed by a tool implementing conditional random fields (CRF). Both perform better than VN. Chen et al. [7] compare the use of GPT-3.5 and GPT-4 for automated domain modeling, applying chain-of-thought prompting to capture complex domain elements. They aim to improve the precision and completeness of generated models, though the study highlights the LLMs' tendency toward omission errors and inconsistencies with best modeling practices. Bragilovski et al. [5,6] evaluated human analysts, a rule-based system, a machine-learning pipeline, Mistral, and GPT-4 on nearly five hundred user stories, showing that although no approach outperforms the performance or experts, LLMs perform similarly to novices.

3   Approach

This section describes the experiment design adopted to answer our research questions. Guided by Wohlin et al. [26], we run a comparative study that contrasts three language models with a rule-based system in the task of domain model generation.

3.1   Research Questions

Over the past few years, automated derivation of domain models from user stories has shifted from rigid heuristic pipelines to language models, but we still lack evidence on whether resource-efficient SLMs can match larger models on semantic quality, and on their error profiles. In this paper, we consider GPT-o1 as a prime example of an LLMs, Llama3-8b and Qwen-14b as examples of SLMs that can be deployed locally, and Visual Narrator as a classic rule-based approach specialized on user stories. We put forward the following research questions:

RQ1 How well do LLMs and SLMs extract domain models from user stories compared to a rule-based system?

    RQ1.1 How complete are the domain models generated by GPT-o1 and the two SLMs relative to those produced by Visual Narrator?

    RQ1.2 How valid are the domain models generated by GPT-o1 and the two SLMs relative to those produced by Visual Narrator?

RQ2 How do the two SLMs differ from each other and from GPT-o1 in model completeness and validity?

RQ3 How do error profiles, particularly false-positive classes and associations, differ among Visual Narrator, GPT-o1, and the two SLMs?

    RQ1 quantitatively explores the performance of GPT-o1, Llama3-8b, Qwen-14b, and Visual Narrator. This work builds on Bragilovski et al. [6], but *i.* introduces Visual Narrator 2.0, an improved version of the state-of-the art rule based domain model extraction tool and *ii.* considers *newer GPT variants as well as two state-of-the-art SLMs*. To measure performance, we use nomenclature from conceptual modeling [10]: validity (akin to precision) and completeness (akin to recall). **RQ2** focuses specifically on a comparison across the language models, while **RQ3** is concerned with a qualitative exploration aimed at identifying patterns in the types of errors generated, which is complementary to the quantitative analysis (the latter aims at statistical testing).

3.2 Experimental Setup

Our experiment comprised four crucial elements: datasets, language models, prompt design, and evaluation metrics. We used the benchmark datasets provided by Bragilovski et al. [6], consisting of nine datasets. Together, there were 487 user stories, along with their corresponding domain models. The domains and brief descriptions of these datasets are summarized in Table 1. While reviewing the benchmark, we followed the guidelines of Blaha and Rumbaugh [4], and found out classes and associations for which we disagreed with the benchmarks. This can be attributed to the fact that multiple domain models may correspond to a set of requirements, depending on their purpose and the level of granularity. To accommodate for such subjectivity, we created a new version of the gold standard; this included extending it with two categories: *mandatory* and *optional*. Mandatory elements are explicitly stated in the user stories, while optional ones are not directly mentioned but can be inferred from domain knowledge. The optional elements are counted as true positives if identified, but are not treated as false negatives if not identified following the guidelines of Blaha and Rumbaugh [4]. Table 1 summarizes the gold domain models prior and after our revision.

    We selected language models that receive regular updates, are easily accessible through an open-source platform[1], and can follow natural language instructions through

---

[1] https://huggingface.co/.

Table 1. Datasets Descriptions and Metrics: US = number of user stories; C_{old} and C_{new} are the number of classes in the old and new gold standard; A_{old} and A_{new} are the number of associations.

Dataset	Description	US	C_{old}	C_{new}	A_{old}	A_{new}
Camperplus	A camp management system for admins, parents, and counselors to track activities and share documents.	55	17	19	23	26
Fish&Chips	A restaurant system supporting takeaway, delivery, and improving outdated kitchen workflows.	50	9	9	8	8
Grocery	A grocery chain's internal system for HR, scheduling, payroll, and employee self-service.	49	9	10	8	12
Planningpoker	An agile estimation tool supporting collaborative story point voting and backlog refinement.	53	6	6	6	6
Recycling	A waste management system for organizing recycling types, locations, schedules, and tracking actions.	51	11	10	11	10
School	A school management system for grades, attendance, messaging, and home-based learning.	61	17	18	23	24
Sports	A CRM system for fitness centers supporting lesson booking, trainer management, and registration.	63	13	13	13	12
Supermarket	An online grocery platform offering delivery, in-store navigation, and personalized promotions.	51	11	12	13	16
Ticket	An event ticketing platform with user profiles, guest checkout, and a resale marketplace.	54	10	10	13	13
Total		**487**	**103**	**107**	**118**	**127**

prompting. We initially evaluated the performance of multiple recent models using the interactive chat interface on Hugging Face, as it allowed for a quick qualitative assessment of model outputs. Models that produced repetitive or unintelligible answers were excluded. The final set of models included GPT-o1 (a reasoning-focused, instruction-tuned model with an unspecified parameter size), Llama3-8B Instruct[2] (an instruction-tuned variant with 8 billion parameters from Meta's Llama series), and DeepSeek-R1-Distill-Qwen-14B[3] (a 14-billion-parameter distilled model from the Qwen series, optimized through knowledge distillation for improved inference efficiency).

We focused on prompt design, as this can influence model performance. Following [25], we adopted three prompting strategies: *i.* persona, *ii.* template pattern, and *iii.* chain of thought. The models were assigned the role of a RE expert and provided with an output template to facilitate processing. We structured prompts into two steps for GPT-o1 and four steps for SLMs, based on observations from our pilot experiment. GPT-o1 could process all instructions, handle the full list of user stories, and follow the instructions accurately to generate the output. However, separating the user stories from the instructions slightly improved its performance. In contrast, SLMs generally failed to follow all instructions when presented at once, often forgetting earlier parts. Therefore, the prompts were divided into four parts for SLMs, with each step delivered separately.

---

[2] https://huggingface.co/meta-llama/Meta-Llama-3-8B-Instruct.

[3] https://huggingface.co/deepseek-ai/DeepSeek-R1-Distill-Qwen-14B.

Our task involved two main stages: *i.* identifying relevant classes and *ii.* determining their associations. Figure 1 illustrates these processes. Although similar, the two tasks differ in their inputs and outputs. For class identification, the input is user stories and instructions, and the output is a set of classes. For association identification, the input includes gold-standard classes, user stories, and instructions, and the output is a set of associations. The process follows Blaha and Rumbaugh's guidelines [4]: candidate classes and associations are first identified, and then irrelevant ones are excluded based on exclusion criteria. Both code and datasets are available online[4].

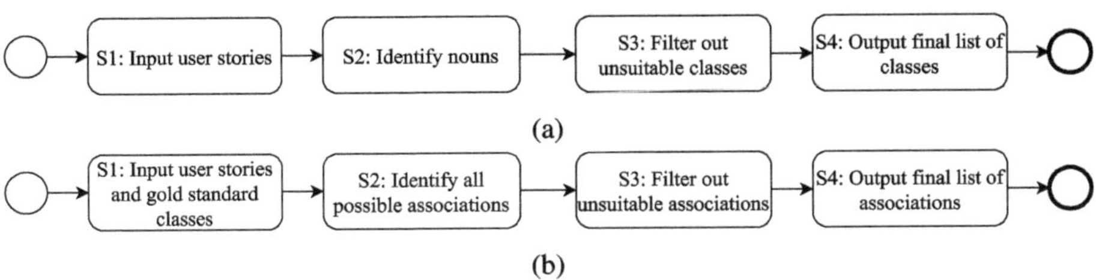

Fig. 1. Steps for extracting (a) classes and (b) associations.

3.3   Evaluation Design

Starting with the quantitative evaluation, we used $F_{0.5}$, F_1 and F_2 scores because they combine precision and recall in a single and interpretable number. $F_{0.5}$ gives more weight to precision while still considering recall, and serves as an indicator of model validity. In contrast, F_2 emphasizes recall and shows the completeness of the model outputs. F_1 provides a balanced point.

Since language model outputs are stochastic, we run of GPT-o1 five times and Llama3-8B and Qwen-14B ten times each, with the differing numbers reflecting budget constraints. By contrast, predictions of VN are deterministic for it is rule based, so a single run per dataset is sufficient. Performance varied across rounds for the LLMs and SLMs, potentially due to random variation rather than systematic effects. Therefore, it was necessary to evaluate whether the observed performance differences among models were statistically significant. Given the small number of datasets in this study and that the independent variable comprised more than two categories, we used the Friedman test to assess whether there is a statistically significant difference among the models. If significant differences were found, the Nemenyi post-hoc test was applied to perform pairwise comparisons and identify differences in performance [9].

In addition to the quantitative evaluation, we conducted a qualitative analysis to gain deeper insights into the models' performance. Following the approach of Bragilovski et al. [6], we considered seven false positive categories for classes (Table 2a) and three for associations (Table 2b), derived from Blaha and Rumbaugh [4]. To ensure repro-ducibility, we constructed decision trees for taggers to guide the classification of false

---

[4] https://github.com/rexchou0715/VisualNarrator-v2.

positives for both classes and associations, which are available in the online appendix. Certain branches of the trees were adapted from [6], and our main addition was a branch designed to handle hallucinated terms as well as verb and noun forms.

Table 2. False Positive Categories, primarily based on [4].

False Positive Category	Description
Irrelevant	A class that has little or no connection to the problem domain.
Implementation	A class that is used for system realization rather than for representing real-world entities.
Operation	A class that represents an operation applied to objects rather than an entity in its own right.
Redundant	A class that represents a concept already expressed by another class; the less descriptive one should be removed.
Vague	A class that is too general or lacks sufficient specificity to represent a distinct concept.
Role	A class that represents a temporary or external role rather than an intrinsic part of the domain.
Attribute	A class whose name primarily describes properties of individual objects rather than independent entities.

(a) FP categories for classes

Irrelevant	An association that lies outside the problem domain.
Implementation	An association that reflects implementation details rather than domain relationships.
Redundant/ Derived	An association that can be inferred or defined through other existing associations.

(b) FP categories for associations

4   Evaluation

Since our research involves conducting multiple rounds of experiments and evaluating their outcomes, a substantial amount of manual effort was initially required. To address this, we developed Virtual Narrator 2.0 (in our appendix) that has two main capabilities: *i.* LLM integration for domain model generation and *ii.* automated evaluation of the generated outputs by comparing them with the given golden standard.

The evaluation process considers not only literal matches between elements but also their semantic similarity. Because language models often produce varied expressions even under instructions, we observed that some outputs correctly refer to an element but use a different term. In such cases, we avoid penalizing the models by creating a synonym dictionary that records all equivalent terms generated during the experiments by the following process. We first let the LLMs and SLMs generate candidate classes (Step 1) through Visual Narrator 2.0. Next, the first author reviewed all false positive and unmatched classes from the gold standard (Step 2) and flagged all false positives that might refer to the same real-world concepts as those in the unmatched list (Step 3). Then, the first author checked the user stories to verify whether each false positive referred to the same concept as the one in the unmatched list (Step 4). The first and the third authors discussed the flagged classes that might refer to the same real-world entities (Step 5) and added the class labels to the synonym dictionary if they agree on their similarity (Step 6). The dictionary has a total of 158 synonyms for 60 classes.

We consider two variants of the original, rule-based VN in line with previous research [5]: VN Precision-Oriented (VN-P) and VN Recall-Oriented (VN-R), both of which are part of the model comparison. VN-P serves as the baseline for RQ1.1, and VN-R for RQ1.2. The difference between these versions is in the threshold that is set for including a noun or a noun phrase as a class in the output (lower threshold for VN-R). Only the classes extracted by VN are considered in the evaluation, as its association extraction does not follow the same guidelines used in our study. Including associations would therefore introduce inconsistencies and reduce the validity of the comparison.

4.1 Quantitative Analysis

Table 3 compares the five approaches for extracting domain models from user stories (GPT-o1, Llama3-8B, Qwen-14B, VN-P, VN-R) on class identification.

Table 3. $F_{0.5}$, F_1, and F_2 scores for class identification, highlighting the best results in yellow and the second best in gray.

Dataset	GPT-o1			Llama3-8B			Qwen-14B			VN-P			VN-R		
	$F_{0.5}$	F_1	F_2	$F_{0.5}$	F_1	F_2	$F_{0.5}$	F_1	F_2	$F_{0.5}$	F_1	F_2	$F_{0.5}$	F_1	F_2
Recycling	0.423	0.453	0.490	0.256	0.318	0.428	0.234	0.274	0.348	0.385	0.286	0.227	0.320	0.370	0.439
Supermarket	0.680	0.764	0.873	0.482	0.499	0.532	0.558	0.632	0.745	0.597	0.640	0.689	0.597	0.640	0.689
Planningpoker	0.643	0.700	0.773	0.365	0.396	0.463	0.437	0.510	0.624	0.682	0.600	0.536	0.588	0.615	0.645
Camperplus	0.791	0.747	0.708	0.601	0.520	0.468	0.658	0.676	0.703	0.672	0.581	0.512	0.479	0.571	0.708
Grocery	0.631	0.688	0.761	0.532	0.564	0.612	0.471	0.545	0.667	0.682	0.462	0.349	0.564	0.608	0.660
Sports	0.689	0.682	0.680	0.562	0.567	0.578	0.579	0.620	0.680	0.536	0.375	0.288	0.379	0.480	0.652
Ticket	0.637	0.648	0.662	0.539	0.545	0.568	0.304	0.356	0.439	0.595	0.556	0.521	0.595	0.556	0.521
School	0.625	0.638	0.654	0.563	0.531	0.515	0.601	0.658	0.739	0.561	0.579	0.598	0.556	0.623	0.707
Fish&Chips	0.613	0.649	0.691	0.410	0.467	0.546	0.387	0.456	0.565	0.476	0.333	0.256	0.217	0.298	0.473
Macro Avg.	0.637	0.663	0.699	0.479	0.490	0.523	0.470	0.525	0.612	0.576	0.490	0.442	0.477	0.529	0.610
Macro SD.	0.097	0.090	0.104	0.113	0.084	0.061	0.143	0.140	0.138	0.100	0.130	0.165	0.140	0.122	0.104

Looking at validity ($F_{0.5}$), GPT-o1 outperforms both SLMs across all datasets and exceeds VN-P in almost all cases, with **Planningpoker** and **Grocery** as the main exceptions (VN-P slightly higher). VN-P also surpasses the SLMs in most datasets. For completeness (F_2), GPT-o1 dominates Llama3-8B, with Qwen-14B and VN-R exhibiting very similar performance (0.612 vs. 0.610) and being the runner-up of GPT-o1 on most datasets. It is remarkable how, although the variants of VN are from a decade ago, they are still up-to-part (if not better) than the examined SLMs.

Statistical tests ($\alpha = 0.05$) confirm these differences. The Friedman test shows significance for both metrics (validity: $p = 0.0001246$; completeness: $p = 0.003283$). Post-hoc (Nemenyi) and Cohen's d effect size tests confirm that GPT-o1 significantly outperforms Llama3-8B ($p = 0.0029$, $d = 2.343$) and Qwen-14B ($p = 0.0056$, $d = 1.929$) in validity, but not VN-P ($p = 0.3543$, $d = 0.842$). For completeness, GPT-o1 only shows a significant advantage over Llama3-8B ($p = 0.0015$, $d = 1.786$), with no significant differences from Qwen-14B ($p = 0.2208$, $d = 0.913$), or VN-R ($p = 0.1532$, $d = 0.997$).

Figure 2 visualizes the distribution of scores of each dataset across different runs using box plots. Note that VN is excluded since its results are deterministic. GPT-o1 achieves higher and more stable scores overall, with performance gaps narrowing for completeness. Qwen-14B becomes more competitive when completeness is prioritized, whereas Llama3-8B remains the least consistent. This is yet another signal of the superiority of GPT-o1 over the two examined SLMs for the task at hand.

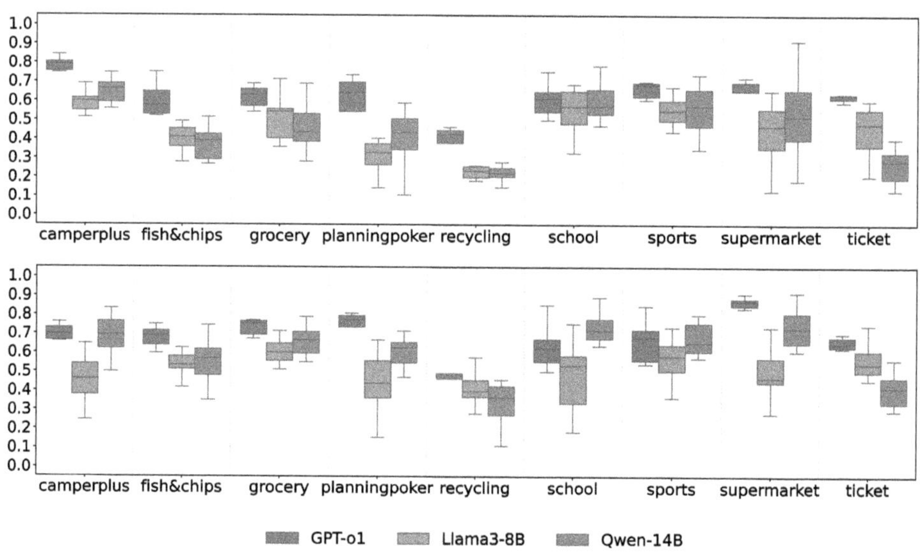

Fig. 2. Class $F_{0.5}$ and F_2 score distribution by model and dataset.

Table 4 reports the $F_{0.5}$, F_1 and F_2 scores for association extraction across all datasets and models. Since we are only comparing three alternatives, unlike Table 3 where we had five contenders, we highlight the best but not the runner-up.

Table 4. $F_{0.5}$, F_1, and F_2 scores for identifying associations.

Dataset	GPT-o1			Llama3-8B			Qwen-14B		
	$F_{0.5}$	F_1	F_2	$F_{0.5}$	F_1	F_2	$F_{0.5}$	F_1	F_2
Recycling	0.525	0.578	0.647	0.469	0.512	0.580	0.426	0.494	0.596
Supermarket	0.929	0.925	0.920	0.728	0.720	0.718	0.718	0.721	0.728
Planningpoker	0.799	0.832	0.871	0.744	0.736	0.741	0.727	0.752	0.779
Camperplus	0.731	0.671	0.621	0.536	0.446	0.385	0.573	0.564	0.557
Grocery	0.738	0.809	0.896	0.580	0.590	0.615	0.556	0.621	0.706
Sports	0.722	0.789	0.870	0.579	0.587	0.598	0.531	0.574	0.640
Ticket	0.877	0.918	0.965	0.618	0.564	0.523	0.718	0.725	0.739
School	0.681	0.682	0.682	0.382	0.358	0.346	0.423	0.472	0.540
Fish&Chips	0.781	0.833	0.896	0.552	0.564	0.590	0.641	0.684	0.738
Macro Avg.	0.754	0.782	0.819	0.576	0.564	0.566	0.590	0.623	0.669
Macro SD.	0.116	0.117	0.130	0.114	0.119	0.133	0.119	0.104	0.088

Looking at validity ($F_{0.5}$), GPT-o1 consistently outperforms both SLMs across all datasets, with scores ranging from 0.525 (Recycling) to 0.929 (Supermarket) and an average of 0.754. The margins vary by dataset, being smallest in Planningpoker and largest in Supermarket and School. Between the SLMs, there is no clear dominance, as Llama3-8B leads in five datasets while Qwen-14B performs better in four, occasionally achieving larger margins (e.g., Fish&Chips, Ticket).

For completeness (F_2), GPT-o1 again demonstrates the strongest performance, with scores between 0.647 and 0.965 (avg. 0.819). It remains above 0.85 in six datasets, indicating strong coverage of relevant associations. Qwen-14B follows, averaging 0.669, and consistently outperforms Llama3-8B (avg. 0.566).

Statistical tests ($\alpha = 0.05$) confirm the significant differences. The Friedman test shows significance for both metrics (validity: $p = 0.0012$) completeness (F_2): $p = 0.0001$, $W = 1$). The post-hoc (Nemenyi) tests further show that GPT-o1 significantly outperforms both Llama3-8B ($p = 0.0062$, $d = 2.113$) and Qwen-14B ($p = 0.0028$, $d = 2.898$) in validity. For completeness, GPT-o1 is significantly better than Llama3-8B ($p = 0.0000656$, $d = 2.267$), while its dominance over Qwen-14B is not statistically significant ($p = 0.0855$, $d = 2.221$), likely due to the limited sample size.

Figure 3 presents the $F_{0.5}$ and F_2 scores for each dataset, showing the variation across different runs of LLMs and small SLMs in the association extraction task. GPT-o1 exhibits higher medians and narrower interquartile ranges, particularly in Supermarket, Camperplus, and Fish&Chips. Llama3-8B shows lower medians and greater variability, while Qwen-14B generally lies between the two, occasionally approaching GPT-o1's performance (e.g., Planningpoker). The patterns for completeness are similar, with GPT-o1 maintaining the highest stability and the differences among models narrowing slightly in Recycling.

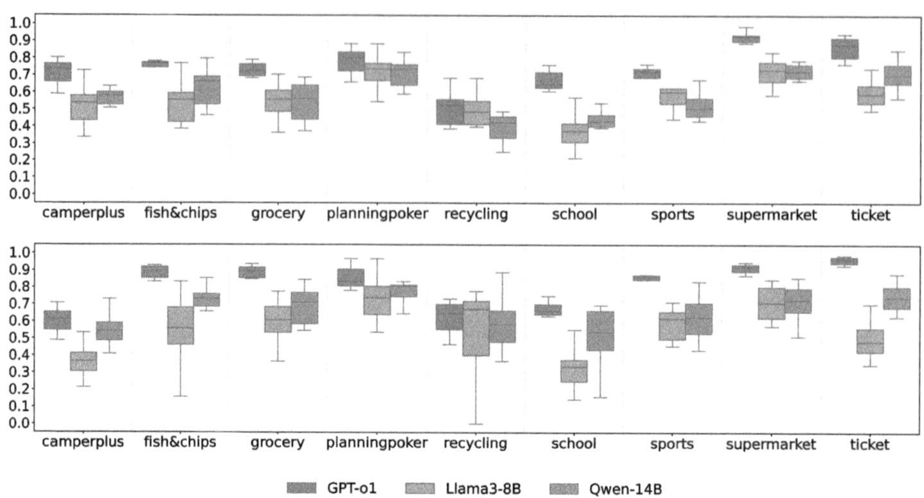

Fig. 3. $F_{0.5}$ (top) and F_2 (bottom) score distribution by model and dataset for association extraction.

4.2 Qualitative Analysis

This section examines false positive patterns in class and association identification. Figure 4 compares the class false positive profiles of GPT-o1, Llama3-8B, Qwen-14B, VN-P, and VN-R. For each dataset, we aggregate all experimental rounds, compute the proportion of each error type, and summarize their distributions using box plots. This visualization highlights error tendencies rather than absolute counts.

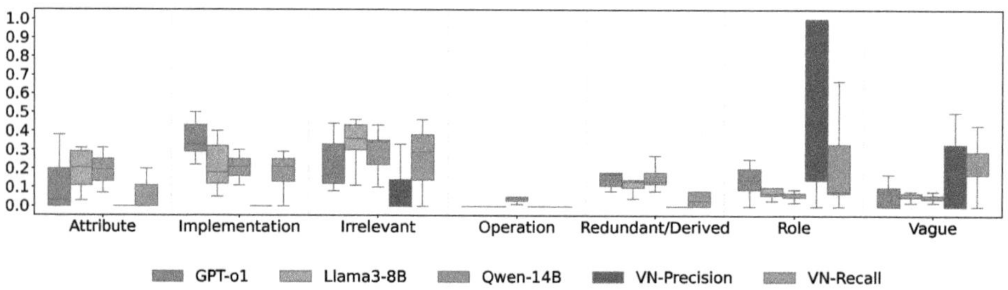

Fig. 4. Distribution of class false positives by error types and models.

VN and language models show distinct error patterns. VN-P produces a narrow range of mistakes, mainly *Role*, *Vague*, and *Irrelevant* errors, while VN-R shows greater variety (because of the lower threshold for class inclusion) but similar patterns. Both variants frequently make *Vague* errors due to difficulty in handling complex nouns (VN uses a classical NLP pipeline). For example, in the Ticket dataset, the system identifies "information" as a class, although it is unclear whether this refers to "artist information" or "event information". They also tend to make *Role* errors by extracting system-oriented entities, such as "admin", as standalone classes. The roles appear frequently in the "As a" part of user story templates, leading VN to assign them higher weights. Occasionally, VN also produces *Irrelevant* errors by identifying relative pronouns, such as "which" or "where," as potential classes, likely due to how sentence chunking.

In contrast, language models distribute their errors more evenly and show a stronger tendency toward *Redundant/Derived* classes, a category that VN rarely triggers. For instance, in the School dataset, Qwen-14B produced both "grade" and "school grade" within the same experiment round. Among the LLMs, GPT-o1 makes fewer *Attribute* and *Irrelevant* errors, whereas both SLMs more frequently confuse attributes with classes or generate out-of-scope entities. GPT-o1, however, shows a slightly higher rate of *Role* and *Implementation* errors. For the remaining categories (*Vague, Redundant/Derived, Operation*), all three models behave similarly. The *Operation* category shows low error rates across all models because language models can effectively distinguish nouns from verbs. Qwen-14B exhibits a slightly higher rate due to its tendency to over-generate elements and extract compound words. For instance, in Camperplus, it identified "consent form submission" as a class; however, the term emphasizes "submission", which is an operation rather than a domain entity.

Figure 5 compares the association false positive profiles of GPT-o1, Llama3-8B, and Qwen-14B. Note that VN is excluded from this part of the evaluation, as explained at the beginning of Sect. 4. *Redundant/Derived* errors are the most frequent across all types. GPT-o1 shows the highest median and widest interquartile range, indicating that it sometimes adds links already implied, for example "Student–Assignment," which can be inferred from "Student–Class" and "Class–Assignment." *Implementation* errors are rare for all models, with GPT-o1 showing the fewest. In the gold standard class list, there is no reference to classes related to the development of a system, *i.e.* technical classes. Any reference to technical classes in the generated output indicates that the model has ignored the instructions provided in the prompt and hallucinated. This phenomenon is especially evident in the SLMs. *Irrelevant* errors occur moderately across models, often from invented or loosely related entities. GPT-o1 has the lowest median but wider spread, while the SLMs display higher medians with less variation.

5 Discussion and Limitations

5.1 Discussion

Our study demonstrates that the GPT-o1 LLM consistently achieved higher validity and completeness than both SLMs and the rule-based Visual Narrator. This result suggests that scale, the training data, and advanced contextual reasoning significantly improve the accuracy of class and association identification. The SLMs delivered performance on the level of the VN; while the SLMs are better suited than the LLMs for educational and resource-constrained environments, the even lighter rule-based VN is still in the same league, if not better, for many datasets.

The first and the third authors manually studied all results and improved the gold standard as well. The analysis revealed recurring error patterns across models. Larger

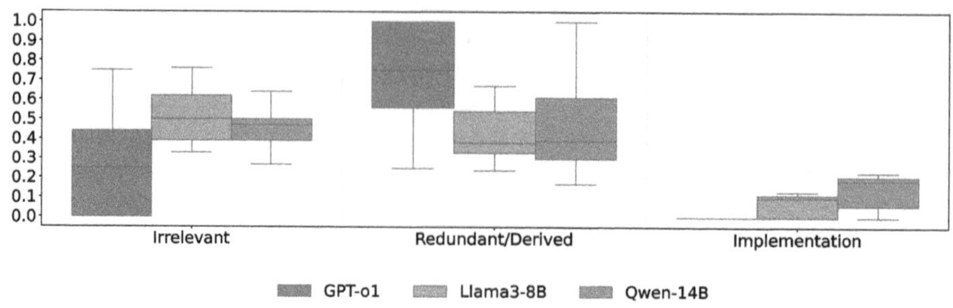

Fig. 5. Distribution of false positives by error types and models for associations.

models tended to generalize associations correctly but occasionally introduced spurious relationships, while smaller models often omitted valid elements or failed to interpret domain-specific terms. These differences highlight that model scale influences not only accuracy but also the types of reasoning errors produced. VN, on the other hand, is fully interpretable and the identified issues could be fixed programmatically.

Our results raise questions about how LLMs reason about software concepts. Despite their generally good performance, they still encounter difficulties with domain-specific semantics, showing that human oversight remains essential. This observation aligns with prior work emphasizing the need for hybrid pipelines [11] that combine LLM automation with manual SE activities. Further research should investigate how prompting strategies, fine-tuning, and feedback loops can balance automation and reliability in conceptual modeling tasks.

Across datasets, our analysis also reveals differences in task difficulty. Some domains appear inherently more challenging for both humans and machines. For example, the Recycling dataset yielded consistently lower scores across all models, mirroring prior observations that even human analysts struggled to construct coherent domain models from its user stories [5]. In contrast, the Supermarket dataset achieved the highest scores, and human participants in the same study also performed well on this domain. These results suggest that dataset characteristics–such as clarity, vocabulary consistency, and conceptual regularity–strongly influence the quality of both human and automated model derivation.

Implications for practice. Large and small language models demonstrate potential to accelerate early modeling activities by extracting preliminary conceptual structures directly from textual requirements, reducing manual effort and without requiring specialized solutions (e.g., classical NLP pipelines). Organizations can integrate such models into existing tool chains to support analysts in identifying classes and associations. However, industrial adoption requires attention to data confidentiality, explainability, and validation workflows to ensure that generated models remain trustworthy and compliant with organizational standards. In such cases, SLMs have an advantage over LLMs for resource consumption, ease of on-premise deployment, and more predictable behavior. With appropriate governance and human oversight, LLM-based model extraction can support faster prototyping, better stakeholder communication, and more consistent documentation across projects. Yet, the effects on humans' cognition need to be investigated, as recent studies [15] have shown how the use of ChatGPT leads to a so called 'cognitive debt', i.e., lower neural connectivity in people's brain.

5.2 Threats to Validity

Following the guidelines by Wohlin et al. [26], we consider potential threats to construct, internal, external, and conclusion validity.

Construct Validity may be affected by the operationalization of conceptual modeling quality, as our metrics focus on classes and associations while omitting attributes, specializations, and behavioral aspects. This is a conscious choice: classes and associations are at the basis of domain models, and other elements (like attributes) are dependent on classes' existence.

Conclusion Validity concerns the interpretation of quantitative differences; to address this, we employed statistical tests and complemented numerical analysis with qualitative inspection. Error profiling is rare in NLP4RE research, and we advocate it as step to go beyond the raw numbers and statistical values. Nevertheless, we have not tested the effectiveness of the generated models in action, i.e., how well they support requirements analysts or developers.

Internal Validity may be influenced by prompt design and random variations in LLM outputs; we mitigated this risk through standardized prompting and multiple runs per model. We were interested in the models' performance with their predefined settings, although an alternative would have been controlling temperature and seed. However, this would not have been possible for GPT-o1.

External Validity is limited by the benchmark datasets, which reflect a specific set of user stories and may not represent all industrial domains or modeling styles. To reduce bias, we have re-tagged the dataset and included mandatory and optional elements, plus a set of synonyms. Nevertheless, replication with larger datasets, additional modeling tasks, and alternative evaluation frameworks will be necessary to strengthen the generalizability of our findings.

6 Conclusions

Our main contribution is a systematic comparison of LLMs and SLMs for conceptual model extraction from natural language requirements. We evaluated three models (GPT-o1, Llama3-8B, and Qwen-14B) against the rule-based Visual Narrator across nine benchmark datasets. The findings confirm that GPT-o1 performs consistently better than the other models and often matches or exceeds the rule-based baseline in both precision and recall. The SLMs demonstrate competitive performance, thereby serving as practical alternatives where computational efficiency is a priority; yet, they do not outperform the lightweight, NLP-based Visual Narrator.

Our research identifies several avenues for future work. We plan to extend the analysis to additional modeling elements such as attributes, multiplicities, and specific relations. We aim to refine the evaluation framework by integrating human judgment metrics and exploring automated semantic alignment techniques. LLM-as-a-judge evaluation setup is also an interesting direction to explore. Finally, we will examine how the insights from this comparison can inform the design of mixed-initiative systems that integrate LLMs into RE workflows responsibly and transparently.

Data Availability. The replication package of this work is available at https://doi.org/10.5281/zenodo.18979158

References

1. Arora, C., Sabetzadeh, M., Briand, L., Zimmer, F.: Extracting domain models from natural-language requirements: approach and industrial evaluation. In: International Conference on Model Driven Engineering Languages and Systems, pp. 250–260 (2016)
2. Arora, C., Sabetzadeh, M., Nejati, S., Briand, L.: An active learning approach for improving the accuracy of automated domain model extraction. Trans. Softw. Eng. Methodol. **28**(1), 1–34 (2019)
3. Arulmohan, S., Meurs, M.J., Mosser, S.: Extracting domain models from textual requirements in the era of large language models. In: International Conference on Model Driven Engineering Languages and Systems Companion, pp. 580–587. IEEE (2023)
4. Blaha, M., Rumbaugh, J.: Object-Oriented Modeling and Design with UML, 2/E. Pearson Education India (2007)
5. Bragilovski, M., van Can, A.T., Dalpiaz, F., Sturm, A.: Leveraging machines to derive domain models from user stories. RequirE. Eng. 1–23 (2025)
6. Bragilovski, M., Van Can, A.T., Dalpiaz, F., Sturm, A.: Deriving domain models from user stories: Human vs. machines. In: International Requirements Engineering Conference, pp. 31–42. IEEE (2024)
7. Chen, K., Yang, Y., Chen, B., López, J.A.H., Mussbacher, G., Varró, D.: Automated domain modeling with large language models: A comparative study. In: International Conference on Model Driven Engineering Languages and Systems, pp. 162–172. IEEE (2023)
8. Deeptimahanti, D.K., Sanyal, R.: Semi-automatic generation of UML models from natural language requirements. In: India Software Engineering Conference pp. 165–174 (2011)
9. Demšar, J.: Statistical comparisons of classifiers over multiple data sets. J. Mach. Learn. Res. **7**(Jan), 1–30 (2006)
10. España, S., Ruiz, M., González, A.: Systematic derivation of conceptual models from requirements models: a controlled experiment. In: International Conference on Research Challenges in Information Science, pp. 1–12. IEEE (2012)
11. Fan, A., et al.: Large language models for software engineering: survey and open problems. In: International Conference on Software Engineering: Future of Software Engineering, pp. 31–53. IEEE (2023)
12. Ferrari, A., Abualhaijal, S., Arora, C.: Model generation with LLMs: From requirements to UML sequence diagrams. In: Model-Driven Requirements Engineering Workshop, pp. 291–300. IEEE (2024)
13. Güneş, T., Aydemir, F.B.: Automated goal model extraction from user stories using NLP. In: International Requirements Engineering Conference, pp. 382–387. IEEE (2020)
14. Honnibal, M., Montani, I., Van Landeghem, S., Boyd, A.: spaCy: Industrial-strength Natural Language Processing in Python (2020). https://doi.org/10.5281/zenodo.1212303
15. Kosmyna, N., et al.: Your brain on ChatGPT: Accumulation of cognitive debt when using an AI assistant for essay writing task **4** (2025) arXiv preprint arxiv:2506.08872
16. Kumar, P.: Large language models (LLMs): survey, technical frameworks, and future challenges. Artif. Intell. Rev. **57**(10), 260 (2024)

17. Lucassen, G., Robeer, M., Dalpiaz, F., Van Der Werf, J.M.E., Brinkkemper, S.: Extracting conceptual models from user stories with Visual Narrator. Requirements Eng. **22**, 339–358 (2017)
18. Pennington, J., Socher, R., Manning, C.: GloVe: Global vectors for word representation. In: Conference on Empirical Methods in Natural Language Processing, pp. 1532–1543. Association for Computational Linguistics (2014)
19. Robeer, M., Lucassen, G., Van Der Werf, J.M.E., Dalpiaz, F., Brinkkemper, S.: Automated extraction of conceptual models from user stories via NLP. In: International Requirements Engineering Conference, pp. 196–205. IEEE (2016)
20. Saini, R., Mussbacher, G., Guo, J.L., Kienzle, J.: DoMoBOT: An AI-empowered bot for automated and interactive domain modelling. In: International Conference on Model Driven Engineering Languages and Systems Companion, pp. 595–599. IEEE (2021)
21. Schick, T., Schütze, H.: It's not just size that matters: Small language models are also few-shot learners. In: Proceedings of the 2021 Conference of the North American Chapter of the Association for Computational Linguistics: Human Language Technologies, pp. 2339–2352 (2021)
22. Sharfuddin, A., Breaux, T.: Generative goal modeling. In: International Requirements Engineering Conference, pp. 92–103. IEEE (2025)
23. Van Nguyen, C., et al.: A survey on small language models. In: Proceedings of the 15th International Conference on Recent Advances in Natural Language Processing-Natural Language Processing in the Generative AI Era, pp. 807–821 (2025)
24. Wang, F., et al.: A comprehensive survey of small language models in the era of large language models: techniques, enhancements, applications, collaboration with llms, and trustworthiness. ACM Trans. Intell. Syst. Technol. **16**(6), 1–87 (2025)
25. White, J., et al.: A prompt pattern catalog to enhance prompt engineering with ChatGPT. arXiv preprint arXiv:2302.11382 (2023)
26. Wohlin, C., Runeson, P., Höst, M., Ohlsson, M.C., Regnell, B., Wesslén, A., et al.: Experimentation in software engineering, vol. 236. Springer (2012)
27. Yue, T., Briand, L.C., Labiche, Y.: A systematic review of transformation approaches between user requirements and analysis models. Requirements Eng. **16**(2), 75–99 (2011)

Author Index

GPSR Compliance
The European Union's (EU) General Product Safety Regulation (GPSR) is a set
of rules that requires consumer products to be safe and our obligations to
ensure this.

If you have any concerns about our products, you can contact us on

ProductSafety@springernature.com

In case Publisher is established outside the EU, the EU authorized
representative is:

Springer Nature Customer Service Center GmbH
Europaplatz 3
69115 Heidelberg, Germany